1895

THE SECONDARY PRINCIPAL'S HANDBOOK

THE SECONDARY PRINCIPAL'S HANDBOOK:
A GUIDE TO EXECUTIVE ACTION

Larry W. Hughes
University of Houston

and

Gerald C. Ubben
University of Tennessee

Allyn and Bacon, Inc.
Boston • London • Sydney • Toronto

Library of Congress Cataloging in Publication Data

Hughes, Larry W   1931–
   The secondary principal's handbook.

   Bibliography: p.
   Includes index.
   1. High school principals—United States.
2. High schools—United States—Administration—
Decision making. I. Ubben, Gerald C., joint author.
II. Title.
LB2831.92.H83   373.1 ′2 ′00973   79-22739
ISBN 0-205-06875-8

Printed in the United States of America

This book is dedicated lovingly to Helen and Peck Hughes, and Ralph Ubben for their unflagging support and selflessness without which two authors never would have made it.

CONTENTS

Chapter Six
Understanding the Community   69

PART TWO/TASKS AND FUNCTIONS   83

Chapter Seven
Guidelines and Goals for Organizing School Programs   85

Chapter Eight
Individual Differences and Student Grouping   95

Chapter Nine
Organizing the Secondary School Curriculum   109

Chapter Ten
Managing the Cocurricular Activities Program   127

Chapter Eleven
Organizing Secondary School Instruction   141

Chapter Twelve
Deployment of Staff   157

Chapter Thirteen
Scheduling Staff and Students   173

Chapter Fourteen
Staffing the School: Recruitment, Selection, and Termination   191

Chapter Fifteen
The Principal as Supervisor   201

Chapter Sixteen
The Principal's Role in Contract Administration   217

Chapter Twenty
Financial Planning and Record Keeping   257

Chapter Twenty-One
Managing the Building and Grounds   275

Chapter Twenty-Two
Techniques to Achieve Good Public Relations   287

PART THREE/MANAGEMENT TOOLS   301

Chapter Twenty-Three
Systematic Planning and Project Management   303

Chapter Twenty-Four
The Effective Management of Executive Time   315

INDEX   331

PREFACE

The secondary school principal performs a crucial role on the education management team. The job is complex. It requires excellent management skills and a repertoire of proven leadership techniques. Our effort in this book is to provide help to practitioners and those preparing to be practitioners in the development and refinement of these necessary skills and techniques. The book relies heavily on exemplary practice now occurring in the field.

Readers will find the book to be a practical guide and daily reference for secondary school principals and those in training for the principalship. It is a comprehensive and straightforward treatment of the roles and functions of the principal. It also provides guidelines for action to assist the reader in the performance of these roles and functions.

When the job of the principal is done well, great things happen; when the school is inadequately managed, young people are materially hindered in achieving their potentials. It is not a job in which one can hide. Yet, persons of Homeric proportions are not required; few such persons exist. What is required is well-trained, intelligent, and humane individuals who have the necessary human, conceptual, and technical skills to lead groups of professionals and clients into rich educational adventures. If the challenges are many and the tasks complex, the outcomes possible in an effectively managed school are well worth the immense efforts required.

There are three parts to the book. The six chapters in the first part focus on the concepts and processes basic to the management of secondary schools, from role definition to legal principles. Part II contains chapters describing the various functional aspects of the principalship. Guidelines for action are suggested in each chapter. The third part is comprised of two chapters each describing an important management tool: systematic planning and effective use of time.

We hope that the pre-service and in-service administrators who study the material contained herein find that material to be immediately useful and sufficient to the task. Best wishes!

PART ONE

CONCEPTS AND PROCESSES

What does it take to be a secondary school principal? Knowledge, skill, and humanity would seem to be basic to the role. The six chapters which comprise Part One focus on conceptual aspects of these three characteristics.

Chapter 1 describes the role of the secondary school principal and makes an important distinction between the principal and principalship. Chapters 2 and 3 examine decision making from two perspectives. First, an analysis is made of the decision-making process and the kinds of decision making which occur. Then, a discussion of decision making is presented as it relates to the human side of the enterprise. Basic to good decision making is effective staff development and participation in organizational problem solving. Chapter 4 focuses on the internal communication process. Chapter 5 contains an extensive review of the legal principles and practices undergirding an effective and humane secondary school. The first part of the book concludes with an examination of the effect of community dynamics on the operation of the secondary schools.

Chapter One

The Secondary School Principal: A Complex Role in a Dynamic Society

INTRODUCTION

"Is the high school principal important?" A suburban Houston principal asked himself this question in a talk before graduate students. Answering his own question he went on:

> Heck yes, he's important. You become a principal and your name makes all the restroom walls. And some of those things I don't even know how to do!

This humorous introduction set the stage for a serious discourse by the speaker about the challenges confronting today's secondary school principal.

It is a challenging position indeed and even if fame, as the principal suggested, is sometimes limited to teenage scatology, the position nonetheless is vital to the success of the school system. The role of the school principal has never been simple, and it is increasing in complexity. From the start, when all it meant was extra duties for the "head teacher," the expectations of boards of education, superintendents, and parents have been demanding. Parents viewed the principal as some kind of all-knowing being, endowed with great authority. This mantle has always been nervously worn. Superintendents and boards, on the other hand, more frequently viewed the position as some kind of glorified clerk. This didn't do much for the self-concept of principals either. The position has developed to the point where it is now one of the most important in the school system, occupied by neither paragons of leadership nor Uriah Heeps. The former are hard to find; the latter are no longer desired by most superintendents.[1]

Schools vary in size and complexity of course. Similarly, the role of the principal and organizational and community expectations may vary from place to place, but the functions performed by the school building executive are quite similar irrespective of where that principalship is located or how large the school is. And this job, which is crucial to the success of the school system, can be performed successfully by mortals. The necessary human, conceptual, and technical skills can be learned.[2]

No enterprise will function well for long without a competent chief executive with well-defined tasks and responsibilities to be accomplished. Effectively executing the responsibilities of the secondary principal will require better deployment of staff, participatory decision making, better utilization of time, and a better understanding of the forces on and in the school. These define the role of the principal.

The Five Functions of the Principalship

Five functions comprise the principalship: school-community relations, staff personnel development, pupil personnel development, educational program development, and business and building management. These rubrics categorize the array of tasks and responsibilities that accrue to the principalship.

Moreover, the principalship has two dimensions. One of these dimensions has to do with effectively managing the enterprise. It is composed of those activities concerned with procuring, coordinating, and deploying the materiel and personnel needed to accomplish the goals of the school.

The other dimension is somewhat more difficult to define but can be summed up in one word: leadership. This is a dimension of quality. It is distinguished by the way principals use themselves to create a school climate characterized by staff productivity, creative thought, and efficient and effective movement toward the goals of the school organization.

The good principal must indeed be a good manager of the enterprise, but this does not mean that the principal must personally perform each specific management task. The principal who does not have time for teachers, or children, or for community relations because the ledgers need balancing is either defining the job too narrowly or is mismanaging time. Boards of education and superintendents of schools who evaluate principals primarily on the basis of balanced ledgers and quiet classrooms would achieve greater economies if they would simply employ husky bookkeepers rather than pay the price for well-trained, lettered school executives.

NEW DEMANDS ON PRINCIPALS

School-Community Relations Specialist

Schools seem to be increasingly under attack and criticism. Why? And what does it mean? How is it possible that groups or individuals can attack such a sanctified institution as education and such a saintly collection of individuals as administrators and teachers? What do

they mean, "schools should be accountable"? Why does there seem to be an "educational credibility gap"? What is this uncertainty? What has happened to the face of education? The answers to these questions lie in an understanding of the growth and changes in society which require a new sort of administrator.

The increasing complexity of society, coupled with the increasing esotericism of the science and art of education, has had a great effect on the relations of the school with its community—if, indeed, one may call collections of large groups of people who simply live in close proximity to each other a community. The dissolution of small closely-knit communities of years past has taken its toll. The effect has been to make the school and community strangers, each rather unsure of the other. Therefore, one new major role that the principal must perform—and is uniquely located to perform—is political and will not occur inside the school, but outside, in the area served by the school. This is the role of a school-community relations specialist. Implied is more than an occasional talk at Kiwanis, and more than a monthly PTA meeting. It means developing effective mechanisms that will involve the many sectors of the typical school attendance area. Neighborhood leaders need to be identified and heard. Neighborhood seminars, parent-teacher conferences, and special advisory groups to focus on single problems are all devices that the principal can employ in addition to the usual bulletins and newsletters that alone are insufficient communication devices.[3]

Why are feedback mechanisms necessary? Five factors contribute to an educational credibility gap: the high cost of public education, changing values, assertive teacher organizations, social discontent, and population mobility.

When a public service is expensive, it becomes highly visible. When an agency is visible, it is scrutinized. School administrators have not been very successful at showing how extra dollars have resulted in a better product. This is what "accountability" is all about.

Because of this first factor—the drive for a bigger share of the public purse—the second factor becomes apparent. (And here again, the need for "proof" of value is important.) In an economy of scarce resources, citizens are forced to make a painful reappraisal of their values.

It is a painful choice—a new car or higher pay for teachers?; a new school or more highly trained and paid police officers and firefighters? This dilemma is a reality with obvious implications to school-community relations programs. Implicitly, it means administrators and teachers ought to be able to point out some results, now. It can't be done with a bulletin sent home, and it can't be done without specific facts. Blind-faith goodwill is not characteristic of society today.

Third, the profession of education is losing the affectionate regard of the public. This has occurred primarily because educators have thrown off a "cloak of sanctity" and a "vow of poverty" in an attempt to gain economic advantages. Many of society's members are shocked and resentful at the assertive attitude that teachers' groups are adopting.[4] Educators ought to recognize that society at large will not accord them the advantages of both sainthood and personal economic advances. Goodwill toward teachers, administrators, and schools will have to be actively sought and based on something more substantial than the sanctity of the educational enterprise.

Fourth, social discontent continues. This factor focuses on the motivation of the poor and culturally different elements of our society. The polyglot nature of our society only recently has been viewed as a positive feature and the melting pot theory put to rest. The implications to the school of multiethnic, culturally diverse population are many indeed.[5]

Two purposes of American mass public education are generally accepted as guideposts. First, public schools are to pass on the accumu-

lated wisdom of the world and teach those skills necessary for continued personal growth. Second, public schools have been viewed as the vehicle whereby social mobility could be achieved so that no child need be victimized by the state of his or her birth. In this regard, the implications of a culturally diverse multiethnic society are manifest. According to many in society's understructure, the public school system has operated to discourage participation in or achievement of the "good life." Members of many groups have argued so persuasively for changed practices in the schools that the courts, legislatures, and educators have been dealing with this very issue for the past two decades. The result has been desegregated schools, bilingual programs, breakfast at public expense, Headstart, Upward Bound, alternative education, magnet schools, and neighborhood miniboards, among a host of programs and procedures designed to reduce blatant inequities and require, as well, closer school-community relationships.

The fifth condition that impels today's principal into an outside role relates to population mobility. If any one factor characterizes most of American society today, it is mobility. America continues to be on the move, and intensely stable school populations are difficult to find. Two kinds of population movements exist—micro and macro—and both have implications for administrative practice.

Macro-population moves relate to certain mass movements of groups of people from one section of the country to another. A current trend, for example, is from the Northeastern United States down the Eastern seaboard and inland to the Southeast and deep South. There is also great movement from several parts of the country to the cities of the Southwest. A continuing trend, albeit of much declining intensity, is from Appalachia to the cities of the near Midwest (Ohio, Illinois, Indiana, Michigan). There are other macro movements and such trends can substantially change the character of a neighborhood or area within a short period of time. These changes may require different kinds of school response patterns, including curricular offerings and public relations programs.

Micro-population moves are most felt in the urban areas, where a change of residence involving a move of but a few blocks results in a change of schools and perhaps even school districts. There is so much of this movement that some urban classrooms reveal as much as 120 percent student turnover in a single school year. Some students' records never do catch up. Coping with such transiency of student population and the negative effect it can have on teaching and learning is one of the great challenges of the urban principalship.

The implication of all of this is that the principal should be spending a large portion of administrative time engaged in school-community relations activities. There will need to be a continuous information exchange and analysis of community and client needs.[6] The problem is even further complicated by the cross-busing and school pairings needed in many school systems to achieve a desegregated student body. In these cases, even the "neighborhood" served by the school may be a dispersed one. The reader may feel that this new role of community relations specialist is overemphasized. The authors don't think so. The closest social institution to the family and to the community, both psychologically and often geographically, is the school. It's "right around the corner," and because of this the school principal enjoys a rare position on the front line between the community and its welfare delivery systems. It is a position in which the principal can perform an important coordinating function.

Educational Engineer

The second new role of the principal is that of educational engineer—a person who makes the school climate a positive and productive one.

Some secondary schools are "up-tight" places, fraught with frustration for children and teachers alike.

The principal sets the tone and standard for the school and there is much good research from which to conclude this. Goldhammer and Becker, for example, reporting a study representing every state in the United States, concluded:

> In schools that were extremely good we inevitably found an aggressive, professionally alert, dynamic principal determined to provide the kind of educational program he deemed necessary, *no matter what*.[7]

Goldhammer and his associates labeled the outstandingly good schools "beacons of brilliance"; those that were extremely poor were called "potholes of pestilence." The potholes of pestilence invariably suffered from weak leadership. The buildings were dirty and in disrepair, teacher and student morale were low, and fear was the basic control strategy. "The schools were characterized by unenthusiasm, squalor, and ineffectiveness. The principals are just serving out their time."[8]

Such conclusions and descriptions are not limited to the Goldhammer study. In a report on innovation and change in American public school systems, Peterfreund Associates reached many of the same conclusions.[9] Among other conditions, these researchers found as correlative of innovation and change was effective school building level leadership. They concluded that, "the school system must have principals who are in tune with the district's objectives and who are skilled at involving and motivating their teachers."[10] Moreover, innovative principals identify their role in terms of educational leadership, of creating an environment for learning. They are less concerned with traditional administrative routine. Leadership implies good communication with the staff, the students, and the community, and these principals have a communication system which allows information and ideas to flow up and down the line. Often they have to be ingenious to overcome limitations in the size of their staff and the restrictions on their time.[11]

The study of the relationship of principal behavior and administrative style to a productive school climate is not a recent phenomenon. Probably the best known studies are the highly respected inquiries conducted by Halpin and Croft in the late 1950s and early 1960s.[12] Halpin and Croft developed an instrument to portray the organizational climate of schools. "Climates" identified by their Organizational Climate Descriptive Questionnaire (OCDQ) range from "Open" on the positive or productive end of the scale, to "Closed" on the negative or nonproductive end.[13] The instrument examines the nature of the interaction between principals and teachers.

Halpin and Croft posit two dimensions to organizational climate: work group characteristics and leader behavior. Developing out of much previous research depicting the successful administrator as one concerned about both organizational task and goal achievement and the personal needs satisfaction of workers, the OCDQ taps both of these dimensions. In schools where both task and personal needs are addressed positively the organizational climate is "open," change acceptant, productive, and adaptive. Discussing this concept, Hughes states:

> The operational definition given to open climate emphasizes that this is a situation in which organizational members derive high levels of satisfaction both from interpersonal relations with fellow workers and from accomplishing tasks assigned to them within the organization.[14]

Further,

> One of the guiding assumptions of the work of Halpin and Croft is that the most effective organizational climate will be one in which it is possible for acts of leadership to emerge easily from whatever source. An essential determinant

of a school's effectiveness noted by Halpin and Croft was the ascribed leader's ability, or his lack of ability, to create a climate in which he and other group members could initiate and consumate acts of leadership.[15]

The role of educational engineer requires a principal who is able to deal effectively with the human side of the educational enterprise while at the same time facilitating maximum organizational goal attainment. "Production orientation" is crucial to building effective leadership, but a high-quality product will not be obtained over the long haul unless great attention is given to the needs and aspirations of the people—pupils and staff—who make up the organization.

THE PRINCIPALSHIP

The "principal" is a person; the "principalship" is a collection of responsibilities and specific tasks. The principal's job is to see that these responsibilities are met and the tasks performed well. A distinction is made between principal and principalship to point out that although the principal is ultimately responsible for what goes on in and around the school, the principal does not have to personally perform all of the management and leadership acts. Some of the tasks will, of course, be performed directly—and should be—because of their complexity or overriding importance or because the tasks are those for which the individual principal has great skill.

Distinguishing between the terms *principal* and *principalship* suggests, therefore, that two of the most important skills a principal must possess are those of the appropriate organization and development of personnel and the delegation of authority. An example of the effective implementation of these skills can be found in the typical physician's office.

Physicians try to draw a tight circle around their professional activities and spend time, talent, and skill doing only those things that they alone can do. Other persons, with varying degrees of professional training and medical expertise, are assigned the tasks that fall outside the circle but are also of importance to the health of the patient. The point is that by doing only those things that he or she alone can do, the physician is able to effectively minister to a great number of patients every day and still frequently make it home for dinner on time. Similarly, the principal can effectively carry out all of the functions of the principalship with the same attention to good administrative practice. It is, of course, somewhat more difficult to draw the circle around the principal's job; but unless this is done, principals will find themselves spending entire days on tasks that someone else could and should be performing.

SUMMARY

Five functions determine the role of the school principal: school-community relations, staff personnel development, pupil personnel development, educational program development, and business and building management. Two dimensions of the principalship are effective management and leadership.

The principal today must be an effective manager, especially in the role of school-community relations specialist and educational engineer. In addition, the organization and development of personnel and the delegation of authority are two indispensable skills a principal must be able to employ.

ENDNOTES

1. The role of the principal as a member of the school management team does continue to be a subject of discussion, however. For example, see Joseph A. Coccia, "Point, Principals: Not Middle Management" and Norman Barea, "Counterpoint, Principals: Yes They are Management," *NASSP Bulletin* 61 (January 1977): 29–84.

2. Regarding this point, Drucker wrote, "Service institutions can, no more than businesses, depend on supermen or lion tamers to staff their managerial and executive positions. There are far too many institutions to be staffed. It is absurd to expect that the administrator . . . would be a genius or even a great man. If service institutions cannot be run and managed by men of normal . . . [ability]; if, in other words, we cannot organize the task so that it will be done adequately by men who only try hard, it cannot be done at all." Peter F. Drucker, *Management* (New York: Harper and Row Publishers, 1974), p. 139.

3. See chapter 22 for a discussion of the variety of communication devices available to the principal.

4. "Assertiveness" on the part of teacher groups (associations or unions) has other implications to the school principal as well. The principal plays a crucial role in the implementation of master contracts and is the "front line" in grievance proceedings. See chapter 16.

5. Insight about the various ways the school principal can capitalize on the richness of cultural diversity and multiethnicity in our society, and the implications such diversity has for school programming and inservice training can be gained from a two-part cassette tape series published by Cassette Services, Inc., St. Paul, Virginia 24283. Request: "The Multi-Ethnic Curriculum" *Principals Audio Journal* (November 1974 and December 1974), Side B.

6. An excellent discussion of the nature of different kinds of neighborhoods complete with analytic techniques and suggested communication devices can be found in Donald Warren and Rachel Warren, "Six Kinds of Neighborhoods," *Psychology Today* 9 (June 1975).

7. Keith Goldhammer and Gerald L. Becker, "What Makes a Good Elementary Principal," *American Education* 6 (April 1970), p. 11. While this nation-wide study focused on elementary schools, similiar conclusions about secondary schools would be justified.

8. Keith Goldhammer et al., *Elementary School Principals and Their Schools: Beacons of Brilliance and Potholes of Pestilence* (Eugene, Ore.: Center for the Advanced Study of Education, University of Oregon, 1971), p. 1.

9. Stanley Peterfreund Associates, "Innovation and Change in Public School Systems," mimeo (Englewood Cliffs, N.J.: The Associates, 1970), pp.

9–11. The study involved over 1200 elementary, junior high, and high schools.

10. Ibid., p. 9.

11. Ibid., p. 10.

12. Andrew W. Halpin and Don B. Croft, *The Organizational Climate of Schools* (Chicago: Midwest Administration Center, University of Chicago, 1963). Original studies focused on elementary schools only; later inquiries examined administrative behavior in other positions including high schools.

13. Halpin and Croft indicate that their use of these labels was influenced by the work of Rokeach in *The Open and Closed Mind* (New York: Basic Books, 1961). They liken climate in organizations to personality in individuals. Thus, an open climate is one that is receptive to new ideas.

14. Larry W. Hughes, "Achieving Effective Human Relations and Morale," in Jack Culbertson et al., *Performance Objectives for School Principals* (Berkeley, Calif: McCutchan Publishing Corp., 1974), p. 138.

15. Ibid.

BIBLIOGRAPHY

Culbertson, Jack A., et al., eds. *Performance Objectives for School Principals.* Berkeley, Calif.: McCutchan Publishing Co., 1974.

Drucker, Peter F. *Management: Tasks, Responsibilities, Practices.* New York: Harper and Row, 1974.

English, Fenwick W. *School Organization and Management.* Worthington, Ohio: Charles A. Jones, 1975.

Goldhammer, Keith, et al. *Elementary School Principals and Their Schools: Beacons of Brilliance and Potholes of Pestilence.* Eugene, Ore.: Center for the Advanced Study of Educational Administration, University of Oregon, 1971.

Goldhammer, Keith, and Becker, Gerald L. "What Makes a Good Elementary School Principal." *American Education* 6 (April 1970): 11–13.

Heller, M. P. *So Now You're a Principal.* Reston, Va.: National Association of Secondary School Principals, 1975.

Hughes, Larry W. "Achieving Effective Human Relations and Morale." in Culbertson, et al., *Performance Objectives for School Principals,* Chapter 5.

Hughes, Larry W. *Informal and Formal Community Forces: External Influences on Schools and Teachers.* (Morristown, N.J.: General Learning Press, 1976.

Hughes, Larry W. "The Multi-Ethnic Curriculum." *Principals Audio Journal* 1, 11, and 12 (November 1974, and December 1974), Side B.

Hughes, Larry W. "The Role of the Principal in the Decade of the Seventies." *Tennessee Education Quarterly* 1 (Summer 1972): 3–9.

Stanley Peterfreund Associates. "Innovation and Change in Public School Systems," mimeo. Englewood Cliffs, N.J.: The Associates, 1970.

William Van Til, ed. *Issues in Secondary Education.* The Seventy-fifth Yearbook of the National Society for the Study of Education. Chicago: The Society, 1976.

Warren, Donald and Warren, Rachel. "Six Kinds of Neighborhoods." *Psychology Today* 9 (June 1975).

Chapter Two

Executive Decision Making

INTRODUCTION

Executive decision making is the essential act of the administrator. Ultimately, of course, all that goes on in and around the school building is the responsibility of the principal. If the school is moving effectively toward appropriate goals, the principal will take the bows; conversely, if things are not all they should be then, justly, the principal will be held accountable. This does not mean, however, that the principal must personally do all of the important decision making that needs to be accomplished in order for the school to be a good one. The principal who attempts to manage by personal direction rather than by exception will do little but spend time reacting to a variety of brush fires with little time left over for either planning activities or working with staff in goal-setting and goal-implementing endeavors.

Much is heard these days about participatory decision making as the way to achieve effective problem resolution. The question that arises in many minds is whether this means the creation of committees for everything, with principals serving as a kind of coordinator and implementor of other people's decisions. The puzzled follow-up to the latter question is another question: "How would anything get done with such an arrangement?"

Set aside, for the moment, all that has been written or said about the term *democratic administration*. This term has become virtually nondefinitive. Instead, think of situations requiring decisions of problems requiring resolution. Further, think about the kinds of people who comprise the professional as well as the noncertificated staff in the school; think about the clients of the school; think about the goals and objectives of the school; and finally, think about the processes that must be used to put all these things together to achieve those goals.

This chapter will describe three kinds of decision-making processes available to the principal and will discuss problem resolution techniques. The chapter immediately following will focus specifically on participatory decision making and the organizational milieu of the school.

THREE KINDS OF DECISION PROCESSES

It is possible to distinguish among three kinds of problem resolution processes: unilateral, majority opinion, and consensus. These labels suggest something about the nature of the involvement of others in the process.

Unilateral Decision Making

By definition the principal is in an authoritative role. To be sure, the degree to which the person occupying this role can make unilateral decisions is circumscribed by public laws, the rules and policies of the school system, the actions of the superordinate decision structure, as well as by informal constraints such as community customs. Nevertheless, in most districts the individual school executive does enjoy a considerable latitude in decision making.

Further, there is both an organizational (superordinate structure) expectation and an expectation of those people within the school building (subordinate structure) that the principal will engage in judgmental actions to insure the maintenance of order and the delivery of services to the appropriate point at the appropriate time. In short, the principal is supposed to keep the school functioning with a minimum of disruption of the teaching/learning act. Such decision making, or problem-anticipation and problem-responding acts, comprise an important part of the principal's role. But not all problems, nor indeed very many complex problems, can be adequately resolved through purely unilateral acts.

Nothing magical occurs when a state department of education confers an administrative certificate licensing a person to be a principal. That person does not, by virtue of certificate, or even, alas, by virtue of training, become all-knowing. It is hoped that the person will have accquired some skills and technical competence and insight into education problems, but no administrator can function effectively from the cloister of the office, ruling by an assumed divine right accorded by a shiny state department certificate.

Is it necessary to state this? The authors would argue that it is because of their observation of the behavior of too many administrators and teachers that suggests while everyone may know better, many act as if all intelligence with respect to the operation of the school building reposes in the principal's office. This misunderstanding of role, often coupled with the inability to distinguish between routine maintenance decisions and futuristic decisions requiring more

complex processes, impedes the school. The lack of skills and mechanisms to tap the collective intelligence of the work group has resulted in uncreative, poorly implemented solutions to the many difficult problems confronting the school.

Majority Opinion

Simple vote taking is an appropriate way to resolve a *simple* problem. It's fast and relatively easy. The issue is described to the group, some discussion of pros and cons ensues, and the group decides, *with one vote over half sufficient to determine the decision*. This process is especially effective when no one in the group really cares what the decision is.

Making a decision should not be confused with implementing a decision. If the decision will require people to behave much differently than they have been behaving, as in the case of an important curricular change or a reorganization of the school, majority opinion is not sufficient. Consider, for example, the faculty that votes 18 to 17 to move to a team-teaching arrangement. It does not require an Indian mystic to predict the outcome of such a venture.

Yet unfortunately, such a process has gone on untold times in the name of "democratic decision-making," and with predictable results. The process is useful for the ultimate resolution of legislative or procedural matters in large groups, but a well-working task group—and a school faculty *is* a task group—seldom can rely on vote taking as a means for creative problem resolution.[1]

If a decision requiring important behavior changes is to be appropriately acted upon, it requies commitment and understanding of the participants. Simple changes in schedules, hours of work, etc., which require only modest behavior changes might rather easily be effected by majority opinion. Issues of curricular change, crisis management, goal setting and goal implementation, and similar questions of overriding importance require a more thoughtful process, such as consensus decision making.

Consensus Decision Making

Consensus decision making is a process that provides: (1) maximum participation of group members in the examination of the issue at hand; (2) sharing of pertinent information bearing on the problem(s); and (3) emergent situational leadership based on expertise concerning the issue being confronted irrespective of formal position in the organization.

The problem and subproblems to be addressed must be clearly defined. That is, the group must understand what it is attempting to resolve. If one is looking for a quick decision, a consensus process is probably inappropriate; if one is looking for a decision that relies on group intelligence and that will receive maximum individual commitment in its implementation, the consensus process offers great possibilities. The consensus process, then, is best employed for policy decision making, for difficult changes requiring substantial organizational readjustment, and for the development of new response mechanisms to anticipated problems of some complexity.

Engaging in a consensus decision-making process does put stress on a task group. In consensus decision making, differences of opinion (conflict) must be expected if the group is to ultimately resolve the problem in a productive manner. Groups lacking cohesion or newly formed groups are less likely to be able to manage this conflict. Therefore, the principal who sees value in forming task force teams to engage in collective decision making should confront such groups initially with problems of low intensity. Hall has found, for example, that established groups (people who have worked on tasks together a number of times before) in the face of conflict will tend to come up with

unique solutions that are creative in nature.[2] In contrast, newly formed groups in conflict situations will tend to rely more on compromise techniques, vote taking, and the like, which often are unsatisfactory to most of the members but do avoid conflict.

The consensus process begins with the creation of a task force team, probably no more than seven or eight people, likely to be affected by a developing problem situation. The composition of the group may at times be cross-sectional in nature as when, for example, the problem to be confronted is building-wide or when several kinds of expertise and insight are needed. At other times, members may represent a complete unit such as a department or the administrative team. Time is spent initially defining the nature of the developing problem, setting the limits of decision-making authority (for example, determining if the group's role is purely advisory or is it charged with final decision making), and identifying any existing rules, policies, and laws that would affect the nature of the decision to be rendered.

Adequate time must be set aside for the tasks. There is no sense attempting to resolve a complex issue through a consensus process if inadequate time exists to thoroughly examine the underlying issues. Time strictures always exist, of course, but when these are too severe, group members quickly recognize it, resign themselves to an inadequate resolution, and refuse to engage in what is perceived to be an exercise in futility. Group members may be polite about this, of course, but when the time allocated is insufficient to provide maximum achievement, it is unrealistic to expect individual group members to address the task very seriously.

The principal's role in a true consensus process is that of a peer among peers; the ascribed authority implicit in the title *principal* must be discarded. If the authority was sufficient to the task, there would be little reason to use the consensus process—unless the principal wishes simply to engage in game-playing involvement. This latter practice, however, is quickly perceived by any intelligent group and, again, while group members may remain polite and play the game, few productive results from such charades can be expected.

Several techniques to facilitate consensus building are available. Brainstorming, discussed elsewhere in this chapter, is one such technique. Figure 2–1 describes yet another

technique. In this process, group members are asked to generate alternative solutions rather than quickly committing themselves to a single course of action. This has the effect of keeping the discussion open and avoids the "one-solution-only blackout." Also important in the process is that attention be given to the anticipated consequences of actions that might be taken in any of the alternatives. In the process, the group attempts to anticipate what the result of

---

The following process is intended to provide general guidelines for a group wishing to methodically, yet quickly, engage in problem solving and action planning activities. An organizational problem is herein defined as any issue the whole group wishes to consider, and which can be planned or decided in a short period of time.

State 1:   Define the problem
Given the issue for which the group has convened, discuss some of its broad parameters as a problem. Why is it a problem? What are some of the facets? What are the underlying issues that present problems?

State 2:   Suggest alternative solutions
Each member of the group should try to think of two viable solutions to the problem. Take some time to think about these solutions and then list them. Share them with the group.

Stage 3:   Choose some solutions (not more than five)
From all of the alternatives the group must choose about five of the most promising solutions. This must be a group decision based on consensus. In arriving at a consensus group decision:

1. Everyone should feel free to state reasons why one or more solutions should be listed among the five.
2. A survey should be taken when actually making the choices.
3. Every member of the group should "own" or be willing to support the five alternatives finally chosen.

Stage 4:   Make some action plans
Based upon the chosen solutions, outline some plans for implementing those solutions and for resolving the problem. The plans should be as specific as possible, including when, where, who, and how. All of the members of the group should agree to help implement the plans. The plans should be recorded and every member of the group should receive a copy of them.

Stage 5:   Evaluation
As the action plan is implemented, its impact on the problem must be checked and any needed "mid-course" corrections made.

FIGURE 2–1.   Problem solving and action planning

Courtesy of C. Brooklyn Derr, Professor of Management, University of Utah.

the action taken will be with respect to any of the receivers of the action.

Training a Group in Consensus Decision-Making As previously noted, newly formed groups often have difficulty with the consensus process largely because it generates conflict as differing views and proposals are advanced and discussed. It is possible, however, to train even newly formed groups in the consensus process rather quickly. One way, mentioned previously, is to initially confront such groups with less complex problems. Another way is to explain the rules of the game and clearly indicate at the outset that conflict and difference of opinion are to be expected. Once a problem-solving group realizes that it is not after unanimity, rarely achieved on a complex problem, but rather after a *maximum feasible decision* to which all can commit themselves, progress in consensus decision making can be made.

A Case in Point

To illustrate and synthesize the concepts presented about different modes of decision making, consider the following case:

You are principal of a recently desegregated high school. Lately you have begun to feel that, while there is little apparent overt hostility, the school may be in for some troubling times. Several things lead to this conclusion.

Student interaction is almost totally within racial and ethnic groups. Social groupings in the cafeteria, halls, and at school-sponsored events reveal this condition. Teachers comment that similiar interaction patterns exist in the classroom, and some end their comments with a statement like, "*They* just don't seem to fit in well." (You have also noticed this same general lack of social interaction among faculty members who represent different racial and ethnic backgrounds, as well.)

Moreover, except for some of the boy's athletic teams, there seems to be little minority participation in school activities. Even athletic participation is limited to junior varsity and varsity sports programs; few minority youth participate in the after-school intramural program. School dances also reveal remarkable separatism. One ethnic group hardly participates at all. Some members of the racial minority have come to you requesting that there be two spring dances held because the band selected for the annual prom by the student prom committee "doesn't play the right kind of music and so why can't we have one of our own?"

You notice, too, after a cursory review of student records and teacher grade sheets, that grades received appear to be significantly different between racial and ethnic groups. It is also apparent that certain curricula and certain courses reflect racial or ethnic separation. Attendance, truancy, and drop out rates also seem to reflect racial and ethnic differences, as do reports of disciplinary action.

Attendance at school open houses and at meetings of the struggling parent-teacher organization is primarily by the majority racial and ethnic group. Almost no minority group parents or students sign up for your regularly scheduled "rap" sessions.

It seems to you that the student body may be "mixed" insofar as total reporting is concerned, but nothing approximating an integrated school setting exists. You have attended enough professional conferences and had sufficient conversations with other principals to know that if these conditions continue to be unmitigated a strong possibility exists for severe interruption of the learning process and perhaps considerable conflict and disorder.

You have arrived at a decision point. Given the information and perceptions, you have alternative routes to take in attempting to resolve this problem.[3] You could, for example, take unilateral action to address the issue. You do some additional reading about "second generation" desegregation problems,[4] discuss the matter with the assistant principal, perhaps consult a leading teacher or two, maybe talk with one of the guidance counselors, and decide to (1) inform the staff at a faculty meeting of your concerns; (2) have the librarian purchase a large number of multiethnic books and materials from recommended lists provided by the American Library Association, The National Council for the Teaching of Social Studies, and the National Council for the Teaching of English; (3) schedule an intensive inservice workshop on cultural awareness and human relations for all teachers; (4) assign the social studies department the task of developing a course in cultural awareness; (5) establish minority/majority ratios for membership in student clubs; and so on.

The program now becomes, in the eyes of everyone in the school, "the principal's new human relations program." *Your* program? Yes, it certainly isn't the staff's, or the students', or the school community's. It's yours—yours to explain, yours to implement, yours to check, yours to evaluate, *yours when it fails.*

None of the ideas mentioned are bad; in fact, some may be most efficacious, but success will require much commitment and psychological investment on the part of those most affected by these ideas. Such commitment is exceedingly difficult, if not impossible, to get solely on the basis of unilateral action by the executive, no matter how good the ideas are. For example, the people who will be charged with implementing any new program are the staff. If the program requires substantially different procedures and materials, it is they who will be required to behave (teach) differently and organize differently than before. Giving up old, comfortable practices and procedures requires a commitment to change.

Other kinds of executive action need to be employed. Implementing new processes that appear to have, on the basis of information and insight, a reasonable chance of solving the problem is very difficult.[5] It is axiomatic that

for a change to be successfully implemented those charged with the implementation must be aware of the need to change (see that a problem exists), be reasonably committed to doing something about it, and be provided with the wherewithal (material resources, decision latitude, and removal of organizational constraints) to facilitate the change.

Unilateral action by the principal may proceed through the same first three steps as before (professional reading, consultation with others, and expressing concern publicly) but following this action the principal should diverge from the previous example. Instead of unilateral action, the principal could begin to tap the group wisdom and collective energy, to use a synergistic approach which would be more likely to result program success.

Consider these steps: Following the initial exploration of the perceived problem by the principal and the beginning data collection process, interested faculty members are contacted to form a task force team. The team's charge might be two-fold: (1) investigate more fully the nature of the problem, and (2) propose alternative solutions to the problem. It is important that the task force team be given some realistic decision-making parameters.

SETTING REALISTIC TASK FORCE DECISION-MAKING PARAMETERS

Few task forces can operate completely unfettered. Real world constraints must always be contended with. Any group charged with completing a task needs to know the "rules of the game" if they are to be expected to render a decision that can be implemented. The following are important considerations and should be the basis for initial discussions between the task force group and the principal:

1. Determine if the task force team is to be advisory in nature, that is, are its decisions

to be suggestions only? (This is not very satisfying to a group that has worked hard, but it is sometimes appropriate and necessary.) Or, is the group to be charged with coming up with a series of decisions which, with your help, will result in a new program?

2. Cooperatively set some realistic target dates concerning the amount of time required for further investigation and data collection, for preparation of final reports, and to generate new program alternatives, as well as the anticipated implementation date, etc.

3. Establish a tentative budget for the project phases. Possible line items include released time costs, materials costs, transportation, etc.

4. Review any district-wide policies, state laws, etc., that might impinge on the nature of any new programs proposed.

5. Set up regular reporting dates to you and to the rest of the staff (interaction sessions) about progress and findings to date.

This procedure is not a magic wand, to be sure, but the prognosis for successful problem resolution is much more optimistic than in the first example given, and the solution will become "our new program" instead of the "principal's new program."

ROUTINE AND NONROUTINE DECISION MAKING

Decisions come in a variety of forms, differing in content, in the process by which the problem is addressed, and in the kind of impact they make on the organization and the people in the organization. Too, there is always the problem of matching the appropriate problem resolution process with classes of decisional situations. When should one make a straightforward, from the hips, unilateral decision, and when

should one involve groups in agonizing consensus?

The answer is not hard to see in the extreme. If the situation is a fire in the basement, one issues the order to clear the building, one does not call a committee together to achieve consensus on which fire exits to use. However, it would be appropriate to involve affected groups or individuals in advance in the development of policies and procedures for coping with such anticipated emergencies.

There are many ways to classify decisions, but beyond a certain point it really doesn't do much good except for retrospective analysis. That is, knowing a taxonomy of decisions would hardly put a person in the position of unerringly knowing when to do what. Unfortunately, that kind of written wisdom doesn't exist. Helpful to this discussion, however, may be some examination of general decision categories occuring in any organization. Decision situations, for example, can be either routine or nonroutine.

Routine Decision Making

Any organization must, of course, accommodate itself to many unanticipated situations, but generally the basis for an orderly goal-oriented school is a "repertory of proven, reliable, productive activities that are activated, monitored, and terminated by an appropriate set of habituated routine decisions."[6]

Many ongoing activities in the school organization are recurring in nature. Although it is important that procedural or routine decision-making practices be reviewed from time to time to make sure they are still adequate to the task (that is, to make sure that the social or organizational conditions to which they respond have not changed), the decisions and decisions processes that respond to these recurring activities should be routinized. The principal can expect certain kinds of problems to recur with frequency, given a particular environment or set of circumstances. Routine response mechanisms to these are expected by the staff so that they can go about their work with a minimum of disruption.

Further, as Gore has suggested,[7] when firm patterns for routine decision making exist:

1. The consequences of action (especially negative) can be more readily anticipated.
2. The most efficient ways of responding have been located through experience, making most [nonroutine] activities appear excessively expensive in terms of time and resources that must be invested to secure a given set of goals.
3. Simply because one is dealing with the familiar and the accepted [routine decisions] are typically accompanied by pleasant, or at least tolerable overtones. On the other hand [a nonroutine decision] characteristically amounts to a leap into the unknown accompanied by individual stress that produces considerable discomfort.

Arranging conditions in the school so that routine, recurring problems are resolved with a minimum of disruption and false starts can be achieved readily. A school building policy and rules and regulations manual carefully developed with the staff and students can provide much assistance. Such a manual should contain statements of basic responsibilities accruing to teachers, counselors, administrators, and classified personnel, perhaps in each of the major decision categories of pupil personnel services, staffing and staff relations, building financial operations, public relations, and curriculum and instructional development. In such a manual the roles and responsibilities of various personnel with respect to matters pertaining to the decision category would be carefully delineated, lines of communication spelled out, and common procedural questions answered.

Delegation of specific management tasks to designated people will also insure a degree of stability, not only because it clarifies the "who is to do what" question, but also because it per-

mits the principal to manage by exception rather than by direct participation in all decisions.

It is important, however, to provide a review process whereby policies, procedures, rules and regulations, and delegation practices are systematically examined to insure that they continue to serve efficiently and effectively. The reason for the development of policies and procedures is to facilitate the delivery of services to classrooms. When it becomes evident that a particular procedure is no longer appropriate, or is actually inhibiting problem resolution, it must be revised. Effective use can be made of a staff-student advisory council for regular reviews of the routine procedures. The question sequence for such reviews is simply: "What are we doing?"; "Why are we doing it?"; and "Can it be done a better way?"

A final word is necessary concerning routine decision making. It should not be assumed that because a decision is termed routine or programmed that that decision is unimportant; it means only that situations often recur, that the school organization has developed procedures for dealing with these problems, and that certain requisite role behaviors have been established.

A properly managed school can carry on the routine day-to-day activities without the constant involvement of the principal. The primary responsibility of the principal is not the building's routine operation, but to create organizational conditions whereby the school may modify its operations to meet changing demands and opportunities.

Thus, routine, regularized or programmed decision making, while encompassing problem situations running the gamut from highly important to mundane, is best formalized to the extent that relatively little stress on individuals or the organization occurs as decisions are promulgated and implemented. Such is often not the case with nonroutine decision making.

Nonroutine Decision Making

Unanticipated problems, unique situations, and fast-changing conditions are also characteristics of organizational life. Decisions concerning these situations often require "leaps into the unknown" that by their very nature produce both individual and organizational stress.

Establishing conditions for creative problem resolution is an important task of the principal—perhaps the most important task. Routinizing responses to recurring problems requires good management skills to be sure; creative problem resolution requires as well both the ability to tolerate ambiguity over a period of time and effective human relations skills.

As noted earlier, the most important resource for creative problem resolution is the combined intelligence and insight of the work group itself, the faculty, classified personnel, and students in the school. Lipham describes this process at its best:

> In heuristic or creative decision-making there is a lack of emphasis upon hierarchical structure. Role behavior is characterized by each individual being free to explore all ideas bearing on the problem, and the processes utilized are characterized by full and free discussion. The emotional or social tone is relatively relaxed and characterized by openness and originality. Working with students or teachers in solving a curricular issue is an example of heuristic decision-making, particularly if there is no agreed-upon method for dealing with the issue.[8]

BRAINSTORMING

Several techniques exist for tapping the collective intelligence of the staff for creative or nonroutine decision making. One technique that has been effectively used is brainstorming.

Brainstorming as a technique for creative problem solving has as its only purpose the generation of ideas, no matter how wild the ideas may seem. The usual kinds of conferences and meetings tend to be rather noncreative. A brainstorming group, on the other hand, devotes itself *solely to creative thinking*. To function properly, the group must remain, during the period of brainstorm, completely divorced from all practical and mundane things of the day. The precise rules described in figure 2–2 must be followed if the maximum result is to be gained from the brainstorming activity.

Logistics The role of the group leader is one of facilitator rather than that of gate keeper. Several methods of recording can be employed. Many brainstorming groups, however, have found that the best method is to record the ideas on flip chart paper.[9] The ideas are thus retrievable in that the paper can simply be taken off the wall and handed to a secretary for duplication on ditto paper or stencil for later circulation.

Judgment and Refinement of Ideas Later, the group reconvenes for the purpose of judging and modifying ideas. This session is one of analysis. Its purpose is to select those ideas that singly, *or in combination with other ideas,* seem to provide a creative solution to the problem.

From the analysis session the group decides on four or five modified solutions that offer a basis for the systematic resolution of the problem. At this point a group may engage in any of a number of systematic planning approaches and work the solutions into an implementation phase.

GUIDELINES FOR EXECUTIVE DECISION MAKING

The overriding question in decision making is what goal or outcome are the pupils or staff attempting to reach and by what process can it be

---

Rules of the Game:

1. *The problem that the group is going to work on must be stated clearly.* That is, everyone must know the problem that is to be solved.

2. *Criticism in the brainstorming session is not permitted.* The group facilitator must not permit any adverse judgment of ideas during the period of the brainstorming. Any idea is a good idea no matter how apparently ridiculous it may seem at the moment to some other members of the group.

3. *"Free wheeling" is welcome and encouraged.* The wilder the idea, the better. The reason for engaging in a brainstorming session is to try to find new ways of approaching a problem. Any group, or any individuals in the group, that become infected with the "that won't work because" syndrome will be most ineffective.

4. *Quantity is what the group is after.* The greater the number of ideas, the more likelihood one or more of those ideas will be a winner.

5. *Combination and improvement are sought.* In addition to contributing ideas of their own, participants should suggest how ideas of others can be combined or changed in some way to produce yet another idea. Idea "stealing" and modification is encouraged; the common rules governing social convention do not apply in brainstorming sessions.

6. *Maximum participation of group members is required.* It is for this reason that brainstorming groups should be kept relatively small, probably no more than ten. Because it is so noticeable, it is hard to drop out when one is in a small group; thus, smaller groups tend to promote maximum participation. Everybody has something to contribute to a brainstorming group and the ideas of everyone are sought.

7. *The only role of the group leader is that of facilitator and participant.* The group leader does not serve as a chairperson in a usual sense and *Robert's Rules of Order* are out. A brainstorming group is a very impolite group.

FIGURE 2-2.   Rules of brainstorming

best achieved. Decision making may be seen as a six-step process:

1. Identifying the true problem and subproblems.
2. Collecting the relevant facts.
3. Identifying alternative actions from which to choose the best course. As a part of this step it is important to anticipate for each of the alternatives what the possible consequences of the action will be with respect to any of several reference groups who may be affected by the decisions.

4. Commitment to a single choice or single course of action.
5. Implementing the preferred choice.
6. Provision for evaluation and feedback about the decision.

What is the Problem?

Until the problem is adequately defined, no effective decision can be reached. Also, the real problem is often not verbally presented or most apparent, and investigation beneath the surface is always justified. Sometimes the real problem may become apparent in the data collection procedure. Thus, the first task is to identify the real problem and the impinging subproblems. When any problem is first presented, an individual or a group is an immediate captive of insufficient data. A staff complaint or parent complaint may simply be an iceberg with the real problem far below the surface. Treating symptoms instead of causes is an administrative trap.

The soundest advice is to initially withhold judgment. Rarely does an immediate seat-of-the-pants decision have to be made. Good decision making requires taking the necessary time to gather relevant facts that have a bearing on the problem at hand. Further, there are usually many sides to an issue or problem, and the avoidance of commitment in the first flush of reaction will stand decision makers in good stead indeed.

Alternative Actions

In dealing with any problem, there are frequently several approaches and several alternative actions that can be taken to resolve the immediate issue. Once all the facts are in, a good way to decide which alternative is the best is to list the alternatives and ask the following questions of each:

1. Does this action treat the real problem or merely the symptom?
2. What kinds of other problems does this alternative decision create?
3. Who and what will be affected by the decision?
4. What probable reaction can be expected from those affected by the alternative?
5. Is the alternative consistent with general school policy, rules, and regulations and with the law?
6. Can the decision be reasonably well understood and implemented?

Six Barriers to Good Decision Making

To summarize the important elements concerning decision making, an examination can be made of six possible impediments:

1. *Improper or inappropriate ordering of decisions.* Some problems by their very nature, or upon even cursory examination, are pressing and critical; others are less so. Analyze the problem. Is it a seat-of-the-pants kind of thing or does it contain very complex elements and subproblems? Is it crucial or doesn't it require immediate attention? It is true that most often decisions do not have to be made immediately, but this gives the principal and the staff time for fact gathering, not vacillation or total postponement of critical issues.

2. *Jumping to conclusions.* This is a result of immediate visceral reaction overcoming cerebral processes and is caused by not asking any questions or by not asking enough of the right questions.

3. *Two-sided thinking.* This barrier refers to putting every issue into a two-value context. In an effort to be extremely fair, the individual or group decides to look at *both* sides of the issues. In fact, of course, issues are rarely two sided. There are probably many sides to be considered and the answer probably lies somewhere around the periphery of the problem circle. Putting issues into an either/or context is one of the quickest ways to restrict creative solutions to complex situations. In issues involving people, it results in a total victory/total capitulation situation which leaves no room for compromise.

4. *The one-solution-only black out.* Often this is a result of pride of authorship by the prime decision maker(s). Such an approach effectively shuts out other decisions, some of which are possibly better. It's related to two-valued thinking and it is a deceptive trap. Some problems, because of their complexity, require

two or more methods to effect a solution or to meet a need. Often, problems can best be solved through a procedure that involves the best thinking of many staff members and the consensus process. It is a wise decision maker indeed who seeks counsel on problem definition, fact gathering, and the development of alternative solutions.

5. *Making unnecessary changes.* This is often a result of failing to ask the question, "Really now, why?" Making unnecessary changes will tend to reflect a degree of inconsistency in principal behavior. Even the most innocuous changes can give off wide ripples if the change has not been well conceived or is not based upon some real need. If there really is no good reason for changing a policy or procedure, then it shouldn't be changed. The principal, thus, should avoid seeming capricious.

6. *Failure to adequately communicate.* If something is important, it deserves to be appropriately understood and accepted in the spirit intended. What the principal is after are sensible decisions so that teachers can teach and learners can learn in a most efficient and effective manner. Little is served in disguising decisions so that no one knows for sure what the decision was.

Good Communication is Essential

Implementing decisions is in large part dependent upon good communication. The way in which the decision is communicated will say much about the importance of the decision. Using the ditto machine to communicate a major policy change says loudly and clearly that the decision is not a very important one. If the problem is a complex one and important behavior change is required in order to have a decision properly implemented, more is required that a simple written statement from the principal's office or the task group. Further, there is

a need to know whether or not those affected by the decision know what it is they are supposed to do. Feedback and evaluation are necessary in any decision process. In its simplest form, the question is, "Is the decision working; was the goal achieved; if not, why not?"

SUMMARY

This chapter has focused on the decision making processes. Three kinds of decision processes are available to the principal: unilateral, majority opinion, and consensus. Each has it's place, but for those decisions that require substantial changes in the behavior of organizational members or considerable organizational readjustment, neither rule by administrative fiat nor one vote over half is sufficient.

Techniques such as task force team development, consensus decision making, and brainstorming are necessary for complex problem solving. Each of these techniques taps the "group wisdom," and provides a strong basis for the effective implementation of solutions.

ENDNOTES

1. The interested reader might wish to examine what Douglas McGregor has to say on the subject of effective problem-solving teams. McGregor describes processes and behaviors characteristic of both good and bad management teams. McGregor, *Human Side of the Enterprise* (New York: McGraw-Hill, 1960), pp. 232–239.

2. Jay Hall, "Decisions, Decisions, Decisions," *Psychology Today* 6 (November 1971): 53.

3. One could, of course, take no action at all and hope the problem would simply go away. This is known as the hemorrhoid approach—one just sits on the problem.

4. Second generation desegregation occurs after the "bodies are mixed," that is, after the racial

and/or ethnic composition of a school is brought into a balance generally reflective of the school district. Moving beyond body mixing to a truly desegregated school presents a much different set of problems and circumstances than those confronted in the initial months of desegregation. See, for example, Frederick P. Venditti, "Second Generation School Desegregation Problems," *Educational Catalyst* 8 (Spring 1978): 100–108.

5.   "New" processes probably are best thought of as "hypotheses to be tested." That is, the effect of the new process should be continually evaluated. The "what are we doing," "why are we doing it," "can it be done a better way" approach is important.

6.   William J. Gore, "Decision-Making Research: Some Prospects and Limitations," in Stanley Mailick and Edward Van Ness, eds., *Concepts and Issues in Administrative Behavior* (Englewood Cliffs, N.J.: Prentice-Hall, 1962), p. 53.

7.   Ibid.

8.   James M. Lipham, "Improving the Decision-Making Skills of the Principal," in Jack Culbertson et al., *Performance Objective for School Principals* (Berkeley, Calif.: McCutchan Publishing Co., 1974), chapter 4.

9.   The recorder's role is simply to jot down the ideas as they are generated, making sure the essence of the idea has been captured. When the group gets moving and the ideas start coming faster and faster use two or more recorders. Depending on the nature of the problem to be addressed, brainstorming groups, both neophyte and veteran, typically generate anywhere from thirty to ninety ideas in a five-minute period or so.

BIBLIOGRAPHY

Bridges, Edwin M. "A Model for School Decision Making in the School Principalship." *Educational Administration Quarterly* (January 1967): 49–61. This work is an analysis of the dimensions and implications of three kinds of arrangements in which school faculties may arrive at decisions.

Drucker, Peter. *Management: Tasks, Responsibilities, Practices.* New York: Harper and Row, 1974.

Hall, Jay. "Decisions, Decisions, Decisions," *Psychology Today* 6 (November 1971): 51–547.

Hughes, Larry W. *Effective Decision-Making: A Principal's Primer.* New London, Conn.: Croft Educational Services, May, 1970.

Hughes, Larry W., and Martha J. Bratton. "Perceived Decision-Making Authority in a Large Decentralized Urban School System," *Catalyst For Change* 7 (Spring 1978): 4–9.

Lipham, James M. "Improving the Decision Making Skills of the Principal," in Culbertson et al., *Performance Objectives for School Principals,* chapter 4.

Mailick, Stanley, and Van Ness, Edward, eds. *Concepts and Issues in Administrative Behavior.* Englewood Cliffs, N.J.: Prentice-Hall, 1962.

McGregor, Douglas. *The Human Side of the Enterprise.* New York: McGraw-Hill, 1960.

Venditti, Frederick P. "Second Generation Desegregation Problem," *Educational Catalyst* 8 (Spring 1978): 100–108.

Chapter Three

Creating a Basis for Participatory Decision Making

INTRODUCTION

It is necessary for the principal to create an organizational climate within which active leadership and good decision making will emerge from the staff.

> Basic to the creation of such a climate . . . would seem to be the principal's assumptions about those with whom he works. If a principal sees his fellow workers—whether they be teachers, supervisors, custodians, or students—as drone-like, lazy, requiring close supervision, and unresponsive [then his] patterns of interpersonal behavior will likely manifest these assumptions.[1]

If these are the assumptions of the principal, creative decision making from the staff cannot be expected. In order to genuinely make use of the group intelligence, one must believe it exists.

Assumptions About the Staff

Douglas McGregor identified two sets of assumptions that administrators might have about subordinates.[2] He labeled these assumptions *Theory X* and *Theory Y*. Essentially, Theory X holds that people are by nature indo-lent, will avoid work wherever possible, and are not goal oriented except perhaps in selfish kinds of ways. The task of the administrator, given these assumptions, is to actively direct the efforts of subordinates, to overtly or covertly attempt to control their actions, and to narrowly describe the subordinate's job so that close supervision is possible. Unless this is done, Theory X assumes, subordinates will be passive, perhaps even resistant to organizational goals. In short, subordinates need to be closely controlled, persuaded, rewarded, and punished; their activities must be directed, otherwise nothing beneficial will get done.

It can be readily seen that there would occur little participatory decision making or little latitude for creative task accomplishment in a management system built on these assumptions. Sadly, many schools are organized in such a way, and inevitably the benefits of the group intelligence in complex problem identification and problem resolution are totally lost. The principal behaving on the basis of such assumptions is victimized and spends time responding to brush fires, controlling by close supervision the activities of the subordinates and interpreting and applying minute aspects of the policy manual. Staff, in responding to such a management system, will indeed be passive and at times resistant, but the management system itself causes these reactions, not an inherent human characteristic.

Theory Y is based on a much different set of assumptions. It assumes basically that most people are capable of self-direction and, given the opportunity, will contribute to organizational goal achievement without intense supervision and close control. It also assumes that creativity and decision-making ability are widely distributed in the population.

Assuming that the motivation, potential for development, capacity to accept responsibility, and a willingness to work toward organization goals are present in all people, the administrator's task becomes somewhat different. The task of the principal under a Theory Y set of assumptions becomes that of arranging organizational conditions so that the staff can satisfy their own personal needs best by directing their efforts toward the objectives of the organization.

Summarizing the application of the *X* and *Y* dichotomy to the tasks of the principal, Hughes has written:

> *Theory X* basically assumes the need for a vast array of external control mechanisms, while *Theory Y* assumes much employee self-control and self-direction and implies a participatory management system. In neither instance are the goals of the organization forgotten, but the means of achieving them vary widely. A principal who accepts the assumptions of *Theory Y* might provide more opportunities for leadership on a particular project or task to emerge from the staff rather than considering himself to be the sole source of initiation. Such a principal would encourage activities designed to enlarge the decision-making authority of individual teachers or groups of teachers, thereby giving them more control over their daily professional life. Clearly, too, performance appraisal of teachers and other employees would result from cooperative target setting, rather than the predetermined expectations of a single administrator. Such procedures require greater faith in one's co-workers.[3]

COOPERATIVE GOAL SETTING FACILITATES DECISION MAKING

It is axiomatic that any well-functioning organization and hence any units of that organization, for example, the individual school building, must have a clear sense of direction—a sense of what the unit or the system is all about, where it is desirably headed (goals), and what it will take to get there (processes). These goals[4] and processes should be the result of the joint thinking of all those to be affected by the school—the staff, the students, the parents of the students, and the community as a whole. Once developed and written down, goals need to be explicated by specific statements of objectives and subjected at regular intervals to a review in the light of: (1) whether or not, or the degree that they are being achieved; and (2) whether, in view of changing social dynamics and social needs, they continue to be appropriate.

Thus, a focus is provided for school system and school building endeavors and a means exists to evaluate the efficacy of these endeavors. New program proposals, responses to problem situations, alternative decisions, all may be evaluated in the light of such goals and objectives. Of course, within the goals, objectives, and processes there must be latitude for individual contribution and creative behavior. Practically speaking, goal setting and the development of specific activities to implement the goals results in a means whereby an individual or department or school staff can show its worth. This is especially important in these days of accountability. Just as important, however, are the positive psychological effects that such cooperative goal setting engenders in a staff. Characteristic of the healthy organization is a considerable degree of congruence between individual goals and objectives and organizational goals and objectives. Where no stated goals or objectives exist, or where there is uncertainty about what they are, one can expect to find at best accidental excellence and incidental staff and client growth, even though individual staff members may be expending great personal energies in the accomplishment of their own professional or personal goals. Without clearly defined and accepted goals, there may be energy in an organization but not synergy.

The key then would appear to be to use the human resources in an organization in such a way that people behave congruent with the organizational goals and, by carrying out their responsibilities in this way, they are also maximally engaged in meeting their own personal objectives and goals. How can this be achieved? The best way is to provide mechanisms and opportunities for participation in goal-setting endeavors and decision making by those who are to be most affected by the goals that are developed and the decisions that are ultimately to be made. Such a mode requires administrative confidence in staff abilities and motivations.

ORGANIZATIONAL JOB LATITUDE

There are many ways to accomplish the specific tasks in the organization. Figures 3–1 and 3–2 depict polar concepts in task assignments. At one end of the continuum are jobs in which behavior is very carefully and tightly defined. Thus, assigning tasks becomes a matter of defining the job and making the person fit that job. In such a job there is little latitude for individual decision making; behavior is controlled by strict organizational expectations. One would not expect to find great job satisfaction in such a "thin" job, although there might be high productivity if the tasks to be performed were simple.[5] At the other end of the continuum exists freedom for the individual to define the job and to enjoy much autonomy with respect to the processes employed in carrying out that job as long as the result was consistent with organizational goals.

Few, if any formal organizations have jobs that are totally at one pole or another. To be sure, in highly mechanized industries the person on the production line often has virtually no autonomy, no decision making about how to carry out the job. Often this person becomes a virtual automaton. Similarly, of course, in very loosely developed organizations of people, such as an artist colony, one may find almost total individual job autonomy.

In the school organization, however, one would seldom observe either extreme in its pure

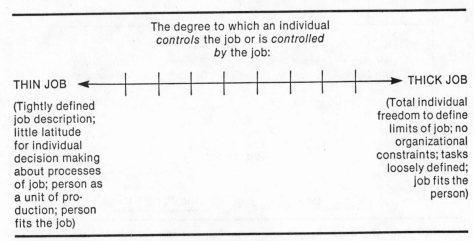

The degree to which an individual *controls* the job or is *controlled by* the job:

THIN JOB ←—————————→ THICK JOB

(Tightly defined job description; little latitude for individual decision making about processes of job; person as a unit of production; person fits the job)

(Total individual freedom to define limits of job; no organizational constraints; tasks loosely defined; job fits the person)

FIGURE 3–1. Organizational job latitude model

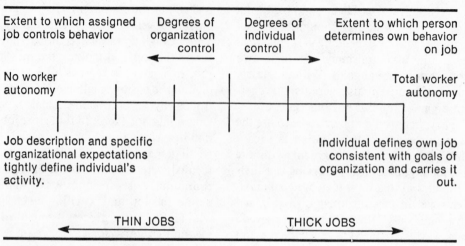

FIGURE 3–2. Organizational job latitude model

form. There are tendencies toward one end of the continuum or the other, however. For example, in the school organization, teachers often have wide latitude for certain kinds of decision making with respect to how the day will be organized and which teaching methodologies will be executed. However, much of the teacher

decision making in traditional schools is confined to the limits of the classroom itself. Figure 3–3 illustrates where various organizational "jobs" might commonly be placed on the continuum.

The authors and most organizational theorists believe that the degree to which the school

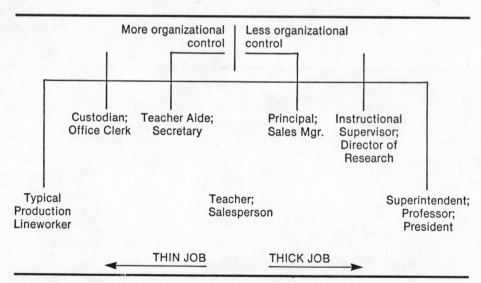

FIGURE 3–3. Organizational job latitude model: Examples of jobs by degree of organizational control and worker autonomy

organization can operate in a mode tending toward the autonomous end of the continuum will determine the degree to which the rich resources of human intelligence in the organization are being appropriately used to provide for effective decision making and organizational goal accomplishment. The work force in the schools is uncommonly well trained. The means for capitalizing on this resource in order to obtain better problem resolution is available to the principal.

All of the positions on the "thin-thick" scale could probably be given more autonomy to good effect. The primary reason for doing so is not to achieve high morale, however; it is to get better results. High morale frequently occurs because of greater job autonomy and this is good, but unless the administrative focus is also to achieve greater movement toward organizational goals, the principal will simply be presiding over a country club. Much energy may be expended, but unless this results in better learning by students, what is the point? There are techniques which the principal can employ to achieve both increased job satisfaction and organizational goal achievement. Job target setting and job thickening are two such techniques.

Job Target Setting

Essentially, individual job target setting requires that the principal and staff member mutually establish for the staff member some year-end goals ("targets"). These targets are to be congruent with the general direction in which the school is desirably headed. It is anticipated that the achievement of these staff goals will result in more effective staff performance and movement to organizational goals.

The principal's responsibility is to help the staff member develop instructional, curricular, and professional growth targets which are realistically addressable and consistent with the curricular goals of the school.[6] It is also the

principal's responsibility to provide the resources (time, budget allocations, technical assistance, etc.) to assist the staff member to achieve the established targets.[7]

It is the responsibility of the staff member to engage in a self and organizational analysis after which appropriate year-end targets are generated for subsequent discussion with the principal. In addition to the target statements, the staff member establishes what will be accepted as indicators of whether or not, or the degree to which, the targets have been reached. Figure 3–4 is an example of a series of targets generated by a teacher in collaboration with the principal; Figure 3–5 shows principal job targets.[8] Care must be exercised to avoid the extremes of either unrealistically high targets or statements of low level accomplishments.[9]

Initially, such a process as that just described may require some intensive inservice training for staff. If the technical expertise is not available in the district, help may be secured from such varied sources as local university departments of administration and supervision, organizations such as the National Association of Secondary School Principals, and private educational consultants including such agencies as The Center for Program Design and Evaluation and Humanistic Management Services, among others.[10]

Job Thickening

Providing a work environment wherein staff may exercise a greater degree of professional or technical autonomy can result in a highly productive and often creative release of energy. The illogic of the person who thinks the principal must make all of the important decisions and closely supervise individual staff member activities has been stressed several times in this book. Stressed too, though, has been that certain kinds of decision making and administrative control logically and expectedly accrue to the principal. Therefore, what are some specific

Professional Targets
School Year_____
Hudson High School

Name_____   Dept._____

I. Instructional Target(s)
Individualize instruction in Basic Algebra course.
Indicators of Achievement:
1. Develop self-instructional modules for Units 1–4
2. Revise pre-instruction assessment instruments for Algebra I (Basic)
3. Devise at least four enrichment activities or games for low-interest students

II. Curriculum Target(s)
Integrate one section of first semester advanced math and physics courses.
Indicators of Achievement:
1. Initiate interdepartmental study group
2. Develop objectives for course
3. Identify potential students
4. Develop syllabus

III. Professional Growth Target(s)
Improve diagnostic and prescriptive skills.
Indicators of Achievement:
1. Review Buros, *Mental Measurements.*
2. Successfully complete FED 638 at University of Houston
3. Revise pre-instruction instrument for Algebra I (same as I-2 above)

FIGURE 3–4.   An example of a teacher's job targets

Activity: Administration of the School Unit

General Objective: Provide for instructional leadership

Specific Targets:
1. The principal will organize his or her time in such a way that he or she visits each classroom in the building for a minimum of one hour per month.
2. The principal will require each teacher in the building to submit behavioral objectives each year for Instructional Council review and will meet individually with each teacher to discuss these.
3. The principal will organize an instructional council which will not meet less than once monthly to advise on school policy curriculum development and instructional practices.
4. The principal will introduce at least one instructional or curricular innovation adjudged by research evidence to be a significant new approach to the teaching/learning process each school year and will develop a PERT network to implement the change.

FIGURE 3–5.   An example of a principal's job targets

decision areas that might best be matters of individual staff member or at least departmental discretion?[11] The following decision areas would seem appropriate for delegation to departments and individuals.

Teaching methodology
Selection of instructional materials
Course content
Inservice training in subject matter
Relationships and roles of teachers and
    students
Student scheduling
Scope and sequence of curricular area
Student scheduling
Assignment of advisors
Evaluation practices and procedures
Scheduling of class periods
Sequencing of instructional modules
Job descriptions and assignments of para-
    professionals
Objectives of the courses, modules, and
    department

The following consideration of the decision area "scope and sequence of curriculum" from Sergiovanni lends further focus to the issue:

Is the curriculum organized in such a fashion which encourages teachers to teach in a mindless way with little regard for the value of the material they cover or for what they are trying to accomplish? Are teachers largely direction-givers implementing a heavily prescribed curriculum and therefore making few decisions of their own? Such situations badly need enrichment. The following questions, though not inclusive, might help decide the extent to which your educational program needs enrichment:

1. Are teachers deciding what will be taught, when, and how?
2. Is the curriculum confining to teachers or does it free them to be innovative and creative?
3. Do teachers know what they are trying to accomplish and why?
4. Are schedules established and youngsters grouped by teachers for educational reasons?

5. Are teachers free to deviate from schedules for good educational reasons?
6. Is curriculum standardization avoided for teachers and students?
7. Is the teacher more accountable for achieving agreed-upon goals and objectives than for teaching the curriculum or operating his classroom in a given way?
8. Do teachers have some budget control and responsibility for their areas?
9. Can teachers team if they wish?
10. Are teachers free to choose their own curriculum materials within budget constraints?[12]

The decision-making responsibility explicit in the foregoing list substantially "thickens" the role of the teacher, providing much job latitude.

WHY PARTICIPATORY DECISION MAKING?

The school executive is looking for the best decision, the maximal feasible solution. Such solutions will not occur in an organization of interacting humans unless processes are employed which make great use of the collective intelligence of these humans.

Four assumptions guide the executive who engages in participatory decision making:

1. People at the working level tend to know the problems best.
2. The face-to-face work group is the best unit for diagnosis and change.
3. People will work hard to achieve objectives they have helped develop.
4. Initiative and creativity are widely distributed in the population.[13]

We hear a lot about trust these days; about how we must "trust" each other if the outcome is to be an effective faculty team and a hospitable organizational environment. Trust is not developed by talking about it or by exhortation. Productive and trusting relationships develop as a result of people engaging in important activities together—through which the strengths and weaknesses of fellow members are revealed—to learn who can be counted on for what kinds of expertise. Knowing where certain kinds of expertise exist permits the principal to constitute effective task force teams to focus on troubling school-wide issues, existent or anticipated.

WHEN TO INVOLVE OTHERS IN DECISION MAKING

It is not possible to unerringly know when to involve others in a decision-making process, who those others should be, or what the nature of that involvement should be. Decision making and decision implementation require varying degrees of expertise and varying degrees of faculty commitment. It depends in great part on the complexity of the problem to be solved and the degree to which those affected by the decision will be required to behave differently in order for the decision to be properly implemented. Using the two factors of technical expertise (quality of decision required) and need for group acceptance (hearty compliance and/or behavior change required) as prime determinants, a quadrant model can be developed to help determine the answer to the involvement question. Figure 3–6 displays such a model.

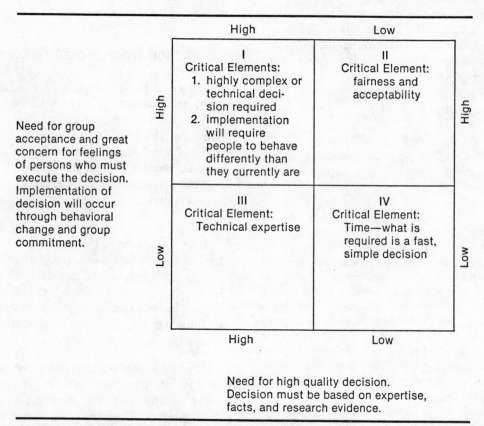

FIGURE 3–6.   **When to involve others in decision making**

Adapted from Jerome L. Franklin, Anne Wissler, and Gregory J. Spencer. *Survey-Guided Development III: A Manual for Concepts Training* (LaJolla, California: University Associates, 1977). Used with permission.

Quadrant I in the model contains those decisions that require much technical expertise and knowledge in order for a high quality solution to be achieved. Quadrant I also describes a situation wherein no matter how technically superior the solution may be, in order for this solution to be put into effect much work group acceptance will be necessary. Hearty acceptance may be questionable for several reasons: because an apparent solution is contrary to present practice or present attitudes; because it requires work group members to perform in ways that are initially more difficult, or for which they have not been trained; because of a simple lack of agreement about the efficacy of the decision; or any number of other reasons including threat, fear, distrust of administrators, or anger. Also, some, if not all, of these reasons may have substance other than emotion.[14]

What kinds of issues might fall within this quadrant? Any curricular change certainly would, as would budget development. Changes in high school policies affecting large numbers of students, and school constitutional questions would also seem to fit here. A problem such as that described in the case study in chapter 2 illustrates this kind of decision situation. Operating in this quadrant will require good human relations skills and technical competence in the subject under review.

Quadrant II depicts those situations where group feelings may be intense, but great technical expertise is not required because the subject is not a complex one. Any number of resolution schemes are available; the appropriate one must be that which is fair and sensitive to the needs and desires of the work group. Assignment of unpaid extra-curricular duties, balanced work schedules for routine duties, school calendar development, among a myriad of decision situations might fall in this category. Among appropriate ways to handle problems in this quadrant would be the formation of advisory committees, complete delegation of decision making to standing or ad hoc bodies, or informal consultation with leaders of the group affected.

Quadrant III contains those kinds of decisions that affect the quality of the operation in a technical sense, but do not impact much on the human side of the enterprise. Equipment selection once needs have been identified, development of conflict-free schedules, design of a management information system, among other examples might be found in this quadrant.

In the fourth quadrant neither great technical competence nor sensitive human relations is a critical consideration. (No decision can ever be entirely devoid of these, however.) What is needed is a simple act to resolve a simple problem. Time is the only critical element. The decision has to be made in a timely manner so that people in the organization can go about their work in an orderly, efficient, and knowledgeable manner.

The model is helpful as an analytical tool. It emphasizes that the good high school principal will have a repertoire of decision-making processes from which to select, and the process selected will be a result of the nature of the problem. Neither committees for everything, nor total exercise of the raw power of expertise will uniformly serve. Also, involvement is a rich term extending from situations where persons will be asked their opinions to situations where broad decision limits will be set and task forces asked to engage in final decision making for the entire high school, with a number of points in between.[15]

IDENTIFYING STAFF INTERESTS, SKILLS, AND NEEDS

How well does the principal know the staff? In order to make the best use of the techniques of job target setting and job thickening it is necessary to have more knowledge about individual staff members than is contained in the typical personnel file. Normal attrition of staff because of transfer, retirement, and resignation, as well as the ordinary difficulty present in any organi-

Title/Position _____   Date _____

Years of Employment _____   Degree _____

Directions: Please place a check in both Columns II and III for each area. Blank columns at the end of the instrument may be used to add special areas you may wish to list.

SECTION A

I. Area	II. Experience				III. Interest		
	Expertise in: experienced practice, and can serve as a consultant	Worked with: in many situations—even though modified	Knowledge of: extends beyond definition but have not worked with	No knowledge of: extends to no more than simple definition	Desire further training in	Desire training in	Do not desire training in
(DIAGNOSTIC AND PRESCRIPTIVE TEACHING)							
Assessing the Classroom Climate							
Teacher-Made Tests							
Standardized Tests							
Grading							
(CLASSROOM MULTI-DISCIPLINARY TEAM)							
(MULTICULTURAL AWARENESS)							
Community Analysis Field Study							
Cultural Communication							
Multilingual Teaching Team							
(DEVELOPING INSTRUCTIONAL MODULES)							

FIGURE 3–7. Teacher/counselor/nurse experience–interest questionnaire

Source: Houston Independent School District.

zation in getting professionally acquainted with all of a large staff even over a period of years, inhibits effective deployment of personnel. Solving this problem is difficult, but some principals have made in-roads by developing relatively simple staff inventories to become better acquainted with the richness of staff resources in a variety of skill areas. Information collected assists administrators in selecting members for special interdepartment and school task forces; providing the basis for a peer diagnostic and supervisory cadre; locating "in-house" instructional experts; and identifying inservice training needs. Figure 3–7 is a portion of an inventory used in the Houston Independent School district. The complete inventory contains such categories as "Teacher Effectiveness Strategies"; "Interdisciplinary Team Building"; "Multicultural Awareness"; "Developing Instructional Modules", among others. A similarly constructed inventory could be used to discover skills and needs of paraprofessionals, custodians, and other noncertificated staff.

SUMMARY

This chapter has focused on ways to effectively deploy staff and achieve greater involvement of the staff in decision making. Increasing the individual staff member's job autonomy by the techniques of job thickening and job target setting does require confidence in the ability of staff members, but the end result will be not only increased staff job satisfaction but, importantly, increased organizational goal accomplishment. Cooperative goal setting and appropriate delegation of decision making results in an effective educational team.

Knowing when and how to involve others in decision making requires great skill. The technical expertise required in order to make a high quality decision and the need for group acceptance in order for the decision to be implemented are the two most important elements to be considered.

ENDNOTES

1. Larry W. Hughes, "Effective Human Relations and Morale," in Jack Culbertson et al., *Performance Objectives for School Principals* (Berkeley, Calif.: McCutchan Publishing Co., 1974), p. 115.
2. Douglas McGregor, *The Human Side of the Enterprise* (New York: McGraw-Hill, 1960).
3. Hughes, "Effective Human Relations and Morale," p. 117.
4. For the purposes of this discussion a goal is defined as a timeless, direction-setting statement of general worth. Goals need to be explicated into a series of more specific and measurable objectives if they are to be put into operation.
5. Country music singer Johnny Paycheck satirized just such a "thin" existence in a hit song entitled, "Take This Job and Shove It."
6. Job target setting is not restricted to the professional staff, however. The same process should be engaged in with noncertificated staff members.
7. In large high schools, with well functioning relatively independent departments and department heads, the principal meets only with the department heads. These meetings would focus on (1) job targets for the head, (2) goals for the department as a whole, and (3) skill development for the head who will in turn work with the particular staff in the development of their individual targets.
8. In chapter 24, Figure 24–3 depicts a basis for the development of a series of principal job targets.
9. Nevertheless, the authors are reminded of the story attributed to Madame Curie. When she was young and just preparing for her career, she received the following advice from one of her teachers with regard to lifetime goals. In an anecdote the teacher said, "A hunter may aim his gun at either a mulberry bush or at the moon. If he shoots at the mulberry bush, he will almost certainly hit it. If he shoots at the moon he will almost certainly miss it. But, what he hits will be *infinitely higher* than a mulberry bush."
10. Center for Program Design and Evaluation, Box 523, Saluda, North Carolina 28773. Humanistic Management Services, 15 Arbor Court, Cincinnati, Ohio 45246.

11. Of course, decision making within these areas should always be consistent with laws, school system policies, and within the bounds of reasonable community expectations and needs. These circumscriptions exist for all persons in all public organizations.
12. Thomas J. Sergiovanni, *Handbook for Effective Department Leadership* (Boston: Allyn and Bacon, 1977), pp. 181–182.
13. Implicit in these assumptions is that group members are competent; a *sine qua non.*
14. The model is equally applicable whether one is dealing with issues affecting faculty, classified personnel, students, or community groups.
15. Many readers will be familiar with the Tannenbaum and Schmidt model which depicts points on a decision continuum from "Boss Tells" to "Boss Accepts any Group Decision," the nature of decision involvement depending on latitudes of leader and subordinate autonomy. Robert Tannenbaum and Warren H. Schmidt, "How to Choose a Leadership Pattern," *Harvard Business Review* 51 (May–June, 1973): 178.

BIBLIOGRAPHY

Argyris, Chris. *Integrating the Individual and the Organization.* New York: John Wiley and Sons, 1964.

Bowers, David G. *Systems of Organization,* Ann Arbor: The University of Michigan Press, 1977.

Herzberg, Frederick. *Work and the Nature of Man.* New York: World, 1966.

Hughes, Larry W. "Effective Human Relations and Morale," in Culbertson et al., *Performance Objectives for School Principals.* Berkeley, Calif.: McCutchan, 1974, chapter 5. At the conclusion of this chapter can be found several specific performance objectives and indicators of achievement with respect to the principal's role in engendering good staff morale.

Maier, Norman R. F. *Psychology in Industrial Organizations.* Boston: Houghton Mifflin Co., 1973.

Maslow, Abraham. *Motivation and Productivity.* New York: Harper and Brothers, 1954.

Moeller, Gerald H. and Mahan, David. *The Faculty Team.* Chicago: Science Research Associates, 1971.

Sergiovanni, Thomas J., ed. *Beyond Human Relations: Professional Supervision for Professional Teachers.* Washington: Association for Supervision and Curriculum Development, 1976.

Sergiovanni, Thomas J. *Handbook of Department Leadership.* Boston: Allyn and Bacon, 1977.

Tannenbaum, Robert and Schmidt, Warren H. "How to Choose a Leadership Pattern." *Harvard Business Review* 51 (May–June, 1973): 176–185.

Chapter Four

Developing Good Internal Communication

INTRODUCTION

Responding to problems in an effective way requires reliable information. Fact gathering, information seeking, perception testing, all initial steps in the decision-making process, require a smooth lateral and vertical flow of information throughout the organization. Two responsibilities comprise the task of administrative leadership. One is the task of moving the organization, in this case the individual school, toward its ultimate goals. At the same time, the school principal has the responsibility of maintaining the organization so it is both efficient and effective. Neither of these responsibilities can be achieved without an effective internal communication system.

A good internal communication system keeps all organizational members aware of what is happening and why it is happening, and attempts to keep them in general agreement that what is being done is correct. This, of course, is the ideal and is rarely totally achieved in any complex organization, but the more nearly it is achieved, the more effective the organization will be. At the very least, personnel in the organization should not work at cross purposes out of ignorance about what the organization is supposed to be doing. Without sufficient exchange of information, the principal and other personnel within the school are victimized when they must respond to a developing problem or make a decision.

Bulletins, Briefings, and Benevolent and Brainy Benedictions

Often a school district will expend much time, effort, and dollars developing a quality external communications program that it labels public relations, but will devote relatively little attention to the nature and needs of the internal communication program. In many school systems the internal communication network is relatively unsystematized, often involving a hit or miss use of a ditto machine or an occasional faculty meeting. At regular intervals, perhaps the superintendent, a member of the central office staff, or the principal will appear on closed circuit TV, radio, or the P.A. system to discuss issues of concern to the system or the building as a whole. Often that's it—and it can simply be labeled bulletins, briefings, and benevolent and brainy benedictions. Such one-way information dissemination techniques provide little opportunity for information exchange.

THE MULTIDIMENSIONAL ORGANIZATION

The educational organization, or for that matter any organization composed of more than two people, has a multidimensional nature. Internal communication must be examined from the standpoint of the nature of organizations and of the ways in which individuals within the organization behave and relate to one another. Without a careful study of the nature of individual behavior within the school, the internal communications effort may easily become ineffective and misdirected, and largely depend upon the three "B's."

Two dimensions, or elements, of the organization can be identified: the institutional dimension and the personal, or individual, dimension. The institutional dimension of an organization is made up of the official roles occupied by individuals. These roles are the dynamic aspects of the positions, offices, and statuses within an organization. They define the official behavior of people holding these positions, offices, or statuses, positions that have, of course, certain normative obligations and responsibilities. Thus, the principal has certain responsibilities and should behave in certain ways. Similarly, a teacher, a student, and a night custodian all have certain responsibilities.

The institutional dimension of an organization can be discerned rather readily from the formal organization chart and the job descriptions of the school system. From a formal organizational point of view, the responsibilities are clear and so the organization would appear to have no difficulty in responding directly and authoritatively to problem situations. The formal organization chart suggests that each role incumbent, each position holder, is devoid of individual personality. It is as if everyone is at the "thin" end of the job latitude model (see figures 3–1, 3–2, and 3–3). A principal is to do these things and react in certain ways; a teacher is to do these things and react in certain ways. This situation would result in a certain predictability of behaviors and reactions, provided, of course, that the individuals in the organization have the same perceptions or nearly the same perceptions about role definitions and what behaviors are appropriate for what roles.

If that was all there was to it, communication would be very easy indeed. Each person would understand what was to be done, would do it, and move on to the next task with a minimum of misunderstanding and false starts. However, official roles in the school are not filled with automatons. Roles are filled with people with individual personalities and no two are the same. This is where the misunderstanding and the breakdown of communications can begin. It is in examining this that the reasons for a good internal communication program can be best illustrated. For, as noted previously, there are two dimensions to the organization—the institutional dimension and the personal dimension.

Personal Dimension of the School Organization

It is not enough to understand the organizational chart and the job descriptions. There must be some understanding of the nature of the individuals inhabiting the various roles or positions in the organization. The individual style each person brings to his or her particular role differs from the style of other individuals performing that same role. In the educational field the individual needs, desires, and ambitions of each student are considered. A good school staff strives mightily to deal with the learner as an individual, to understand the learner's basic drives and why individuals behave as they do, as a unique entity. Schools do this in an effort to provide a more efficient and effective learning program, to help the student develop into a productive, self-satisfied being. Transfer this knowledge about the individual learner to the personnel within the school organization. The adult worker also has needs and ambitions, and any effort to derive the greatest productivity from the individual worker must take these into consideration. Social psychologists call these *needs-dispositions*.

In large part, an individual's needs-dispositions comprise the personality and determine how the person acts and reacts to other people and situations. They help determine what information will be accepted and what information will be rejected; how closely the person is "in-tune" with the school operation; or for that matter, how closely the person is in-tune with his or her own assignment within the organization. A more precise way of saying in-tune is to say that the person's goals and the organizational goals are congruent. The greater the degree of congruency between person and job, and person and organization, the more effective the person will be.

Is the way to facilitate communication and provide for a productive environment then to explain precisely to each person what the specifics of the job are, lead the person to a desk in a classroom, ring a bell, and let the work begin? Congruence is, of course, more complex than this. How people behave, where people think they stand in relation to others and the organization in general, and how much they understand is dependent upon their own perceptual framework. People see and understand what their individual backgrounds permit them to see and understand. Once this is recognized, the internal communication program ought to begin to mature. It then becomes apparent that bulletins, briefings, and benevolent and brainy benedictions simply are not enough, except for low level communication.

A great error is made by assuming that when an individual works in an organization that individual really understands the goals of the organization, agrees with them, or for that matter, even thinks about them. The person may not join a school staff in any particular capacity because of a deep commitment to education. In fact, he or she may even be antagonistic toward it as it is being practiced. The person may simply have wanted a job. To expect each worker within the school organization to have deeply internalized feelings about the significance of the job or the significance of the organization itself is not realistic. Zeigler has written with great insight:

It is not merely a person's occupation which colors his attitudes, but it is his perceptions of his occupation and the extent to which the occupation is functional in maintaining an integrated personality. On the other hand, there is the question of commitment to the occupation. To some persons the occupation is a major component of their identity. Others look at the occupation in a more casual fashion, viewing it primarily as a money-making device and not so much a portion of a total lifestyle.[1]

Informal Groups

Many informal groupings of people not found on the organizational chart function within the formal framework of any school organization. These nonofficial groupings are characterized by a feeling of general agreement, not necessarily spoken but tacitly understood, about certain values and goals. These are groupings of people who tend to see things somewhat similarly, who meet over a cup of coffee or cigarette during work and perhaps socialize together afterward. This highly personalized system of interaction operates to modify the effect of the formal organization on individuals. The groups may or may not tend to agree with the institutional goals or the expectations of the formal organization, although overtly they may behave as if they do. Leadership within the informal organization is earned through power, personality, or prestige, rather than being ascribed as in the formal organization. Further, the informal organization lies outside of the formal communications channel.

Commonly one thinks of the professional teaching staff as being the most important locus of informal groups, but informal groupings also may be found among administrators, noncertificated employees, and students. In some cases, there may be a mixing of role incumbents, as in the "boiler room gang" which might include a custodian or two.

There are, then, loosely organized but potentially influential groups of people operating outside the formal organization of the institution. As previously indicated, these groups have their own norms, values, and needs. The individual members may perceive their functions as being somewhat different than the official organization would define them. In the negative extreme, these groups may actually operate in such a way as to inhibit the school as it moves toward its goals. The more congruence in terms of values and goals that the informal and formal organization can develop, the more successful the school will become.

One function of administrative leadership is to maintain the institution while moving it toward its goals. The administrator must be aware of the functioning of the informal dimension and its various needs, and must seek to achieve a congruence between the two. Further, a rich source of information and leadership exists in the informal dimension—a source that the perceptive principal will tap in the problem resolution process.

Because of their nature, informal groupings do not have an intensely stable organization. There are shifts in the leadership as members leave the system or the building, or as other leaders emerge. The principal must be aware of these shifts and the implication that they may have to the effectiveness of the communication channels that may have been set up. Informal groups are a natural part of any organization and provide for a sense of personal significance within what may be a very impersonal structure. Also, there is not only one group operating within the information structure but a number of groups. Thus, different ways of relating and dealing with these groups must be developed, depending upon the situation and the group.

How does all of this affect the development of a good internal communication system? It clearly means that principals should make use of several mechanisms in the communications effort. Attempting to change behav-

ior just because it's "good for the organization" will not be a sufficient argument for many members of the staff. The development of mechanisms to involve teachers and non-certificated employees in significant tasks of a school nature that affect their job will be important to the success of the school. In other words, there must be means to provide for group attention to the problems affecting the organization. Tapping the group's intelligence will result in better problem resolution as well as engender support for the final decisions.

Certainly, bulletins, briefings, and benevolent and brainy benedictions are not enough for good communication and problem resolution. Such one-way devices do not provide an adequate opportunity to learn the reactions of the various people in the organization or to secure additional information that may materially affect problem resolution.

LEVELS OF COMMUNICATION

So far, the subject of effective communication has been treated almost as if communication "A" is the same as communication "B." It is not necessary to deliver all information in person to each individual within the organization, nor do all messages require group meetings. There are different levels of communication. Some matters can be taken care of adequately by a bulletin and a ditto machine. Others, however, require different approaches. For lack of a better classification, the levels of communication might be called low level, middle level, and high level. The distinction between these levels are made largely on the nature of the communication, the significance of it, and the ease with which the request or the concept being explored can be understood and implemented.

Thus, a *low level* of communication covers those simple little directives such as when pay day is or when a report is due. These are simply the things that the staff member must know and can forget until the next time. They would require very little explanation and are easily implemented.

The *middle level* of communication includes important information about the district (new policies and procedures, for example), new programs the district is involved in, the appointment of textbook adoption committees, etc. This information would require somewhat more detail and would cause a greater expenditure of energy on the part of the personnel to whom it is directed, both in comprehending the message and in implementing it.

High level communication is concerned with items of a more conceptual nature, such as major changes in direction for the district or the school, major policy changes at the school board level that would have great effect throughout the district or that deal with developing problems of some magnitude. Examples of such high level communication would be a dramatic change in the achievement levels of students, the changing nature of the student population, and other situations that have implications for school programming and instructional procedures.

The more difficult the nature of the idea that is being conveyed, the more important it is that the sender receive a reaction from the receiver. The best communication of all is face-to-face communication since it provides the best chance to avoid misunderstanding. One can tell by immediate action, facial expression, or response whether or not the message has been received and understood and, most important, whether it will be acted upon in a positive way. Good communication then requires:

1. The appropriate device.
2. A clear statement of the problem or the issue.
3. Understanding by the receiver.

FEEDBACK

The informal groupings and informal communication channels in the system cannot be disregarded. Informal groupings provide a most effective way of gaining feedback and information. Of course, it is difficult for the principal to have access to or to be a member of many of the informal groups that exist within the school. This is apparent to any person who has walked unexpectedly into the teachers' lounge and sensed the dramatic change in the nature of the conversation or interrupted the secretarial pool at coffee break time. Yet it is possible, once the existence of the informal groups has been recognized, to develop clear and open relationships with these groups, or with certain individuals within them, to secure information and do some perception testing. It is possible to use many of these groups or leaders of these groups as sounding boards and as devices to get the word out about items of interest and concern.

Very few communication systems work as fast as the informal network in most organizations. For example, consider how long it takes for the word to get out to the affected teacher that a supervisor is in the building. The informal network can hardly be depended upon as the sole means of communication, but the principal ought to be aware of it and use it to best advantage.[2]

SUMMARY

Good communication within the school organization is not an accident. It occurs as a result of careful attention by the principal. The communication system must be fast, reliable, and appropriate to the message being conveyed.

The organization is made up of many different kinds of people with different backgrounds, different perceptions about their work, and different motivations. There is an informal dimension to the organization which frequently does not even approximate the formal organization depicted on a chart. This confounds the problem of transmitting important messages.

The key to a good internal communication system is to use a variety of media; the medium selected needs to be appropriate to the complexity of the message.

ENDNOTES

1. Harmon Ziegler, *The Political World of the High School Teacher* (Eugene, Ore.: Center for the Advanced Study of Educational Administration, 1966), p. 3.
2. It is sound practice to establish a committee structure in the building so that the insights and decision-making ability of the staff are tapped in addition to the committee serving as a means to effectively convey messages. Some specific suggestions for committee structuring are contained in chapter 12, "Development of Staff."

BIBLIOGRAPHY

Argyris, Chris. *Integrating the Individual and the Organization.* New York: John Wiley and Sons, 1964.

Hughes, Larry W. "Effective Human Relations and Morale," in Jack Culbertson et al., *Performance Objectives for School Principals.* Berkeley, Calif: McCutchan Publishing Co., 1974, chapter 5, see pp. 127–30 especially.

Sergiovanni, Thomas J. *Handbook for Effective Department Leadership.* Boston: Allyn and Bacon, 1977, see especially chapter 3.

Ziegler, Harmon. *The Political World of the High School Teacher.* Eugene, Ore.: Center for the Advanced Study of Educational Administration, 1966.

Chapter Five

The Legal Rights and Responsibilities of Students, Staff, and Administrators

INTRODUCTION

"Ignorance of the law excuses no man, not that all men know the law, but because 'tis an excuse every man will plead, and no man can tell how to refute him."[1] It is most important that the principal have firm understandings about the legal framework within which the school operates. This is not to say that a principal should be a member of the bar in order to carry out the functions of the job, but it does suggest that knowledge about certain legal principles is important. Roe and Drake provide a perspective:

> . . . A hunter must know the hunting laws; the fisherman the fishing laws. The car driver is responsible for knowing traffic laws. We all must know right from wrong, not only morally, but also legally. . . .
>
> It follows that a school administrator must know the law concerning his professional field—education and the schools. One would not expect a school principal to consult a lawyer every time he made a professional decision, yet, to carry a point to the extreme, to be on the safe side he would have to do so unless he had a working knowledge of school law.[2]

In many states, school districts, as extensions of the state, still receive protection from court action under the medieval doctrine of sov-ereign immunity. ("The king can do no wrong.") Increasingly, however, this doctrine is being replaced, and even in those states that have not totally done away with school district immunity from tort liability many hold the district accountable at least in certain instances.[3] However, principals and teachers are seldom immune to litigation regardless of the extent of protection which their district may have. Further, with the growing complexity of school programs, legal implications increase. As societal attitudes change, so does the nature of many judicial interpretations.

This chapter will not attempt to replace a graduate course in school law. It cannot do so. Nor could any graduate course in school law prepare an administrator to be an attorney. But, there are recurring legal issues and fundamental legal bases which need to be addressed in a book about the principalship to provide a firm legal footing for the day-to-day operation of the schools.

There is one caveat: rules of law are not universally accepted. Different courts, especially between states, often take similar cases and hand down conflicting decisions. Further, the interpretation of the law changes as societal attitudes change. It is important to keep abreast of these changes as well as important court decisions throughout the country.[4]

Legal Structure of the Schools in the United States

By law, public school districts are state organizations; board of education members are state officers; school personnel are state employees; and school district buildings are state property. In practice, of course, the support and control of the public schools is a partnership between local, state, and federal governments. Even private and parochial schools are not totally autonomous because these school systems must meet certain state curricular and teacher certification standards. Often, too, federal regulations impinge on their operation when these schools accept financial support for certain programs.

The legal framework within which school systems operate is manifest in the acts passed by federal, state, and local legislative bodies; court decisions, constitutional law, and rules and regulations enacted by regulatory and administrative bodies such as the state departments of education or health departments, for example. A further source of legal guidelines are state attorneys' general opinions that stand until tested in a court of law or modified by subsequent legislative acts. Within this legal framework, local administrators have latitude in developing policies, rules, regulations, and procedures. The authority for local school board and administrative action is depicted in figure 5-1. One extra-legal impingement exists: community sanctions, attitudes, and belief structures that serve to modify, often very directly, the development and implementation of local policies.

Limitations on local authority also depend on prevailing court philosophy in any state. In some states, the prevailing philosophy is that boards of education may adopt any reasonable policy not specifically prohibited by statute. In other states, courts insist that there be specific statutory permission before a particular policy can be adopted. Generally speaking, courts have tended to hold that boards of education may adopt any reasonable policy within the

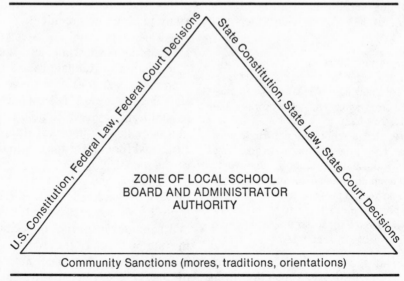

FIGURE 5-1. Circumscribed local authority for school operation

Adapted from Larry W. Hughes. *Education and the Law in Tennessee* (Cincinnati: W. H. Anderson Co., 1971), p. 5.

law. Courts in all states do insist on strict adherence to laws concerning management of public funds, however. School boards and administrators must find clear statutory authority for the expenditure of funds derived from public revenues.

The rule of reason is particularly relevant to principals and teachers, since it is at the school building level that the policies of the school board and laws governing education are most often implemented. It is also at the school building level that most of the litigation involving the school occurs. Laws and policies injudiciously applied, or incorrectly interpreted, at this level may result in children and personnel inhumanely and illegally treated. More and more frequently, the result is litigation naming principals and teachers as defendants. This chapter will focus, therefore, not on the entire spectrum of school law, but on legal issues common to the operation of the school building.

STUDENT AND PERSONNEL RIGHTS: ESTABLISHING A FRAMEWORK

It is important to establish that although students and staff may not always be right, they always have rights. This means that there are certain fundamental rights which all people in the country have simply by virtue of being born here or being naturalized as citizens, and these rights cannot be abrogated by any public or private agency. It means, too, that agencies are obligated to inform employees and clients about their rights and to work diligently to insure that everyone in the organization is accorded those rights. Withholding information from anyone within and about the school organization—students, teachers, parents, or classified employees—about their rights is immoral and inconsistent with the tenets upon which this country was founded. The law insures, in short, the fairest "shake" for every-

one. Attempting to keep people ignorant of the laws, and thus their rights, violates this.

Essentially, people have no more rights today than they did in the past, but the according of these rights is under increasing review by the courts. Unfortunately, school administrators have sometimes trapped themselves into acting simultaneously as judge, jury, and prosecuting attorney—in many instances overstepping their authority and jurisdiction. Sometimes teachers, administrators, and other school employees have behaved *in loco deo* rather than *in loco parentis,* and have frequently placed themselves in untenable legal positions.[5]

Most of the individual rights enjoyed in this country derive from the Constitution of the United States, and are largely located in the first ten amendments of the Constitution, the Bill of Rights, and in some subsequent amendments, notably the Fourteenth Amendment. Basically, those amendments of special relevance to the operation of the schools are:

Amendment One deals with freedom of religion, expression, and rights to peaceful assembly and petition. It grants, in part, the rights of all citizens to peacefully assemble and to petition the government for redress of grievances. Amendment One has often been cited in civil rights cases involving students.

Amendment Four focuses on the rights of persons and states; in part, that the people and property shall be protected against "unreasonable search and seizures," meaning that appropriated warrants must precede such police action. The educational implications here affect the confidentiality of records, interrogation of pupils, and the proceedings of juvenile court.

Amendment Five guarantees due process of law. It says that certain rights are inviolate and people cannot be deprived of them without due process of law. Essentially it says that no person may be deprived of life, liberty, and property without due process of law.

Amendment Six provides for judicial procedure and public trial, an impartial jury, information about the nature of the charge, confrontation by witnesses against the party, the right of the accused to obtain witnesses in his own behalf, and the right to have counsel.

Amendment Eight prohibits cruel and unusual punishment and excessive bail.

Amendment Nine is the "rights of the people" amendment. It states that the enumeration in the Constitution of certain rights shall not be construed to deny or discourage other rights retained by the people. This simply means that even if the Constitution is explicitly silent, it does not mean that other rights are not enjoyed.

Amendment Ten is the reserved power amendment. It indicates that the powers that are not delegated to the United States by the Constitution nor prohibited by it to the states are reserved to the states respectively or to the people.

After the Civil War, the Fourteenth Amendment, often called the "States Bill of Rights," was adopted. It states, in part, that "no state shall make a law which abridges the rights of citizens in the United States nor deny anyone the equal protection of the law." It states further that all persons, whether born or naturalized in the United States and subject to the jurisdiction thereof, are citizens of the United States and of the state wherein they reside. Thus, the state must guarantee the same rights to its citizens that are guaranteed by the federal Constitution. It is important to call attention to the phrase "all persons." The amendment does not say all adults, it says all persons, and that includes children.

This then sets a legal framework for a discussion of student and faculty rights. In a very real sense it also sets a moral or ethical framework as well because the laws of the land reflect the morals of the land, and it is the spirit on which the law is based which is pervasive. The spirit of the law applies equally to students and nonstudents; just because a person is young, he or she cannot be denied certain fundamental rights.[6]

In general, the courts have made it clear: constitutional protections apply to students both in and out of school. Freedom of expression and other basic rights, if not always clearly defined in the school, are well established in the law. Courts require that there be specified procedures to safeguard those rights against the abuse of institutional authority. The matter of procedural due process, which will be discussed later in this chapter, guarantees certain rights by the fair application of rules and regulations.

Some principals and teachers may argue that there have always been adequate means for dealing with student complaints and grievances, that the "latchstring" has always been on the outside of the door, and that staff members have always been willing to listen to complaints and grievances. However, the capacity to take appropriate corrective action when such action is essential to sustain student rights is even more important than listening, for, as pointed out in *Tinker* v. *Des Moines School District,* "Students do not shed their rights at the school house gate."[7]

One of the major goals of school personnel should be to establish a trust based on humaneness and respect for others. A child or adult who feels unrespected and not accorded basic human rights will not respect others. The authors especially like the court's language in the 1943 case of *West Virginia* v. *Barnette:*

> The Fourteenth Amendment . . . is now applied to the State itself and all of its creatures—boards of education not excepted. These (i.e., boards of education) have, of course, important, delicate and highly discretionary functions, but none that they may perform except within the limits of the Bill of Rights.

Further, this same court said in what is very perceptive pedagogy:

> That they are educating the young for citizenship is a reason for scrupulous protection of constitutional freedom of the individual *if we*

*are not to strangle the free mind at its source
and teach youth to discount important principles of our government as mere platitudes.*
[Emphasis supplied.][8]

In other words, and educators must know this
is true, *responsibility cannot be learned in the
absence of freedom.* Shannon puts the issue in
good perspective when he writes:

> Controversy over . . . issues of public school
> governance and administration is actually
> symptomatic of the robust health of our system
> of government. Education has assumed an
> importance in our society that it did not have
> just a few decades ago. Today, we are in a time
> of profound change in society. It is natural that
> public education would be the subject of
> spirited community discussion and debate, as
> competing values and philosophies of our poly-
> glot society are filtered into courses of action on
> educational policy matters. Instead of weak-
> ness, community involvement, although some-
> times rancorous and bitter, is in reality a
> strength of the public school system and augers
> for continuing improvement in educational
> offerings to meet the changing demands of our
> changing world. As frustrating and difficult as
> controversy may be at times, it is a hallmark of
> our open and free society. Instead of rejecting
> it, we must learn to live with it—even in educa-
> tional matters—which, in the final analysis, is
> clearly an area of life where reasonable opinions
> may differ.
>   Finally, the wide publicity accorded student
> misconduct by a media bent on entertaining as
> well as informing people, often gives the erro-
> neous impression that student misconduct is
> more prevalent than it actually is and that
> school authorities are inept in dealing with it.
> Moreover, "misconduct" is often the word
> used by the people as a result of media cover-
> age, of conduct by students which the courts say
> is fully protected by the expanding First
> Amendment "free speech" right. And, "devel-
> oping due process" rights characterized by
> elaborate hearing procedures, for students
> accused of misconduct which could result in
> their suspension or expulsion is sometimes mis-

taken for authoritarian softness and permissive-
ness by parents whose children were never
accused of serious misconduct in schools.[9]

RULES AND REGULATIONS

The efficient routine operation of any complex
organization requires a well developed, well
understood, and consistent set of rules and
regulations. It is axiomatic that if staff and students are to be held accountable for certain
standards, then these official expectations must
be established and promulgated *ahead of their
application* in a manner that makes them easily
disseminated, learned, and understood. A principal has the right to prescribe reasonable controls for the efficient day-to-day operation of
the schools, but, of course, this does not imply
that the school building is a fiefdom and staff
and students are serfs.

What is "reasonable"? A rule of thumb
applied most frequently by the court is, "Does
the regulation enhance the education of the
children, promote their interest and welfare,
and is it for the common good of education?"
Implicit is that the regulations be within the
legal authority of the school district. Regulations beyond the province of the school board
are not enforceable. A long-standing decision
has held that ". . . boards are not at liberty to
adopt according to their humor regulations
which have no relevance to the schools' purposes."[10] It follows that this would be no less
true in the matter of rules and regulations which
the principal might prescribe.

Moreover, while it is sound management
practice to develop procedures and guidelines
that provide for consistency of school operation, the authors of this book would hold that
the rule of parsimony should be followed.
Developing long lists of do's and don't's in an
attempt to cover every contingency can create a
school climate in which the name of the game
becomes "beating the system," a climate in
which staff and students derive a perverse joy

from testing the limits—in a kind of grim cat and mouse game. Rules and regulations that attempt to define every type of situation and recourse are not necessary. In fact, the enumeration of prohibited actions may foreclose any discretion on actions not so listed. It is better to have some general guidelines and a few specific dictums to cover the hazardous situations and common management problems than to go overboard.

The Out-of-Date Rule

Rules and regulations should be subject to regular review to insure their continued appropriateness and efficacy. Outdated, misunderstood, inappropriate, or unnecessary rules only breed contempt for other rules. A few years ago, one of the authors and a colleague were members of a Southern Association of Schools evaluation team participating in a routine accreditation review of a large urban high school.

After a morning of review activities, some of the consultants had lunch in the school cafeteria. Finding the food not quite seasoned enough for our taste, two of us looked for the salt and pepper shakers on the table. There was none. Further, as nearly as we could tell as we looked around the room, there was no salt or pepper on any of the tables. We asked a nearby student, "Where is the salt and pepper?" The student's reply was, "We don't get salt and pepper." "Why?" was our response. To this the student shrugged his shoulders.

Again and again, we repeated our query to students about the location of the salt and pepper. Each time the response was, "We don't get salt and pepper," and each time when we rejoined with, "Why?" the response was nearly the same—a shrug, a glance at the ceiling, or an "I dunno." One of the students said that he had run for student council president the previous spring on a "Bring Back the Salt" ticket but had not been elected.

Having nothing to do for another half-hour or so, we begain to pursue this deepening mystery. Cafeteria personnel were queried about the salt and pepper. Their response was that it was a rule that students were not to recieve salt and peper, but no one knew why. "Has it always been a rule?" we asked. Two employees, who had indicated that they had been there for at least four years, said that to their knowledge it had always been a rule. "Does it seem to be a sensible rule?" we pursued. There was no response to this question, and as we developed the issue somewhat further, it became clear that our presence was really no longer desired.

The head cook was of no help, nor was the cafeteria manager, so we took our problem to the principal's office, avoiding the assistant principal because she had only been on the job a couple of years.

The principal indicated that he thought the rule was one which the cafeteria manager had issued but confessed that he really didn't know why. We should have gone to the teacher's lunchroom, he said, "They have salt in there." "That's not the point," we replied, "we're just curious about why there is a rule against salt and pepper." At this moment a teacher who had been in the school for some time came in and, overhearing the conversation, grinned at both of us and simply said "It was a punishment because several years ago we had a rash of students unscrewing the tops of the salt and pepper shakers so that when they were used the tops would come off, dumping the contents on the food."

Further conversation determined that this had all occurred some seven or eight years previously and the rule had been invoked, presumably until just the end of the school term. Subsequent to that, the principal had left and the cafeteria manager continued to apply the rule, unthinkingly, unquestioningly. So what had been a temporary punishment for some normal adolescent hijinks had become a school tradition summed up in the lament, "We don't get any salt."

Silly? Certainly, but it is this sort of unthinking application of rules that have long since ceased to have any relevance that creates a general disrespect for rules that do have relevance. Rules and regulations that guide the school's routine operations should regularly be subjected to a review. The questions asked should be: What is this rule for? Does this rule work? Is there a better way?

Establishing Good Rules and Regulations

Three general guidelines provide good rules and regulations:

1. The principal's own good management sense will provide some insights into the kinds of rules and regulations needed to routinely guide the school. The orderly development of a school program requires certain specified times when activities are to begin, when the school lunch period will be, common standards of good conduct, and teacher responsibilities, for example. These rules and regulations should be appropriate to the maturity of the students under the school's charge.
2. Rules and regulations developed for a particular secondary school must be consistent with the general policies of the school district.
3. A faculty/student advisory committee should be constituted to help identify areas needing more specific regulations and to serve as a review board for existing rules and regulations.

Neither the extreme of rules for every occasion nor, its opposite, no rules at all, is sensible. It has been established that principals and teachers have the right *and the obligation* to determine reasonable policies governing the conduct of their charges, not only to maintain a proper educational climate, but also for safety. When challenged in the courts, particular rules and regulations will in all probability be upheld, provided, of course, the rule is a reasonable application of an educational function and not contrary to a higher enactment by the school board or federal and state bodies.

The principal is the person most often responsible for the promulgation and enforcement of rules and regulations.

> It is he who must require that certain instruction be given in order to comply with local and state regulations. . . . Whether the principal acts in an authoritative manner, suggested by the "line" concept and makes all assignments himself, or whether he employs a cooperative plan, the legal relationships between the principal and employee are the same. Regardless of the "method" of getting things done, the principal cannot relieve himself of the legal responsibility his position entails.[11]

DUE PROCESS

The general issue addressed by due process considerations is that of the constitutional rights of personnel and students balanced against the duty of the school board to control and protect the school system and protect the rights of students to obtain an education. There are two kinds of due process: substantive and procedural.

Substantive Due Process

Substantive due process is concerned with the basic legality of a legislative enactment. School policies, rules, and regulations must stand the test of substantive due process. A person punished or denied the right to behave in some way by an existing law, rule, or regulation when it is contrary to certain constitutional guarantees has legal recourse to set aside the punishment or denial and make the rule invalid. Moreover, substantive due process requires that there must be sufficient evidence or documentation of violation to warrant action by school officals, or sufficient reason to believe that if the rule is not invoked current or subsequent acts by the parties involved will result in disruption of the educational process. The burden of proof rests with the school officials, not the transgressor.

The *Tinker* case is often cited in reference to presumed disruption.[12] Rules are invoked because the school principal says, in effect, "If this rule is not enforced and obeyed, the process of education in the school will be impeded." In the *Tinker* case, students were suspended for wearing black armbands to school in mourning for American military personnel who had died in Vietnam, as well as to protest continued U.S. involvement in that country. The school promulgated a rule prohibiting this, subsequent to which some students continued to wear the armbands in open defiance. Two important legal principles of a substantive nature were applied by the Supreme Court in holding for the students: (1) There was no disruption, therefore the presumption of the rule was false and students had the constitutional right to defy the rule, and (2) the wearing of the armbands was analogous to free speech (a First Amendment guarantee) and the students had the right to express themselves.

The two rules of thumb that must be applied are: Will the behavior cause substantial disorder to the education process or normal operation of the school? Will the behavior be an invasion of the rights of others? If the school principal believes the answer is yes, the burden of proof lies on the principal. Courts are critical of administrator action predicated on presumption.

Moreover, the collection of sufficient evidence to show reason for administrative action is vital. For example, the dismissal of

teachers for incompetence is often interrupted for this reason. In an Illinois case a probationary teacher, in his third year, would have been given tenure in his fourth year.[13] However, he was given a notice of nonrenewal instead. A hearing was held on seven charges stemming from the evaluation system used in the district. The teacher claimed that no one had advised him of the evaluation form (no prior knowledge of the conditions), no one had supervised or observed his teaching (no collection of evidence), and that no one had advised him of needed improvements. The court ordered him reinstated as a tenured teacher.

Guidelines to Insure Adherence to Substantive Due Process

School policies, rules, and regulations and the administrative actions enforcing these should be subjected to the following guidelines:

1. *Legality.* Is there a basis in state and federal constitutional and legislative law for the policy, rule, or regulation? Are the constitutional rights of those for whom it was written protected?
2. *Sufficient specificity.* Are the conditions under which the policy, rule, or regulation will be invoked detailed? Are the terms and phraseology used definitive? Vague and unclear statements are sufficient to cause the courts to abrogate.[14]
3. *Reason and sensibleness.* Does the rule or regulation really enhance the educational climate; that is, is it really necessary? Is there sufficient reason to believe that without the rule, the rights of others will be unprotected or the school will be disrupted? A rule may be declared unreasonable in and of itself *or* in its particular application.
4. *Adequate dissemination.* Has information about the rule been distributed in such a way that persons affected can be expected

to know about it, what it means, and what the penalties are?

5. *Appropriate penalties.* Are the punishments appropriate to the nature of the infraction? Severe penalties for minor transgressions must be avoided.

Procedural Due Process

Procedural due process is an orderly established process for arriving at an impartial and just settlement of a conflict between parties.[15] It entails the elements of fair warning and fair hearing.

Fair Warning Fair warning simply means that a person must be made cognizant of the rules to follow or behavior that must be exhibited and the potential penalties for violation. In the Illinois teacher dismissal case, the element of fair warning was missing; the teacher did not know what the evaluation system was and was unaware that he was performing inadequately.

The age of the person and the length of experience must be taken into consideration as well. Moreover, there must be a correlation between the penalty and the type of rule that has been broken.

Fair Hearing A fair hearing is composed of the following specific aspects:

1. *The individual must be given a written statement of the charges and the nature of evidence.* This is often called a "Bill of Particulars." Clarity is very important. The accused, and in the instance of pupils, the parents of the accused, must comprehend the contents of the written statement. The background and educational level of the individuals involved and the complexity of the statement to the parents should be taken into account. This would provide an opportunity for clarifying questions, and would be appropriate at times. The precise nature of the charges and the evidence must be incorporated in the statement. Vague rules and imprecise charges have resulted in the reversal of more school board and administrative decisions than any other defect.

2. *The individual must be informed of his or her procedural rights.* As noted earlier in this chapter, having rights but being kept unaware of them is the same as not having rights. Individuals must be provided information specifying the appeals and defense processes available. Information such as to whom the appeal can be advanced, and other elements of procedural process is necessary.

3. *Adequate time must be provided to prepare a defense.* In serious issues ordinarily a minimum of five days should be provided for an individual to prepare a defense; ten days almost certainly will be acceptable to a court.[16]

4. *The opportunity for formal hearing must be accorded.*[17] There are five components in the proper conduct of a formal hearing:

- The case must be presented to an impartial hearer. The school official bringing the charge may not also serve as hearer. One person may not serve at once as judge, jury, and prosecuting attorney.
- The individual must have the opportunity to present evidence on his or her own behalf.
- The individual has the right to know and confront whomever brought the charges and to question that person or those persons.
- The individual has the right to produce witnesses and to cross-examine witnesses. The individual must have the opportunity to disprove the accusations of a hostile witness and include testimony of those who can explain the defendant's side of the issue.
- The individual has the right to counsel. This does not necessarily mean an attorney. It may be simply a friend, parent, or citizen on whose advice the defendant wishes to rely. It would be a foolish board of education or administrator,

however, who would try to prohibit an individual from having an attorney present, even though at this writing there has been no court decision mandating legal counsel at hearings such as these.

COMMON TORT LIABILITY SETTINGS

A *tort* is defined as an act or an omitted act, incuding breach of contract, that results in damage, injury, or loss to the injured person(s) who then may seek relief by legal action. Torts may be intentional, or the result of negligence or careless acts. School employees are liable for their individual acts of negligence,[18] for failure to carry out prescribed duties, or failure to carry out these duties correctly. School employees are expected to behave in a reasonable manner in the discharge of their duties, avoiding acts that are capricious, arbitrary, or negligent.

Familiarization with the elements of tort liability is a must for all school employees. Tort liability suits usually demand adequate evidence of the following:

1. A prescribed or implicit duty on the part of the defendant for the care of the plaintiff.
2. An error of commission or omission by the defendant.
3. Damage, loss, or injury sustained by the plaintiff.
4. Indication of a cause and effect relationship between the error and the circumstance at issue.
5. Absence of contributory negligence on the part of the plaintiff.[19]

The principal who devotes some inservice training time with staff to legal aspects of the school operation will be performing an important service. The best defense against law suits is proper precaution. Principals and teachers cannot be expected to be prescient, but they are expected to anticipate possible dangers. The discussion that follows will examine common liability settings and describe certain aspects of the legal environment.

Student Injuries

One does not usually think of a school as a hazardous place, but students frequently do sustain injuries in and about the school. Most of these injuries are accidental and minor, the result of normal behavior of the young and immature as they hurry through the processes of learning and growing. Nevertheless, teachers and administrators do have a responsibility to provide reasonable and prudent protection for their charges, and they are legally liable in tort for injuries arising from their negligence.[20] The main test of negligence is "foreseeability"; that is, the behavior of an individual would be called negligent if an ordinarily prudent person would have foreseen that certain actions, or failure to act, would lead to injury to another.

The principal is responsible for taking all steps to promote the well-being of the students within the school and to guard the welfare of the staff. Therefore, to both staff and students, the principal has a particular duty to plan and supervise so to minimize the possibility of injury. At the very least, this involves supplying information to staff members about their legal responsibilities and cooperatively developing a set of rules and regulatons that, if carefully followed, would result in protection for students and the elimination of negligent behavior. Student injuries are most likely to occur in the following settings.

Physical Education, Athletics, Field Trips, and Other Cocurricular Programs Sports, other cocurricular programs, and the physical education curriculum itself are inherently more hazardous than the regular academic program. They require greater supervision to avoid liability as a result of negligence, and it is especially important that there be carefully developed and well understood written rules and regulations for their governance.

Adequate regulations should cover such categories as pupil conduct while a participant or spectator, medical examination for participants, medical care for sick and injured participants, transportation to and from the activity, duties of teachers and/or adult supervisors, and notification and approval in advance by parent or guardian.[21] Figures 5–2 and 5–3 illustrate request and permission forms.

The Classroom Teachers are normally in charge in the classroom and thus are most frequently held responsible for the safety of the students there. However, the principal has some responsibilities that, if not met, may result in a charge of negligent behavior. The primary responsibility of the principal with regard to classroom activities is to insure that there is a teacher or a responsible adult present at all times. Therefore, a plan should exist whereby the principal is always aware of a teacher's

---

Please fill out this form and send it and its duplicates to the Director of Instruction one week prior to the date of the trip. Upon approval of the trip, the white copy will be returned to the principal to be filed; the yellow copy will be given to the supervisor; and the pink copy will be kept by the superintendent.

Date Submitted_____ School_____

Grade, Subject, or Organization_____

No. of students making the trip_____ Date of trip_____

Method of transportation_____ When bonded carriers are used, give

the per pupil cost_____ How will these costs be defrayed?_____

Time of departure_____ Time of return_____

Destination _____

Purpose of trip (state the relationship to current study)_____

_____

What are your plans to follow up and evaluate the trip?_____

_____

Will parent permission slips be filed with the principal prior to the off-campus trip?

_____

List staff members and other adults who will make the trip.

_____   _____

_____   _____

Requested by:_____
                   Teacher

               _____
                   Teacher

Approved: _____
                   Principal

               _____
                   Director of Instruction

FIGURE 5–2.   Off-campus trip request

Date_____

Dear Parents:

In order for your child to be allowed to go on an off-campus trip, we must have the following agreement signed by his or her parent/guardian giving permission.

Sincerely,

William M. Gordon, Principal

Please allow_____to go with his or her group to_____ on the date set for the trip. By signing this statement I give my full permission for my child to go on this off-campus trip.

| _____ | _____ |
| Date | Parent/Guardian |

FIGURE 5-3.   Parent permission slip

absence from the classroom. Failure to have such a plan to provide for student supervision when a teacher becomes ill or is tardy to class could cause the principal to be charged with negligence if an injury should result while the students are unsupervised. For example, a common practice is to have a sheet for teachers to "sign in" in the morning so that the principal can know immediately of any unanticipated absence or tardiness of personnel who have responsibility for the supervision of children.

Generally speaking, however, the temporary short-term absence from the classroom by a teacher would not, in and of itself, be considered a negligent act of general supervision. If, for example, a pupil misbehaves and in so doing injures another pupil during a teacher's brief absence from the room, a court would not ordinarily find negligence because the teacher's absence was not the proximate cause of the accident. However, in all cases, the age, maturity, and intelligence of the students will bear on the question of teacher negligence in such absences. The best rule is not to leave pupils unattended.

Laboratories and Shops These two instructional areas present more hazards than any other in the school. The hazards of operating equipment powered by gas or electricity and engaging in activities requiring the use of chemicals, for example, are apparent. Moreover, good educational practice in teaching science involves such outside classroom events as off-campus field trips and on-campus land laboratory activities.

Constant and immediate supervision is expected of teachers functioning in these educational spheres. It is of great importance that teachers adequately instruct students in the care and use of equipment they will be operating. If there is evidence that a pupil has been permitted to use a particular tool, or perform an experiment, before being trained, or the consequences of improper usage explained, negligence will be difficult to disprove. Greater care is expected of teachers supervising students who are exposed to dangerous equipment. Obviously, in a room where a class is engaged in hazardous activities, teacher absence from the room, no matter how temporary, is very risky indeed.

Activity Areas Where supervision is regular, planned, reasonable, and proper, a negligence charge in a case of pupil injury is less likely. Things to be taken into account in determining the suitability of supervision include the kind of equipment in use, the size of the area, and the number and age of the pupils to be supervised.

The courts generally appreciate the fact that a teacher is unable to keep every student within view and out of hazard at all times; nor is the teacher expected to be prescient. Nevertheless, negligent supervision is often held to be proximate cause of injury. If, for example, a teacher permits a pupil to leave a supervised group and the pupil is injured in a known existing hazardous condition, then the teacher may be liable. If a teacher assigned to an activity area leaves the post for no good cause and a pupil is injured in a known or foreseeable dangerous condition, there may be tort liability because of negligence.[22] Also, while teachers are not expected to repair equipment, if they permit pupils to use equipment which is known to be faulty, and injury is sustained, negligence may be found.

The principal, in providing for the organization and administration of playground use, has responsibility in three major aspects. First, proper rules of behavior, consistent with good safety practices must be developed and implemented. Second, the management system should provide adequate adult supervision in the activity areas when students are present. Third, the principal must provide for frequent and regular inspection of the areas and the equipment, report any hazardous conditions, apprise staff and students of these, and see to it that the condition is corrected.

Regulating Student Conduct

Even in the best run schools, students misbehave. Principals and teachers may prescribe reasonable controls against the misconduct of pupils, and many kinds of disciplinary action are available to school administrators and teachers when there is a violation of school policies and rules. These include such minor punishments as short-term removal from the classroom, withholding certain privileges, detention after school, isolation from the rest of the class, and so on. The courts have generally upheld the right of school administrators and teachers to impose such minor punishment. Other forms of disciplinary action, however, such as suspension and expulsion from school,[23] or the use of corporal punishment, are more often tested in the courts. Hence, greater care must be taken by school administrators and teachers in the prescription of these punishments. A good beginning is to make a clear report, as shown in figure 5-4.

In any case, the question of both substantive and procedural due process is extremely important.[24] The reasonableness and legality of the rule or regulation which was violated must be examined with care, and the legal issue of whether or not the student has a right to a prior hearing is important.

Clearly, care should be taken in minor as well as major punishments to insure that pupils or personnel to be punished are treated fairly and not victimized by capricious and/or arbitrary action.

Corporal Punishment Corporal punishment is defined as disciplinary action by application of physical force. As a means of modifying behavior, it is probably the oldest disciplinary tool. It also may be one of the most inefficacious. More recently, acts of corporal punishment are probably the cause of more court cases than any other single action.[25] However, under the legal concept, *in loco parentis,*[26] the courts continue to uphold the right of teachers and principals to use "reasonable" force to insure proper conduct, or to correct improper conduct.[27]

Date_____

Student's Name_____Homeroom_____Grade_____

Time_____ Location_____

Person Reporting _____

Title of Person Reporting_____

Nature of Offense:

Student's Account:

Action Taken:

I have had a chance to tell my side._____
                                   (student signature)

Date of Hearing_____ Person Conducting Hearing_____

Time_____ Other Person(s) Present_____

Infraction: State Law_____ School Policy_____

                 Board of Education Policy _____

                 Central Office Policy_____

                 Teacher Rule_____ Common Sense_____

FIGURE 5–4. Report of disciplinary action

Important guidelines, however, must be followed if the use of corporal punishment is to be adjudicated as prudent and reasonable. Corporal punishment is generally held to be prudent providing:

1. The state law and the local policy permit it.
2. The punishment takes into consideration the age, size, sex, and health of the student, and is not excessive.
3. There is no malice, and the punishment is given for corrective purposes only and is not immoderate.
4. The student understands why the punishment is required.
5. An appropriate instrument is used.

Sometimes other attendant circumstances, such as whether there was permanent injury suffered as a result of the punishment, are considered by the courts.

To avoid legal suit and to insure the fairest treatment possible for the student, it is important for the principal and the teacher to establish reasonable rules and make certain that the punishment for breaking these rules is suitable. It is also important to reasonably administer the rules and apply them equally to all students. It is possible to administer a reasonable rule so improperly that it becomes unreasonable. Any vindictiveness or viciousness in administering corporal punishment must be avoided. If the teacher or the principal knows that he or she is uncontrollably angry, then is not the time to punish the child corporally, or any other way for that matter. In all cases, it should be remembered that the purpose of punishment is for the child's benefit, not for the vindication of the schools' posture.

Suspension/Expulsion Suspension from school has been defined as a dismissal, most often by the principal, from the school for a specific, but relatively short length of time. Expulsion means permanent or long-term dismissal from school. In most states, expulsion can only be accomplished by the board of education, permanent exclusion usually being outside the authority of any school administrator. Attendance at a public school is generally viewed as a right rather than a privilege, but the enjoyment of this right is conditioned by the student's willingness to comply with reasonable regulations and requirements of the school. Violations of these may be punished by suspension or, in extreme cases, by permanent expulsion. Under a suspension, a pupil is usually required to meet some set of conditions established by the administrator before he or she is readmitted.

The dividing line between a short- and a long-term exclusion from school is not clearly defined, but as a result of *Goss* v. *Lopez* has probably been established as ten days.[28] Longer exclusions, irrespective of what they are called, will require greater attention to all the vestments of due process because they clearly bear more heavily on a student's right to an education.

In *Goss* v. *Lopez,* the court clearly established the right of school administrators to suspend students to maintain order in the school system. However, the court did find school officials in violation of the students' constitutional right to procedural due process. In this instance, nine students were temporarily suspended from school *without a hearing,* and thus were held to be denied due process. The school board had contended that due process was not applicable to suspensions because there was not a "constitutional right" to public education. The court disagreed with this, indicating that:

Although Ohio may not be constitutionally obligated to establish and maintain the public school system, it has nevertheless done so and has required its children to attend. Those young people do not "shed their constitutional rights at the school house door. . . ." The authority possessed by the State to prescribe and enforce standards of conduct in its schools, although concededly very broad, must be exercised consistently with the constitutional safeguards.[29]

Second, the school board argued that even if public education was a right that was protected by due process, then in this instance the due process clause should not apply because the suspensions were limited to ten days and this was not a severe nor grievous infringement on the students' right to an education. The court disagreed here also, and faced the question of what kind of process is due in the instance of short-term student suspensions. The court held that only rudimentary process was required to balance student interests against the educator's need to take quick disciplinary action. The court said:

> [T]he student [must] be given a written notice of the charges against him, if he denies them, an explanation of the evidence the authorities have and an opportunity to present his side of the story. . . . There need be no delay between the time "notice" is given and the time of the hearing. In the great majority of cases the disciplinarian may informally discuss the alleged misconduct with the student minutes after it has occurred. We hold only that, in being given an opportunity to explain his version of the facts at this discussion, the student first be told what he is accused of doing and what the basis of the accusation is.[30]

This is important because it may be implied that while due process provisions must always be present, even in less than major punishment, the nature of the punishment and the infraction will determine the degree to which one must engage in elaborate vestments of due process.[31] In minor infractions it would be necessary only to provide rudimentary forms of hearing. Even here, however, the important lesson is that the child to be punished must, in all instances, be treated fairly, and that there be clear indication of the absence of capricious action.

Goss v. *Lopez* has not stripped the school administrator of authority. It simply prescribes safeguards against the abuse of authority. The principal who acts reasonably and behaves in a manner consistent with the general guidelines for substantive and procedural due process will have little difficulty with the courts.

For example, in *Sweet* v. *Childs*,[32] students were suspended by radio. They had left school during regular hours to march on the superintendent's office and did not return. There was a substantial disruption of the academic process, and conferences with the students and their parents were held by the principal after the term of the suspension. The court ruled that under the circumstances such action was not inconsistent with the *Goss* case. In a much different case, a group of students was suspended for hazing new club members. The principal called each one to the office and asked if he had been a participant in the hazing. This action was upheld by the court, which said that the proceedings in the principal's office complied with the minimum standards of due process.[33]

Caution must be the byword, however. In New Hampshire, a student was informed that he had behaved improperly *but* was not informed that he might be suspended for such behavior. Moreover, he was not given specific reasons for his suspension prior to it taking place. The Federal District Court ruled that he was not provided minimum due process. However, since the suspension was not, in the court's opinion, the result of capricious and arbitrary action by the principal no damages were awarded.[34]

Earlier, in *Wood* v. *Strickland,* the Supreme Court had established that pecuniary damages could be awarded if school officials violated the rights of students.[35] The Court said, in what many feel is a far-reaching decision:

> [A] school board member who has voluntarily undertaken the task of supervising the operation of the school and the activities of the students, must be held to a standard of conduct based not only on permissible intentions, but also on the knowledge of the basic unquestioned constitutional rights of his charges. . . . In the specific context of school discipline, we hold that a school board member is not immune from liability for damages . . . if he knew or reasonably should have known that the action he took within his sphere of official responsibility would violate the intention to cause deprivation of constitutional rights or other injury to the student. That is not to say that school board member has acted with such an impermissible motivation or with such disregard of the student's clearly established constitutional rights that his action cannot reasonably be characterized as being in good faith.[36]

The courts are acting conservatively in their interpretation of *Wood* v. *Strickland,* however. The Eighth Circuit Court of Appeals has set forth criteria which define "good faith":

1. The action must be taken without malice or ill will.
2. The school must balance the interests of the individual against its own legitimate governmental interest.
3. Basic rights of procedural and substantive due process must be followed.
4. The rights allegedly violated must be unquestioned constitutional rights.[37]

And, if administrators and other school officials have operated in good faith, most courts have held they will be free from personal damages.

There is growing opposition to the use of suspensions and expulsions as punishment for misconduct. The authors support the following statement detailing four counterproductive effects of the exclusion of children from school:

> While precise measurement of the psychological and educational harm done by suspension is impossible, it is clear that any exclusion from school interrupts the child's educational process. . . . It is not clear what good such punishment does. In fact, it may work against the child's improvement in at least four ways. First, it forbids the child from participating in academic work. If children with discipline problems are also weak in their studies, their missed classes, assignments and exams may doom them to fail completely. Second, suspensions merely remove troubling children. They do not set in motion diagnostic or supportive services that might uncover and remediate causes of a child's misbehavior. Thus, suspensions deny help to children. Third, suspension is a powerful label that not only stigmatizes a child while in school (or out of it), but follows the child beyond school to later academic or employments pursuits and fourth, suspensions are highly correlated with juvenile delinquency. Putting children out of school, leaving them idle with no supervision, especially when they are demonstrating they have problems, leaves children alone to cope with their future.[38]

Many schools are developing a disciplinary procedure called in-school suspension as a means of avoiding the disruption and negative effects cited above.

The in-school suspension usually involves taking the student out of the regular classroom for a period of time and placing the student in another learning environment within the school, either in an independent learning situation with supervision or in a designated special class. When this procedure is coupled with counseling by the principal or the guidance counselor or some other clinician to diagnose and treat the problem, it is a sound practice.[39]

Detention   It is well established that principals and teachers do have the authority to temporarily detain students from participating in cocurricular activities and even to keep children after school as a punishment, providing, of course, the student has a way of getting home. As in other punishments, the detention must be reasonable. False imprisonment may be claimed if the principal or a teacher either wrongfully detains a student or detains a student for an unreasonable amount of time as a punishment.

In this, as in all other punishments, the main test is one of *fairness*. If school officials act fairly and in good faith in dealing with the students, their actions will probably be upheld by the courts.

Participation in Cocurricular Activities

Aspects of cocurricular activities continue to be litigious. The basic issue has been whether or not participation in cocurricular activities is a right or a privilege. More recently, the issue has been equality of opportunity for the sexes. These related issues are a source of much concern for school administrators, and most frequently become apparent at the secondary school level.

Right or Privilege?   Whether or not participation in cocurricular activities is a right or privilege has more often and historically found its way into court on the issue of married students. Some courts have excluded married students from participating on the basis that while attending a public school was a right, cocurricular opportunities were not.[40] For example, the Utah Supreme Court declared in 1963 that cocurricular activities "are supplementary to the regular classes of the academic curriculum and are carried on under the discretionary powers granted to the board of education."[41] This position, however, no longer seems likely to prevail. Mawdsley has written:

The U.S. Supreme Court will ultimately have to resolve the question of whether extracurricular activities are a right or privilege, but given the prominence of the constitutional arguments and the importance of extracurricular programs in schools, especially sports, it is probable that the courts will declare such activities to be a right rather than a privilege.[42]

In 1972, a federal district court in Ohio stated that "extracurricular activities in the modern thinking are an integral part of the school program," and held that to deprive a student of the aspect of the program would violate state policies that provide for the establishment of a system of education.[43] Moreover, as far back as 1929, a court in Mississippi held that the establishment of two classes of students in the field of extracurricular activities (those that were permitted to participate and those who were not) amounted to an unreasonable classification and thus was in violation of the equal protection clause of the constitution.[44]

It appears that participation in cocurricular activities will be viewed as a right, and as such, exclusion from these activities will have to rely on substantive and procedural due process. In *Warren* v. *NASSP,* a student was ordered by the court to be reinstated in the National Honor Society of his high school because the Society had violated its own rules in suspending him, and not on the basis of whether or not his expulsion from the club was for just cause.[45]

No Discrimination on the Basis of Sex Title IX of the 1972 Education Act amendments established, among other things, that participation in organized athletic programs in the public schools was to be accessible irrespective of sex.[46]

Discrimination in athletics on the basis of sex has been a subject of much controversy and litigation. Much of the litigation was based on the equal protection clause of the Fourteenth Amendment.

There are two situations in which equal protections claims have arisen. First is the complete failure of a school district to fund and provide a team for a specific sport for its women students. Then, while not providing a particular team for the women students, the school district prohibits them from joining the men's team of that sport. The issue in these cases was not whether a woman has a constitutional right to participate in a particular sport, but whether the state, having provided an athletic program, can deny an opportunity for equal participation to members of one sex. This asserted protective purpose in maintaining separate teams was determined upon the conclusion that women cannot compete effectively with men in sports because of the inherent physical differences between the sexes; thus it was argued, separate teams were reasonable, indeed necessary. Several courts accepted this conclusion, but held they could not sanction a failure to provide an athletic program for women.[47] Separate but equal athletic programs are also statutory law in section 86.41 of Title IX (b) on the "Administration of Athletics." An alternative provision is included if a school district does not fund and offer separate athletic programs for women.

> However, where a recipient operates or sponsors no such team for members of the other sex, and athletic opportunities for members of that sex have previously been limited, members of the excluded sex must be allowed to try out for the team offered unless the sport involved is a contact sport. For the purpose of this part, contact sports include boxing, wrestling, rugby, ice hockey, football, basketball and other sports the purpose of major activity of which involves bodily contact.[48]

The second situation presents a more complex problem. This is where a separate program for women does exist, but the plaintiff wishes to play on the male team. In *Ruman* v. *Eskew,*[49] the plaintiff sued to compel the high school to permit a girl to try out for the boy's tennis team even when there was a tennis program for girls. The Lake Superior Court denied a preliminary injunction and the plaintiff appealed. The Court of Appeals of Indiana denied the appellant's petition. In *Bucha* v. *Illinois High School Association*[50] the plaintiffs sought to gain entry to the men's swimming team, despite the high school association's rule prohibiting girls' participation when the high school offers a girl's swimming program. The district court ruled in favor of the defendants again in this case.

Courts do not always agree. The Sixth Circuit Court of Appeals in *Morris* v. *Michigan State Board of Education*[51] affirmed the district court's issue of a temporary injunction prohibiting the exclusion of women from varsity interscholastic athletics with one exception. The lower court had banned sex segregation in athletics generally, but the court of appeals modified the order, making it applicable to noncontact sports only.[52] The *Morris* decision illustrates the dichotomy in treatment accorded contact and noncontact sports. Women are allowed to try out for and participate in all interscholastic noncontact sports including all boys' teams even if the school does provide a team only for them, according to the *Morris* case.

The courts have generally assumed that women are incapable of competing on an equal basis with men in contact sports such as boxing, wrestling, rugby, football, and basketball. But if the suit is not a class action and if the plaintiff has demonstrated her ability to compete, it would seem that a rule prohibiting women from competing would have to be found to discriminate against that particular plaintiff. The argument becomes even stronger when all men are permitted to participate on a team, regardless of athletic ability. In *Darrin* v. *Gould*,[53] the court expounded upon the list of inferior female physical characteristics which was presented by expert testimony. Even so, a court may find it difficult to justify why an unqualified male may be allowed to try for a team position while a qualified female may not. A rule that gives one sixteen-year-old greater discretion over the use of his body than another has over hers is unacceptable to the skilled woman athlete of high ability.

One solution to the dilemma that has been suggested is to offer both separate and mixed athletic programs. Structurally it would consist of three independent teams per sport. The varsity would consist of the best male and female athletes. Varsity team membership would be based only on ability, and no distinction would be made between contact and noncontact sports.

The question of equity in cocurricular activities is manifested more often in the athletic program because of its sheer magnitude in most secondary schools and because it is in the athletic program where the inequities have been the most blatant, both with respect to access and with respect to budget allocations.

Privacy and the Confidentiality of Student Records

The question of the confidentiality and accuracy of student records is an important one. Since the passage in August of 1974 of Public Law 93–380, "The Family Educational Rights and Privacy Act" (FERPA),[54] the issue has been legally clarified. This act provides that students and parents are permitted to inspect and review records, and must be given a copy of any part or all of the educational record at the request of a student or parent. Further, it is required that in any dispute concerning the contents of a student's educational record, due process must be provided. Where a record is found to be inaccurate, the inaccuracies must be expunged.

In essence, to protect the privacy of individuals, the act, among other things, requires that the schools and other agencies permit an individual to:

1. Determine what records pertaining to him or her are maintained in the system of records.
2. Gain access to relevant records in such a system of records and to have copies made.
3. Correct or amend any record pertaining to him or her.

Further, the records about an individual may not be disclosed to outsiders except by the consent of the individual in question. The consent must be in writing and must be *specific* in stating to whom the record may be disclosed, which records may be disclosed, and, where applicable, the time frame during which the records may be disclosed. In some instances, disclosures may be made without the consent of the pupil or the pupil's parents. Information may be disclosed within the school to teachers or guidance counselors who have a "need to know," where there is a court order, where there is required disclosure under the Freedom of Information Act, and for routine usage such as publication of names of people who made an honor roll, or information for a directory such as class lists or sports brochures, which might include such information as the student's name, address, sex, or birthplace. Even in this latter instance, it would be advisable to get prior permission through some sort of routine process. Figure 5–5 describes one state's response to the problem.

MEMORANDUM

TO: The School Official Addressed
FROM: M. L. Brockette, Commissioner of Education
DATE: March 15, 1978
SUBJECT: Release of Student Directory Information

Several school districts in Texas have requested information regarding the release of student directory information to various groups and organizations without violating the provisions of the Privacy Act. The purpose of this communication is to clarify what information may be released and to whom it may be provided.

1. Directory information which may be released is limited to the following:
   - Student's name and address
   - Telephone number
   - Date and place of birth
   - Major field of study
   - Participation in officially recognized activities and sports
   - Weight and height of members of athletic teams
   - Dates of attendance
   - Degrees and awards received
   - The public or private school most recently attended by the student
2. Directory information may be disclosed by all school officials.
3. Under no circumstance can directory assistance be disclosed to private or profit-making entities other than employers, prospective employers or representatives of the news media.
4. Directory information may be released to requesting private schools, colleges, universities, and military recruiting officials.

FIGURE 5–5. A state education department responds to FERPA

The Family Educational Rights and Privacy Act simply legalizes what should have been, and was in many places, common administrative practice with regard to student records.[55] (The fact that it was not all that common gave rise to the act.) It is important for schools to take voluntary action to build confidence on the part of the school constituency and to create an atmosphere of trust. The implementation of good policies for the management of pupil records is as good a place as any to begin to increase this confidence.

General guidelines to assist principals in developing fair policies about student records might include the following, suggested by the Russell Sage Foundation.[56]

1. *Principals should develop procedures to insure that all parents and students know what kinds of information are contained in school records at a given time and are informed of their rights concerning control over the process of information collection and recording.* Schools should be diligent in the effort to provide parents with information about pupil records and this information should be in a readily understandable form.

2. *Encourage mature students and their parents to inspect the records.* As was noted in the discussion of FERPA, the rights of parents to do this are now well established but most parents are unaware of these rights. Increased communication and greater trust on the part of the parents might be a major benefit, especially because such a policy might provide a substantially more accurate record. Unfortunately, current practice in most schools allows clerical and other kinds of errors to be perpetuated. The best check on the accuracy of records is the parent or the student. More important, if either the objective or the subjective judgments contained in the official records cannot be justified to the student and parents, then such judgments have no place in a permanent record.

3. *Develop systematic procedures to obtain explicit and informed parental or pupil consent before information contained in school records is released to outside parties, regardless of the* *reasons for such release or the characteristic of the third party.* Most schools will, on occasion, give out information to law enforcement or other agencies without obtaining consent from the student or the student's parents. Aside from the possible legal implications of a violation of privacy, this practice can have no other effect than that of discouraging a mutually trustful relationship between the parent, the student, and the school.

SUMMARY

This chapter examined legal principles undergirding the operation of the school. Knowledge about the laws governing school practice is important for principals and teachers, not just in order to stay out of court, but to provide the kind of orderly, productive, and humane school climate essential to the furtherance of a democratic society. The authors agree with McIntyre's statement:

A moral school principal . . . is one who takes seriously the school's accountability for helping individual human beings to realize their potential. . . . He is a believer in law and order, and he demonstrates his belief by operating a school in a lawful and orderly manner—including observance of laws, court decisions and ethical principles pertaining to race, religion and freedom of expression. He is more concerned with the depth of students' understanding than the length of their hair. He is outraged by the erosion of citizens' constitutional rights, and he scrupulously protects the rights of the citizens in the classrooms. He is, in short, a thoroughly *human* being who is dedicated to the proposition that the schools can be significant instrumentalities in the fulfillment of the American dream—a democracy with liberty and justice for all.[57]

And, while school officials cannot, in the language of the Supreme Court, "be charged with predicting the future course of constitutional law,"[58] they are expected to stay abreast of current legal requirements and behave accordingly:

> There can be no immunity even where an official has acted without intending to deprive the plaintiff of his constitutional rights, if a reasonable man in the defendant's position would have realized that his actions would have that effect.[59]

ENDNOTES

1. John Seldon (1584-1654), *Table Talk: Law.*
2. William H. Roe and Thelbert L. Drake, *The Principalship* (New York: MacMillan Publishing Company, 1974), p. 52.
3. The replacing principle is *in respondeat superior.* For an explication of this principle and the implications it has to school districts, see Larry W. Hughes and William M. Gordon, "Frontiers of Law" in *The Courts and Education* (Chicago: National Society for the Study of Education, 1978), pp. 340-341.
4. Several services are available to the school administrator to assist in this endeavor. For example, the National Organization on Legal Problems in Education (NOLPE), 1501 West 21st Street, Topeka, Kansas 66606, distributes the monthly *NOLPE Notes* to members who deal with current legal matters involving the school. The various professional principal organizations have publications containing legal foci. Also, many of the national educational journals such as the *American School Board Journal* contain regular legal features. NOLPE promotes an interest in and an understanding of school law. In addition to meetings and membership response systems, it issues regular publications on school law subjects and serves as a clearinghouse for information on research and legal publications. It does not take official positions on policy questions, but does attempt to provide broad information about current issues in school law.
5. *In loco parentis,* as a legal principle, is a common law measure of the rights and duties of school authorities relative to pupils and schools, and holds that school authorities stand in the place of the parent when the child is at school. It simply means that school personnel may establish rules and require obedience of these rules for the educational welfare of the child. Further, school personnel may inflict punishments for disobedience. The legal test is whether a reasonably knowledgeable and prudent parent would so act, and the doctrine is used not only to support the rights of school personnel, but also to establish a responsibility of these same school personnel regarding such occurrences as injuries that may befall pupils. It is a presumption of the law that those having such authority will exercise it properly, and generally speaking, in claims of improper application of authority, the burden of proof falls on the person making the claim. Thus, for example, a parent who may object to a rule or to a punishment generally must prove "unreasonableness."
6. In Dayton, Ohio, an agency entitled the Center for the Study of Student Citizenship has provided a *Student Rights Handbook,* wherein students are informed of their rights and responsibilities under the law. The center's address is 1145 Germantown St., Dayton, Ohio 45009. Copies of their booklet are quite inexpensive and most useful. Also see Alan H. Levine and Eve Cary, *The Rights of Students, an American Civil Liberties Union Handbook,* rev. ed. (New York: Avon Books, 1977).
7. Tinker v. Des Moines Independent Community School District, 393 U.S. 503, 89 S. Ct. 733 (1969).
8. West Virginia v. Barnette, 319 U.S. 624 (1943).
9. Thomas A. Shannon, *Current Trends in School Law* (Topeka, Kan.: The National Organization on Legal Problems of Education, 1974), p. 5.
10. State v. Fond du Lac Board of Education, 63 Wis 234, 23 N.W. 102, 53 Am Rep 262 (1885).
11. William E. Gauerke, *Legal and Ethical Responsibilities of School Personnel* (Englewood Cliffs, N.J.: Prentice Hall, Inc., 1959), p. 127.
12. Tinker v. Des Moines Independent Community School, 393 U.S. 503, 89 S. Ct. 733 (1969). See also, Burnside v. Byars, 363 F.2nd 744 (5th Cir. 1966).
13. Illinois Education Association v. Board of Education, 320 N.E. 2nd 240 (Ill. App. 1974).
14. For example, a policy which prohibits "extreme hair or dress styles" is too vague. What an "extreme style" is varies with individual interpretation. In just such a case, Meyers v. Arcata Union High School, 75 Cal. Rptr 68, (Cal. App. 1969) 89 S. Ct. 668 (1969), the school regulation said to the students. "If you wear an extreme hair style you'll get suspended." The California court ruled, "This regulation is too vague and, therefore, cannot be enforced, and

therefore the students have the privilege of disobeying it. We do not dispute the authority of the schools to regulate grooming and personal appearance but they must do so in clear terms so that students know what conduct or appearance is required of them, with some particularity."

15.   The seriousness of transgressions ranges widely, from minor misbehavior problems of students and minor infractions of staff to major infractions capable of inflicting bodily harm or questions of incompetence and subsequent dismissal of personnel. The seriousness of the proposed penalty will determine the degree to which specific due process protections are officially and publicly accorded the person. Nevertheless, even in the instance of a minor punishment, such as making a child stand in the hall for whispering in class, the teacher should mentally go over the guarantees if for no other reason than to test the fairness of the punishment. The teacher should also be sure that the child being punished is the child who committed the offense.

16.   Procedural due process legislation varies from state to state and often depends on the issue. The question of a time line for various appeals often varies and is specifically established in many laws. This is especially true in such issues as personnel terminations. It is always wise to check the specific law with the school attorney or the state code.

17.   It is important to remember that while this process takes on some of the vestments of a court of law, it is not a court of law. It simply is a provision for fair and impartial treatment. After the process is complete, the individual still has the right to "take his case to court" if it is felt that the act for which punishment was rendered was not a punishable one, or that the punishment was too severe. Nevertheless, according the aspects of procedural due process will be most influential with the courts. It avoids the charge of capricious action and is both legally and morally sound.

18.   Negligence is usually defined as failure to do something that any reasonably prudent person would have done in a similar situation.

19.   Contributory negligence is determined by whether or not the party who was injured exercised the degree of caution others of the same age, sex, maturation level, and experience would have exercised under the same conditions. Obviously more supervision would be expected of those in charge of young children; teachers and principals in the elementary school have less chance of avoiding a law suit by claiming contributory negligence than those who are charged with the supervision of older children. Nevertheless, a student who disregards or acts in direct defiance of an admonishment by a teacher or a principal would probably be held to be guilty of contributory negligence if by doing so he or she was subsequently injured.

20.   Of course, not all injuries to pupils are actionable; some are simply unavoidable, the result of pure accident. Only those injuries resulting from negligence provide the injured with the right to recover. See also the meaning of contributory negligence discussed earlier.

21.   However, advance approval by a parent or guardian for participation of a child in an activity such as a field trip or an athletic event *does not* waive the right of the child to sue for tort in case the child is injured. It does perform an important function, however. It informs the parent, and the mere fact that such advance approval was required is some evidence that care was exercised by the school.

22.   See, for example, Tymkowiez v. San Jose Unified School District, 312 p. 2d 388 (1957). The court let the case go to jury on the question of adequacy of supervision. The court stated that the teacher had "a duty to be present" to supervise pupils during a recreation period, "when it may reasonably be expected to result in rough, rowdy, and dangerous conduct."

23.   Suspension generally is defined as dismissal from the school for a specific, although generally short-term period of time (two or three days, or often a week). Usually the principal of the school has the authority to suspend. Expulsion is defined to mean permanent dismissal and normally is an action which can legally be taken only by the school board. There is some question as to whether or not a pupil, otherwise within the legal age of school attendance, can be permanently excluded from a public school; although it has been established generally that for good cause the student can be permanently removed from a regular public school provided that he or she is placed in an appropriate special school.

24.   In the instance of suspension, one of the most favorable due process cases for students is Mills v. Board of Education, 348 F. Supp. 866 (1972) in which the court ordered that there must be a hearing prior to a suspension invoked for any period in excess of two days. In Goss v. Lopez, 95 S. Ct. 729 (1975)

the U.S. Supreme Court ruled that basically school officials must accord students and school employees their constitutional right of due process even in routine disciplinary actions. In the Goss v. Lopez case, it was held that a junior high school pupil suspended for as much as a single day is entitled to due process. Further, in Wood v. Strickland, 95 St. Ct. 992 (1975) the U.S. Supreme Court ruled that school board members and school officials can be held personally liable for pecuniary damages when students (and by logical extension one must suppose school personnel as well) are denied constitutional rights, even by accidental omission.

25. If a teacher or a principal uses excessive force or causes untoward injury, he or she may be held liable for battery. There is often confusion among lay people about the terms *assault* and *battery*. Battery means the actual unlawful inflicting of physical violence on another. Assault is a threat to commit battery. There can be assault without battery; battery always includes assault.

26. *In loco parentis, supra*, p. 6.

27. A Supreme Court case has affirmed the right of school personnel to use corporal punishment. The Supreme Court upheld a lower court ruling that corporal punishment may be administered provided that only "reasonable force" is used and provided that pupils know beforehand that certain behavior or actions will result in physical punishment. Baker v. Owen, 385 F. Supp. 294 (1975).

28. Goss v. Lopez, *loc. cit.*

29. Ibid., p. 736.

30. Ibid., p. 740.

31. Expulsions are a different matter. In the instance of expulsion, it would seem clear that all of the vestments of procedural due process should be followed.

32. Sweet v. Childs, 518 F. 20 320 (1975).

33. McNaughton v. Circleville Board of Education, 345 N.E. 2d 649.

34. Kelly v. Johnson, U.S. D.C. New Hampshire, No. 75-91, February 12, 1976.

35. Wood v. Strickland. The facts of this case involved three tenth grade girls who were suspended from school for three months for allegedly "spiking punch" at an extracurricular school event. The girls and their parents sued school officials for monetary damage, claiming violation of due process rights, and the Supreme Court ultimately ruled in their favor. Wood v. Strickland 420 U.S. 308 (1975).

36. Wood v. Strickland, at 322.

37. Sullivan v. Mead Independent School District No. 101, 530 F 2d 799 (1976).

38. Children's Defense Fund, *Children Out of School in America* (1974), p. 135.

39. See chapter 19 for a more complete discussion of in-school suspensions.

40. Cases decided on this basis within the last two decades include Kissick v. Garland Independent School District, 330 SW 2d 708; Board of Directors v. Greene, 259 Iowa 1260, 147 N.W. 20 854; State ex rel Baker v. Stevensen, 27 Ohio op. 2d 223, 189 N.E. 2d 181; Starkey v. Board of Education, 14 Utah 2d 227, 381 p. 2d 718.

41. Starkey v. Board of Education, at 720.

42. Ralph Mawdsley, "Constitutional Rights of Students," in Hooker, ed., *The Courts and Education* (Chicago: National Society for the Study of Education, 1978), p. 170.

43. Davis v. Meeks, 344 F. Supp. 298 at 301 (N.D. Ohio, 1972).

44. McCleod v. State, ex rel Colmer, 154 Miss. 468, 122 So. 737.

45. Warren v. NASSP, 375 F. Supp 1043 (1974).

46. 20 U.S.C. 1681 et. seq (Supp. 1975).

47. Brenden v. Independent School Dist, 342 F. Supp. 1224, 1242-43 (D. Minn. 1972): Haas v. South Bend Community School Corp. 259 Ind. 515, 522-24, 289 N.E. 495, 498-500 (1972); Gilpin v. Kansas State High School Ass'n. 377 F. Supp. 1233, 1242 (D. Kan. 1974.); Hoover v. Meiklejon, 430 F. Supp. 164 (D. Col. 1977); Carnes v. Tennessee Secondary School Athletic Ass'n. 415 F. Supp. 569 (E.D. Tenn. 1976); Reed v. Nebraska School Activities Ass'n. 341 F. Supp 258 (D. Nebraska, 1972).

48. 20 U.S.C. 1681 et. seq (Supp. V, 1975).

49. 333 N.E. 2d 138 (Ind. App. 1975).

50. 351 F. Supp. 69 (N.D. Ill. 1972).

51. 472 F. 2d 1207 (6th Cir. 1973).

52. Ibid. After the preliminary injunction had been entered and perhaps because of it, the Michigan legislature enacted the following law: "Female pupils shall be permitted to participate in all noncontact interscholastic athletic activities. . . . Even if the institution does have a girl's team in any noncontact interscholastic athletic activity, the female shall be permitted to compete for a position of the boy's team."

53. Darrin v. Gould, 540 p. 2d 882 (1975).

54. FERPA is also commonly known as The Buckley Amendment.

55. Privacy regulations were slow in coming to school administrators. Following the passage of FERPA in August, 1974, the Department of Health, Education and Welfare was charged with the responsibility for developing guidelines for school administrators. The complete guidelines can be found in the *Federal Register* and have been published in two parts, the first appearing in the March, 1976, edition of the *Federal Register* and part two in a subsequent edition.

56. The Russell Sage Foundation has developed very helpful guidelines for the management of pupil records: *Guidelines for the Collection, Maintenance and Dissemination of Pupil Records.* Single copies are free from the Russell Sage Foundation, 230 Park Avenue, New York, New York 10017.

57. Larry W. Hughes, "Achieving Effective Human Relations and Morale," in Culbertson et al., *Performance Objectives for School Principals* (Berkeley, Calif.: McCutchan Publishing Company, 1974), p. 133, chapter 5.

58. Wood v. Strickland, at 322.

59. Chaudin v. Atkinson, 406 F. Supp. 188 (1975).

BIBLIOGRAPHY

Current Trends in School Law. Topeka, Kan.: National Organization on Legal Problems of Education, 1978.

Gatti, Richard D., and Gatti, David J. *Encyclopedic Dictionary of School Law.* West Nyack, N.Y.: Parker Publishing Co., 1975.

Gauerke, William E. *Legal and Ethical Responsibilities of School Personnel,* Englewood Cliffs, N.J.: Prentice Hall, 1959.

Gee, E. Gordon, and David J. Sperry. *Education Law and the Public Schools: A Compendium.* Boston: Allyn and Bacon, 1978.

Hogan, John C. *The Schools, The Courts and The Public Interest.* Lexington, Mass.: D.C. Heath, 1974.

Hooker, Clifford, ed. *Courts and Education, Seventy-seventh Yearbook of the National Society for the Study of Education.* Chicago: University of Chicago Press, 1978.

Hughes, Larry W. "Achieving Effective Human Relations and Morale," in Jack Culbertson et al. *Performance Objectives for School Principals.* Berkeley, Calif.: McCutchan Publishing Co., 1974, chapter 5.

Hughes, Larry W. and Gordon, William M. "Frontiers of Law," in *The Courts and Education, Seventy-Seventh Yearbook of the National Society for the Study of Education.* Chicago: University of Chicago Press, 1978. chapter 13.

Hughes, Larry W. *Education and the Law in Tennessee.* Cincinnati: W. H. Anderson Company, 1971.

Inequality in Education (a series of thirteen legal reviews on educational issues). Cambridge, Mass.: Center for Law and Education, October 1969 to December 1972.

Ladd, Edward T. "Regulating Student Behavior Without Ending Up in Court." *Phi Delta Kappan* 54 (January 1973): 38–43.

Mawdsley, Ralph. "Constitutional Rights of Students," in Hooker, ed. *The Courts and Education.* Chicago: NSSE, 1978, chapter 7.

"Negligence—When is the Principal Liable." From the series *A Legal Memorandum,* Reston, Va.: National Association of Secondary School Principals, January 1975. (A bibliography of previous issues may be secured from NASSP, 1904 Association Drive, Reston, Virginia 22091).

Nolte, Chester M. "Legal Issues in Education." *American School Board Journal* (regular feature in this monthly journal). See especially, "Why You Need A Student Grievance Plan," Ibid., 162 (August 1975): 38–40.

Nolte, Chester M. *School Law in Action: 101 Key Decisions With Guidelines for School Administrators.* West Nyack, N.Y.: Parker Publishing Co., 1971.

Piele, Philip K., ed. *The Yearbook of School Law.* Topeka, Kan.: National Organization of Legal Problems of Education, 1975. (Published annually since 1972.)

Roe, William H., and Drake, Thelbert L. *The Principalship.* New York: MacMillan Publishing Co., 1974.

Student Rights Litigation Packet, Cambridge, Mass.: Center for Law and Education, 1972.

Von Brock, Lewis. "Coping with Suspension and The Supreme Court," *NASSP Bulletin* 61 (March 1977): 68–76.

Chapter Six

Understanding the Community

INTRODUCTION

Meredith Wilson's popular musical, *The Music Man,* opens with a group of turn-of-the-century salesmen describing their occupation while riding a train to the next town. The refrain is that to be a good salesman, "you gotta know the territory." No better phrase could be used to describe the most pressing need of the secondary school principal who wants to develop good school-community relations. In these days of rapid social change, however, the nature of the territory often changes very fast, causing traditional communication mechanisms to be insufficient.

Redrawn attendance zones in response to a desegregation plan, rural school consolidation, or the impact of suburban sprawl on a heretofor sleepy village can quickly complicate the external role of the secondary school principal. Miscommunication and distrust often result when the "neighborhood" served by the high school suddenly reflects wide cultural and ethnic diversity and students with even more widely varying needs and interests. The territory for many principals has become vast and indeed complex. This chapter will examine important social phenomena which impinge on the activities of the principal.

Societal Change

The obvious societal changes that have occurred over the past century have taken their toll, as can be seen by examining the common relationships between school and community. One need not be a graduate sociologist to consider the impact of such phenomena as industrialization, technocracy, urbanization, and the increasing complexity of social relationships on the relationship between school and community. The increasing esotericism of professional education practices, a concomitant of these changes, has also had the effect of widening the gap of understanding between school and community. The dissolution of small, closely-knit communities of years past has made strangers of the school and those served by the school, each rather unsure of the other, as well as of itself or themselves. The same situation occurs in the medical profession and other welfare delivery agencies that attempt to cater to the varied, complex and multifaceted needs of people who live in a community. The term *community* has come to be used in a most unsociological sense to simply mean a group of people living in close proximity to each other and served by many of the same social and governmental agencies.

A Slowly Dying Myth

In times past, two patterns were characteristic of the school's role in the community and the relationship it had with its clients. First, there was a general lack of threat and mystery about what the school was doing or was supposed to do. Ideologically, unified communities of the past viewed the school primarily as an extension of the home; as an instrument for passing on the eternal verities, for teaching children how to read, write, and cipher, and to somehow enculturate these same children into the appropriate ways of behaving. Further, the financial outlay for the support of such a school was relatively small. The school itself may have been built by willing hands in the community, much as groups of farmers might come together to build barns for each other. Out of such an environment one might have expected rather broad community cooperation and support for the local educational system.

Of course, such a bucolic wonderland probably did not adequately describe this nation, but it did describe many communities in the rural heartlands. Whether or not it ever generally existed and even if it still exists today in some few isolated places isn't really the important point. The fact is that for many educators, the state of the school-community relations program continues to be based on the notion that such a well-ordered and ideologically unified situation does exist or should exist. That's where the trouble begins.

The school has become a broad institution serving a very complex society. Out of this complexity and perceived educational esoterism, and the new roles and responsibilities being expected of the school, has developed a mystery about just what schools do. Coupled with the mystery is that the school itself is the single most expensive public welfare delivery subsystem. Further, ideological unity is not characteristic of very many cities and towns; thus, there is distrust, disenchantment, misconception and a general depth of concern by many in society about the school and its performance and its cost. This is an age characterized generally by criticism and skepticism about public agencies and their efficiency.

The need for the development of better mechanisms to provide for effective communication between the school and the community is glaringly apparent. The principal who relies on informal relationships that may have served adequately in less complex times is operating in a precarious position indeed.

Ideological Disunity

The concept of ideological unity needs some consideration. Ideological unity in a community context refers to a community that is inherently in tune with itself; with well understood belief structures and mores, and where the eternal verities are indeed eternal and true for all. This type of community has been described by sociologists as *sacred* in orientation. It does not describe very many places in this country today.[1] What does describe much of American life today is the term *secular*. A secular community struggles with conflicts in values, with old virtues being viewed by some as being hypocritical or evidence of blind conformity, and with people unified largely by civil units rather than by any kinship ties. There is a great division of labor and proliferation of organizations, each with its own special membership and interests. Very formalized social controls set up by law and enforced by various civil agencies. Secular communities also create a basic anonymity to the extent that people are living *in* the community but are really not *of* the community.

> The problem in an urbanized society such as we live in with its evident cultural pluralism, is that various groups and individuals will reflect differing points on the sacred-secular continuum, and thus will hold different perceptions of what the institutions serving that community ought

to look like. The politics of confrontation and conflict within which the school and other social institutions are caught is simply a manifestation of this.[2]

Role of the School

The mass public education system of this country is generally considered to have two primary roles: (1) to serve as an instrument by which the important knowledge and skills needed to be a productive human being are acquired in an effective and efficient manner, and (2) to provide for a fluid social structure.

Attending to the demands of the first role produces about as much conflict as the second, although the conflict is often of a more specialized nature. Most citizens would agree that this is indeed the *raison d'etre* for the public school system, but there is much controversy about the processes that should be used to achieve mastery of the important knowledge and skills. Further, responses to the question, "What knowledge is of most use?" vary widely and cause misunderstanding and conflict.

The second role of the school, that of providing for a fluid social structure is more honored in the breach than in the practice. It is generally accepted that the United States and Canada do not have the rigid class lines of many countries and that it is important that mobility be facilitated up the social scale. Class lines in America do tend to be blurred. However, members of minorities will point out that this has been primarily true only if you happened to be a white, Anglo-Saxon Protestant (WASP), or at least have an ethnic or cultural background that facilitated a one-generation amalgamation of WASP characteristics. Moreover, it is possible to have so many impinging negative variables present that even if one has the appropriate ethnic characteristics, the American Dream ("If one tries hard, one can succeed.") becomes impossible for many members of the poverty-ridden social understructure.

The idea that the school's role is to provide for fluid social structure therefore continues to be under fire and, in the authors' judgment, will continue to be so in the foreseeable future. The concept is generally well accepted, but perceived aggressive efforts on the part of school leaders to implement the concept by bussing, breakfast programs, compensatory education programs, reorganizing school district boundaries, bi- and tri-lingual instruction, among a host of policies, procedures, and processes now ongoing in many schools, are met with resentment, misunderstanding, downright hostility by many in the majority culture. Similarly, perceived or actual nonattention to inequities in school programming, organization and instruction receive hostile reaction and frequent precipitative action by members of groups outside the mainstream.

The public school system has been viewed as an instrument of social reform for more than a century, but only in the last few decades has it overtly engaged in activities that have occurred mostly as a result of outside forces, such as federal and state legislation, acts of the courts, pressures from the down-trodden, etc. Sadly, with some notable exceptions of course, school leaders have largely been content to avoid the issue and have provided organizational structures and response systems—PTA's, newsletters, standardized curriculum—that are somewhat out of touch with social reality and based on the presumptions of ideological unity and automatic equity.

Enlightened School-Community Relations

It's no wonder, then, that schools are caught in a crossfire at times as first one group or individual and then another attempts to make the school reflect the image of the particular part of the world to which they subscribe. Because of the nature of the public educational enterprise, the school must derive its very support from the outside world. People who influence policies in the community that affect the school reside in that outside world, and inevitably they seek ways to develop policies for the schools in conformity with their own desires and values. If all of this suggests there is a need for a broadly based, carefully organized community-school relations program, then the intent of these opening paragraphs has been met.

Progress in education today depends in large part on the consent of parents and other citizens in the community as well as upon relationships that the school maintains with other community agencies and government. In an economy of rising costs and an expanding sense of cultural pluralism and multiethnicity, the acquisition of additional support for the education program, or at least the development of firm understandings about the nature and role of education, assumes increasing importance. The problem, however, of securing adequate support for the schools (psychological support as well as fiscal support) goes well beyond the understanding of fiscal need alone. Citizens are interested as never before in the various dimensions of the educational system, and the demands made on individual schools are indeed great.

A sound school-community relations program is necessary to gain this needed support if the public education system is to make progress, or even survive as a viable institution in the decades ahead. The role of the principal is an important one, for the principal serves as administrative head of the closest public agency to neighborhood or community residents, in both a literal and figurative sense. In geographic proximity, the school is "just around the corner"; thereby making it the first line of communication with the neighborhood or the community it serves. It is closer than the mayor's office, and even closer in many cases than the fire station. The school affects the community's most prized possessions—its children and its pocketbook.

THE PLURALISTIC COMMUNITY

In the pluralistic community, schools serve many publics, each of which may have different values and orientations. In such a setting, the role of the school administrator often becomes that of mediating conflicts between various competing pressure groups. This simply means that educational administrators must be able to work successfully with the many publics who often are pulling in conflicting directions. The importance of identifying key community or neighborhood influentials and the development of informal working relations with these cannot be overemphasized, not because the persons or groups are always right, but because they usually represent the best thinking of the community and are most influenced by a rational approach to problem solving.

Confounding the problem of communicating with school patrons is that more and more frequently districts are reorganizing school attendance zones to achieve desegregated student bodies. Thus, as bussing and noncontiguous pairings of schools occur, the neighborhood served by the school may be quite dispersed. Conventional parent and patron groups, such as booster clubs and PTAs, may be difficult to maintain because of time and distance problems. Such groups are worth the energy to maintain, however. Beyond this, it is apparent that a considerable portion of administrative effort will be required to work with existing community groups in the various neighborhoods from which students come, as well as to develop school-wide advisory groups with cross-sectional representation.[3]

Neighborhood Influence Systems

Neighborhoods have influence systems that may be especially important in the principal's sphere of interaction. As urban and suburban communities have become more and more complex and power sources diffused, neighborhood influence systems have become increasingly apparent, at least partly in response to a perceived lack of responsiveness of certain community welfare delivery systems such as schools. More often, such influence systems also reflect racial or ethnic homogeneity. Individual schools may serve as effective mechanisms to receive information from and to dispense information to neighborhood leadership. Research suggests that an individual community member's decision to support or not support any particular community issue is more often than not based on the influence of friends and neighbors rather than on the presence of any outside objective data. It would seem, therefore, that the perceptive school principal should become familiar with the leadership structure of the particular microcosmic society the school serves.

Every social group has a leadership structure that, with diligence, can be identified. The principal who wishes to begin a new kind of dialogue with the immediate community will do well to engage in this endeavor, for what is generally true of community power structure—that it represents some of the best thinking of the community—will also be true of neighborhood influence systems.[4]

During the early part of the Johnson administration the Community Action Programs (CAP) were implemented. Some readers may remember that an important aspect of CAP was the initial constitution of a local policy-making and decision-making body that had under the law the task of governance of the several programs. The provision establishing the governing board of the Community Action Program required that there be representation in substantial numbers of those people who were to be helped by the programs; that is, the policy and advising board would be composed of a large number of the poor. "But, who?" was the question most often raised in local government circles and among those charged with getting the programs going. At first, in many communities

no one knew just how to go about *locating* individuals who might be interested in serving on such advisory boards. Surprising to many, was the discovery that there was indeed a leadership structure among the understructure, and it could be readily identified, often through reputational means by surveying the storefront churches, the local welfare agencies, the less well-known social clubs, the membership of small union locals, among any number of other somewhat formal sources. Not very helpful were such agencies as PTA/PTO, the well-known churches, and the well-known civic clubs. There is a lesson here for the principal who wishes to engage in a new kind of relationship with the community, especially if that community is characterized by heterogeneity in racial, ethnic, or social makeup. Further, a neighborhood leadership structure may not be composed of or contain very many people who are also parents of children attending the schools.

The major point is that for a secondary school principal interested in developing effective school-community relations programs based on mutual trust and a ready willingness to examine issues of mutual concern, the old mechanisms for doing this may not suffice. The authors of this book have nothing against the usual parent-teacher groups. Without question, in many places these formal groups have performed very important services for the schools. Neither do the authors have anything against well-known civic and community groups, for they too perform many needed community services. It is simply that such well-known groups as these often do not have a membership comprised of anything approximating the real nature of the community or the neighborhoods served by the schools. There may exist, well outside these more conservative groups, a structure with important things to say to the schools, but for which there has been no regular communication channel. School administrators should not engage in self-delusion about the nature of the leadership pattern in the neighborhoods the school serves. An examination of the membership rolls of the usual local formal organizations and a comparison of certain characteristics of these people with general demographic characteristics of the student body of the school may reveal that different kinds of people are missing entirely. If different kinds of people are missing, one can be sure that many key neighborhood influentials are not being reached by school messages. Principals, like most of the rest of us, are most comfortable when surrounded by persons who reflect a background similar to their own. Principals tend to be most comfortable when speaking with other professionals. This fact alone, then, may suggest a careful analysis of the procedures currently being used to tap community leadership sources.

People in the community are also often members of an array of different formal and informal groups that may impinge upon the schools. They are members of clubs and associations, as well as other more general self-help groups such as the American Indian Movement, the Congress of Racial Equality, or a group such as the DAR or the American Legion, for example. All of these organizations demand loyalty from their membership and may oppose certain school system procedures and policies. Membership in what may at times be adversary groups may be the source of much community-school conflict.

> In sum, then, characteristic of our complex society are communities which are more generally reflective of cultural pluralism. The fact is that many people in the community will not derive their normative behavior from white, middle class heritage—and by extension, of course, neither will the student body; nor the teaching staff. Responses to traditional control and decision systems in the school and the community may vary from hostile acquiescence to open challenge. Teachers and administrators must learn to cope with this great diversity.[5]

It is apparent that school leaders need to identify the influential people and groups in the community or neighborhoods. Influence systems vary from community to community and neighborhood to neighborhood. To assume that all influentials in a particular neighborhood or community feel similarly about school issues and that there is unanimity is unwise. There is an indeterminacy and amorphousness about influence systems, but the degree to which various leaders in the community are able to agree on a direction that education ought to take and the degree to which they are able to accept certain principles and guidelines that school leaders determine, will ascertain, in great part, the extent of reform, modification, and growth of the educational institution in the community.

There are many instruments available to assist school leaders in gauging the nature of interest in the schools, the degree of educational enlightenment, and the nature, extent, and identification of influential people and groups in the community. The school administrator should subject the area that the school serves to a community analysis, not only to develop good public relations strategies, but, more important, to utilize the resources and problem-solving ability manifest in neighborhood or community influentials. This will thereby provide a foundation for cooperative development and growth of both school and community.

Conflict is not inevitable, but it is frequent in any society. Conflict is not necessarily disruptive or negative. In fact, it is often out of conflict that greater understanding results, provided the situation is characterized by positive acts of openness, a willingness to compromise, and well-understood procedures for resolution.

Negotiating with Pressure Groups

From time to time, all school administrators will be confronted with requests from organized groups of people who represent a particular point of view about a school-related issue. Frequently, such pressure groups begin their inquiry at the individual school level in the principal's office. The issues may run the gamut, from complaints about teachers, textbooks, or specific courses of study to alleged institutional racism and demands for more equitable staffing or pupil personnel decisions.

Pressure groups can be distinguished from the normal community decision system because of the somewhat temporal nature of their activities and their tendency to form about single issues or causes, frequently in response to specific decisions made in the school. Often they display a legitimate concern, and they must always be dealt with sensitively and sensibly. The following guidelines may help the besieged principal:

1. *An early identification should be made of the group that is in opposition or is likely to be in opposition to certain school programs.* Who are they, and more important, who are their leaders?

2. *Can the group and its leaders be talked to?* Once the opposing group and the leader(s) of that group have been identified, it is appropriate to contact them for a closed-door session to explore the elements of the issue. The principal may gain some more definitive notion of just what it is that is troubling the group. This meeting or series of meetings may develop ways, if the cause is legitimate, for the school to help the group achieve its goals. It may require great insight to find out what the real issue is because stated "reasons" for opposition to this or that school issue are often at variance with the real causative factors. It is important to know what the real reasons are if the group is to be dealt with effectively and if subsequent negotiations are to be successful. (At this point, it is also important to apprise the central office of the potential hostile situation and seek counsel.)

3. *Following these informal meetings, reach a decision.* Some important points must be deter-

mined at this time, including the question about how strong the opposition really is. Do they have a good chance to beat the school in its present position? Most important, do they have a good solid point on which to differ with the school? It is at this time that the principal must decide whether or not the issue will be fought out on the basis of the initial position of both sides or whether some areas of accord are possible. Before a decision is made to fight it out, there is an alternative.

4. *Is there room for compromise?* The political system under which we operate functions on compromise. Politics is the delicate art of compromise. Professional educators view themselves as experts who know what is needed for good education, but it is within this context that educational administrators often show a lack of political sophistication. The greater good sometimes demands compromise solutions where they can be achieved without compromising principles or without loss of integrity.

Of course, compromise may not be necessary. Perhaps simply sitting down with members of the pressure group, explaining the school's position and the facts, may dissuade the group from further action. Administrators who have engaged in potential community conflict situations over the years would suggest that compromise through negotiations may be the more likely result. The pressure group's motives may be highly complex. Its needs and goals are every bit as important to its membership as the needs and goals of the particular administrator or school system in question.

In any effort to influence or achieve compromise, timing is important. One really can't wait until the organized campaign is underway to effect compromises or modify points of view. The time to influence a pressure group is before the particular group has made its initial fussilade and before the school or the administrator is totally committed to a position. Common sense says that it is increasingly difficult, if not impossible, to change someone or some group when there will be much loss of face, real or imagined, by doing so.

5. *Seek help from other community members.* Assuming that all efforts to appease the opposition are unsuccessful, what does the administrator try next? The first step is to find out who is on the school's side, or who it appears ought to be on the school's side.[6] Some community analysis can be conducted even at this stage and may prove fruitful. Who besides the school really stands to lose? School principals should not forget about other less organized neighborhood groups of people who, while seemingly have a low potential for power, might have a high potential for unity on the particular issues, and who could be called upon for counsel and other help.

In all situations, it is implicit that it be known what the real goal is and what results or gains can be expected from the achievement of that goal. In other words, is the school's position or is the school administrator's position on the issue tenable? If so, evidence must be presented to substantiate why it is tenable. Many school administrators have ended up in hot water because of a refusal to negotiate or compromise, or because of tenaciously sticking to their guns on irrelevant points of contention. Further, it must be remembered that it is clearly the right of citizens to protest when they feel that the school is failing to accomplish the right thing. It is a wise school administrator who looks to community opinion as an invaluable source of information about the quality of decisions made at the school.

Need for Well-Developed Policies

If conflict can be expected on educational issues, if total ideological unity is not characteristic of very many complex communities, and if criticism can be expected as a part of the normal life of the administrator of any public

institution, what can be done to modify the divisive effects such actions might have and instead capitalize on the rich diversity of views and opinions to improve schools? Foremost would be to provide a broad set of policies, both at the school district level as well as at the school building level, that establish a framework within which diverging views can be heard in a regular and systematic manner. Such a framework provides, in effect, procedural due process whereby dissident factions in the community can formally register their views. Perhaps a specific example would help.

The Oak Ridge Example The Oak Ridge, Tennessee public school system achieved nationwide recognition for its public relations policies that build upon the rich diversity of that community and reflect as well an acceptance by the school board and the individual school administrators that the citizens of Oak Ridge are most interested in having a quality school program. The illustration to be used concerns the criteria employed for the selection of instructional media other than state-adopted textbooks. The school system's policy statement on this is as follows:

1. Subject to the review of the board of education, the superintendent of schools is responsible for developing procedures for the selection of instructional media other than state-adopted textbooks. Instructional media include books (hard and paperback), newspapers, periodicals and other printed materials and audio-visual resources purchased by the schools or received as gifts.

2. Selection of instructional media shall involve the professional staff. The principals shall be accountable for the administration and supervision of the curriculum in their schools, including coordinating the selection of instructional media and making recommendations for purchase to the assistant superintendent. The responsibility for evaluating and selecting instructional media for use in the classroom shall rest primarily with the teachers, with other

members of the department or grade level being involved at times. In making selections, the professional staff should be aware of reputable, unbiased, professionally prepared selection aides and resources.

3. Instructional media to be used in the Oak Ridge Schools shall be selected for the purpose of helping the student to become a literate citizen, sensitive of and educable to new and changing problems within the democratic framework. Media should aid in preparing the student to offer solutions to the problems.[7]

Thus, a general framework was established, and roles and responsibilities in the selection of instructional material were assigned. Implicit confidence was placed in the superintendent, the principals, and the teachers for appropriate selections. Specific criteria by which the materials should be selected were also established:

1. Instructional objectives.
2. Needs and interests of the students.
3. Needs of the individual schools.
4. Appropriateness both in relation to the student and the curriculum.
5. Balance in materials that present differing points of view concerning problems and issues of our times.
6. Factual accuracy.
7. Recency of publication.
8. Timeliness.
9. Effectiveness of presentation.
10. Technological production.
11. Availability and cost.

This school system also anticipated that the instructional materials used in the school might, from time to time, be subjected to criticism from various people or groups in the community. In fact, of course, the use of certain instructional materials has, in many communities, resulted in much controversy and conflict. Therefore, a supportive policy was developed for handling public criticism of selected educational media. That policy statement is as follows:

The board of education recognizes the right of citizens to offer suggestions, criticisms, and complaints concerning the use of certain instructional material in the school system.

Since the principal bears the major responsibility for the administration and supervision for the curriculum in his school, he, therefore, must assume the major responsibility for receiving and handling complaints.

The policy goes on to describe the procedures that should be used by principals and teachers if there is a complaint. Those procedures include explaining the rationale for the use of the particular media, or informing the complainant that an inquiry will follow after a report is made.

The person is then informed that he or she may formally submit the objections, using an appropriate form provided by the principal, to the office of the superintendent if the issue is not satisfactorily resolved after the hearing. The form, entitled, "Citizen's Request for Reconsideration of Educational Media" is explained as is the process for filing the complaint. (See figure 6–1.) The final responsibility of the principal is to inform the superintendent or the superintendent's designate of the complaint if, in the principal's judgment, it is likely to become an issue. The responsibility of the superintendent's office is to review the complaint and determine the appropriate course of action. Each policy statement establishes clear channels of responsibility, and each person who has responsibilities is required to inform others who may also be affected. Thus, communication of potentially hot issues is encouraged.

Note that the complaint form contains some important categories. The complainant must identify the specific media, as well as make personal identification, indicating whether he or she is the only one involved or represents an organization or group. Then the complainant is asked to become very specific. The objection must be stated precisely and refer-

Title of media:_____

   Type of media: (circle)

      Book   Film   Filmstrip   Recording _____

                                                               (other)

   Author/artist/composer/other: _____

   Publisher/producer (if known): _____

Request initiated by:_____ Phone:_____

Address:_____

Complainant represents

      _____ self

      _____ (Name of organization)_____

      _____ (Identify other group)_____

1. After having read/viewed/listened to the item in question, to what do you object and why? (Please be specific; cite pages, frame, other)_____

   _____

2. What do you believe is the theme of this item?_____

   _____

3. What do you feel might be the result of students reading/viewing/listening to this item?_____

4. For what age group would you recommend this item?_____

   _____

5. Other comments _____

   _____

   _____

   _____

_____   _____

      Date   Signature of Complainant

FIGURE 6-1.   Citizen's request for reconsideration of educational media

enced to the particular work in question. Further, the person is asked to describe what is believed to be the theme of the work and what possible consequence it is felt will occur if students are generally exposed to it.

Two important defusing aspects are apparent in this process. First, the complainant receives a fair and careful hearing. The person receives an opportunity to register a complaint, important for both psychological reasons as well as because of the information exchanged.

Second, the complainant knows that if there is dissatisfaction with the action which the principal proposes, and appellate procedure is open. Clearly, however, the board of education and the superordinate administrator must rely on such a policy in an undeviating manner. If it becomes apparent that the policy will not be adhered to in any kind of systematic way, superordinate administrators and board members can prepare themselves for a general onslaught from anyone who wants immediate action.

This type of procedure will not solve all of the problems, of course, but it will provide a regularized response mechanism that may eliminate many problems quickly and satisfactorily.

Using Review Boards Individual principals would also be wise to constitute some kind of review body on whom the principal could rely for advice, counsel, and the development of criteria for judging potentially controversial instructional materials. Help is available to such a professional review body from such agencies as the National Council for Social Studies or National Council for Teachers of English, as well as other sources. Such a review body might consider the policy depicted in figure 6–2.

The importance of involving a wide array of appropriate personnel in the development of policies to anticipate problems is important because it provides the basis for information sharing and good decision making. Principals cannot be expected to be all-knowing. No principal should expect to be able to respond instantaneously to a critic. The advice and counsel of the school staff, as well as the community, and the development of broadly based policies and policy review boards is needed to provide for effective decision making and intelligent responses to questions.

Yes or No Before reading further, respond to the test in figure 6–3.

How did you respond? The person who mixes responses is in trouble! On what basis can some of these groups' materials be denied entry into the library? How can you decide which to tell yes and which to tell no? Many principals or those preparing to be principals will base their judgment on the name of the organization itself, often saying no to those organizations which they perceive to be unacceptable to the community, and yes to those organizations that they know or think they know. Some of the organizations on the list, despite their patriotic or religious names, however, are products of the authors' minds. Those respondents who mix their answers often will say yes to the "God is

---

In training for effective citizenship it is frequently necessary for pupils to study issues and use instructional media which may be controversial. In considering such issues and media, the *teacher's responsibilities* shall be:

1. To determine whether the treatment of the issue in question is within the maturity, knowledge, and competency of the students.

2. To confer with members of the department or grade level and/or the principal concerning the acceptability of certain issues and media. In every case the principal shall be informed about such instructional media to be used.

3. To have clear educational goals when dealing with controversial issues and materials.

4. To approach controversial topics objectively.

5. To provide study materials and other learning aids from which a reasonable amount of data pertaining to all aspects of the issue can be obtained *and from which alternative selections may be made.*

6. To utilize only as much time as needed for satisfactory study of the issue.

7. To see that the issue is current, significant, real, and important to the students.

8. To bring out facts concerning controversial questions, and when expressing opinions, to see that the teacher's opinions are recognized as personal and not to be accepted by the students as an authoritative answer.

FIGURE 6–2.   A policy for selecting potentially controversial material

You are a principal and your school does not have a library materials selection committee:

1. The Association of American Parents for Better Sex Education wants to provide free materials for your school library. Do you tell them Yes or No?   YES   NO
2. The American Legion?   YES   NO
3. The NAACP?   YES   NO
4. The AFL/CIO?   YES   NO
5. The John Birch Society?   YES   NO
6. The Associated Groups for a Better America?   YES   NO
7. The Gay Liberation League?   YES   NO
8. The Black Coalition?   YES   NO
9. The Women's Christian Temperance Union?   YES   NO
10. The Society for Equal Rights for Women?   YES   NO
11. The Daughters of the American Revolution?   YES   NO
12. The Southwest Council for LaRaza?   YES   NO
13. The "Four Square for Our Flag Society"?   YES   NO
14. The Sons of Italy Club?   YES   NO
15. The God is Love Circle?   YES   NO

FIGURE 6–3.   Free materials for your school library

Love Circle" and the "Four Square for Our Flag Society" merely because the title of the organization suggests goodness. This is a trap. The next best response to the test is to say yes to all; again because there is no basis for judging. If one is going to accept free materials from one organization on no basis, there is no legitimate reason to say anything except yes to all of the others. The principal will stay out of court this way, although the library might become the repository for a wide array of useless propagandizing pamphlets.

The best answer is to say no to all, given the statement at the beginning of the test that the particular school in question has no library material selection committee, nor implicitly, a selection policy. This is the best decision not because some of these organizations don't have useful education materials, but because without policies for judging educational appropriateness, it is better to refuse them all.

There is a need, then, for systematic policy development and the establishment of appropriate review bodies at all levels of the school organization in order to provide good decision making and appropriate mechanisms for response to community needs and community inquiries. The principal who views his or her role as one or coordination and facilitation will be on firm ground.

SUMMARY

This chapter described the multiplicity of forces that interact with and act upon the school. The nature of neighborhood influence systems, pressure groups, and other organized community groups has much implication to the kinds of response patterns and information-seeking devices that a successful school administration uses. The responsive school has well-developed policies which provide legitimate avenues for citizens to use to make their concerns known.

American society is characterized by great cultural and ethnic diversity. Frequently, organized public relations efforts fail to take this into account, seemingly assuming instead an ideological unity that is characteristic only of much simpler societies.

"Knowing the territory" the school serves is the principal's job because the school derives its support from the community it serves. The educational enterprise depends upon the consent of parents and other community members. Consent issues from understanding.

ENDNOTES

1. For an insightful view of the nature of an ideologically unified community, refer to the Broadway musical, *Fiddler on the Roof*. The opening number, entitled, "Tradition," lyrically describes just such a community—with roles carefully spelled out and understood by one and all. The play, of course, does go on to detail the dissolution of this community because of forces within as well as forces without.

2. Hughes, Larry W., *Informal and Formal Community Forces: External Influences on Schools and Teachers* (Morristown, N.J.: General Learning Press, 1976), pp. 2–3.

3. An especially good reference for working within neighborhood society structures is Donald J. Warren and Rachel B. Warren, "Six Kinds of Neighborhoods," *Psychology Today* 9 (June 1975): 74–80.

4. It is often not easy because, almost by virtue of the person's position as principal, there may be some suspicion and distrust on the part of various community members. Vidich and Bensman cite several studies which indicate that the school administrator or any professional educator who is removed from direct contact with children and parents is considered the "alien expert" who "knows the ways and laws of the world and who uses this knowledge *to shape the community as it bears on him and his ends which are necessarily in the selfish interest of education*" [emphasis supplied]. Arthur J. Vidich and Joseph Bensman, *Small Town and Mass Society* (Princeton, N.J.: Princeton University Press, 1968) p. 195.

5. Hughes, *Informal and Formal Community Forces,* p. 19.

6. There may develop many untapped resources among these groups. Into these groups may fall labor unions, civic clubs, mother's groups, garden groups, veteran's organizations, and so forth.

7. *Oak Ridge Tennessee Administrative Bulletin* 10 (November 1970).

BIBLIOGRAPHY

Brandt, Richard M. et al. *Cultural Pluralism and Social Change.* Syracuse, N.Y.: National Dissemination Center, School of Education, Syracuse University, 1977.

Hughes, Larry W. *Informal and Formal Community Forces: External Influences on Schools and Teachers.* Morristown, N.J.: General Learning Press, 1976.

Hughes, Larry W. "Know Your Power Structure." *American School Board Journal* (May, 1967): 33–35.

Hughes, Larry W., Gordon, William M., and Hillman, Larry W. *Desegregating America's Schools.* New York: Longman, Inc. 1980. See especially chapters X and XI.

Koerner, Thomas F. "Some Isms of School Public Relations." *Illinois Education* 58 (October 1969): 8–9.

Lipsky, Morris. "Toward a Theory of Street Level Bureaucracy," in W. D. Hawley et al., eds. *Theoretical Perspectives on Urban Politics.* Englewood Cliffs, N.J.: Prentice-Hall, 1976, pp. 196–213.

Mann, Dale. *The Politics of Administrative Representation.* Lexington, Mass.: Lexington Books, Inc., 1976.

Ryan, Thomas K. and Ryan, Martin D. *Power and Influence in a Rural Community.* Knoxville, Tenn.: Bureau of Educational Research and Service, The University of Tennessee, 1974.

"School Storm Centers" *Phi Delta Kappan* (December 1974): 262–267.

Vidich, Arthur J. and Bensman, Joseph. *Small Town and Mass Society.* Princeton, N.J.: Princeton University Press, 1968.

Warren, Donald J. and Warren, Rachel B. "Six Kinds of Neighborhoods." *Psychology Today* 9 (June 1975): 74–80.

PART TWO

TASKS AND FUNCTIONS

This part is composed of several chapters, each of which examines a task area or a functional aspect of the principalship. Guidelines for action as well as underlying principles are contained in each chapter. The purposes of the section are to provide insights about the functional responsibilities which accrue to the principal, describe successful practices, and offer suggestions for implementation.

The five functional aspects of the principalship are treated in the following order: curricular and instructional development including co-curricular activities (five chapters); staff personnel (five chapters); pupil personnel (three chapters); financial and building management (two chapters); and public relations. The effort has been made to stimulate creative thinking about these task areas rather than to simply prescribe a single approach, although where it is appropriate prescriptive material does appear.

Chapter Seven

Guidelines and Goals
for Organizing School Programs

The person basically responsible for the quality of the curricular and instructional program in the school building is the principal. A school is as good or as bad, as creative or as sterile, as the person who serves as the head of that school.

> . . . Principals are about the most important people around when it comes to generating the reforms we need in secondary education . . . . You have more direct and immediate impact over what goes on in your school than any other state or local official. . . . Your decisions about how your school is run and what it offers in the name of education can permanently alter, for better or for worse, the attitude of teachers towards teaching and students toward learning. . . . You sit in the pivotal seat in secondary education.[1]

The principal is the one person in a school who can oversee the entire program because of the interest in the success of the school in its entirety. Therefore, the principal is in the best position to provide the necessary balance to the various aspects of the school. For example, serious problems develop if an overly zealous music teacher is convinced the entire school program should center on the school choir and band, expecting all the other teachers in the school to give way to his or her demands for students' time, space, and even funds, for the music program; or if the librarian develops a

schedule when classes may come to *his* or *her* library without adequate communication with the classroom teacher. The principal must provide the necessary balance in deciding what is best for the entire school and each individual in the school.

These examples are obvious problems that require immediate attention. However, many of the problems of balance within the school organization will be more subtle, more difficult to solve, and will require greater conceptual and technical knowledge of curriculum, instruction, and learning. The task can be carried out most effectively if the school program is founded in a strong philosophy of education and has established specific goals and objectives toward which to work. The principal must have the necessary understanding to find proper and just solutions to these problems and many others like them. This chapter presents direction in establishing balance as well as direction for the establishment of goals and objectives.

INTERDEPENDENCE OF THE SCHOOL'S
ORGANIZATIONAL COMPONENTS

The school program is organized into a series of interrelated components. Each of these components is dependent upon and influences the others. One component, for example, is the curricular organization of the school. Other components include instructional processes, practices in grouping children, the organization and utilization of staff, scheduling learning time, and organization and use of the facility. (See figure 7-1.) Decisions about the organization of each of these six components must be made for every school and they *must* be made under the leadership of the principal. If not, special interest groups may attempt to organize the school for their own needs and preferences.

Three factors msut be considered in making decisions about the six-program organization components: compatibility, balance, and flexibility.

Program Compatibility

The interdependence of program components demands that attention be paid to all six areas when a change is proposed for any one. It is analogous to a six-piece jigsaw puzzle. If the shape of one piece is altered, the puzzle can be made complete again only if the shapes of the adjacent pieces are also altered.

For example, if a decision is made to individualize the instructional program, attention must likewise be given to altering student group patterns and staff organization as they will be affected by the decision to individualize. Curriculum, scheduling, and facility utilization will probably be affected also.

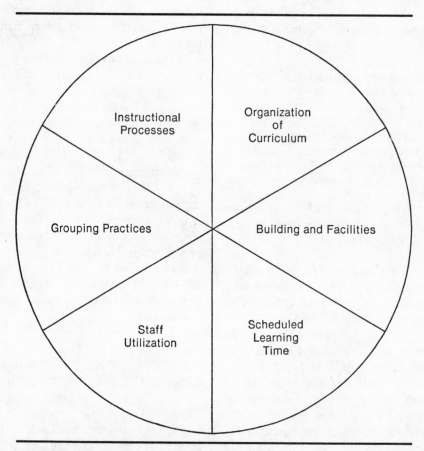

FIGURE 7-1. Program organization components

Many mistakes have been made in implementing innovations for organizational components because adequate attention has not been given to program component compatibility. Many of the efforts to implement ideas such as team teaching were unsuccessful because of this lack of proper attention to component compatibility. Somewhere in the organization the decision was made to be innovative and utilize a new staffing pattern called team teaching. Being basically conservative in nature and not wanting to change the program too radically, planners limited the change to the one component. No changes were made in instruction or scheduling or student grouping. As a result, the innovative idea was not effective and gradually faded away.

Organizational Balance

The second major concern that the principal must have for the organizational program components is in balancing how much of each component is needed. Concern for this point is particularly important when contemplating a change or implementing an innovation.

A case in point is the technique of individualized instruction. Two excellent aids in individualized instruction have been the use of learning packages and the use of independent study. Both are good ideas, but either done to excess is doomed. Children can be papered and penciled to boredom with the overuse of learning packages, even if they are good ones. The same is true of too much independent study. Used with discretion, independent study is an excellent tool, but overdone, as was necessary in some of the "unscheduled time blocks" of early modular schedules, it can be disastrous.

Any good innovative idea carried to an extreme or emphasized out of balance with its counterparts is not good. Instructional patterns, curriculum, student grouping, staffing, scheduling, and facility ultilization must be in balance.

Organizational Flexibility

Adults, as well as children, usually like order, uniformity, consistency, and simplicity. Therefore, the attempt is often made to organize schools along pure, simple lines; the more alternatives built into a system, the more complex it becomes and the more difficult to implement. Moreover, the varying needs of learners require flexibility. The school principal must be willing to overcome some of the desire for simplicity and ease of operation and recognize that a good instructional program is indeed complex and must be flexible.

How often has a lesson that is still going strong been interrupted as the bell rings? How many times are field trips turned down because of the inability to schedule them into the everyday timetables? What about the student who needs additional work or reading skill development but must go to the social studies lesson with the rest of the group? The inability to adjust for each of these things is the result of inadequate flexibility in arranging organizational components of the school. The organizational components should be arranged to allow the administrators and staff to vary or adapt them to a particular need, preferably without reconstructing the entire schedule of the school.

While the principal's role is providing instructional leadership and balance, this should not be looked upon as isolated role, however. As discussed in chapter 3, it is extremely important to have faculty involvement in the decision-making process, and it is probably most important in this area of organizing instructional programs. A principal's advisory council made up of lead teachers, team leaders, or department heads is an excellent way to obtain faculty involvement for instructional decisions.

The principal's role in program organization is to provide balance between and among the various interests of the school. No aspect of the school should be allowed to become out of balance with the other components. The principal also insures the compatibility of the several organizational components by not letting new ideas be thrust upon the school without considering the overall goals of the school and the necessary adjustments in the total program that will result from changes. The principal must insure program flexibility, allowing and encouraging desired changes and adjustments in the program to take place by encouraging an openness to planned change through proper setting of goals and objectives.

SETTING PROGRAM GOALS

The goals of the school should relate to social expectations, wants and needs, and the individual differences of children. How does one organize such a program in a school?

The structure of a school program requires that specific thought be given to each of the several organizational components of the school program: (1) curricular organization, (2) instructional processes, (3) student grouping practices, (4) staff organization, (5) scheduling learning time, and (6) facility utilization and design. While the six components can be separated for discussion purposes, the program that results for any particular school must give detailed attention to both the contribution that each component makes to the achievement of the goals and objectives of the school, as well as the development of each component in such a way that it is compatible with the other five components. For example, a goal statement may speak of meeting the individual needs of each child. From this goal an individualized instructional format might be selected. This instuctional format must then be supported with a student grouping plan, staffing plan, and schedule. In turn, if the staffing selection proposes team teaching, the facility utilization design should provide appropriate work spaces for teaching teams.

The organizational components are not independent entities, nor are they equally im-

portant. Decisions regarding the organization of the curriculum and instructional program should be made first, but they must be logically based on the goals and objectives for the school. The other four components serve the first two. Goals should be discussed first, then decisions should be made regarding the curricular and instructional program, and finally decisions regarding grouping, staffing, scheduling, and facility utilization should be made.

GOAL DETERMINATION

What are the goals of the school, how are they determined, and by whom? Are they determined by teachers, administrators, students, or community? In many cases, they are made by classroom teachers by default because no one else has made them or because the classroom teachers are not aware of goals previously set by others. Only when someone disagrees with what goes on is the issue of goals brought to light.

In reality, each of these groups should contribute either directly or indirectly to establishing goals. The principal has the opportunity to bring goals or objectives into focus where they can be considered in a rational manner. Of course, goals can remain a somewhat vague set of assumptions upon which school decisions are based, but the problem with vague objectives is that many important decisions relating to the organizational structure of the school rest upon these goals. To leave them as vague, unfocused assumptions does not provide a sufficient foundation upon which to base decisions.[2] The following guidelines can be helpful in determining goals and objectives:

1. Relevance of the statement of philosophy to the larger purpose of the American democratic commitment.
2. Attention to intellectual, democratic, moral, and social values, basic to satisfying the needs of the individual and his culture.

3.   Recognition of individual differences.

4.   The special characteristics and unique needs of secondary school children.

5.   Concern for the nature of knowledge and for the nature of the learning process as they apply to learners and their total development.

6.   Consistency of philosophy with actual practice.

7.   Identification of the roles and relationships expected of the community, the student, the teacher, and the administration in the educational process of the school.

8.   The role of the secondary school program of the school district and the importance of the articulation with other elements of the overall educational program.

9.   The responsibility for making a determination as to a desirable balance among activities designed to develop a cognitive, affective, and psychomotor demands.

10.   The relationship of the school and all other educational learning centers.

11.   The responsibility of the school toward social and economic change.

12.   The accountability of the school to the community it serves.[3]

A statement of philosophy expresses direction and contributes to firming up the goals of the school. A statement of objectives identifies more specifically the direction that the school program will take and should be compatible with the school philosophy. Suggestions for statements of objectives would include the following:

1.   General objectives of the local school system.

2.   Desirable characteristics of the pupil's total educational environment.

3.   Recognition and appreciation of sound learning theories which have been supported by research.

4.   Respect for individual differences among children and ways of providing these differences.

5.   Recognition of the obligation to provide citizenship experiences necessary to function in a free American society.

6.   Development of social and occupational awareness.

7.   The physical, mental, emotional, and social maturation of all the pupils in a rapidly changing culture.

8.   Continuation of the development of essential learnings.

9.   Recognition of a need to provide for research and innovation.

10.   Provide for a wide range of exploratory and socializing experiences and activities for all students.

11.   Help children develop a positive self-concept and to recognize and accept his potentials and limitations.

Community Input

School goals, as expressed through a statement of philosophy and objectives, should be developed with active involvement from the professional staff, students, parents, and the community at large. Community input is critical at all stages of the development of school goals. It is particularly important in the initial stages where an assessment of community attitudes provides the initial input to the faculty for its deliberations. It also alerts the community to the fact that the school staff is rethinking the direction for the school and wishes to have the community's input. A survey instrument to identify community thinking can be developed in the form of a needs assessment. A community needs assessment can take several shapes, from being very open-ended to asking a community respond to a specific list. Materials such as the *Phi Delta Kappan* Educational Goals and Objectives[4] provide an excellent list of eighteen goal statements regarding the school to which the community may reply. The PDK model suggests a series of work sessions with community input and discussion as a means of formulating goals. Or, this list of eighteen goal statements can be mailed to a broad cross-section of the local community, asking each respondent to identify the most important and least important items on the list. Once returned, the responses can be tabulated and used as input to the faculty in developing its statements.

Faculty Input

Meanwhile, faculty input can begin through a series of work sessions or preferably a concentrated workshop. Every faculty member should be asked to contribute to the completion of the following series of incomplete statements, showing his or her personal philosophy regarding school:

1. We believe that students . . .
2. We believe that learning . . .
3. We believe that teaching . . . .
4. We believe that teaching and learning can best be accomplished . . .
5. We believe that the role of administration . . .

By spacing these beginning statements over several worksheet pages, leaving adequate space for response, the entire faculty can have opportunity to consider and generate ideas which can be organized through committee action into a statement of philosophy. The faculty can be organized into five teams with each team consisting of a cross-section of the faculty, including representation from the several departments, men, women, new teachers, veteran teachers, as well as a representation of different approaches to education. Each team should be given all of the responses to *one* of the five questions and asked, as a committee, to generate a philosophy statement based on the faculty responses to that statement. When each committee has had the opportunity to put together a statement, one representative from each of the five committees should bring their collective statements together with those of the other committees and combine and rework those statements until one fairly concise statement of philosophy and goals has been developed. Figure 7–2 is an illustration of a statement gen-

erated by the Manor High School faculty following this process. It is organized into three parts: philosophy, purpose and goals, and functions. This seemed like the best solution for organization as this faculty worked through the problem. Yours may come up with a different arrangement.

In order to make a statement of philosophy, goals, and objectives operational, it must be accepted and acted upon by all. Therefore, after the basic set of statements has been put together, opportunity must exist for it to be shared with all concerned. This must be in a way that it is meaningful and understandable. Parents and other community members who have responded to the original needs assessment and statement of setting of goal priorities will be interested in seeing how the faculty has taken their ideas and responded. Hence, both the results of the original needs asessment and the resulting goal statements should be published and shared with the community. Also, adequate copies of the philosophy, goals, and objectives statements should be published and placed in prominent locations—inside the front cover of the faculty handbook, in the student handbook, and posted in faculty offices.

The fulfillment of goals, however, will take place only as a result of specific planning and implementation. A series of questions must be asked regarding the implementation of each goal. One way of doing this is to refer back to the original six areas of school organization which are dealt with in the following chapters. Each goal or objective often can be implemented in some specific way within a particular area of school organization. On the other hand, school organization frequently can violate a particular goal or objective. For example, if a goal is to teach independence and responsibility to the individual yet no opportunity exists within the school structure to express independence and responsibility, then school organization is probably lacking. If a function is to provide a success-oriented school environment yet the grouping structure within the school or the

We believe that Manor High School is a unique educational environment. Its uniqueness is exemplified in certain aspects of its design. It is designed to meet the individual needs of a larger percentage of students than is possible in the traditional system; to avoid a mass-produced, molding effect; to provide a distinctly pleasant atmosphere for learning; to foster respectful relationships; and to serve the community.

We believe that all students have needs which must be fulfilled. We believe that all students are unique as individuals—that they develop at different rates and in different manners. We believe that students have a natural desire to learn independence, responsibility, self-assertion, democratic ideas, and the skills necessary to solve present and future problems.

We believe the role of the student is to involve himself responsibly in the learning experience.

We believe that learning is evidenced by a behavioral change. It is a continuous process which takes place in the home, community, and school.

We believe that the role of the teacher is (1) to design learning opportunities and (2) to provide each student for whom he is responsible the freedom to learn what he needs to take a productive and rewarding part in society. The teacher is an advisor and sharer.

We believe that teaching and learning can best be accomplished through interaction and involvement of students, staff, administration, and community.

We believe that the administration is responsible for supplying and maintaining all the physical accouterments of the school. The principal shares with students, teachers, and community the task of facilitating and coordinating learning. His leadership should be democratic not authoritarian.

FIGURE 7–2a.   Philosophy of Manor High School

PURPOSE: The purpose of Manor High School is to establish a student and community learning center designed to facilitate stimulating learning experiences and harmonious social interactions in which each individual has the opportunity to realize his full potential.

GOALS: Before stating the following goals it should be noted that in each case we firmly believe that every individual has some degree of the qualities outlined. It is our endeavor to develop these qualities to a higher degree through conscientious and dedicated guidance and instruction. These qualities are:
1. The self-evaluative ability of the individual.
2. The positive attitude of the individual towards himself and others.
3. The independence and responsibility in the individual.
4. The creativity in the individual.
5. The ability to be self-assertive.
6. The acquiring of knowledge relative to both the mental and physical needs and abilities of the individual.
7. The critical thinking and decision-making ability of the individual.
8. The ability of the individual to contribute to and to make his way in our society.

FIGURE 7–2b.   Manor High School purpose and goals

1. To allow the pursuit of individual interests while assuming a working knowledge of basic disciplines.

2. To provide an atmosphere of freedom which will encourage creativity.

3. To provide multi-method instruction to facilitate various student learning styles.

4. To provide a success-oriented school environment.

5. To provide the student with experiences in which responsibility is desired, delegated, and/or assumed.

6. To expose students to various cultures and ethnic groups through school interaction and course content.

7. To expose the student to current, community, state, national, and world problems.

8. To allow students to use their talents to fulfill self-directed goals.

9. To involve students, teachers, and community in decision-making concerning school policies.

10. To encourage community participation in the learning process through the use of school facilities.

11. To provide a faculty and staff that is skillful and imaginative, and also serves as an advisor, a team participant, and an instructor to help the individual achieve his maximum potential.

12. To provide a physical laboratory containing modern educational equipment which has been designed to promote creative learning.

13. To involve the student in the evaluation of the learning experience.

14. To encourage learning as an integral part of daily living.

FIGURE 7–2c.   Manor High School functions

grading practices of the school provide a failure-oriented school environment for a portion of the student body, then once again some oversight exists.

Goals and objectives must be kept active if they are to be of any value. Frequently, objectives and goals can be organized as checklists. Each team or department is asked each marking period to evaluate its progress in the implementation of school objectives as a regular part of its reporting process. Each teacher or team should select particular goals to emphasize during certain segments of the year. Goals and objectives for the school should be part of the regular staff evaluation process and entered into that process early in the evaluation planning process.[5]

If direct action to bring goals and objectives alive is not done, philosophy, goals, and objectives frequently become relegated to an unused file cabinet serving no purpose in the daily operation of school and being used only once every ten years when the accrediting association comes around for its review. Well-designed goals and objectives deserve more than that. They deserve to become the basis by which our schools are operated each day.

Goal statements generated from these points can be commonly applied to curriculum development projects to determine what is to be taught in the school. The application of these goal categories to the development of the curriculum is a necessary step. Moreover, these goal categories need to be applied to other facets of the school's organization as well. For example, using the first goal category, that of establishing goals consistent with democratic ideals, a curriculum goal relating to democratic ideals might be fulfilled through some aspect of the social studies curriculum. On the other hand, another objective consistent with democratic ideals might be the creation of independent learners capable of continuing their learning in a systematic way after leaving school. The objective probably will be best approached through one of the organizational components, such as instruction or scheduling. Here, through independent study techniques, the skill of becoming an independent learner could be practiced and applied directly to the democratic ideals goal.

The goal of fulfilling human needs may be manifested in attention to other organizational components. A curriculum can be designed to provide the student with certain skills that will allow that student, as an adult, to generate the necessary income to meet basic human needs. On the other hand, needs don't begin with adulthood. How are children's human needs being met today in the organization of the school? Do hungry children learn well? Psychologists will say no. Do insecure children make good social adjustments? Probably not. Are children who lack love or affection capable of concentrating on higher order needs and thus motivations toward academic learning, and finally, self-actualization?

The climate created within the school has a direct bearing on the mental attitudes of students and teachers alike and thus on the productivity of the school.

SUMMARY

The goals of the school are statements of intent or direction for the organization. They are important to the organization because every objective and every action should be planned to move the organization toward the goals. It is important that all members of the staff and school community are cognizant of the goals, and it is preferable that they have had a hand in their development or modification. Goal understanding on the part of the members of an organization is a sound basis for their coordinated action in moving the organization in the desired direction.

The principal has the responsibility to provide the leadership to the faculty and the community for the development of these educational goals and objectives, to keep the current goals and objectives constantly in front of the staff in order to maintain direction, and to see that goals are frequently reviewed and revised when desirable.

ENDNOTES

1. Terrel H. Bell, "The Principal's Chair: Pivotal Seat in Secondary Education," *NASSP Bulletin* 391 (May 1975): 13–18.
2. The publication, "We Agree" Workshop, by IDEA is an excellent planned program to involve staff in goal development.
3. *Elementary School Evaluative Criteria,* National Study of School Evaluation, A Guide for School Improvement (Arlington, Va. 1973): 39–40.
4. Educational Goals and Objectives, *Phi Delta Kappan* (Bloomington, Ind., 1975).
5. See Step 1 of the evaluation process (chapter 7).

BIBLIOGRAPHY

Bell, Terrel H. "The Principal's Chair: Pivotal Seat in Secondary Education." *NASSP Bulletin* 391 (May 1975): 13–18.

Billot, Fred. An abstract of "Methodologies for Ascertaining Local Educational Needs and for Allocating Developing Resources." In *Literature Searches of Major Issues on Educational Reform,* edited by Allen Schreiber. Washington, D.C.: ERIC Clearinghouse, February 1974.

Educational Goals and Objectives, *Phi Delta Kappan* (Bloomington, Ind., 1975).

Elementary School Evaluative Criteria, National Study of School Evaluation, 4th ed. National Study of School Evaluation. Arlington, Va., 1970.

Evans, William, and Sheffler, John. "Assessment of Curricular Implementation." *Planning and Change* 7 (Fall 1976): 80–85.

Glasser, Wiliam. "Roles, Goals, and Failure." *Today's Education* 60 (October 1971): 20–21.

Goodlad, John I. "Schools Can Make a Difference." *Educational Leadership* 33 (November 1975): 108–117.

Gronlund, Norman E. *Determining Accountability of Classroom Instruction.* New York: MacMillan Publisher, 1974.

Holzman, Seymour. *IGE Individually Guided Education and the Multi-Unit School.* Washington, D.C.: National School Public Relations Association, 1972.

Kinghorn, Jon R., and Benham, Barbara. *The "We Agree" Workshop.* Dayton, Ohio: Institute for Development of Educational Activities, Inc., 1974.

Lipham, James M., and Fruth, Marvin J. *The Principal and Individually Guided Education.* Reading, Mass.: Addison-Wesley, 1976.

Matthews, Kenneth M., and Brown, Crovin L. "Schooling and Learning: The Principal's Influence on Student Achievement." *NASSP Bulletin* 60 (October 1976): 1–15.

McIntyre, Kenneth E. "Administering and Improving the Instructional Program." In *Performance Objectives of School Principals,* edited by Jack Culbertson et al. Berkeley, Calif., McCutchan Publishing Co., 1974, chapter 6.

Wright, C. Dan. "Five Important Considerations for Planning Individualized Instruction." *High School Journal* 60 (December 1976): 111–116.

Chapter Eight

Individual Differences and Student Grouping

The concept of individualized instruction has reached prominence in the past few years. Underlying all of the efforts to provide greater individualization is the knowledge that children grow and develop at different rates and learn in different ways.

What is the nature of the child? What differences count when organizing the school? Differences can be found in children's abilities, height, weight, age, sex, interests, needs, ethnic background, learning styles, achievements, and personalities. Before determining which differences matter in school organization, we should consider what these differences really are. Obviously, as children mature, differences increase. By the time they enter high school the differences are often extreme. Many characteristics can be measured against accepted fixed scales and spoken of in fairly concrete terms. Items such as sex or ethnic background remain fixed and can usually be described in specific terms also. However, factors such as ability, interests, needs, learning style, and personality are much more difficult to assess. They are far more complex, varied, and changeable. As a result, our efforts to classify people become more dependent on other constructs for definition, and therefore, less exact. For example, rarely will a single continuum suffice in a description of ability. Ability to do what? To be meaningful, ability descriptions must also be scaled in

some way. Ability compared to what or to whom? Ability to do something or do something better than someone else? Comparative information, then, is necessary in studying or determining differences in abilities because of the abstract nature of terms such as creativity, ability, personality, learning style, etc.

ACHIEVEMENT VS. ABILITY DIFFERENCES

One purpose for looking at individual differences is to determine the conditions they may set for organization. Individual differences obviously affect the way instruction and curriculum are organized. Contributing to these organizational decisions will be decisions relating to grouping children. Achievement is most often used as a basis for predicting ability. As a result, the two terms become inappropriately interchanged. Achievement can be measured with a fairly high degree of accuracy, but translating achievement into ability is fraught with dangers because of our inability to always know of, or adequately place in the formula, those factors contributing to a student's opportunity to achieve.

For example, a child may have the ability to be an excellent swimmer, but if he or she has never been swimming, future performance is uncertain. Thus, to take past achievements in swimming as a predictor of future success would be erroneous. More thought about the conditions or circumstances under which past achievement occurred needs to take place before making instructional decisions.

If one is not going to look at ability but rather at achievement as a determinant for organizing children for learning, what kind of differences should be expected to be found in a school population? Studies done at the University of Minnesota a number of years ago established a simple rule of thumb to indicate an

achievement range. "The achievement range of an age group of children is equal to two-thirds of their chronological age."[1] A group of twelve-year-olds will have an eight-year achievement range. A group of fifteen-year-olds will have a ten-year range. In other words, in an average high school sophomore class within a given subject the slowest students will be functioning at approximately a fifth-grade level (five years below), while the best students will be functioning at a college junior level (five years above). Figure 8–1 illustrates the formula for school-age children. Note particularly the

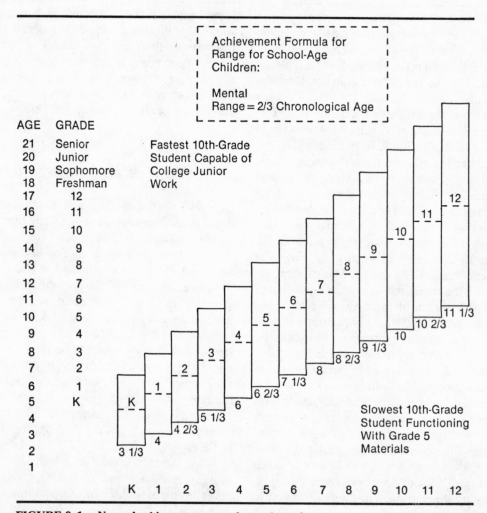

FIGURE 8–1. Normal achievement range for each grade

overlap of achievement for any three- or four-year age span as shown by the last four bars on the graph. It should also be noted that the achievement range held in common by freshmen through seniors in high school is by far greater than the area in those grades which indicate differences.

Differences in Learning Styles

A second factor in individual differences that merits attention for organizational programs is learning styles. How do children learn best? An identification of how children learn has tremendous implications for how we teach. If there are different learning styles, different teaching styles should be developed when instruction is organized.

Russell French has suggested that every child may have a unique personal learning style. From a sensory intake point of view the list might include the following styles:[2]

Style	*Characteristic*
Print-Oriented	Dependency on reading and writing
Aural	A listener; doesn't say much
Oral (Interactive)	A talker; learns through discussion
Visual	Must have many visual stimuli and visual representations
Tactile	Has to touch everything and everyone
Motor	Has to move about while learning anything
Olfactory	Learns through taste and smell

A learner probably uses several of these styles in concert, moving from one to another or using a combination of styles at different times. Each of us can probably think of a particular student that generally fits each of these categories. Another view of learning styles offered by French is:

Style	*Characteristic*
Sequential	Must perceive orderly relationship (B follows A)
Logical	Uses processes of reasoning to reach conclusions
Intuitive	Perceives truths and facts directly without benefit of extensive reasoning
Spontaneous	Relies on impulse
Open	Uses combinations of the above or each of the above at different times

This list relies on internal thought processes rather than the five senses for its logic. Again our own experience can give us many personal examples of children who use these styles. The striking thing about this list is the remembrances it creates of particular children who at times seemed to learn intuitively or spontaneously, while at other times or in other subjects only understood after the most detailed sequential instruction. French suggests that these two style lists might be combined into a matrix as shown in figure 8–2, resulting in thirty or more combinations or personal learning styles.

Student Growth and Maturity

Any discussion of individual differences must obviously pay heed to effects of maturation changes in student interests and needs. Several notions in particular are significant when considering the organization of the school. The first is that all children do not mature at the same rate. Maturity differences in boys and girls are quite obvious, physically and mentally. The same variation in size, mental capacity, interests, and needs also exists within children of the same sex at a given age, only to be in a dif-

	Sequential	Logical	Intuitive	Spontaneous	Open
Print-Oriented					
Aural					
Oral (Interactive)					
Visual					
Tactile					
Motor					
Olfactory					

FIGURE 8–2.   **Matrix of personal learning styles**

ferent balance or relationship after several more years of maturation. This, of course, needs to have a bearing in instructional techniques and curriculum offerings, as well as ways of grouping students.

As children mature, their interests, needs, and mental capacities expand and change. Interests begin to broaden as they come into contact with more and more of the world. Curiosities continue to expand. Needs change and their requirements for safety, security, love, affection, and self-esteem take on new dimensions. The source of need fulfillment transfers successfully from the home and parents to the teacher and then to a peer group—first of the same sex and finally to a peer relationship with the opposite sex.

Quite often in organizing schools we tend to resist responding to these basic drives. The child who seeks attention, the child who needs a friend, the child who comes to school hungry, the child who needs status often cannot find solace in the school. This is often because adults in the school feel that since fulfilling these needs is not listed anywhere in the curriculum outline or specifically mentioned in someone's lesson plan, they are inappropriate concerns of the school.

Psychologists believe that every human being has needs that are constantly seeking fulfillment. Some theorists suggest that these needs can be classified into categories such as physiological (food, warmth); safety and security (safety from bodily or mental harm now and in the immediate future); love and belonging (a need to be wanted, appreciated, understood, and a sense of being part of a group); self-esteem (a sense of self-worth, self-concept); and, finally, a need for self-actualization (the opportunity to be or become what one wants). Some psychologists believe there is an ascending order to these needs, and that basic needs (those first on the list) must be satisfied before the individual will consider higher-order needs. In other words, needs for hunger or warmth (physical) must be met before needs for safety and security, which in turn must be fulfilled before concern for love and belonging surface. Need fulfillment also operates on several wavelengths. Hunger, obviously, is a recurring need that demands satisfaction several times daily. Other needs, once fulfilled, may sustain themselves for an extended period of time without reinforcement.

Several important lessons can be found in the application of needs theory to school organization. Most desired educational outcomes occur in the realm of the higher-order needs of self-esteem and self-actualization. If lower-order needs must be satisfied before higher-order needs, then as educators we must create an environment that satisfies the physiological, safety and security, and love and belonging needs of the student. The hungry, the fearful or insecure, and the left out will all experience a great reduction in learning if those needs are not fulfilled.

Second, since a need creates a drive or motivation on the part of the individual, planners should create learning environments that emphasize rewards of love and belonging, self-esteem and self-actualization. Group learning, praise for achievement, and opportunity for self-direction can all be directed to achieve both personal and school goals. Finally, knowing that needs change as children mature, we can design curriculum using needs theory. The curricular organization, through the establishment of course sequences, has become more responsive to changes in mental capacity, but in

the area of matching school organization to student interests, the school has been only partially successful.

For example, the graded curriculum represents an effort to adapt the content to the levels of student capacity. It is possible to look at various curriculum materials and make a fair judgment of their appropriate intended maturity level through the degree of difficulty of the materials. On the other hand, instruction tends to look very much alike from the lower elementary grades through college. The way children are grouped, the way school staffs are organized, and the way facilities are used look very much the same at all grade levels. It would seem that if varying interests and needs motivation of students were being considered, differences would be apparent. Our lack of adequate attention to school program organization and to developing needs and interests to motivate students may be partly behind certain students' year-to-year increased disenchantment with school. If the activities and outcomes educators have planned for schools are not congruent with the needs and interests of the students, the increasing disinterest on their part is only natural and leads to a greater apathy and to activities outside those planned by the school.

The problem of lack of congruence between school programs and student interests and needs is illustrated by figure 8–3. Circle A represents the planned activities and outcomes of the school, such as social studies, language arts, math, science, health, P.E., music, and art. Circle B represents those things that actually occur for children through their interaction with the school environment, such as frogs, rubber bands, paper airplanes, bicycles, girls, boys, telling stories, graffiti on restroom walls, fights on the playground, motorcycles, hot rods, sex, drugs, what you are going to do when you finish school, and on and on. Area C represents the area of congruence or the area in which what was planned actually occurred.

A school with a program highly tuned to students' needs, interests, and differences will

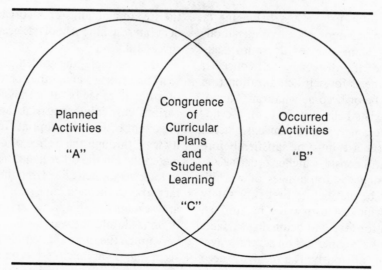

FIGURE 8–3.   Impact of students' interests and needs on planned vs. occurred student activity

have a high percentage of congruence between Areas A and B, resulting in a large Area C. This congruence will probably not exist for the school that pays little attention to these factors.

Adequate attention to individual differences and varying maturity rates and levels will recognize student achievement interests and needs as being broadly based. The principal and staff must use this information about these needs, interests, and capabilities in all their diversity in the organization of the school and the way the students are grouped.

GROUPING STUDENTS

Instruction in any normal school setting requires numerous decisions about grouping students. Basically, these decisions will relate to three variables: group size, group composition, and group tenure. The basic purpose of grouping students is to bring about the highest quantity and quality of instruction possible. Grouping practices should be consistent with curricular decisions and should be compatible with each student's needs and interests. These

lofty goals must be tempered by two factors. The first is recognition of the complexity of the individual learner, as has been discussed. The second factor is the practical consideration of the cost of a particular organization design in comparison to its related effectiveness. For example, group size usually suggests certain staffing patterns that can be converted into dollar costs. A school might conclude that a staffing ratio of three-to-one would give the best quality and quantity of learning per student, but that it would be too expensive. Instead, grouping designs must consider more economical staffing ratios, most likely in the range of fifteen-to-thirty students per staff member.

Group Size

Research studies indicate that the quantity of learning does not improve each time the size of a class is reduced by one.[3] Reducing class size from thirty to twenty-nine and then again from twenty-nine to twenty-eight probably will not result in any observable increase in learning on the part of students. On the other hand, significant behavior changes do occur in the classroom when student/teacher ratios are reduced from a high of thirty-five or forty to one to under twenty-five to one. If the ratio is larger than twenty-five to one (assuming little or no assistance from aides and volunteers), teachers seldom vary their instruction or accommodate various learning styles within the group. The reason may be that attempting to individualize instruction with a large group is so overwhelming that experience suggests that it is better to try to keep the children together for most of the learning activities and teach to the middle. When ratios fall below twenty-five to one, teachers seem to provide more individualized instructional styles.

As group size drops to fifteen and lower, cross-member interaction and discussion tend to increase because it is possible for every member to participate in discussions. Finally, when the ratio is reduced to five (or less) to one, a tutorial style of instruction begins to emerge, with teachers assigning work to children on a one-to-one basis.

For many years research did not show any significant relationship between class size and student achievement. Recent research, however, now indicates that when class size is substantially reduced to a range under fifteen to one, significant increases in student learning, as shown by standardized achievement scores, do occur. Large differences do not occur until reductions to the fifteen to one level are reached, however. According to authors Jean V. Glass and Mary Lee Smith, this inverse relationship between class size and achievement does not differ significantly across different grade levels, pupil I.Q. levels, or subjects taught, although it seems slightly stronger in secondary grades than in elementary grades.[4]

Administrative Decision Making About Group Size

In the past administrators have used group size as a constant and forced instructional decisions

to be made based on group size. Instead, instructional decisions should be dominant, and decisions regarding group size should be secondary in nature. Therefore, if the instructional purpose demands a tutorial approach, a staffing ratio of five to one will be both effective and efficient. For purposes of group discussion and maximum interaction among all members, a group size of fifteen is about the maximum. If the instructional demand on teachers includes individualization of instruction, a ratio of not more than twenty-five to one apparently is needed. Finally, if instructional plans require the presentation of basically the same material to all members of the group with the need for only one-way communication, any sized group is appropriate. The limiting factors become those of space and the number of students available. Further discussion of variability of flexibility in group size requires a discussion of variations in staff utilization.

Group Composition

What should be the basis for organizing students into groups? Obviously efficient instruction requires groups. The question of group composition has been intriguing and controversial among educators for years with debates on practices such as homogeneous ability grouping and retention and their accompanying problems. Alternative grouping patterns based on interest, age, skill, and achievement as well as discussion of group flexibility and tenure need to be considered also.

Ability Grouping A common practice is to organize or group students on the basis of their supposed ability, creating a tracking system with a two-, three-, or four-group continuum consisting of the high-ability, average-ability, and low-ability students. This grouping strategy is then often converted into a college track, a business track, and a general education track.

The basic assumption underlying this pattern of student organization is that by subdividing children from the extremely broad ability continuum found in any normal school population, teachers will be better able to focus instruction on the needs of the children in any particular group. Thus, ability groups supposedly narrow the range of abilities within any group and make it more possible for the teacher to organize and prepare materials for a narrower range of abilities.

Factors used to determine group composition have included achievement test scores, I.Q. scores, previous grades, and teacher opinion. Serious problems develop when any of these criteria or combinations are used as the basis of organizing students on a permanent basis or for long periods of time. This method of grouping is usually not very effective. Earlier this chapter presented a discussion of individual learner differences in such areas as achievement, interest, and learning styles. Differences exist from student to student for each of these variables. The pattern for each student is also different. No common denominator can be found for long-term grouping across disciplines or even within disciplines. For example, interest can greatly change productivity within a discipline, overriding previous supposed ability measurements.

Students can be successfully grouped according to one factor to obtain a degree of homogeneity, but the group remains heterogeneous on all other aspects of curriculum and instruction. For example, homogeneity in mathematics can be obtained by placing in a group all students who know how to solve quadratic equations, but they remain a heterogeneous group for the rest of the curriculum, including other areas of mathematics.

When the descriptors of homogeneity are based on broad measures such as previous math achievement, an I.Q. test score, or all previous grades, almost all useful definition of homogeneity is lost; for in almost any specific skill or knowledge, some students placed in the lowest group on one basis will exceed the knowledge level of other children placed in the highest group on another. Homogeneous grouping, therefore, as a broad-based or permanent grouping design simply does not work, and the homogeneity is a figment of the staff's imagination. (Figure 8–4 illustrates how students will group differently from skill to skill.)

Many teachers and administrators have argued strenuously that ability grouping does work and that definite differences exist among students. Of course, differences can be seen, but the point is that the overlap in abilities is far greater from group to group than most of us imagine, and, most important, homogeneous grouping overlooks the individual student.

Several attitudinal factors must also be considered in a discussion of homogeneous grouping. The phenomenon of the self-fulfilling prophecy enters into the ultimate outcomes of ability grouping. This prophecy says that students become what we say they are or what they think they are.[5] Research about self-concept has shown that a student's own attitude towards himself or herself as a person and his or her assessment of personal abilities represent major factors in the ultimate success or failure of the student in school. Teacher attitudes as well as student self-concept contribute greatly to a student's ultimate success or failure in school. The placement of a child in a group on the basis of perceived ability can seem to prove itself correct by adjustments in a productivity on the part of the student that in fact occur as a result of the placement, thus fulfilling the prophecy. Over the past forty years, numerous research studies have considered ability grouping. A massive review of many of these studies was reported in 1973 with the following conclusions.[6]

1. Homogeneous ability grouping as currently practiced shows no consistent positive values for helping students generally, or partic-

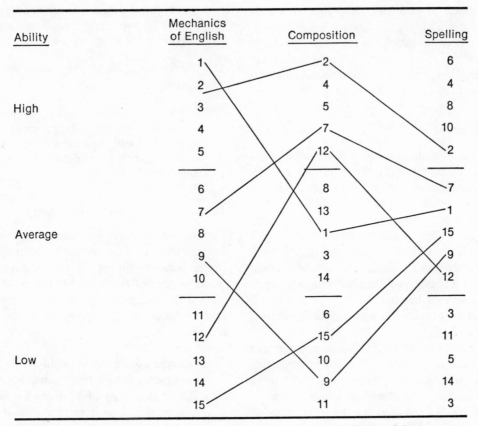

Ability	Mechanics of English	Composition	Spelling
	1	2	6
	2	4	4
High	3	5	8
	4	7	10
	5	12	2
	6	8	7
	7	13	1
Average	8	1	15
	9	3	9
	10	14	12
	11	6	3
	12	15	11
Low	13	10	5
	14	9	14
	15	11	3

FIGURE 8-4. Variations in student rankings that confound efforts of homogeneous grouping

ular groups of students, to achieve more scholastically or to experience more effective learning conditions. Among the studies showing significant effects, evidence of slight gains favoring high-ability students is more than offset by evidence of unfavorable effects on the learning of students of average- and below average-ability, particularly the latter.

2. The findings regarding the impact of homogeneous ability grouping on affective development are essentially unfavorable. Whatever the practice does to build or inflate the self-esteem of children in the high ability groups is counterbalanced by evidence of the unfavorable effects of stigmatizing those placed in average- and below-average ability groups as inferior and incapable of learning.

3. Homogeneous ability grouping, by design, is a separative educational policy, made ostensibly according to test performance ability but practically according to socioeconomic status and, to a lesser but still observable degree, according to ethnic status.

4. In cases where homogeneous or heterogeneous ability grouping is related to improved scholastic performance, the curriculum is subject to substantial modification of teaching methods, materials and other variables that are instrinsic to the teaching-learning process, and that, therefore, may well be the causative fac-

tors related to academic development wholly apart from ability grouping per se. Similarly, with respect to social development, evidence that points to variables other than ability grouping tends to relate substantially to personal growth or lack of growth.

Retention

One form of ability grouping that is often overlooked is the result of the retention policies operating in many school districts. Retention places a student with a less intellectually and socially mature group based on his or her demonstrated ability or achievement. Therefore, it is an instance of ability grouping, of adjusting the placement of the student to fit a curriculum and instructional level thought more appropriate for him or her, rather than bringing that appropriate curriculum and instructional level to the student.

Retention is as ineffective an approach to the grouping of students as the previously discussed method. A poorly achieving tenth grader is not more like ninth graders. Such a student is still more like his or her peers and will be more successful with them than if he or she were retained and placed with a younger group of students. At any grade level the achievement range will spread over a number of grade levels. The Cook studies concluded that:

> When pupils in the lower 10 percent of the classes are failed because of low achievement, they do not become better adjusted educationally or socially in the retarded position. The available evidence indicates that, on the average, they achieve as much or more by being given more regular promotions.

The study goes on to point out that:

> When attempts are made to reduce the range of abilities and achievement in a school by retarding slow learning pupils and accelerating fast

learning pupils, there is an increase in the proportion of slow learning pupils in each grade. Average grade achievement is lowered.

The study concluded, somewhat tongue-in-cheek, that:

> If the major concern of the teachers is to maintain grade level standards, the more effective way of increasing achievement standards in a school is to retard the bright and accelerate the dull pupils.[7]

Appropriate Bases for Grouping

Groups are necessary for school organization, but retention and homogeneous ability grouping as semi-permanent forms of student organization are not effective. What should be the basis for grouping? The following principles and techniques for organizing students are sound:

1. Grouping can be used on any known common factor found among students.
2. The homogeneity of a group of students is improved directly in ratio to the specificity of the grouping criterion.
3. The ensuing curriculum and instruction can assume commonality among students only according to the single factor used as a basis for the grouping. On all other factors, the group must be considered to be heterogeneous.
4. Most grouping criteria, if they are fairly specific, are valid for only a short period of time. As learning takes place, students who were grouped to learn a specific skill need to be regrouped for other skills. Students who have been grouped on the basis of interest must be regrouped when either that interest area is completed or the student's interests change.
5. Age is not necessarily a factor in grouping. In other words, students of various ages

may be grouped together if some other appropriate criteria is being used; single skill development, for example.

6. No grouping practice should damage the self-concept of a student or create stereotypes in the eyes of other students or teachers toward particular children.

7. In most instructional settings a variety of grouping criteria should be used and integrated into the various parts of the school day.

With these criteria in mind, a tremendous variety of grouping bases is available. Possible designs include the following:

Heterogeneous Grouping A heterogeneous group is a group created to represent a cross-section of the available student population. Planned heterogenity is not the same as that which may occur by simply placing together an available group of students. Many factors within the school can indirectly affect the availability of students for heterogeneous groups. If true heterogenity is sought, care must be taken to insure the distribution of students in some uniform fashion across the various groups being created. By definition, unlimited heterogenity would even include a proportionate number of students from each age group within the school. In other words, if the school consisted of grades ten through twelve, the group would consist of students from each of those age categories.

Age Grouping Students of a particular age or range of ages are placed into a single group. The group may still be heterogeneous in all other factors except age.

Multi-age Grouping A common practice is to not limit age groupings to a one-year span, but to group students over a two- or three-year span. Therefore, students between fourteen and sixteen or sixteen and eighteen are eligible for membership in particular groups.

Interest Grouping This technique brings students directly into the decisions regarding grouping. Based on individual interests and needs, the students select the group according to whatever criteria have been established for group organization. Regular electives and mini-courses at the secondary level are compatible curriculum components to accompany interest grouping.

Skill Grouping Children are grouped on the basis of possessing or not possessing particular skills that are usually quite narrowly defined. Skill grouping is often used in conjunction with a curricular area of a skills nature that lends itself to a detailed continuum of learning with a logical sequence and order. By diagnosing previous student skill acquisition, a current skills placement can be identified for each student. A choice of several appropriate learning activities is then available. Instructional modules are usually short, requiring from one to five hours of student and teacher time. Students needing a particular skill are placed together in a group for instruction on that particular skill. When the skill has been learned, a new group is found for them. The new group may consist of the same children or new children, depending on the progress of the other children in the group and the availability of other children for inclusion in the new skill area. Reading and mathematics represent two basic skill subject areas where such groups can be organized. With available diagnostic instruments, students can be accurately placed and organized into groups where similar needs exist. The major problem with skill grouping is that a relatively large group of approximately one hundred children is usually desirable as a base group from which to create the skill groups. This allows for the creation of skill groups large enough for efficient use of teacher time but limited to a relatively narrow range on the skills continuum.

Achievement Grouping Achievement grouping is similar to skill grouping but is somewhat less specific, covering a wider range of previous learning. It is based on demonstrated achievement, not predicted ability. It should be as narrowly defined as possible, rarely expanding outside of a single discipline, and preferably representing a subset within a discipline. For example, an achievement group might be established within language arts on the basis of previously demonstrated competence in composition writing. The same grouping should not be used for spelling, grammar, reading, or literary analysis. Each of these would need their own achievement groups. Within the area of composition, a whole series of subskills could be defined for the further breakdown of groups into skill groups. Achievement groups are usually used where minuté skill details cannot be adequately diagnosed, are not needed for intended instruction, or would create groups too small for efficient instruction. Achievement groups are based on previously demonstrated achievement. Achievement should not be confused with ability, which is a prediction of potential rather than a measure of past achievement.

Group Flexibility

How long should an established group remain intact? When groups are reorganized, how extensive should that reorganization be? At what level within the organization should decisions for group reorganization take place? These questions relate directly to the ultimate flexibility that can be obtained for grouping within any school organization.

Groups should remain intact until they have accomplished their skills objective. Once the original purpose for the grouping has been achieved, the group must be reorganized. This may be after one hour of instruction in a skills group, or it might be after three years together as a heterogeneous multi-age group. Skill groups, interest groups, and achievement groups should be designed so they can be reorganized daily if necessary.

Problems of Regrouping The need for frequent regrouping in the school presents several problems in school organization. First, it is impractical to refer all grouping decisions to the principal since the quantity and frequency of needed grouping decisions would overwhelm that office. More significant, most of the information needed for intelligent grouping decisions is found at the teacher-student level.

To give the teacher-student level an opportunity for flexible grouping decisions, the school is best organized into learning communities consisting of teams of two or more teachers, their students, and an extended time block. With this arrangement, students and teachers can group students. The fluid block design for school organization with a team of teachers, aides, and a group of 75 to 150 students is a good example of this organization.[8]

A number of tools is available to aid teaching teams in the mechanical details of internal team grouping. Skill continua and diagnostic tests are available in many subject areas to aid in the placement of students. In some cases, the item analysis from standardized tests can serve this purpose. In other cases, criterion-referenced tests should be used.

The important concept here is that the principal has passed the decision making regarding grouping directly on to the teachers. Once the components of the learning community have been designated, the principal's role becomes one of giving advice to the teams for internal grouping decisions. The teachers, in turn, then organize the groups or may directly pass on to the students many grouping decisions based on interest. Students can group themselves according to whatever ground rules are established by the learning community team. Student-selected learning packages are a good illustration of this technique.

SUMMARY

Student grouping is necessary for school organization. For purposes of assigning students to individual teachers or teams, a heterogeneous or mixed grouping plan is usually best. Homogeneous grouping should take place in the classroom and be done by teachers. The basis for internal class grouping can be interest, achievement, skills, age, or designed heterogenity.

Homogeneous grouping should be kept flexible with several different grouping patterns used. All homogeneous groups are usually of short duration. Flexibility is necessary because of the changing nature of groups and the problems of negative student self-concept or poor teacher attitudes that can develop from rigid homogeneous grouping patterns.

Some of the concepts discussed in this chapter may seem to be somewhat strange considerations in the secondary school, largely because this is not the way we have tended to organize. The concepts, however, are valid. New conceptualizations in curricular and instructional organization need to be developed to accommodate what we know about individual differences.

ENDNOTES

1. Walter V. Cook and Theodore Clymer, "Acceleration and Retardation," *Individualized Instruction, 1962 Yearbook of the National Society for the Study of Education,* Nelson B. Henry, ed. (Chicago: The Society NSSE, 1962), pp. 179–208.

2. Russell L. French, "Teaching Strategies and Learning Process," *Educational Considerations* (Spring 1975): 27–28.

3. Martin N. Olson, "Ways to Achieve Quality in School Classrooms: Some Definitive Answers," *Phi Delta Kappan* (September 1971): 63–65.

4. Jean V. Glass and Mary L. Smith, *Meta-Analysis of Research on the Relationship of Class Size and Achievement* (Boulder: Laboratory of Educational Research, University of Colorado, September 1978).

5. A study by Rosenthal investigated the concept of the self-fulfilling prophecy and found that teacher attitudes and expectations about a child do have a direct bearing on the child's performance. Robert Rosenthal and Lenore Jacobson, *Pygmalion in the Classroom* (New York: Holt, Rinehart, and Winston, 1968).

6. Dominick Esposito, "Homogeneous and Heterogeneous Ability Grouping," *AERA Journal* (Spring 1973): 163–179.

7. Walter W. Cook, "Effective Ways of Doing It," *Individualized Instruction, 1962 Yearbook of the National Society for the Study of Education,* Nelson B. Henry, ed. (Chicago: The Society NSSE, 1962), chapter 3.

8. Gerald C. Ubben, "A Fluid Block Schedule," *NASSP Bulletin* 60 (February 1976): 104–111.

BIBLIOGRAPHY

Bruner, Jerome S. "The Process of Education Revisited." *Phi Delta Kappan* (September 1971): 18–21.

Cook, Walter. "Effective Ways of Doing It." *Individualized Instruction, Yearbook of the National Society for the Study of Education.* Chicago: The Society NSSE, 1962, chapter 3.

Dewey, John. *The School and Society.* Chicago: University of Chicago Press, 1900.

Dirr, Peter J. "Individual Instruction: A Bibliography." ERIC (August 1974) ED 105 678.

Dunn, Rita, and Dunn, Kenneth. "Learning Styles, Teaching Styles: Finding the Best Fit." *NASSP Bulletin* 59 (October 1975).

Esposito, Dominick. "Homogeneous and Heterogeneous Ability Grouping." *AERA Journal* (Spring 1973): 163–179.

French, Russell. "Teaching Strategies and Learning Processes." *Educational Considerations* (Spring 1975).

Glass, Jean V., and Smith, Mary L. *Meta-Analysis of Research on the Relationship of Class Size and Achievement.* Boulder: Laboratory of Educational Research, University of Colorado, September 1978.

Goodlad, John I., and Anderson, Robert H. *The Nongraded Elementary School.* New York: Harcourt, Brace and World, Inc., 1959.

Goodman, Steven, ed. *Handbook on Contemporary Education.* New York: R. R. Bowker Co., 1976. See especially Part VII, "Teaching and Learning Strategies."

Hadermann, Kenneth. "Ability Grouping—Its Effect on Learners." *NASSP Bulletin* 60 (February 1976): 85–89.

Hoen, Robert T. "An Evaluation of Multi-Age Classes at Carnarvon School 1971–1972." *ERIC* (June 30, 1972) ED 076 649.

Hunter, Madeline. "A Tri-Dimensional Approach to Individualization." *Educational Leadership* 34 (February 1977): 351–355.

IGE Unit Operations and Roles. Institute for Development of Educational Activities. Dayton, Ohio, 1970.

Koons, Clair L., "Nonpromotion, A Dead End Road." *Phi Delta Kappan* 58 (May 1977): 701–702.

LaBenne, Wallace D., and Green, Bert I. *Educational Implications of Self-Concept Theory.* Pacific Palisades, Calif.: Goodyear, 1969.

Martin, Lyn S., and Pavan, Barbara N. "Current Research on Open Space, Non-graded, Vertical Grouping and Team Teaching." *Phi Delta Kappan* 57 (January 1976): 310–315.

Mitchell, Joy, and Zoffness, Richard. "Elementary Pupils Favor a Multi-age Class." *Education* 91 (Fall 1971): 270–273.

Moffett, James. *A Student Centered Language Arts Curriculum, Grades K-13: A Handbook for Teachers.* Boston: Houghton-Mifflin, 1973.

National Society for the Study of Education. *Individualizing Instruction.* Sixty-First Yearbook of the National Society for the Study of Education. Chicago: The Society NSSE, 1962.

Neill, Shirley. "Self-Starting School: Multi-Age Grouping Program." *American Education* 11 (October 1975): 25–29.

Olson, Martin N. "Ways to Achieve Quality in School Classrooms: Some Definitive Answers." *Phi Delta Kappan* (September 1971): 63–65.

Purkey, William W. *Self-Concept and School Achievement.* Englewood Cliffs, N.J.: Prentice-Hall, 1970.

Rosenthal, Robert, and Jacobson, Lenore. *Pygmalion in the Classroom.* New York: Holt, Rinehart and Winston, 1968.

Shumsky, Aida. "Individual Differences in Learning Styles in Learning Performance and Individual Differences." *Essays and Readings,* Len Sperry, ed. Glenview, Ill.: Scott Foresman and Co., 1972, pp. 122–123.

Smith, B. O.; Stanley, W. O.; and Shores, J. H. *Fundamentals of Curriculum Development.* New York: World Book Co., 1957. Old, but a classic.

Toffler, Alvin. *Learning for Tomorrow.* New York: Vintage Books, 1974.

Wiles, Hilda L. "Multi-Age Team Teaching Program." *Educational Leadership* 29 (January 1972): 305–308.

Chapter Nine

Organizing the Secondary School Curriculum

In an article published several years ago in the *Phi Delta Kappan,* the author, Maurice Gibbons, told of a film that he had recently seen entitled "Walkabout."[1] In the movie, a young aborigine, a native Australian boy, was on a six-month-long endurance test called a walkabout, which he must survive alone in the wilderness and return to his tribe as an adult or die in the attempt. Gibbons relates that in the film the young aborigine survives not only with skill but with grace and pride as well, through the stalking of a kangaroo in a beautiful but deadly ballad or seeing the subtle signs of direction by merely standing and watching. In contrast, the film showed two suburban young people who became lost in the Australian desert who met up with this young aborigine and whose lives were saved by his skill. In the contrast, it was evident they had no similar skills that even allowed them to succeed to a similar degree in their suburban life.

In a more recent famous television series based on Alex Haley's novel, *Roots,* a young African boy, Kunte Kinte, in the early part of the film was trained in the rites of manhood and was turned into the jungle for a period of time to demonstrate his skill before he was allowed to return to the tribe as a warrior. Anthropologists tell us of many similar rites from around the world as part of the manhood experience for young people. By contrast, the

graduation experiences for our high school seniors with the prom, the validictorian speech, the parade of candidates to the sounds of pomp and circumstance, the silly notes written in the yearbook, the all night parties, and the painting of class of '80 on the local water tank leave much to be desired, but it may on the other hand be a relatively accurate reflection on the significance of four years of high school towards one's success in life.

In his article, Gibbons proposes a walkabout as a youthful model to guide us in redesigning our own rites of passage and thus much of our high school curriculum. What would an appropriate and challenging walkabout for students in our society be like? Or, put another way, what sensibilities, knowledge, attitudes, and competencies are necessary for a full and productive adult life in our technological society? What kinds of experiences will have the power to focus our children's energy on achieving these goals and what kind of performance will demonstrate to the student, the school, and the community that the goals have been achieved? The walkabout test would be a measure not of what a child can do under a teacher's direction, but what a teacher has enabled that child to decide and to do on his or her own. The focus on the curriculum, then, would be towards developing specific skills for success in our society as well as independence of learning and ability to make decisions regarding that learning. The walkabout proposes that children complete their high school education by presenting in front of teachers, family, friends, and peers a demonstration of their competencies in the areas of challenge.

The curriculum organization within a school obviously should reflect the goals of the school. Chapter 7 proposed a way to organize an indepth look at curricular and instructional goals. Ultimately the curriculum should provide learning opportunities to match cultural, vocational, and career goals as well as other individual needs. It is the function of the principal to provide the leadership to see that it does!

CURRICULAR STRUCTURE

How is school curriculum to be organized? Our analysis of curriculum usually defines both a vertical and horizontal dimension. The vertical dimension considers what content is to be presented or what objectives are to be met at a particular maturity level with sequence as an important aspect of the vertical dimension. The horizontal dimension focuses on the array of subjects or concepts available or taught to a student or group of students simultaneously.

The graded curriculum of many of our schools has both a vertical and horizontal dimension. The vertical organization of the math program of an elementary school utilizes graded math texts based on knowledge about what an average child at a particular grade level is ready to learn. The horizontal dimension of the graded mathematics curriculum includes as much information regarding topics such as numeration, fractions, addition, and subtraction that a child can assimilate at a particular time. As specialization develops at the high school level, this horizontal dimension becomes vertical, with the offerings of subjects such as algebra I, geometry, algebra II, and trigonometry, sequenced through the four years of high school.

The horizontal dimension of curriculum usually includes all the subjects available to a student at a given time. When a student participates daily or weekly in social studies, English, science, mathematics, health, art, music, and P.E., the student participates in the horizontal dimension of the curriculum. The horizontal structure of most of our schools is relatively uniform, and curricular areas are almost standard among schools and among grade levels. The horizontal balance remains about the same from year to year, providing students with equal doses of each subject area. Schools that are departmentalized, such as most junior and senior high schools, have an additional problem with horizontal organization. The departmentalization creates *compartmentalization* and the several disciplines being taught are not well-coordinated or -integrated for the student, but are taught as totally separate unrelated bodies of knowledge.

CURRICULAR FLEXIBILITY

If individual differences are to be recognized, both the vertical and horizontal dimension of the curriculum require flexibility. Figure 9–1 illustrates the three different rates of learning. Since most children vary from the norm, the curriculum needs to be organized to allow each child to progress individually, as shown by lines A, B, and C.

The organization must allow both child B and C access to appropriate information as it is sequenced according to the difficulty of concepts and materials. The achievement of the student over time will depend, therefore, on the capability of the student to learn and the time committed to that subject.

In subjects such as reading and mathematics, where we traditionally have assumed that all basic skills are taught in the elementary school, we must now recognize that, because of their slow maturation rates, a large portion of our children have in fact not learned these basic

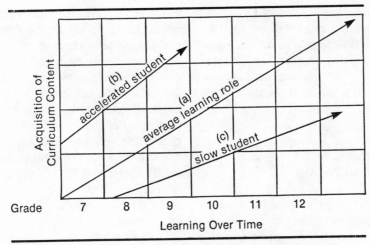

FIGURE 9-1. Impact of individual differences in rate of learning

skills to a level satisfactory for efficient high school learning by the time they have entered high school. Therefore, these, as well as other elementary subjects, must still be available for our high school students.

Varying Curricular Emphasis

Curricular emphasis can also be varied by the flexible use of time. The distribution of time over the curriculum does not necessarily need to be equal. One student might spend five hours a week in language arts, one hour in science, three hours in social studies, ten hours in music, and three hours in P.E. Another student might spend ten hours in language arts, three hours in science, one hour in social studies, two hours in music, and five hours in P.E.

In order to accomplish curriculum variation, schools require a greater variety of curricular offerings. Also, because of the varying rates of progress caused by either differences in ability or in time commitment, a major portion of any skill-sequenced curriculum must be available for instruction at any time. Variations in curriculum should also be available to fulfill student needs and interests.

Curricular Continuity

How much freedom should a student have to reflect needs and interests in determining curriculum selection? Should a student have unlimited choice or should he or she be guided according to some plan? How can the school program curricular opportunities for a student who can move rapidly up a vertical skill sequence ladder, for a student who progresses at a slower rate, for a student who wants or needs an extremely broad range of content areas, or for the student who must concentrate on basic skills? In the past we have not differentiated for the individual student but have provided a very basic curriculum for everyone, allowing for variation only through our high school elective program.

One proposal for high school curricular organizations suggest that one hour per week be devoted to each basic subject area of the curriculum for each high school student on a continuous basis throughout the student's high school career as the minimum of the common learning and basic skills core. Included would be language arts, social studies, math, science, fine arts, P.E. and health, and home and shop arts. The one hour per week is devoted to either high-interest motivating presentations in that subject or continued skill proficiency in areas including reading, math, or previously taught foreign languages.[2] The balance of the students' time would be taken by the required and elective subjects.

PROBLEMS OF DISCIPLINARY CURRICULAR ORGANIZATION

Another major dilemma of continuity in high school curriculum lies with the "compartmentalization" of the disciplines. A subject curriculum is organized around a narrowly defined discipline and is usually planned so it can be easily explained (i.e., simple to complex, full to part, past to present), with all learning activities taking place within that field of knowledge. Most of our high school course offerings are organized as a simple subjects curriculum such as English, history, biology, chemistry, etc. A broad fields curriculum involves combinations of closely related subjects resulting in area subjects such as social studies, language arts, or general science. In some cases, a broad fields approach is used such as in social studies (by combining history, geography, economics, political science, etc.), or language arts (which includes components of English, speech, literature, spelling, reading, and grammar). Seldom, however, are subjects ever combined outside of an accepted broad fields area, and only in the language arts area has the broad fields been effectively implemented in our secondary school program.

A core curriculum involves establishing meaningful relationships between and among subjects, and is, in that sense, interdisciplinary. It often implies a problem-solving approach to learning designed around a series of broad social problems or themes. Efforts in past years to develop an "interdisciplinary core curriculum" or a "problems of living curriculum" which jump across broad fields to combine areas such as language arts, social studies, or subject areas have generally met with failure. Several reasons are given for this failure: (1) poor content selection; (2) lack of appropriate material, such as adequate textbooks; (3) difficulty in teaching such a diverse content area which must include lesson preparations in a variety of disciplines; (4) teacher certification; and (5) organizational problems relating to scheduling, assigning of students, and the assigning of teachers to more than one department.

The advantages of such an interdisciplinary curriculum are many, however. They include: (1) the integration of knowledge; (2) an opportunity to deal with broad themes that cut across disciplines, such as major social problems; and (3) the opportunity for teachers to work with students for an extended period of time during the school day. The solution to the problem of an interdisciplinary curriculum probably rests in part with a revamping of some of the other components of school organization. As pointed out in chapter 7, methods of instruction, grouping, scheduling, staffing and facility utilization often enter into a solution when revisions are to be made in other major areas such as curriculum. An interdisciplinary curriculum can best be organized with an interdisciplinary teaching team operating on a multi-hour block schedule. This solution also correlates with the efforts to improve school climate, as discussed in chapter 11, to deal with student guidance on a more personal level as well as to provide greater flexibility for diversified instruction.

The next section of the chapter presents three models of curriculum implementation that attempt to incorporate the current ideas for innovative curriculum organization. Included are mini-courses, action learning and a walkabout model.

Mini-Courses

A mini-course is a short course usually offered for one marking period of six to nine weeks, and it is frequently nontraditional in its content and organization. Mini-courses are a functional method of creating desired variety, flexibility, and open-access to content within a high school curriculum.

The concept of the mini-course is to offer to students a learning experience either within one of the given disciplines or from a multidisciplinary approach in an effort to better meet their needs and interests. When a great variety of mini-courses is offered, the curriculum is broadened. When mini-courses are available on a nonsequenced basis, maximum access to the curriculum is obtained. When necessary, some sequencing can be accomplished through the use of an introductory course within a particular discipline, followed by a series of mini-course options. But, in many cases, sequencing to meet individual student needs is carried out internal to course structures.

Figure 9–2 illustrates how a basic course can be offered as a mini-course within a par-

---

ACADEMIC BIOLOGY

The courses offered in Academic Biology are designed to prepare Phase 3, 4, and 5 students with the basic information needed for a college preparatory knowledge of biological science. All students will be required to enroll in Biology 211 the first quarter to receive training in the fundamentals of science.

To receive a unit of credit in biology, the student must enroll in and successfully pass four quarters of work.

COURSES

211 Basic Principles of Biology

An introductory course of penural biology that will include the study of scientific method of research, an indepth study of microscope usage, animal and plant cell physiology and anatomy, and the history and development of biology.

212 Survey of Animal Kingdom

A study in comparative anatomy and physiology beginning with sponges and ending with mammals. Laboratory work will consist of dissections of preserved specimens and the study of living organisms.

213 Survey of Plant Kingdom

A study of comparative anatomy and physiology of plants beginning with mosses and ending with flowering plants. Laboratory work will deal with plant morphology and physiology.

214 Genetics   Required for Phases 4 & 5

An indepth study of inherited characteristics. Laboratory experiences will include the study of the fruit fly.

215 Ecology

A study of the environment with laboratory work being conducted primarily in the field.

FIGURE 9–2. A mini-course series with a common introductory component

CENTRAL HIGH SCHOOL
DEPARTMENT OF ENGLISH

Period	Quarter A	B	C	D

1	Orientation
	Grammar II
	Vocational English
	Black Studies
	Supernatural
	  Literature
	Oral Interpretation
	Informative &
	  Entertaining
	  Speech
		Grammar I
		Grammar I
		Composition
		Creative Writing
		Fundamentals of
		  Reading
		Children's
		  Literature
		Group Discussion
		Vocational English
		  II
			Grammar II
			Fundamental
			  Reading
			Reading
			  Appreciation
			Introduction to
			  Literature
			Mythology
			American Fiction
			Persuasive &
			  Convincing Speech
				Vocational
				  English III
				Introduction
				  to Literature
				Reading
				  Appreciation
				20th Century
				  Poetry
				Science Fiction
				Supernatural
				  Literature
				Comprehensive
				Literature of
				  the Bible
				Journalism
				Acting

2	Orientation
	Grammar II
	Grammar II
	Grammar II
	Vocational English
	  III
	Literature of the
	  Bible
	Supernatural
	  Literature
	Persuasive &
	  Convincing
	  Speech
	Science Fiction
		Advanced
		  Composition
		Vocational English
		  I
		Reading
		  Appreciation
		Introduction to
		  Literature
		Fundamental
		  Reading II
		Mythology
		Grammar II
		Oral Interpretation
		Informative &
		  Entertaining
		  Speech
			Grammar I
			Grammar II
			Composition
			Introduction to
			  Literature
			Creative Writing
			Black Studies
			Children's Literature
			Journalism
				Grammar I
				Creative
				  Writing
				Fundamental
				  Reading II
				Reading
				  Appreciation
				American
				  Fiction
				Science Fiction
				Comprehensive
				Acting
				Group
				  Discussion

3	Orientation
	Grammar II
	Grammar II
	Grammar II
	Vocational English
	  I
	Literature of the
	  Bible
	Mythology
	Acting
		Grammar I
		Reading
		  Appreciation
		Introduction to
		  Literature
		Vocational English
		  III
		American Fiction
		Supernatural
		  Literature
		Composition
		Journalism
		Persuasive&
		  Convincing
		  Speech
			Grammar I
			Advanced
			  Composition
			Fundamental
			  Reading I
			Fundamental
			  Reading II
			20th Century Poetry
			Supernatural
			  Literature
			European Novels
			Oral Interpretation
			Informative &
			  Entertaining
			  Speech
				Composition
				Vocational
				  English II
				Creative
				  Writing
				Introduction
				  to Literature
				Black Studies
				Children's
				  Literature
				Comprehensive
				Group
				  Discussion
				20th Century
				  Poetry

ticular subject and then be followed by course options based on the interest and needs of the student.

Mini-courses offer students many curricular areas of interest that traditionally cannot be achieved within single or even multiple track curriculums. In order to create mini-courses, some schools take their traditional curricular format and divide their regular instructional units into mini-course components. Other schools, with the input of students and parents, create new curricular areas for mini-course activities either within or outside of the traditional disciplines.

The utilization of mini-courses varies from school to school. Some create a special mini-course hour within the schedule, with each student electing one mini-course per marking period in addition to the traditional curriculum. Other schools offer a variety of mini-course options within each discipline, as well as multidisciplinary mini-course options that make up virtually the entire curriculum. Some schools will operate a mini-course program within only one department, such as English, with the remainder of the school maintaining a traditional design. Figure 9–3 illustrates the mini-courses offered by an English department in the four quarters of the school year and the options available to the students each period. This is an illustration of the modification of a fairly standard curriculum into a mini-course approach. Previously taught units were converted to the mini-course format with the addition of several new mini-course topics to broaden the mini-course English curriculum.

Another approach to mini-course design is the creation of a series of special interest topics with high appeal to the student's special needs. Figure 9–4 is an example of such a proposed list of mini-course topics that was created jointly by teachers and students in a mathematics department. Topics such as trigonometry, statistics, and calculus offer opportunities for advanced mathematics students; while students in need of basic skill development have basic operation as well as a variety of mathematical applications for everyday use that would appeal to all.

Trigonometry
Slide Rule
Statistics
Calculus
Theory of Equations
Fractions, Decimals, Percent
Exponents
Probability—Gamblers
Computer Science
Vectors
Math for Athletes
How to: Make Charts
　　　　Read Rules
　　　　Measure (as in home economics)
Reading House Plans
Drawing to Scale
Basic Operations—Addition, Subtraction,
　　Division, Multiplication
Interest—as in Banks
Stocks and Bonds
Money—How It Works
Invoices
Graphs—How to Read
Use of Drafting Instruments
Income Tax
Use of Calculators
Logarithms
Solving Equations
Word Problems
Metric System
Equivalents—As in pounds to ounces,
　　miles to feet
Sets
Map Reading
Analytic Geometry
Logic
Solid, Plane Geometry—Area, Volumes

FIGURE 9-4.　Mathematics mini-course ideas

If desired, mini-courses can be classified into traditional subjects, such as history, political science, economics, or geography, but when organized as mini-courses, student interest is often enhanced, the curriculum is broadened, and open access can be achieved through nonsequencing. Flexibility in scheduling and improved individualization of instruction provide for a wider range of student abilities. Examples of mini-course topics from a social studies department are shown in figure 9–5.

"Honest Politicians: Is There Such an Animal?"
"Voting and Elections Knowledge"
"Local Political Structure"
"Women's Role in Politics"
"Foreign Affairs"
"Media's Influence on Politics"
"Foreign Conflicts"
"Domestic Strife"
"Depressions and Recessions"
"What and Why of Inflation"
"Consumerism"
"Famous Boycotts"
"The Bermuda Triangle"
"How Do You Learn?"
"How to Study" ("So You Want to Earn an A")
"Why Did You Do That?"
"Strange People in Strange Lands"
"The Development of Man in Society"
"How to Deal With Parents" ("Are Adults
    Really People?")
"How to Deal With Peers" (dating, sex, etc.)
"How Do You Like Yourself?"
"History Oddballs"
"Profiles of Courage"
"Tennessee Folk Culture"
"Stonehenge Revisited"
"Religious Studies"
"Outer Space in Ancient Time"

FIGURE 9–5. Social studies mini-course ideas

ACTION LEARNING

Four hundred seniors in a midwestern high school performed tasks in the community as part of their twelfth grade social studies class. More than 90 percent of the senior class chose to do community service instead of writing a research paper. The students worked in a variety of endeavors including political campaigns, voter registration drives, elementary and junior high schools, day care centers, nursing homes, county recreation departments and other places where they were needed. The only criterion for selecting placements was that the students work with people, not in clerical jobs. Finding placements for such a large number of students was facilitated by holding a community fair each fall. Those community agencies that desired student assistance set up tables or booths and the students shopped around for a volunteer opportunity that interested them and met their time and transportation limits. Students did their volunteer work during unscheduled time during the school day or after school.

Action learning is based on the concept of young people learning by doing, and tying this concept into the idea of learning by serving. It is learning through a combination of direct experiences and associated instruction or reflection. The purposes that action learning can serve and the student experiences can offer vary greatly from school to school. The emphasis can be on "service learning," which is volunteering in projects that fulfill community needs, or "experimental learning," which connotes activities focused on self-development. All the varied approaches, however, put the emphasis on the personal involvement of young people in the wider community and the recognition that learning does and should take place outside the classroom. Actual learning situations can include volunteer services, internships, community surveys and studies, social and political action, shadowing a person to explore a career role, living in another culture, and work experience. Of course many of these activities are very common to some of our vocational programs, but in fields such as math, English, health, history, and government, the practice to go along with the theory is less common.

Action Learning Objectives

Schools that offer action learning identify a variety of objectives for their program. Included are:

1. Contribution to a young person's social development and his or her sense of responsibility for the welfare of others.
2. Intellectual development—academic subjects take on added significance when students can apply their classroom knowledge to real problems.
3. Career education—being able to see first hand and participate in a variety of possible job roles.
4. Benefits to the school—breaking down the barriers between school and the wider community.
5. Benefits to the community—the ability to provide many community services that would not have been possible without student volunteer help.

Organizing for Action Learning

Many different action learning programs have been implemented, each with its own unique characteristics. Analyses of these different programs show five basic types of action learning situations, ranging from the minimum integration with the school program to almost total involvement. From least involvement to most, the action learning programs can be described as follows:

A Volunteer Bureau   The school or the student identifies volunteer activities. The work is done during unscheduled time, study hall time, or before or after school. In some cases, arrangements are made for half-day release of all students participating in the volunteer program on a particular day of the week. The staff coordinator of volunteer programs is valuable in providing coordination to the program by identifying and placing students, following up, and reviewing the student's work. The student usually has the prime responsibility for initiating his or her community experience, with the school providing a coordinating function.

Community Service for Credit   The same basic plan arranged as a volunteer bureau can be carried out, adding to it some form of academic credit for student participation. The school may actively promote the program or the student may possibly still be the initiating agent.

Laboratory for Existing Course   Projects organized in conjunction with regular courses are used often in lieu of research papers or other assignments. Students may engage in community activity during school hours or after school, depending on their schedule. Often, as the students become more involved in community projects, course content begins to be altered toward the more practical useful information, emphasizing teaching systematic observation, data gathering, and community involvement.

Community Involvement Course   A formalized course in community involvement draws on the major features of the laboratory idea (from the previous model) along with the service for course credit concept. The course, though, has its entire structure organized around community involvement, and draws all of its data for the course directly from the community. A course title such as Student Community Involvement might be appropriate.

The Action Learning Center The center carries the students and teachers into the community, where they gain their total experience. This type of course is often interdisciplinary in nature and may be staffed by specialists who repeat the experience several times each year for different groups. Projects such as mountain camp-outs, canoe trips, rebuilding deteriorated homes, or other forms of community action are illustrative of this idea.[3]

Guidelines for directing action learning programs have been proposed by the National Association of Secondary School Principals:[4]

1. The program must fill genuine needs of adolescents and of society of involving youth in tasks that are recognized as important by both young people and adults.

2. It must provide a real challenge to students, offering them an opportunity to extend their skills and their knowledge.

3. An opportunity for guided reflection on the service experiences is necessary and this opportunity should be continued during the period of service.

4. Successful programs provide participants with the sense of community, that special feeling that comes from sharing a goal and working toward it with others.

5. A learning by serving experience should contribute to the knowledge that adolescents need regarding career options open to them in the adult world and some opportunities to work cooperatively with competent adults who are models for these options.

6. In format the program must be both structured and flexible. Many projects have failed because they were too rigid to respond to changing conditions, or others have been unsatisfactory because they were too loosely structured to have brought out a clear and continuing sense of direction.

7. The program must promote a genuine maturity by allowing young people to exercise adult responsibility while at the same time being held accountable for their actions. This means among other things that they should actively participate in decision-making and governance of the project in which they are learning by serving.

8. The stimulus for a worthwhile project or program can come from innumerable sources so keep your eyes and minds open for leads as to needs, people, and places. Be particularly alert to hints that young people themselves may drop. They often are closer to the subtle but serious needs out of the community than school teachers and administrators are.

9. Try to determine the optimal life span for a given learning by serving project and make this an element in planning and administration of the program. Probably more than most other aspects of secondary school curriculum, learning by serving programs have a constant need for new blood.

WALKABOUT

Major revision in secondary curriculum is a monumental task, but many forces are at work that may require such revision—dropping test scores, the basic skills movement, questions regarding compulsory attendance, growing dropout rates, and a general feeling that secondary education is failing. The walkabout experience, described by Maurice Gibbons at the beginning of this chapter, offers some interesting proposals for a major overhaul in our secondary curriculum. The *New Secondary Education*[5] focuses around the real-life experiences demanded by our society or desired by its members instead of the artificial world of academic tradition that no longer represents reality. Proposed for this curriculum are a series of preparatory activities to the walkabout challenges that are the components of study or graduation activities.

The report, which extended Gibbons' original walkabout article in the May, 1974, *Phi Delta Kappan* issue, proposed the following challenge areas as the basis for the new curriculum:

- physical or psychological adventure
- creativity
- service to others
- rational investigation
- practical skill
- work experience
- academic mastery
- social, recreational programs; community events

Prior to the involvement in the senior challenge curriculum for ages fifteen to seventeen, students would receive preparatory work in the junior segment of the program for ages thirteen to fifteen. Action learning courses of concentration for the junior school, as proposed in the report, are: art; wilderness adventure and craft; practical investigation procedures; advanced academic studies; humanities and life skills; world study; practical, productive skills; and self-directed program development. Through both the junior and senior portions of the program, the students would be involved in a core skills program.

Each of the program segments functions as a two-month full-time experience for the student. Students entering from the elementary schools join one of the eight program centers focusing on a singular purpose for nine weeks. The student gradually gains sufficient range of awareness in the area to choose and pursue a particular indepth focus.

When the nine-week period is over, the student moves on to other centers, completing all of them in a maximum of three years. Figure 9–6 shows the structure of the junior centers, the core skills training, the senior challenges, the community programs, the social and recreational facilities, as well as the continuation of the core skills into the senior segment.

The eight centers of the junior program are described by Gibbons as follows:

1. The Center for the Fine, Applied, and Performing Arts (FAPA): A wide range of experiences in the ways people express artistic imagination, study in one or more art forms, and progress in one or more forms of artistic expression, such as sculpture, musical instruments, engraving, fashion design, pottery, industrial design, and silversmithing.

2. Wilderness School: Experiencing solitude on solos and individual projects and teamwork in field studies of nature, ecology, and conservation, as well as adventure challenges in the mountains and on the rivers.

3. The Local Bureau of Investigation (LBI): Experiences in a wide range of investigative procedures used by police, chemists, city planners, archaeologists, reporters, and engineers. Study and application of modes of inquiry leading to individual and group investigations.

4. Workshop in Practical Activities: Inventing, designing, making, constructing, repairing, assembling, problem-solving, in the practical world of machines, electronics, buildings, plumbing, instruments, farming, manufacturing, selling, and city planning. Emphasis is on learning how by doing, leading to individual or group projects.

5. The Institute of Advanced Studies: Intensive academic studies leading to the acquisition of a body of knowledge, concepts, operations, and broad framework of principles in at least two disciplines, and culminating in a presentation and oral examination by a community committee. Theoretical in emphasis, studies are nevertheless related to concrete experience and practical application.

6. The Humanities Center and Life Skills Laboratory: Focus on personal values and relationships with others through the study of literature, media, and actual behavior; guided self-analysis, role playing, and skill training; and working with community service groups and younger students. Total family participation in the family segment is recommended.

7. Center for the Study of the World: Experience, study, and practice in the dynamics of social, legal, and political processes at local, state, national, and international levels. Learning responsible, active citizenship in the community and the world.

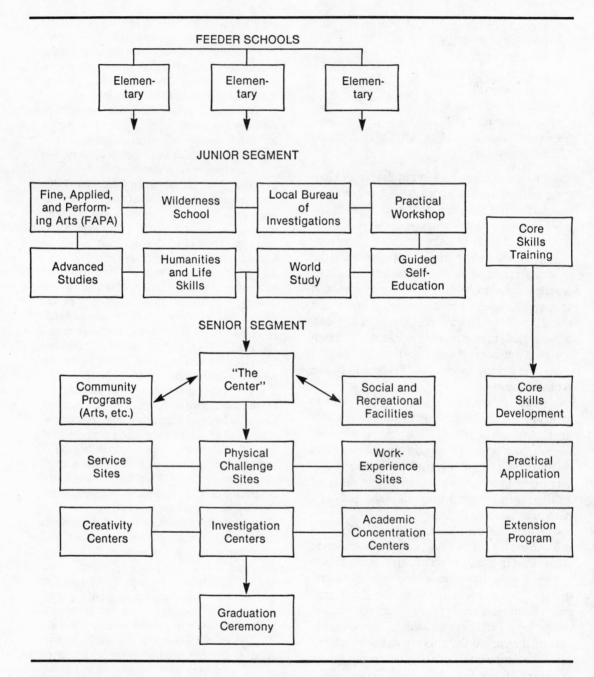

FIGURE 9–6.   Outline of elements in the secondary levels program

Maurice Gibbons, *The New Secondary Education,* a Phi Delta Kappa Task Force Report (Bloomington, Ind.: Phi Delta Kappa, 1976), p. 116. Reprinted with permission.

8. School of Guided Self-Education: Students learn to identify interests and abilities, explore alternatives, assemble resources, decide on a focus, set goals, plan a program, confront difficulties, seek appropriate assistance, manage time, and evaluate their own effort and accomplishment. Emphasis is on personal decision making, planning, and performance without the support of a learning grid structure.

In order to insure a well-balanced instructional program, the Phi Delta Kappa report suggests that each segment of the curriculum involve a personal dimension, an interpersonal dimension, and an academic dimension to be dealt with in three learning modes—by experience, by study, and by productive activity. Figure 9–7 illustrates how this instructional grid might appear for elements of instruction in the local bureau of investigation curricular area. The eight program segments of the curriculum are to prepare and train students for the increased responsibility of the senior segment.

Early in the senior program, plans are to be made involving the students, parents, and teachers, mapping out the goals in the eight senior challenge areas. Students with similar interests or needs are grouped together where appropriate. Learning grids similar to figure 9–7 are developed for the exploratory parts of the challenge program, with advisors later helping students prepare specific competency ladders to meet their goals. The eight senior challenge areas proposed in the Phi Delta Kappa report are:

1. Physical (Psychological) Challenge: A challenge to the student's daring, endurance, and skill in an unfamiliar environment.
Examples: Build a kayak and run a river, conduct a solo expedition on the Pacific Crest Trail, learn to climb a 55° slope, arrange an exchange with an African student, develop a particular athletic skill to a level of excellence, solo in a light plane, develop a program in meditation or yoga, and so on.

2. Creativity Challenge: A challenge to the student's ability to explore, cultivate, and express his own imagination in some inventive or aesthetically pleasing form.
Examples: Sculpting, writing poetry, acting, decorating, welding, political cartooning, creating Japanese decor and gardens, playing rock music, forming a jazz group or string quartet, performing a stand-up comic's act, cooking gourmet foods, constructing and designing furniture, creating inventions, and so on.

3. Service Challenge: A challenge to identify a human need for assistance and provide what is necessary to fulfill it; to express caring without expectation of reward, preferably through personal interaction with individuals or groups.
Examples: Volunteer work with the young (old, ill, deformed, or retarded), develop such services as a games program for the handicapped, a big brother program for the retarded, trips for shut-ins, activity courses for the aged, crisis work with peers, day-care programs or tutoring for younger children.

4. Investigation Challenge: A challenge to formulate a question or problem of personal importance and to pursue an answer or solution by systematic investigation.
Examples: How does one navigate in space? How much can I control my mind and body through biofeedback? How exactly does a starfish regenerate a lost arm? Can the validity of any psychic experience be proved? What natural, organic means can I use to protect my crops from disease?

5. Practical Skill Challenge: A challenge to explore a utilitarian activity, to learn the knowledge and skills necessary to work in that field, and to produce something of use. This is work one may always do for oneself though perhaps never as a job or profession.
Examples: Write a movie review for a local paper, construct a telescope with hand-ground lenses, develop and manage a section of a farm, create an expert repair service for gas furnaces or electrical appliances, mount a conservation program for an endangered species, design and build a mountain cabin.

	Personal	Interpersonal	Academic
Experience	• Share the experience of someone active in reporting, policework, or small business operation. • Experience a number of shops, newspapers and precincts as a client and participant. • Experience and record your personal attitudes and responses to the work involved.	• Find out how the adult you are working with feels about his job, what it means, what he experiences. • Interview people; try selling someone something. • Share your experiences and responses with others.	• Work-study: take over or help with some part of the job. • Experience micro teaching, writing from the wire services, investigating simulated crimes.
Study	• Outline the skills of investigation involved in one of these jobs. • Plan a personal program of study, practice, and activity to master the skills of investigation. • Design a competency ladder for developing an important skill involved in the job.	• "Apprentice" to the reporter or teacher learning from them what they do, how, and why. • Establish a base group with others to discuss problems encountered. • Plan an investigation or study of the job with others. • Practice interviewing, selling, teaching others.	• Study technical sources about the work suggested by the teacher or other adult. • Attend the police academy, a night school course in small business management. • Set up classes at the Bureau.
Productive Activity	• Research and write newspaper articles until one is accepted locally for publication. • Prepare and teach a lesson or unit. • Study catalogues, sales, and the market and prepare an order for the business. • Teach others what you have learned.	• Launch a newsletter about the activities of others at the Bureau. • Plan and institute a short-lived small business at the Bureau with others. • Set up a tutoring bureau for younger students.	• Conduct investigations of problems your tutor-model is solving. • Consider other approaches which might be employed and suggest them.

FIGURE 9–7. Some possible elements in a learning grid for the Local Bureau of Investigation (police work, small business management, reporting, teaching)

Maurice Gibbons, *The New Secondary Education,* a Phi Delta Kappa Task Force Report (Bloomington, Inc.: Phi Delta Kappa, 1976), p. 119. Reprinted with permission.

6. Work-Experience Challenge: A challenge to work on the job in the community and learn the information, skills, and procedures involved while working closely with a skilled adult or adults.
Examples: Factories, mills, construction crews, animal hospitals, professional offices, social services, offices, newspapers, maintenance crews, local government, private business, artist's studios, stores, and clubs.
7. Academic Challenge: A challenge to organize a coherent program of academic studies—which may include tutoring, laboratory work, and formal courses—in a specific discipline and achieve significant progress beyond baseline performance in it. Wherever possible, academic challenges should be directed toward theoretical understanding of a performative activity.
8. Extension Program: An optional challenge enabling students to pursue one area further, develop a second focus in any challenge area, or create a new challenge which combines areas or establishes a new one.[6]

Students in the senior segment will spend two to three months in each challenge area preparing for the graduation presentation. Resources for study are to be internal as well as external to the school depending on the

student's needs and where appropriate assistance can be located. The public library, community agencies, skilled instructors, and artisans are all used where appropriate.

The basic skills component of the model merits special attention. Gibbons defines such skills as those which enable people to learn, to experience, and to study and perform better. He proposed that they be taught in relationship to ongoing activities and not in isolation prior to the involvement in real learning situations. People often learn best if they have understanding about what they are learning. One way of achieving this is to experience the whole before studying the parts. Learning basic skills also needs to have available direct application in the form of productive activity. These three ideas of experiencing, learning, and applying are designed into a basic skill training loop as shown in figure 9–8.

The meaningful application to real life situations is designed into the basic skills program to improve incentives for skill instruction as well as to improve understanding.

Basic skill training is intended to apply to more than proficiency in just reading and mathematics. All educational programs that culminate in the ability to perform an activity must

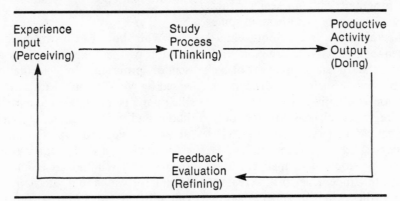

FIGURE 9–8.   Skill training loop

Maurice Gibbons, *The New Secondary Education,* a Phi Delta Kappa Task Force Report (Bloomington, Ind.: Phi Delta Kappa, 1976), p. 125. Reprinted with permission.

develop skills. The training in specific basic skills must then be coordinated with various junior segments as well as senior challenges. Included would be problem-solving skills, inquiry skills, interviewing skills, analytical skills (such as organizing data to discover patterns), and basic decoding skills (in areas such as reading and mathematics).

The graduation exercises of walkabout consist of each graduate reporting on the eight areas of his or her investigation. These reports are the major part of the graduation activities. The last years of the student's high school career focus on preparing for these culminating activities and choosing a final selection from a variety of ideas. The walkabout idea, of course, represents a major departure from our traditional approaches at organizing curriculum where the emphasis is placed on the culminating activities as a means of forcing a reorganization of the activities experienced along the way. This may be a far better answer to measuring the proficiencies of our high school graduates than the minimum competency tests being proposed by many of our legislatures.

Caution is urged in any attempt to put walkabout into effect. In some cases, past innovators have simply attempted to put old content into the new programs with no real restructuring of learning experiences. Others, in some of the most liberal of the free schools, eliminated all content and directive instruction, and instead relied on the student's discovery of his or her own program. Such a leadership or authority vacuum is usually left unfilled, and this laissez-faire approach has created only chaos. If we remove the structure of subjects, disciplines, courses, lessons, texts, etc., it is essential that we develop other superstructures that will support the student's effort to create a structure of his or her own. The superstructure must be one of assisting the students in developing their own learning skills and intrinsic motivation, and to have this decision-making ability in order for them to make wise choices.

Recognizing the fact that a school faculty and principal are simply not going to throw out existing structures and enthusiastically embrace a total curriculum entitled "walkabout," what can be done to more gradually move a school in the direction of providing meaningful culminating experiences along with appropriate developmental opportunities for their students along the walkabout theme? Gibbons has suggested four levels of implementation that will allow a school more gradual access:

1. Walkabout can be an extracurricular activity in which all planning and work is done during out-of-school time.
2. It can be one element of a curriculum that is included in the schedule like a course, giving students time for planning, consultation, and training.
3. It can be the core of the grade twelve program, one in which all teaching and activity is devoted to preparing for trial.
4. It can be the goal around which a whole new curriculum is designed for the school or for a school within a school, staffed by interested teachers for interested students, which of course is what the 1976 Phi Delta Kappa report suggests.

Walkabout can be arranged for a limited portion of the student body as an alternative school program. Implementation could be eased by working only with students who have their parents' permission to participate in walkabout and with volunteer staff that is excited about this type program. Even then, the transition may be eased by starting the students in their regular school courses and allowing them to opt for walkabout alternatives as they successfully prepare learning contracts for walkabout type experiences. There are several schools in the country that have had very successful adoptions of walkabout using this approach.[7]

Walkabout is just one of a number of examples of the kinds of innovations that might be carried on in high schools. Whether it is walkabout or some other innovative notion, the important thing is to accept innovation, plan for it, nurture it, reword it, and improve it.

SUMMARY

A variety of curricular concepts have been outlined in this chapter. In summary, they are as follows:

1. Curriculum has a vertical dimension, which is the sequencing of a particular discipline over time.
2. Curriculum has a horizontal dimension. It includes the several components of a discipline that are taught at the same time or the combination of the several disciplines that are included for a student at a particular point in time.
3. Curriculum should be organized flexibly so that students can move to a sequence of learning experiences at different rates (vertically).
4. Curriculum should be organized so that more or less time can be spent by a particular student in certain aspects of the curriculum as needed (horizontally).
5. Curriculum should be organized flexibly to provide open access to meet the various needs and interests of children (exploratory, electives, specialization).
6. Curriculum should be organized so that all subjects are taught to some degree each year through high school (common learning, basic skills).
7. Action learning offers a way to expand the curriculum.
8. Mini-courses offer a way to provide more flexibility and open access.
9. Curriculum may need a total overhaul to meet the challenge of a changing society.

ENDNOTES

1. Maurice Gibbons, "Walkabout Searching for the Right Passage from Childhood and School," *Phi Delta Kappan* 55 (May 1974): 596–602.
2. The skill proficiency development could answer the current demand for improved basic skills on the part of high school students prior to graduation and would assist them in the passage of proficiency tests now being required in many states.
3. Dan Conrad and Diane Hedin, *Action Learning in Minnesota.* Center for Youth Development and Research, The University of Minnesota and the Minnesota Association of Secondary School Principals, undated.
4. "Community Service One Path to Learning," *Curriculum Report,* National Association of Secondary School Principals 4 (May 1975).
5. Maurice Gibbons, *The New Secondary Education,* a Phi Delta Kappa Task Force Report (Bloomington, Ind.: Phi Delta Kappa, 1976).
6. Ibid., pp. 120–122.
7. The North Central High School of Indianapolis, Indiana, under a project called "learning unlimited," has developed an excellent alternative program as a school within the school. Approximately 350 students participate in the North Central alternative walkabout program.

BIBLIOGRAPHY

Abel, Billy L. "Humanizing Secondary Schools: Words or Action." *NASSP Bulletin* 60 (October 1976): 63–68.

Barr, Robert D. "The Development of Action Learning Programs." *NASSP Bulletin* 60 (May 1976): 106–109.

Bloom, Benjamin S. "Affective Outcomes of School Learning." *Phi Delta Kappan* 59 (November 1977): 193–198.

Brandstitter, John, and Foster, Charles R. "Quality Integrated Education in Houston's Magnet Schools." *Phi Delta Kappan* 57 (April 1976): 502–506.

Clements, Zacharie J. "Taking All Students from Where They Are." *NASSP Bulletin* 60 (April 1976): 104–108.

Clements, Zacharie J. "Humanizing and Back to Basics: The Perfect Blend for the '70's and Beyond." *NASSP Bulletin* 61 (May 1977): 98–108.

Combs, Stanley B. "A Summary of a Survey on Student Involvement in Curriculum." *Journal of Secondary Education* 25 (October 1970): 243–249.

Connelly, T. Michael. "The Functions of Curriculum Development." *Journal of Secondary Education* 25 (October 1970): 161–177.

Duff, Charles F. "Meaningful Career Education in the Middle School." *NASSP Bulletin* 62 (April 1978): 60–63.

Egginton, Everett. "Is Vocational Education Meeting Its Objectives?" *Phi Delta Kappan* 59 (April 1978): 533–534.

Fenwick, James. "Arts Education: A New Place in the Sun?" *Phi Delta Kappan* 59 (March 1978): 467–469.

Fox, Robert S. "Innovation in Curriculum: An Overview." *Journal of Secondary Education* 25 (October 1970): 243–249.

Gibbons, Maurice. " 'Eleusis' The Secondary School Ideal." *Phi Delta Kappan* 57 (June 1976): 655–660.

Gibbons, Maurice. "Walkabout Searching for the Right Passage from Childhood and School." *Phi Delta Kappan* 55 (May 1974): 596–602.

Gottesman, Alexander M. "Applying a Model in Curriculum Planning." *NASSP Bulletin* 61 (October 1977): 24–30.

Gow, Doris T. "The PIC (Process Individualization Curriculum) Model: Structure with Humanistic Goals." *ERIC* (1975), ED 104 286.

Guenther, John, and Ridgeway, Robert. "Mini-Courses: One Way to Provide More Humanistic School Programs." *NASSP Bulletin* 60 (April 1976): 12–15.

Hanks, Nancy. "The Arts: An Integral Part of the School Curriculum." *NASSP Bulletin* 61 (December 1977): 94–97.

Harmer, Earl W. "Veteran Teachers and Curriculum Development." *Phi Delta Kappan* 58 (June 1977): 751–752.

Hepburn, Mary. "Political Field Experiences in Secondary Social Studies." *NASSP Bulletin* 50 (December 1976): 4–15.

Jarrett, James L. "I'm For the Basics, But Let Me Define Them." *Phi Delta Kappan* 59 (December 1977): 235–238.

Jennings, Wayne, and Nathan, Joe. "Startling/Disturbing Research on School Program Effectiveness." *Phi Delta Kappan* 58 (March 1977): 568–572.

Johansen, Don. "Tell Me What You Do." *NASSP Bulletin* 60 (December, 1976): 63–65.

Keefe, James W., and Georgiades, Constance J. "Competency-based Education and the High School Diploma." *NASSP Bulletin* 62 (April 1978): 94–108.

Kimball, Roland B. "A Case for Teaching the Humanities in the High School." *NASSP Bulletin* 60 (April 1976): 31–38.

McGregor, Warren. "The Changing Twelfth Grade." *NASSP Bulletin* 60 (May 1976): 115–121.

Popham, W. James. "A Competency-Based High School Completion Program." *NASSP Bulletin* 62 (February 1978): 101–105.

Roller, Lawrence W. "Career Education: An Alternative High School Program." *NASSP Bulletin* 62 (April 1978): 47–49.

Simonson, Michael R. "Global Awareness: A Curriculum Plan for World Study." *NASSP Bulletin* 61 (October 1977): 75–79.

Smith, Vernon H. "Alternatives in Secondary Education." *NASSP Bulletin* 60 (May 1976): 110–114.

Trump, J. Lloyd, and Miller, Delores F. *Secondary School Curriculum Improvement.* Boston: Allyn and Bacon, Inc., 1968.

Tuckman, Bruce W. *The Student-Centered Curriculum: A Concept in Curriculum Innovation.* New Brunswick, N.J.: Rutgers University, HEW, Bureau of Research, ERIC (March 1969), ED 032 616.

Tyler, Ralph W. "The New Emphases in Curriculum Development." *Educational Leadership* 34 (October 1976): 61–71.

Whealon, Terry O., and Whealon, Janet K. "Curriculum Integration Via Career Education." *NASSP Bulletin* 60 (December 1976): 66–68.

Wilson, L. Craig. *The Open Access Curriculum.* Boston: Allyn and Bacon, Inc., 1971, p. 303.

Chapter Ten

Managing the Cocurricular Activities Program

INTRODUCTION

Probably no single aspect of the high school program provides as many headaches for the principal as cocurricular activities.[1] These activities are frequently the source of heated debate both inside and outside the school. Several factors account for this: the program is expensive; is highly visible; requires careful staffing; is typically highly diverse; and is easily thrown out of balance by the overemphasis or greater community involvement in some aspects such as interscholastic athletics. Despite the managerial and public relations problems that cocurricular activities often cause, few educators would want to see a high school without them because these activities can contribute especially to the orderly development of two of the four interacting "selfs" within the learner: the physical self and the social self.[2]

The issue of student activity programming is not new. Over fifty years ago it was the subject of a yearbook of the National Society for the Study of Education,[3] and a book entitled, *Extra-Curricular Activities in the High School.*[4]

Over the years, attitudes about the function of cocurricular activities have changed to the point where these activities are less frequently viewed as "extra" and more often seen as an integral aspect of secondary school programming. Moreover, recent years have seen more and more court opinions expressing the position that participation in these activities is a right rather than a privilege. An Ohio court, for example, stated that "extra-curricular activities . . . are an integral part of the school program" and went on to hold that to deprive any student of such an aspect of the school would violate the particular state's principles in establishing its own system of education.[5]

DEVELOPING THE PROGRAM

The development and operation of a sound cocurricular program issues from a well understood and agreed on philosophy and a series of specific objectives explicating that philosophy. The philosophy and objectives should be firmly rooted in an understanding of the nature and needs of adolescents and knowledge about the power of the four interacting selfs which comprise the learner. This understanding provides a necessary perspective and will help prevent the program from becoming a narrow one devoted to the needs of only a few students who happen to excel in some particular interest area. The educational goals of the cocurricular activities program are many, but may be summed up as:

1. Social and physical development.
2. Opportunity for leadership development.

3. Opportunity for greater development of student responsibility.
4. Practice in democratic processes.
5. Improvement of school morale.

Moreover, the program needs to be subjected to regular and continuous evaluation in the light of its objectives.[6] Figure 10–1 depicts certain essential steps in the organization and administration of the cocurricular activities program.

The scope of the program should be broad. Opportunities must be provided for all students if the program is to be considered a successful one. With respect to scope, Stoops and his associates have stated cogently that a good program provides

> opportunities in athletics and physical development; speech and drama; journalistic and creative writing; music; recreation; hobbies; social development and academic and other interests not covered in a regular curriculum, clubs and student government.[7]

Participation in cocurricular programs should be extensive. If it is not, obviously something is wrong with the program. A high school that has less than 70 percent of its students participating in the cocurricular program is cause for great concern. Possible conditions affecting the number of total participants include narrow scope of activities, high cost of participation, rigid membership requirements, low faculty interest, inadequate financing, and low-level administrative commitment. Any one of these is sufficient to keep the program from being successful.

The Needs and Interest Assessment

Given the educational goals noted in the previous section, and given the fact that communities and student bodies differ somewhat in their expectations, needs, and interests, how might the school administration provide for an effective cocurricular activities program? A needs and interest assessment followed by a discrepancy analysis provides a sound approach. Students, staff, and community should all be a part of such an approach for all are crucial to the success of the program.

Elements of the Needs and Interest Assessment   A needs and interest assessment is not difficult to accomplish. The simplest way is to

---

1. Establish and reach agreement on a philosophy and the objectives of the cocurricular program.
2. Survey the interests, needs, and opinions of students, staff, and community.
3. Establish procedures, rules, and regulations for cocurricular groups and activities.
4. Define the roles of personnel engaged in supervising and sponsoring the various activities.
5. Determine the administrative structure for managing and supervising the program.
6. Establish financial procedures, including bookkeeping and any fund-raising policies.
7. Provide a systematic way of evaluating the several aspects of the program.

FIGURE 10–1.   Essential steps for organizing and administering a cocurricular activities program

use a survey format, such as suggested in figure 10-2. This example would probably require local adaptation but most surveys will need to contain its essential elements if good insights are to be gained. With further adaptation, the same instrument can be used to survey faculty, staff, and community about their perceptions.

In order to get maximum student and faculty response, the survey form should be distributed during an assigned period and collected immediately. If finances permit, the community form of the questionnaire should be mailed to a random sample and contain a stamped return envelope. A good alternative to this is to publish the questionnaire in a local newspaper (perhaps a weekly advertiser which serves the same neighborhood as the school) and have several collection points around the area.

The Discrepancy Analysis

The administrator hopes to acquire valid information and perceptions that a variety of people have about the existing cocurricular activities program, their notions about its value and shortcomings, and suggestions for improvement.

The biographic information requested will assist in determining whether there are certain activities that reflect an exclusivity when responses by various categories of individuals are compared. Moreover, it may reveal that significant numbers of students' needs and interests are not being addressed. In urban areas, asking respondents to indicate the neighborhood in which they live will, in most instances, provide insight about the socioeconomic level of respondents without being unnecessarily provocative.[8]

Responses to questions will not only give insight about the breadth and scope of the program, they may also uncover some unobserved negative characteristics and suggest modification of the existing program.[9] Data should

also be collected about the nature and kind of participation in the existing program and compared to the responses to appropriate questionnaire items.

Elements of a Good Program

What characterizes specific activities in a good program? The following are essential:

1. Membership is open to all students.
2. The group or activity has a charter that is consistent with the philosophy and objectives of the cocurricular program.
3. Adequate facilities exist and are allocated for the activity.
4. The activity is student-centered and provides the opportunity for student leadership.
5. The activity is subjected to regular evaluation in the light of (a) whether it is meeting its defined purpose; (b) how well it is meeting its defined purpose; and (c) its continued relevance to the quality of student life.
6. Adequate financing with no or low cost to participants.
7. Adequate faculty sponsorship and administrator commitment.

Economics of Student Participation: A Caution

Frequently participation in cocurricular activities is marked by stark aspects of the social and economic realities of the larger society. Many activities require a considerable expenditure of money by participants or participants' parents. This often results in many members of the student body being excluded from some activities. This has been the subject of much concern for many years, and it seems unlikely to receive resolution until the cocurricular program is entirely funded from the general school district fund. Sadly, it is often the economically deprived student who is in greatest need of the en-

---

Cocurricular Activities Survey
Herrscher Senior High School
Our Cocurricular Activities Program*

We would like to have your opinion about the Senior High School student activities program. Your ideas will make the program a better one. Please be frank.

Part I

_____ Age   _____ Grade
_____ Sex   _____ Racial or Ethnic Group
_____ Neighborhood in which you live

Part II

Objectives and Operation of Cocurricular Activities:

- To provide leadership opportunities and growth in responsibility.
- To provide practice in democratic processes.
- To assist in social and physical development.
- To keep school morale high.
- To provide opportunities for students of all ages, sexes, ethnic backgrounds, and economic levels to come to know each other better.

1. Given the objectives and philosophy just stated, how would you rate our program? (Circle one)

1	2	3	4	5
The best	Good	So-so	Falls short	Really bad

2. Where is it good? (Which objectives and/or activities are best?)
3. Where does it need improvement? (Which objectives and/or activities need improvement or need to be added?)
4. Do you think the philosophy and objectives are good ones? (If no, what is wrong with them?)
5. How could more students be encouraged to participate?
6. Do you feel any of our activities are over-emphasized?_____ (Which?)
7. Do you feel any of our activities are under-emphasized?_____ (Which?)
8. If there could be only three cocurricular activities for the entire school, what should they be?

_____   _____   _____

9. What new activities should be added?

(continued)

---

*It might be helpful to include a list of currently offered activities with this questionnaire to better inform respondents of the possibilities.

10. Would you be interested in leading (or sponsoring) any of these?_____ (Which?)

11. Who (if anyone) would you suggest should lead (or sponsor) such an activity?

12. Do you know of any others who would be interested in this activity?_____ Who? (Name three or four.)

13. What cocurricular activities do you now participate in?

14. Can you think of an activity you are interested in but don't participate in? _____ What is that activity?_____ Why don't you partici- pate? (Check all that apply.)

_____ Not offered at Herrscher
_____ Costs too much
_____ Parents won't let me
_____ Held at a bad time
_____ My friends don't participate
_____ Other (Please say why)_____

_____

15. Cocurricular activities cost money. How should these be financed? (Check all that apply.)

_____ By the board of education from general funds
_____ Extra student fees from all
_____ Extra student fees from those who participate in the activity
_____ Fund-raising schemes such as bake sales and carnivals
_____ Donations from patrons and businesses
_____ Admission charges
_____ Others (Please state)_____

_____

16. When should cocurricular activities be scheduled? (Check all that apply.)

_____ During regular school hours
_____ Extend school day
_____ After school only
_____ Weekends
_____ Other (Please state)_____

_____

_____ Depends on the activity (If this is your choice, please state what you mean.)_____

_____

Thank you very much!

Lloyd A. Williams
Director of Student Activities
Herrscher Senior High School

FIGURE 10-2.   An example of cocurricular needs assessment-student form*

*This same form with appropriate editing can be used for faculty and community members.

riching experiences provided by the myriad of activities in the cocurricular program.

Research monographs and articles in the periodical literature about the effect of cost of participation are extensive, from an early work by Harold Hand to the present. Hand studied the problem for the years 1931–1937![10]

> Hand . . . observed that many parents of low income simply could not find the money to keep their children in high school with the drain on the family budget becoming increasingly acute as the children progressed from ninth to twelfth grades. . . . Many children of the poor do not want to stay in high school when it means that their poverty would prevent them from maintaining themselves on a social level with fellow students.[11]

If the cocurricular program contains important and even necessary educational experiences consistent with the goals of the school, then it should be organized and administered so that there is student access to all aspects of the program irrespective of the economic condition of the student.

MANAGING THE PROGRAM

Except in very small schools, the principal will probably have assistance in the management of the cocurricular program. Frequently the program will be extensive enough to require the attention of a full-time person. One person or many; the principal or a delagatee, the tasks accruing to the manager of the cocurricular program include financial management (including budgeting), scheduling, securing equipment and supplies, personnel recruitment and assignment, and evaluation. Delegating these tasks to a subordinate, of course, does not change the fact that it is the principal who is ultimately responsible for the proper conduct of the program. Figure 10–3 contains a representative position description of a Director of Student Activities.

Position Description: Director of Student Activities

Qualifications: Counselor's certificate

Supervisor: Principal

Responsibility: The role of the director of student activities involves the coordination of student cocurricular activities. The director of student activities

- plans and implements development of vocational and avocational clubs
- provides direction to the student Congress or Council
- coordinates use of building facilities
- plans and coordinates assembly programs
- assumes responsibility for the collection of money from cocurricular activities
- coordinates faculty and student parking facilities
- promotes positive school and community relations through effective communication and involvement of students and community members
- interprets school policies relative to student activities

FIGURE 10–3. Position description: Director of Student Activities

Interscholastic Athletics

Most often the largest single cocurricular activity in a school district, in terms of expense, if not active participation, will be the interscholastic athletic program. In systems where this is so, there frequently will be a district level administrator whose responsibility it is to coordinate the program district-wide with the assistance of the principals of the district. Insight about the magnitude of this responsibility can be gained by examining the position description in figure 10-4.

While the position described in figure 10-4 is for a person with district-wide responsibil-

ities, it is of special value to the secondary school principal because it clearly delineates the responsibilities and tasks which accrue to anyone charged with managing this activity. In small school districts these will fall to a single athletic director in a high school, some of the responsibilities probably to be shared with the principal. In still smaller districts it may be that they will be the sole responsibility of the principal.

Similar descriptions should be developed for all individuals who direct, sponsor, or manage any of the activities in the cocurricular programs. It should be clearly evident whose responsibility it is to oversee the particular

---

1. Prepares, with the assistance of principals and head coaches, a handbook of athletic policies, regulations, plans and procedures.
2. Evaluates policies within the area of responsibility and makes recommendations to the principals and superintendent for changes.
3. Determines, with the assistance of principals and head coaches, staff needs of the junior and senior high schools and offers assistance to the assistant superintendent for administration in securing qualified personnel.
4. Assists in planning and implementing staff development programs and activities to strengthen identified areas needing improvement.
5. Prepares a budget, with the assistance of principals and head coaches, for the total athletic programs based on identified needs and priorities of the District.
6. Administers the athletic insurance program.
7. Secures needed transportation for athletic teams.
8. Cooperates with the police department concerning school safety matters related to athletics.
9. Supervises and evaluates, with the assistance of principals and head coaches, professional and nonprofessional staff assigned.
10. Supervises the general management and care of the stadium and grounds, baseball field, auxiliary field, and District practice fields.
11. Monitors an inventory of athletic equipment prepared at each secondary school.
12. Schedules all athletic contests with the assistance of the head coach and the principal involved.
13. Prepares news releases as needed which are connected with athletic programs.
14. Represents the District in the Interscholastic League.

FIGURE 10–4.   Position description: Coordinator of Athletics

activity and precisely what tasks need to be accomplished.

Keeping a Perspective   Balancing the needs of students with the interests, needs, and desires of the education establishment and the community is sometimes difficult. Students need to be guided into a variety of activities if they are to develop maximally. Communities need to be helped to see the value of the variety of cocurricular activities even though individual community members may have interest in only one or a few of the more visible activities. It's not easy sometimes but it is encumbent on the educator, especially on the building executive, to assume the responsibility for providing a cocurricular activities program sufficient to meet the needs of all students, and one which is a logical extension of the regular curricular offerings. The best example we can use to illustrate what is meant by the need for cocurricular being a logical extension of the regular curriculum and sufficient to meet the needs of all students can be drawn from the health and physical education program.

In most states students are required to be enrolled in and successfully complete a curricular sequence in physical education and health. Why? Because it is well understood that the development of a healthy body and sound health practices are vital to a productive and full life. It is a recognition of the interaction of mind and body. Long before education was a profession and curricula were formalized in books and treatises, intellectual activity was interspersed with rigorous physical activity and all students participated. Thus, it is not surprising that health and physical education is an integral part of the regular curriculum.

What flows out of this into the cocurricular? The obvious, of course, is interscholastic athletic events, and it is at this point that the need for a broadened perspective with regard to cocurricular activities becomes apparent. It is also at this point that the question of meeting the needs of the greatest number of students can be raised.

Leading schools in the nation do not make the leap from required physical education for all students to interscholastic athletics for the few who excel. Something is missing in such a leap and that something is a program of physical benefit to the huge number of students who are thrilled to play, want to play, can play, will derive great educational advantages from playing, but do not excel sufficiently to ever make a varsity or even junior varsity team. So what does the alert principal and the good school do? Capitalizing on the interests and the needs of youth, an intramural program is provided.

Our point is that, in order to be educationally justifiable, the cocurricular program must be organized in such a way that it addresses the needs of large numbers of students and must not be inherently restrictive so that its values are possible to only a few. The regular academic curriculum provides a wide variety of opportunities for students to participate in academic learnings in specific subject areas—essential learnings for all; electives for those who are interested or wish to explore; and highly advanced coursework, seminars, and independent study for those who excel. This same approach should be reflected in the cocurricular activities program.

Figure 10–5 graphically depicts the physical education analogy with a series of consentric circles indicating numbers of participants. All students are participants in the curricular health and physical education program; many have the opportunity to learn additional skills as participants in competitive athletics through intramurals; the few who excel are provided a varsity athletics program. Unless adequacy exists in the larger two circles (HPE and Intramurals), there is no justification for the smallest circle (Interscholastic)!

This same analogy can be made for all interactions between the curricular and cocurricular. It is no less true for the fine and per-

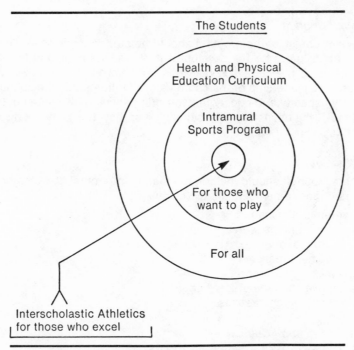

The Students

Health and Physical
Education Curriculum

Intramural
Sports Program

For those who
want to play

For all

Interscholastic Athletics
for those who excel

FIGURE 10–5. Keeping the cocurricular program in perspective: An example of school programming and the development of the physical self

forming arts program or the social activities program. If the senior prom is the major social event—an expensive undertaking indeed—and there are few other social events on the school calendar whereby certain social skills can be learned, then it is clearly an instance of detrimental over-emphasis. The point is that cocurricular activities do exist for an educative purpose, and a continual assessment must be made by the administrator about how well that purpose is being served by the existing program.

Policies to Govern the Student Activities Program

The best way to insure a good balance in the cocurricular activities program is to develop a series of policies, rules, and regulations for governance. Such a policy would begin with a general statement of purpose and then focus on

such important aspects as administration of the program, acceptable sponsorship, criteria for judging appropriateness, and specific rules and regulations.

Student Leadership In an effective activities program there are many opportunities for leadership by the students themselves. Governance of the program as well as managerial responsibilities can be a joint effort of administrators, faculty, and students. To illustrate the wide range of possibilities, we turn to the exemplary program maintained at the Baker Senior High School in Fairborn, Ohio. Illustrated in figure 10–6 is the governance structure for the intramurals program. The program is administered by a faculty intramural coordinator who functions with a council comprised of students and faculty.

The Intramural Council

To every extent possible, the program should be student controlled. The council provides an opportunity for the development of leadership among the students. The membership of the council should be drawn from both faculty and student groups. Under the leadership of the coordinator of intramurals, the council serves in an advisory capacity and concerns itself primarily with intramural policy. Periodic meetings of the council may be scheduled or they may be held on call by the coordinator.

Personnel for Council

The intramural council should include the faculty intramural coordinator and faculty advisors. Student members should consists of:

- Student intramural manager
- Student assistant managers
- Student record manager
- Student equipment manager
- The points award manager
- A representative from the student council
- The home room representatives.

Duties of the Intramural Council

1. To formulate or adopt a body of rules and regulations.
2. To rule on the eligibility of players.
3. To decide all questions or protests.
4. To decide all controversial questions not taken care of in the regular rules and regulations.
5. To act as a liaison between the organization of the intramural program (scheduling, etc.) and the home room.

FIGURE 10–6. Student administration of a cocurricular program

STUDENT GOVERNMENT

Among the many student leadership opportunities in the cocurricular program, the most traditional is the student council. It is also frequently the most ineffective because it is seldom given anything important to do. An obvious effort to provide a framework wherein students may learn principles and practices of a republican form of government, it often reflects the sort of rubber stamp congress characteristics of those nations in the throes of a government by benevolent despotism.

Obviously no principal, nor any school district, would give total control of the school to an organized group of students no matter how democratically elected. However, if the student government organization is to be something more than play acting, it must have responsibility for some significant aspects of student life. Moreover, the value in having a strong student government extends beyond simply providing leadership opportunities for students and teaching the principles of representative democracy in an action setting. It can provide administrators, faculty, and community with important insights and excellent decision-making to enhance all aspects of the school program. A rich source of wisdom exists among students, and it is a wise school staff who uses student government as one way to tap this wisdom.

Student Government as a Problem-Solving Group

The best way to make maximum use of the organization for the benefit of students and school is to follow the same principles of conduct that should be followed in the constitution of any task force team. These principles, amplified in chapter 2 are as follows:

1. Define the problem to be addressed. Whether it's an increase in vandalism or vitriolic complaints about the school lunch program, solicit opinions about root causes and lead the group to the development of a problem statement. Getting to the real problem will require an examination of symptoms.

2. Determine whether the group is to be charged with decision making or whether it is to be advisory. The degree of final decision-making authority with respect to a solution to be implemented will vary by issue, by the maturity level of the group, and by the level of problem-solving sophistication of the group. Care should be taken by the principal or the student government advisor to provide at least some decision-making latitude and responsibility for the group, however. Students, as well as adults, soon tire of simply being a "sounding board." Little is learned beyond a soon reached point if the only responsibility is to venture an opinion. Moreover, the administration is after help and the reason for engaging in decision involvement is to get better decisions.

3. Establish essential conditions which decisions must fit if the student governmental body, or a task force from this body, is to be given at least some active responsibility. All decision-making bodies must operate within a world of constraints. Review laws and school district policies with the group. Discuss community attitudes. Advise the group about budgetary constraints. Develop a list of essential conditions that must be met for a decision to be acceptable. This list need not be elaborate; it is simply to keep the student task force from expending great amounts of energy in developing a solution which can't be implemented. This latter will only result in great disappointment, resentment, and the loss of credibility by the principal or advisor.

4. Cooperatively set realistic target dates for completion of the phases of the project. Establish regular reporting dates and provide help to the group. Use the systematic planning procedure discussed in chapter 23.

What kinds of projects are possible? The following are some of the possible areas of general importance to the school and its students which a student government organization can investigate and assume at least some responsibility for:

- Organize tutorials for students
- Volunteer work programs for school or community improvement (services might include clerical and custodial)
- Intramural program
- Tutoring in the elementary schools
- Mini-courses
- Social and political action programs
- Cafeteria, including participation in menu planning
- Needs assessment of student activity program
- Program evaluation

This is not to suggest that the student government body should not also be involved in the more traditional social activities, such as sponsoring dances and rallies. It is just that such an organization can also provide a wide variety of useful services as well, and it is in the performing of these services that the greatest opportunity for leadership development may come.

SUMMARY

This chapter has examined the several aspects of the high school cocurricular activities program. Cocurricular programs are not inherently balanced and must be deliberately planned if the program is to be educationally sound. Good management practices are crucial. Certain essential steps in the organization and administration of the program should be followed, beginning with a sound and agreed on philosophic base and including needs assessments, rules and regulations, job descriptions of those who will serve as advisors and managers of program components, financial procedures, and a system of evaluation.

ENDNOTES

1. We prefer the term *cocurricular* to *extracurricular* primarily because we view these activities as an integral part of the high school rather than as an adjunct.

2. See chapter 17 for a discussion of the four selfs: intellectual, emotional, physical, and social.

3. L. V. Koos (ed.), *Extra Curricular Activities* (Bloomington, Ill.: Illinois Public Schools Publishing Co., 1926).

4. Charles P. Foster, *Extra-Curricular Activities in the High School* (Chicago: Johnson Publishing Co., 1925).

5. Davis V. Meek, 344 F.Supp. 298 at 301 (N.D. Ohio, 1972). A complete discussion about the issue of whether participation in cocurricular activities is a right or a privilege is contained in chapter 5.

6. The evaluation effort provides an excellent opportunity to involve students and community members in a useful activity. It is an important task because it creates a situation wherein the community can better understand the several purposes of the program, and it will give the administrator new insights as well.

7. Emory Stoops et al., *Handbook of Educational Administration* (Boston: Allyn and Bacon, 1975), p. 472.

8. One could, of course, simply ask respondents what their income is, but this is often resented. What the administrator wants is to be able to assess the degree of heterogeneity of participants in the various activities, and the suggested questionnaire item is probably sufficient to do this.

9. Expressed student interest in a particular activity does not always indicate the amount of participation that will result if the activity is incorporated. I remember, with amusement, an interest assessment conducted when I was principal of a small high school in Michigan several years ago. On the basis of a survey, a mixed chorale was initiated and students who had responded affirmatively to the question, "Should Waldron have a modern music chorale?" were scheduled for an organizational meeting. Janet was one such student. She came to me and informed me that she was not going to attend the meeting. "Why not?" was my reply. "I don't want to sing in such a group." "Then, why did you respond as you did on the questionnaire?" "Well, Mr. Hughes, I think we should *have* such a chorale; it would be good for some of the kids, but I certainly don't want to be a part of it!"

10. Reported in Bruce Evans and Hilmar Wagner, "Have Student Activities Costs Gotten Out of Hand?" *NASSP Bulletin* 55 (September, 1971): 22–23. This article contains a good bibliography on the subject.

11. Ibid., p. 24.

BIBLIOGRAPHY

Buser, Robert L. "What's Happening in Student Activities in the Schools of the Seventies?" *NASSP Bulletin* 55 (September 1971): 1–9.

Coleman, James S. *Youth: Transition to Adulthood.* Chicago: University of Chicago Press, 1974.

Evans, Bruce, and Wagner, Hilmar. "Have Student Activities Costs Gotten Out of Hand?" *NASSP Bulletin* 55 (September 1971): 22–33.

Foster, Charles P. *Extra-Curricular Activities in the High School.* Chicago: Johnson Publishing Co., 1925.

Frederick, Robert W. *The Third Curriculum.* New York: Appleton-Century-Crofts, 1959.

Keith, Kent. *The Silent Majority: The Problem of Apathy and the Student Council.* Washington D.C.: N.A.S.C., 1971.

Koos, L. V. (ed.) *Extra Curricular Activities.* Twenty-Fifth Yearbook of the National Society for the Study of Education, Bloomington, Illinois: Illinois Public Schools Publishing Co., 1926.

Robbins, Jerry H. "Hot Spots in Student Activities: How to Deal with Them." *NASSP Bulletin* 55 (September 1971): 34–43.

Stoops, Emory; Rafferty, Max; and Johnson, Russell E. *Handbook of Educational Administration.* Boston: Allyn and Bacon, 1975. (See chapter 18 especially.)

Student Activities in Secondary Schools: A Bibliography. Reston, Virginia: National Association of Secondary School Principals, 1974.

Chapter Eleven

Organizing Secondary School Instruction

If curriculum can be defined most simply as *what* is taught in the school, then instruction is the *how*—the methods and techniques that aid students in their learning. The emphasis in instruction should be on learning and not on teaching, but obviously both are significant.

Instruction is the lifeblood of the school. It is the process by which content or curriculum is transported to the student. Instruction, however, requires a learner who gains insight, acquires information, and forms values not only from the context of the curriculum but also through the processes by which the content is presented—instruction. Therefore, the entire learning environment of the school constantly provides content for learning. This entwining of curriculum and instruction forces school administrators to look very carefully not only at what they teach in the schools but at how they teach it, for the medium is truly the message.

Consideration of instruction as the process of providing content to the learner presents several major problems to the thoughtful organizer of the school program. These can best be presented as four questions:

1. What instructional processes should be used?
2. How do these processes accommodate individual differences?

3. What curricular overtones will be created by specific instructional styles?
4. What are the implications of these instructional processes for the other organizational components of the school?

Answers to these questions are not necessarily required, but principals should be aware of the implications of each.

DIVERSIFIED INSTRUCTIONAL PROCESSES

Instruction can take place according to different formats. Types of instruction can be divided into several basic categories:

1. Lecture presentation or demonstration
2. Discussion
3. Laboratory Activities
   a. Group or individual
   b. Independent study

Each category presents a different mode for student learning. The purpose of instruction and the expected outcomes should be major factors in determining which instructional type should be used. For example, if the purpose of instruction is to introduce or present an overview of a topic, a lecture presentation to a large group might be best. On the other hand, if the anticipated outcome is the modification of values, then an instructional format that directly involves the learner (such as a laboratory or discussion) would be more effective. Figure 11-1 presents the major purposes of different categories of instruction. Note that each category also has certain group size recommendations.

Accommodating Individual Differences

The question of how these processes allow for individual differences may be viewed from three different perspectives:

1. Instructional process applied to student ability.

2. Instructional process applied to different individual learning styles.
3. Instructional process applied to individual human or psychological needs.

Earlier we considered factors regarding the nature of the learner, such as the range of student achievement levels as well as the internal variation in talent or ability levels within a child. The complexity of the variations between and within children show the futility of efforts to provide any type of permanent or semi-permanent grouping of children for instruction based on ability and achievement. The variation in talents would require many groups, and they would need constant reorganizing. While certain kinds of learning groups are necessary,

I. Presentation	II. Discussion
Build concepts through information Stimulate inquiry Enrich course Relate course to reality Make assignments	Raise questions Report experience Discuss ideas Generalize Form opinions Plan independent study
Usually most efficient and effective in large groups.	Usually most efficient and effective in small groups (7–15 persons).

III. Laboratory Activities

Individual Study	Purpose	Independent Study
Student performed directed	Build concepts and principles through action and viewing Practice skills	Student directed planned performed evaluated
Teacher directed planned evaluated managed	Apply ideas Develop investigative skills Develop problem-solving techniques Develop evaluation skills	Teacher advised

These activities may be small-group (2 or more) or individual in nature. These activities can be either scheduled or unscheduled.

FIGURE 11-1. Categories of instruction and major purposes

they must be kept flexible in order to provide for the individual differences within the group. In order to do this, the entire curriculum needed by the slowest to the most advanced student must be available.

The problem of instruction is further complicated by the differing student curriculum needs previously discussed.

The flexibility required to achieve the extent of diversification of instruction necessary to meet the high degree of differences within any group of children will demand techniques different from those most often used in traditional classrooms. A great deal of independent learning is necessary unless tremendous improvements occur in the traditional student-staff ratios. Students must be able to work without the constant direction of the teacher because of the directions they must go.

Student self-direction can be accommodated in two ways. One way is not to attempt to meet every individual difference or need, but to simply say, "It is not humanly possible to individualize instruction; therefore, I won't worry about it and I'll simply do the best I can in a group situation." The second approach is to accept the philosophy that students need to develop the skill of independent learning and that instruction can be organized for them in meaningful ways for individual consumption. Students learn independent learning skills by practicing them, and with practice all students can become proficient independent learners. Obviously, neither answer in its extreme form is satisfactory, but together they represent a continuum along which instruction can take place. There should be balance between group activities and individual tasks.

No matter what the organizational design, it is apparent that within any classroom a great variety of instructional activities must be going on simultaneously in order to begin to meet demands of individual differences. However, the differences in learning styles as described by French,[1] in addition to the relationship of instruction technique to intended outcomes,

should prevent one from thinking that individualized instruction always means independent work. Our knowledge of human needs indicates that, more often than not, small group activities will best meet security and belonging needs as well as those associated with self-esteem.

Influence of School Climate on Instruction

Most experienced educators will say that they can go into a classroom and after only a few minutes have a very good feel for the amount of learning that is taking place in that room. What are they feeling? How can they make such a quick judgment? Words such as *warmth, busyness,* and *climate* are usually part of their answers. Numerous studies have tried to determine the implications of teacher behavior for student learning and attitude development. The organization of instruction as well as the behavior of individual teachers affects what is actually learned in the school. For example, a child will learn independent study skills only if given numerous opportunities to practice them. A child will learn how to think and discuss in a group situation only if given numerous opportunities to practice discussion. Some of the more recent studies on nonverbal teaching behavior also show that teachers increasingly direct student learning simply by their support or rejection of actions.

Instructional Implications for Program Organization

In a system of instruction where a great variety of activities are going on simultaneously and where many independent activities occur, special care should be taken for the actual progress and development of the individual child. A real danger exists that teachers may become so busy running a complex individualized system that they lose sight of the individual child in the process.

Even a school that is doing all the right things to create a proper individualized instructional system can create a serious problem if individual children are neglected in the process.

INDIVIDUALIZED INSTRUCTION

Schools must give adequate attention to placing individual students in the learning environment. Two basic but overlapping approaches exist for matching students to the proper learning activities. One method is to identify common needs of students and place them in a group formed for the purposes of offering instruction to fulfill that need. (Grouping methods and techniques are discussed in the next chapter.) The other approach requires no particular grouping consideration for the placement of a child into a class, other than possibly heterogeneity, but rather deals with individual differences in a diagnostic-prescriptive manner after the students are assigned to the classroom.

Diagnostic-Prescriptive

A diagnostic-prescriptive approach to teaching begins with a basic set of learning goals and objectives for the students. A general, as well as specific, diagnosis is conducted for each pupil in order to determine which goals and objectives have been previously met. This serves as a basis for determining what objectives would be appropriate for the next block of instructional time. The diagnosis can assess students' skill development, determine needs, and explore learning styles. Based on the diagnosis, a prescription is prepared as a list of objectives to be met. Upon the establishment of a prescription, a plan is constructed consisting of appropriate lessons and activities designed to meet the objectives. The plan can be in the form of a teacher-directed lesson for all students working on the same objective, or it may be carried out as a lab activity, discussion group, learning package, or independent study project. The amount of time spent on directed group teach-

ing is often reduced from around 90 percent to somewhere around 50 percent when a diagnostic prescriptive approach is used. In an individualized system, the balance of the teacher's time is taken up by the functions of diagnosis, preparation of prescriptions, planning, and evaluating.

Evaluation has unique characteristics in an individualized system. With individual student pacing, as well as students working on different learning goals, evaluation no longer can be a tightly scheduled function. Unit tests given to every pupil at the same time are no longer appropriate. Instead, tests are given to students who have indicated they are ready or when the teacher thinks they should be prepared. Teachers, of course, are at liberty to schedule an examination, but the decision is based on the knowledge of an individual student's progress and not on the basis of class progress or administrative convenience. Evaluation in the diagnostic-prescriptive format also must be tied directly to the objectives established at the beginning of the program. If, for example, the objective was for the student to be able to identify the main idea of a story, then the evaluation item must test whether the student can identify the main idea of the story—nothing more, nothing less. (See figure 11-2.)

Diagnostic-prescriptive teaching works best for those areas of instruction where specific skills can be identified and where it is important for a child to be able to perform a particular skill before a more advanced learning can take place. Secondary school subjects where this system is most effective would include certain language arts skills such as composition writing, mechanics of English, and grammar; social studies, geography skills; science, basic laboratory skills; and mathematics, all basic functions. Many excellent diagnostic-prescriptive programs can also be developed in foreign languages, physical education, health, industrial arts, home economics, and in many of the vocational areas.

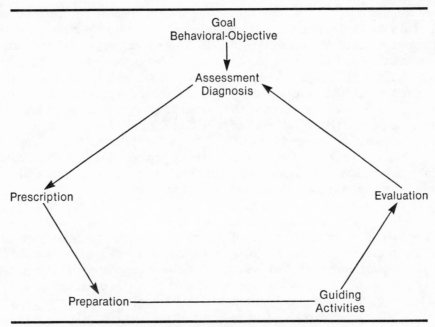

FIGURE 11–2.   A model for diagnostic-prescriptive teaching

Behavioral Objectives

A key element for most of the independent instructional tools is the adequate specification of instructional objectives. In most cases, well-stated behavioral objectives are desirable because they provide good direction to the student in knowing how to chart his or her independent learning course. A good behavioral objective has four major characteristics:

1. It is written for the learner, using terms that students can understand.
2. It states the conditions or "givens" under which the student is to perform or be tested.
3. It identifies the specific behavior or action expected of the student.
4. It indicates a performance level or how well the student must do on that objective. Example: Given six short stories and a list of possible main ideas for each, you will identify the correct main idea for five of

the six stories. This objective (a) is written to the student, (b) states the conditions, "given six short stories and a list of possible main ideas," (c) identifies the specific behavior desired, "identify the correct main idea," and (d) indicates the performance level, "for five of the six stories."

Many of the materials published today include lists of behavioral objectives that can be used by teachers to create independent learning materials.[2]

Instructional Tools for Individualization

We have emphasized individualized instruction and the need to provide a variety of self-instructional activities for students in order to make such a system functional. The logical question is how to organize or create materials for self-instruction. Must each teacher develop materials?

Excellent commercial materials are now available for individualized systems, and more are becoming available each year. In areas such as reading and math, schools can purchase an entire system for a wide range of student achievement levels. Other material can be organized and coordinated for instruction by teachers using that material. Teachers, of course, should also continue to use their own material.

The real problem, however, is organizing materials in a systematic way so that they are adequately available to students when they need them, adequately self-instructional so that the teachers using that material. Teachers, of and adequately organized to assure proper instructional sequencing, recording, and evaluation.

Several techniques have been developed in recent years to achieve these goals. Among them are the use of learning packages, independent study contracts, and learning laboratories. Each represents a way of matching instructional goals to appropriate learning objectives, and in turn to appropriate materials, resources, and activities.

Learning Packages

Simply stated, a learning package is a prepackaged self-instructional lesson. It includes:

1. A statement of purpose.
2. Specific goal(s) and objective(s).
3. A list of resources or activities designed to aid the student in achieving the stated objective(s).
4. A form of evaluation to allow the student and the teacher to determine if the instructional goal has been achieved.

The basic purpose of the learning package is to organize an instructional module or lesson in such a way as to make it as self-instructional as possible, thus providing individualized instruction in the classroom. The teacher's role in this kind of learning activity is to assign, or help

the student select, a particular set of learning packages and to help explain anything in the learning package that is not understood. This is done either on an individual basis or with several students with similar problems. Learning packages are designed to be self-instructional in order to provide necessary teacher freedom as well as flexibility for individualized instruction.

The basic strategy for movement through a learning package follows the diagnositic-prescriptive format, and is illustrated by the flowchart in figure 11-3.

Learning packages are largely teachermade, often with teams of teachers sharing in their construction. Some commercial packages are available and some package exchange arrangements are possible. However, the fact that specific resources often unique to the teacher-author-school are necessary for the effective use of the package make the transfer to other schools difficult.

Learning packages can vary greatly in length and complexity. A learning package may be a simple one-page lesson, or it may be a multiple-page complex unit of instruction with many objectives and several sublessons within it.

Learning packages are to be used as a form of directed independent study. The underlying purposes are to aid in the individualization of instruction by freeing the teacher from constant presentation of material to students, and providing students with learning activities appropriate to their instructional needs. This then allows the teacher to concentrate on other aspects of instruction.

The learning package should, however, not become the only instructional method used. It must be used in conjunction with learning laboratories, lectures, discussion groups, and other forms of instruction, including independent study. If used to excess it will not be successful. There are numerous resources available that go into greater detail regarding construction of learning packages. A number of these are listed in the bibliography of this chapter.

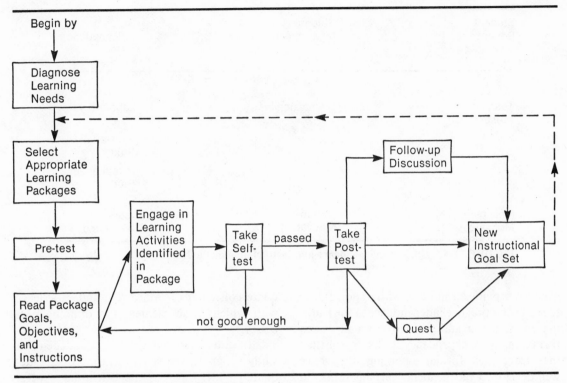

FIGURE 11-3.   Learning package flowchart

Independent Study

Two of the generally stated goals for secondary student development are "the development of independence" and "the development of purpose." Traditional approaches to organization of instruction tends to limit, restrict, or inhibit these desired goals, however. Instruction that is heavily teacher-directed tends to foster dependence rather than independence. If student interdependence and independence with purpose are desired, then instruction must be organized to achieve it. This is one of the underlying themes of the walkabout concept of Gibbons discussed in chapter 10.

The categories of instruction shown in figure 11-1 describe the four different forms of instruction, but no judgments are made on any particular desired instructional behavior. However, once consideration is given to concerns of

student dependence, interdependence, and independence, certain desired patterns can be established. When applied to a dependence-independence continuum, instructional formats can be shown to contribute heavily to goal achievement. (See figure 11-4.)

There is a need for every student to develop a personal model for learning and behavior that is applicable to everyday life. There's an old Chinese proverb that says, "Feed a man a fish and he will eat for the day; teach a man to fish and he will eat for a lifetime." This applies directly to the needs for students to become independent learners. In order to move students toward independent learning, there must be a planned program of instruction in which the student is expected and allowed to become a purposeful independent learner, i.e., a responsible individual who is less dependent upon the teacher and others. Consequently, the school

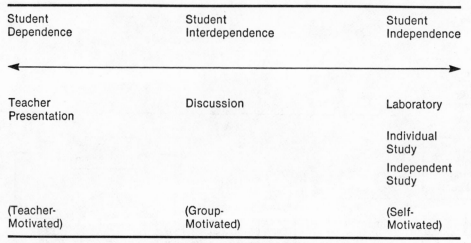

Student Dependence	Student Interdependence	Student Independence
Teacher Presentation	Discussion	Laboratory
		Individual Study
		Independent Study
(Teacher-Motivated)	(Group-Motivated)	(Self-Motivated)

FIGURE 11–4. Student independence and instructional methods

needs to provide all students with opportunities to study and practice independence in the learning environment and then to gradually ween them away from dependency so that by the time they leave their formal schooling, they have well-developed independent learning skills. In order to achieve the desired outcomes, each student must assume a responsible role in his or her own educational growth. Their responsibility cannot develop unless some intellectual and physical freedom exists. Students can be expected to grow in their ability to be supervised less frequently only if they are given opportunities to function without supervision for longer and longer periods of time.

Through a cooperative effort among students and teachers, the student should learn how to learn in proportion to his or her capabilities and interests. Eventually, the learner should become the manager of major aspects of his or her own educational program. As the student assumes a greater share of this responsibility, the role of the teacher becomes proportionately less that of an instructional manager and more that of an adviser. It must be recognized that it is necessary for the student to have developed and continue to maintain an ade-

quate collection of knowledge and experience with which to supplement the thinking processes.

In order to implement a good independent study program, the school must provide adequately staffed and equipped learning spaces. These spaces must reflect the needs and interests of the students in their educational development. General library services as well as specialized departmental learning centers are desired.

A variety of type of learning experiences may be considered as independent study program activities. Students may participate in homework and depth projects, walkabout challenge projects, enrichment courses, regularly scheduled classes, informal discussion, and other activities that are consistent with the purposes of the independent study phase of instruction.

Specific independent study objectives for students include the following:

1. Assume an increased responsibility for making decisions relative to his or her education.

2. Develop an increased control over his or her impulse behavior.

3. Become a more purposeful, independent learner by achieving the higher degree of interdependence, venturesomeness, resourcefulness, goal directedness, and persistence.

4. Develop an increased capacity to solve problems and learn to use the critical and creative thinking processes.

5. Acquire relevant subject matter content.

6. Develop an increased interest in learning.

7. Achieve emotional independence of parents and other adults.

8. Achieve more and more mature relationships with peers of both sexes.

9. Desire and achieve socially responsible behavior by becoming more self-disciplined.

10. Acquire a set of values in an ethical system and a guide to behavior.

The implementation of an effective independent study program will be a new activity for many schools. Consider the following list of suggestions to implement such a program:

1. Provide time for students and staff members to plan, perform, and evaluate the various independent study activities.

2. Provide adequate facilities and equipment for the program.

3. Encourage staff members to implement the program.

4. Create a department of independent study.

5. Assign a regular member of the staff, preferably in a full-time position, as the independent study coordinator.

6. Have the coordinator implement an orientation to independent study program for students, staff, and the community.

7. Implement a preparatory and inservice education program for the staff.

8. Coordinate all aspects of the program through the department of independent study and librarians.

9. Have all teachers participate in the program as independent study advisors.

10. Designate one member of each department as the independent study coordinator for that department.

11. Require all students to participate in the independent study program at a level commensurate with their ability, interests, and needs.

12. Grant credit to students who successfully complete their required components of the independent study program.

13. Establish the independence program at a number of formal levels, including homework, depth projects, quest projects, and enrichment courses.

14. In order to adequately prepare students for independent study, teachers should:
   a. Provide students with the opportunity to develop skills necessary to continue learning.
   b. Provide investigative, laboratory, and independent study opportunities.
   c. Consider the learning style of the students.
   d. Encourage creativity on the part of the student.
   e. Encourage greater independence on the part of the student.

15. Well-designed independent study activities should:
   a. Allow the student to *perform* the activity.
   b. Allow the students to *share in the direction* of the activity.
   c. Provide increased time spans between formal supervisory contacts as the student progresses through the course.
   d. Provide opportunity for student evaluation of the performance and direction phases.
   e. Provide opportunity for group student planning of all phases of the learning activity.
   f. Include opportunity for individual student planning for all phases of the learning activity.

16. Each student participating in advanced forms of independent study should sign an appropriate contact that states purpose, completion date, conference dates, etc.[3]

See figure 11-5 for a complete independent study planning document.

Date Proposed_____

Date Approved_____

Date Due   _____

5 copies:

1. Student
2. Advisor
3. Dept. Quest Coordinator
4. School Quest Coordinator
5. Parents

High School Quest Agreement

_____ Homeroom #_____ Grade_____

Last Name   First Name   & Teacher

                            Subject Teacher _____ Room_____

Subject _____ Advisor _____ Room_____

Minor _____ Minor _____ Room_____

Subject(s)   Advisor(s)

_____ _____ Room_____

Community _____ _____ Room_____

Resource(s)   Organization   Contact Person

Quest Title_____

Brief Description:

1. What do you want to do?

2. Why do you want to do it?

3. How do you want to do it?

4. How do you want to present and evaluate it?

   a. Presentation: (check one)   Written   _____

                                    Oral   _____

                                    Seminar   _____

                                    Model   _____

                                    Other: (specify)_____

   b. Evaluation: Method used as mutually agreed upon between advisor and student:

Comment:

5. Approximate time required to complete quest project: (check one)

   a. year _____   c. quarter _____

   b. semester _____   d. no. of weeks _____

I, _____, enter into the above described Quest Agreement with full knowledge and acceptance of the following:

1. I assume full responsibility for my regular class attendance and assignment as required by the individual department.

2. I assume full responsibility of my conduct during scheduled and unscheduled time for pursuing my quest project.

3. I assume full responsibility of out-of-school visitation through regular school procedure of obtaining excursion permit.

4. I assume full responsibility of meeting conferences, appointments, and deadlines with my advisor and/or other significant person.

(continued)

5. I assume full responsibility of any other activities which may be mutually agreed upon.

6. I agree that the end product of my quest project may be submitted to the school library for display and sharing.

If I fail to comply with the above mentioned conditions, appropriate action will be taken as mutually agreed upon by my advisor and myself.

Comment: _____

_____

_____

_____

_____

Class attendance: Check appropriate boxes
Large Group: excused ☐   unexcused ☐
Small Group: excused ☐   unexcused ☐   Signed_____
Medium Group: excused ☐   unexcused ☐   on this____day of_____19___.
Grading/Credit: (check one)
    Quest Grade and Credit   ☐
    Regular Class Grade and Credit   ☐   _____
                                  Signature of Advisor

High School Quest Agreement   3 copies:
Conference Schedule   1. Student
                                     2. Advisor
                                     3. School Quest
                                        Coordinator

                                     Grade_____

_____
     Last Name   First Name

Advisor_____

Quest   Title:_____

It is agreed that both the student and advisor will keep this Conference Schedule current. A copy of this schedule is to be submitted to the School Quest Coordinator at the completion of the quest project.

Conferences: Comment

_____   _____
      date   _____

_____   _____
      date   _____

_____   _____
      date   _____

_____   _____
      date   _____

_____   _____
      date   _____

(continued)

_____ _____
date   _____

_____ _____
date   _____

_____ _____
date   _____

_____ _____
date   _____

Quest Evaluation

Date Approved _____   Date Completed _____

Project Completed for: (check one)

_____   _____ _____
Name of Student   Grade R. R. Teacher

1. Quarter:

_____   _____
Advisor   Dept.

1st__ 2nd__ 3rd__ 4th__

_____   _____
Minor Advisor (if any) Minor Dept. (if any)

2. Semester:
   1st_____ 2nd_____
3. Year:_____
4. Number of weeks____

_____ had successfully completed his/her quest project titled
Name of Student

_____
_____

and is evaluated as follows:

   1. In place of regular class:_____ _____
                               Name of Course   Grade

   2. Recognition for quest: (check one if applicable)
     A. In place of regular class_____
     B. In addition to regular class_____

   3. Quest for credit:_____ _____
                               Name of Course   Grade

6 copies:
   1. Student
   2. Advisor
   3. Dept. Quest Coordinator
   4. School Quest Coordinator
   5. Counselor
   6. Parents

_____
Signature of Advisor

_____
Signature of Minor Advisor (if any)

FIGURE 11–5.   Independent study contract

Learning Laboratories

Independent study takes many different forms. The learning package previously discussed represents one form of independent but teacher-planned activity. The independent study contracts represents another. Still another is the resource laboratory, or learning laboratory.

Independent study usually requires gathering resources for student use on special projects and investigations that go beyond the normal function of a library or media center. Often, homework or class-assigned independent study activities require the use of teacher-prepared materials, such as worksheets, learning packages, special textbooks, or other teacher-gathered items. More advanced independent study may require sophisticated equipment, needing the expertise of departmental staff to supervise and monitor, such as lab equipment, computer equipment, or various kinds of tools. For these reasons, a strong independent study program often needs to be supported by a series of specialized learning labs operated and maintained by instructional departments. The following suggestions and guidelines are proposed for such learning laboratories:

1. Each department operates a learning laboratory that is fully equipped with investigative and manipulative equipment that are considered to be the tools of the trade.
2. Within each learning lab are learning aids such as books, filmstrips, maps, newspapers, motion pictures, pamphlets, periodicals, phonograph records, slides, pictures, and video and audiotape equipment.
3. Each lab is equipped with individual study stations that are quiet and free from distraction.
4. Each lab provides quiet areas for student-teacher conferences.
5. Each learning lab is open for individual and group investigations throughout the day.
6. The learning lab is staffed by instructional staff members.
7. The learning lab is supervised throughout the day by a noncertified staff member who has received some training and supervision in library activities.
8. Each learning lab has an environmental climate appropriate to the nature of the activity and subject matter studied.
9. The library or media center is still the headquarters for the network of resource or learning centers.
10. All carriers of information and ideas are catalogued in the library.
11. Study in the library is restricted to that necessitating the use of library carriers.
12. The learning lab is opened to all study activities related to that particular discipline. Teacher offices or work space are adjacent to the learning lab.
13. The chairperson of the department is responsible for staffing and maintaining the learning lab in such a way as to maximize its available use to students.
14. All teachers within a department contribute to supplying and supporting the learning lab.
15. A separate classroom, or in some cases a designated area within the media center, is available to each department to develop as a departmental resource area.

SUMMARY

A diversified system of instruction requires a new role for most teachers. Extensive preparation is needed to develop a variety of learning goals, objectives, and activities, so that an individualized plan can be developed for each student. The teacher's role in the classroom is largely one of management, guiding students through a variety of activities, such as learning packages, independent study, or learning laboratories that have been prepared in advance of the class session.

The principal must have an understanding of diversified instruction and exhibit an expectation of such instruction from the teachers rather than an expectation for large group, teacher-presentation recitation style.

ENDNOTES

1. Russell French, "Teaching Strategies and Learning Processes," *Educational Considerations* (Fall 1975): 27-28.
2. Instructional Objectives Exchange (IOX), Box 24095, Los Angeles, Calif. 90024. IOX has collections at the secondary level in the following areas: language arts: reading, comprehension, structural analysis, composition, reference skills, listening, oral expression and journalism, grammar, mechanics and usage, English literature. Other areas include general mathematics, business education, home economics, auto mechanics, electronics, general metals, mechanical drawing, woodworking, American history, geography, biology, and Spanish. A current catalog can be obtained by writing to the above address.
3. Quoted from Lee Renz, an excerpt from a 1970 rough draft of a dissertation.

BIBLIOGRAPHY

Coppedge, Lloyd L. "Characteristics of Individualized Instruction." *Clearing House* 48 (January 1974): 272-277

Dagnon, Carol, and Spuck, Dennis W. "A Role for Computers In Individualizing Education and It's Not Teaching." *Phi Delta Kappan* 58 (February 1977): 460.

Davidson, Helen H., and Lang, Gerhard. "Children's Perceptions of Their Teacher's Feeling Toward Them Related to Self-Perception, School Achievement, and Behavior." *Journal of Experimental Education* 29 (December 1960): 107-118.

Duchastel, Philipe C., and Merrill, Paul F. "Effects of Behavioral Objectives on Learning: A Review of Empirical Studies." *Review of Educational Research* 43 (May 1973): 53-69.

Everson, Margaret. "Recipe for Continuous Progress." *American Secondary Education* (June 1971): 13.

Gilstrap, Robert L., and Martin, William R. *Current Strategies for Teachers: A Resource for Personalizing Instruction.* Pacific Palisades, Calif.: Goodyear, 1975.

Glines, Don E. *Creating Humane Schools.* Mankato, Minn.: Campus Publishers, 1971, pp. 11-20.

Gronlund, Norman E. *Individualizing Classroom Instruction.* New York: MacMillan, 1974.

Henderson, Judith E., and Lanier, Perry E. "What Teachers Need to Know and Teach (for Survival on the Planet)." *Journal of Teacher Education* 24 (Spring 1973): 4-16.

Hunsaker, Johanna S., and Ray, Will. *The Group Centered Classroom: Alternative to Individualized Instruction? Educational Leadership* 34 (February 1977): 366-369.

Individually Prescribed Instruction. Philadelphia: Research for Better Schools, Inc., undated (promotional literature).

Kraener, James D. "Individualized Education: Some Implications for Media." *Programmed Learning and Educational Technology* 10 (September 1973): 342-346.

Ritter, Myron W. "Individualized Study in Coatesville." *National Association of Secondary School Principals Bulletin* (November 1970): 70-78.

Stuckley, Michael H., and O'Dell, Robert T. "The Open Learning Model Using Computer Instruction." *Educational Technology* 26 (February 1976): 39-42.

Trump, J. Lloyd. "The Future in American Secondary Schools." *American Secondary Education* 6 (March 1976): 4-7.

Trump, J. Lloyd, and Georgiades, William. "Doing Better With What You Have: NASSP Model School's Project." *National Association of Secondary School Principal's Bulletin* (May 1970).

Ubben, Gerald C. "A Look at Non-Gradedness and Self-Paced Learning." *Audio-Visual Instruction* (February 1970).

Ubben, Gerald C. "Individualized Instruction: Why Open Spaces?" *Education Technology* (November 1974): 28–29.

Ubben, Gerald C. "The Role of the Learning Package in an Individualized Instruction Program." *Journal of Secondary Education* 46 (May 1972): 206–209.

Ubben, Gerald C., and Gargurich, Thomas. "Independent Study, Cherry Hill High School East: An Interview." *The Principal's Audio Journal* I (December 1974) Side A.

Weinstock, Ruth. *The Greening of the High School.* New York: Educational Facilities Laboratories, Inc., 1973, p. 19.

Chapter Twelve

Deployment of Staff

One of the greatest responsibilities assigned to the principal is organizing and assigning staff in the school. Included in normal staffing responsibilities is the deployment of all employees and volunteer workers to the instructional program and service functions of the school. Often, central office administrators and supervisors have a hand in these assignments, but the basic responsibility usually rests with the principal.

Inherent in any good staffing design is optimal utilization of staff.[1] Staff planning must take into account the present needs and functions of the members of the organization as well as the long-range goals and plans of the school that might modify hiring practices in the future.

Traditionally, staffing has been by simple unit-classroom analysis, that is, one teacher, one group of students, one room, sometimes one instructional format, and sometimes one subject. Staffing plans have been built and modified from year to year using this basic classroom unit. Such a procedure is very restrictive, and can be dysfunctional, particularly when used in conjunction with some of the curricular, instructional, and grouping ideas presented in previous chapters.

STAFFING ANALYSIS

There are three basic dimensions to staffing: single-to-multiple staff assignments, general-ized or specialized curricular assignments, and division of teaching functions.

Single-to-multiple staff assignments describe the number and kinds of people that are to work together in the organization. Such assignments might require a single staff member or multiple staffing arrangements. The simplest is the single teacher. The complexity of staffing patterns can be increased by adding teacher aides or forming a collegial team arrangement with co-equals. Finally, assignments might fulfill a differentiated staffing pattern that includes several teaching levels, such as master teacher, teacher, and teacher intern, as well as several classifications of support personnel, including instructional aide, clerk, student aides, volunteers, etc. (See figure 12–1.)

The continuum of generalized and specialized assignments relates teacher assignments to the curricular and instructional program of the school. A generalized assignment requires one teacher to teach many subjects, the extreme being the one-room school house where the teacher has responsibility for all grades as well. Specialization is introduced through the gradual narrowing of the grade span and content areas for which a teacher has responsibility. Instead of teaching a dozen or more subjects, as is commonly done in elementary schools, a teacher would share the age span and instructional load with other teachers and would be responsible for preparations in a few subjects

157

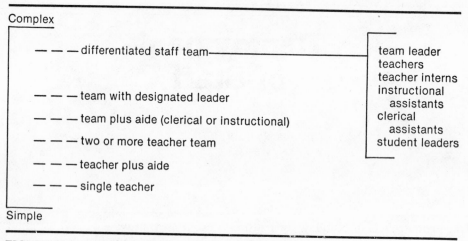

FIGURE 12–1. Staffing assignments—simple to complex

or a fused curricular area, such as social studies or language arts. The extreme of specialization is responsibility for a single subject offering within the school for a homogeneously grouped class. These last two specialization categories have led to a departmentalized form of staffing within the school. (See figure 12–2.)

The relationships of staffing to curriculum and staffing to instruction can be analyzed by considering the two-dimensional relationship of single teachers to teaching teams, as well as the relationship of generalized curricular assignments to specialization. As a result of this analysis, four major staffing relationships emerge: (A) the one-teacher unit in a self-contained classroom with responsibility for all sub-

jects; (B) the one-teacher unit with subject specialization, usually referred to as departmentalization; (C) a teaching team with subject area specialization, referred to as a disciplinary team; and (D) a team with responsibility for all subjects, referred to as an interdisciplinary team. These four staffing relationships are illustrated by the four quadrants of figure 12–3.

None of these four categories are mutually exclusive. Many variations are possible with slight alterations in either the staffing or curricular dimension, including whether the student grouping is heterogeneous or homogeneous. Using the four lettered quadrants of figure 12–3, several common staffing patterns can be described as follows:

Generalization				Specialization
All subjects multi-age	All subjects except P.E. music art	Teach only L.A. S.S. Sci. or Math	Teach only L.A.	Teach only reading or P.E. or science

FIGURE 12–2.

1. A + B requires a one-teacher unit for most curricular areas plus specialists also operating in a one-unit fashion for subject areas such as music, art, and P.E.
2. C/D requires an interdisciplinary team, with teacher specialization of subjects within the team, and a common group of students.
3. C/D + B requires an interdisciplinary team as above with the addition of self-

contained subject specialists for the other parts of the curriculum such as art, music, and P.E.

As can be seen, an almost endless variety of combinations is possible, depending on the particular desires and needs within a given school.

The third staffing dimension, instructional functions, can be added for further analysis to

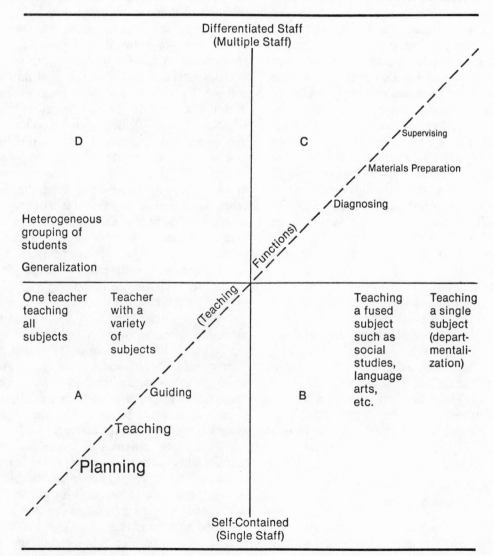

FIGURE 12–3.

any of the designs, particularly a team dimension, permitting specialization in the planning, teaching, guiding, diagnosing, materials preparation, and supervising dimensions. The teaching functions of planning, teaching, guiding, evaluating, developing materials, diagnosing, and supervising represent another way of analyzing the differentiation between specialization and generalization.

A teacher may fulfill the functions for a particular subject or all subjects, or, in concert with other staff members, may carry out increased or reduced responsibilities within these functions. A teacher working alone obviously must always do them all. However, when teachers work within a team arrangement, one member of the team might be responsible for planning and coordinating the reading program, several other teachers might carry out the plan and assume direct teaching responsibility for reading, while yet another staff member or aide may provide only general supervision of children related to reading. This dimension of staffing must be considered as a major factor in determining team working relationships. (See figure 12–3.) Each of these functions must be performed by someone, no matter what the staffing pattern.

Teaching function analysis is useful when designing staffing patterns other than the single-unit system. Teachers are not equally talented at planning, teaching, guiding, evaluating, diagnosing, developing materials, or supervising students, nor do they have the time to do a good job in each of these areas for the entire curriculum. These functions present a way of subdividing responsibilities when multi-unit or team approaches are used in organizing schools.

Considerations for Selecting Particular Staffing Models

Since such a wide variety of staffing patterns is possible, how can anyone determine what is best in a particular situation? The following discussion may be helpful in making such a determination.

Generalization versus Specialization The question of generalization or specialization has gone on for many years under the guise of discussions relating to self-contained versus departmentalized school arrangements in the one-teacher unit classroom. The major argument for generalization has been that one teacher who operates the entire curriculum has ample opportunity for contact with each student across a broad segment of school life. The teacher gets to know a student extremely well over an extended period of time and thus can consider the student in a broad range of social as well as academic settings. The teacher in this situation is aware of the student's development in all subjects. If the student is having difficulty in a particular subject, the teacher may be able to determine the source of difficulty from knowledge about the student's development in other subjects. The major problem of the self-contained, all-subject classroom is the burden placed on the teacher for preparing such a broad range of subjects. It can be overwhelming and ultimately prevent the teacher from adequately preparing in all but a very limited number of subjects.

This problem leads directly to the argument favoring specialization. A teacher with the responsibility of preparing for a reduced number of subjects can do a much more thorough job and can come to the classroom much better prepared. This is particularly important as students become older and require more knowledge from the teacher.

The major weakness of specialization is that a teacher is aware of only a limited portion of the curriculum and is knowledgeable about a student's growth and learning only in that portion of the curriculum; thus, the teacher is not in a good position to judge total learning. If the student is having difficulty in social studies, the teacher may not be aware that the student also has a serious reading problem that may be the underlying cause of the difficulty. A further criticism of specialization is that it forces the teacher to work with a much larger number of children during the day, again reducing the contact with each individual child. Both the arguments for and against specialization and generalization are logical. The best solution probably lies somewhere between the two extremes or may be most effectively resolved with the inclusion of some kind of team teaching.

Single Staff versus Multiple Staff Persuasive arguments can be given on both sides of this question. Reasons favoring self-contained classrooms are as follows:

1. Teacher training and experience traditionally have been for the self-contained classroom. Many teachers favor it because they know it best.
2. Buildings are designed for self-contained classrooms, not for team arrangements, and they simply do not lend themselves to team teaching.
3. Teachers, when placed on teams, develop difficulties in interpersonal relationships because of different personalities, teaching styles, philosophies, etc.
4. Team teaching requires a great deal of additional time on the part of the teacher in planning that could be devoted to students or to preparation of lessons in the self-contained classroom.

Arguments in favor of team teaching are:

1. A teaching team provides variation for the students as they have contact with a set of teachers.
2. Teacher productivity generally increases under a team arrangement since teachers tend to support each other in achieving goals.

3. Flexibility of grouping becomes possible and building level scheduling can be greatly simplified when teachers are working together in a team.
4. The advantages of both specialization and generalization can be obtained when teachers specialize in either or both the curricular and instructional dimension within the team and still have the opportunity to observe the whole student as that student works with the team over the major portion of the day.
5. Individualized instruction can more easily be attained with the team of teachers sharing the variety of instructional tasks necessary to successfully implement an individualized program.
6. Greater consideration of curriculum can be obtained in interdisciplinary programs through a team approach with team members coming from several different disciplines. This results in a school within a school design which allows for greater accountability for learner development.

Departmental versus Interdisciplinary Team Design

Teaching teams can be organized on either a departmental basis where all members of the team teach in the same subject area, or teams can be organized on an interdisciplinary basis where several subjects are combined within a team like language arts, social studies, or science. While initially it would seem that disciplinary teams would be the most compatible with traditional secondary school curricular design, in fact it is often not the best solution to team organization because they are somewhat dysfunctional.

Interdisciplinary teams of the D type or D/C type (figure 12–3) seem to be most functional. Two major problems occur with the creation of disciplinary or C-type teams. They require many students to satisfy the hour-by-hour demand on the team. For example, a team of four social studies teachers could teach from 100 to 120 students per hour for each hour that it operated. This requires not only a fairly large school to supply adequate numbers of students, but it also places very stringent demands upon scheduling priorities.

Disciplinary teams have more difficulty with interpersonal relationships than interdisciplinary teams. When two or more teachers within a given discipline are placed together, the potential for disagreement increases since the opportunity for philosophic and teaching style conflicts is greatest when people have virtually identical assignments. In addition, one teacher's desire for domination conflicts with the attitudes of other members of the team. Interdisciplinary teaming does not face this problem because each teacher has a given area of specialization within the team. Other members of the team do not come into direct conflict over that assignment.

Interdisciplinary teams also have a tremendous advantage for maintaining control and accountability in the large high school. A team of teachers, collectively responsible for a large block of the curriculum and instruction for a particular group of students, can work with them for the majority of the day in a given portion of the building. This provides an environment where control of students is much improved by reducing anonymity, increasing the concentration of instructional knowledge about the student, and increasing responsibility for the education of the student. (See chapter 23 for more details.)

Team Compatibility   Efforts should be made to provide as much team compatibility as possible when teams are initially organized (as well as when making additions or replacements). Some of the items to consider in determining team compatibility are as follows:

1. Do the members have similar teaching philosophies and styles?

2. Do they have similar work habits? Do they come to work early or stay late, have a clean room or a messy room, follow a fairly rigid schedule or a somewhat irregular schedule?
3. Do they fit together with an appropriate combination of curricular and instructional interests and talents?

When formulating teams, the overriding consideration should probably be the individual acceptance by each teacher of the particular staffing and instructional model to be used in the school. This acceptance, of course, can be greatly enhanced by involving the staff in the initial determination of the design. Personnel not accepting the design should be allowed to make other arrangements. Transfers now will greatly ease implementation later. If no other schools in the system can take transfers, dissatisfied staff members will have to be accommodated into the new system. There are three possibilities of what to do with these staff members:

1. The teams can be balanced by assigning dissatisfied members equally among the teams, hoping to reduce their impact or convert them through involvement. However, experience has shown that "One rotten apple *can* spoil the whole bushel."
2. These members of the staff can be grouped together on teams to concentrate their influence in a limited area, hopefully reducing their impact on the entire school. This allows the principal to maintain, at least on paper, a uniform staffing pattern throughout the school.
3. A school can have some teams as well as self-contained classrooms, allowing those unwilling to try a team arrangement to continue to operate in the traditional way.

This latter approach has been found to be desirable. Its major advantage is that it creates an alternative to the team situation not only for the teachers but also for the students and their parents, some of whom may prefer, at least initially, a self-contained situation.

Team Planning

One of the most crucial factors in a successful team operation is adequate planning time and efficient utilization of that time. If at all possible, team planning should occur during the regular school day. Planning should be regularly scheduled, and at least two hours per week are needed in a minimum of one-hour blocks. Each team meeting should have an agenda, prepared by the team and distributed in advance, and each meeting should have a designated chairperson. A secretary for the team should keep minutes of the meeting.

The principal's major task is to develop a schedule that provides adequate planning time and training for the faculty for the efficient utilization of this time. Basically, it requires that all members of the team have their preparation hour at the same time at least twice each week.

A variety of different planning tasks of both a long- and short-term nature needs to be carried out by each team. Effective use of planning time can usually be enhanced by focusing on a particular purpose during a meeting. The following five types of planning meetings are suggested with recommendations regarding frequency.

Goal Setting Meeting   One goal setting meeting should be held each semester to look at the philosophy of the school, the curriculum guidelines existing for its direction, and the identification of goals for the particular group of students for whom the team is responsible. These goals would be long-range in nature and would be things to work toward over a semester or year.

Design Meeting   A design meeting is a planning meeting to select instructional topics and develop instructional units. Principles, objectives, and general ideas for the unit are considered. After the topic has been selected, one team member is usually assigned the responsibility for drafting the unit. When the draft is ready, the team modifies and builds on the design. Specific objectives are listed, overall responsibility for each member of the team is outlined, and the calendar of events is developed with specific target dates. Methods of student evaluation are also planned. One of these meetings is necessary for each new unit, and a minimum of one each quarter or marking period is essential.

Grouping or Scheduling Meeting   This planning meeting outlines activities for the next week or two, defining specific instructional plans, organizing students into appropriate groups, and constructing the weekly calendar and daily schedule. One of these meetings is needed at least once every two weeks, if not weekly.

Situational Meeting   This meeting focuses on individual students. Various students within the group are discussed by the various members of the team to coordinate information and develop plans for learning activities for that child. The teacher/advisor for the particular student has the responsibility of carrying out team decisions. These meetings should probably be held each week, with each teacher/advisor determining which students need to be discussed by the team.

Evaluation Meeting   The major focus of this meeting is the evaluation of the instructional program and units. Questions asked are: Did we achieve our goals? What were our strengths? What were our shortcomings? How well did we function together as a team? One of these meetings should be held immediately after the close of each quarter or immediately after the completion of a major unit.

STAFFING PATTERNS FOR SECONDARY SCHOOLS

Different staffing patterns are possible for any situation from the traditional single teacher, single discipline classroom to a variety of team and differentiated staffing models.

General ideas have been presented for staffing design, curricular arrangements, and instructional strategies. How does a school operating in a traditional mode begin to make the transition to incorporate some of these ideas into an operating model? This section of the chapter takes an existing high school with the staff of 67 professionals and 1260 students and shows a number of staffing alternatives for their organization. Each staffing pattern takes into account some of the ideas previously discussed in the chapters on curriculum, instruction, and grouping of students. The first model shows how the school is organized at the present time in a traditional departmental staff organization.

Departmental Staff Organization

The standard departmental staffing arrangement shown in figure 12–4 divides the high school into nine departments: language arts; social studies; science; math; foreign language; physical education, health and driver education; fine arts; vocational; and special services. The school is a comprehensive high school with a large vocational program. The special services department is somewhat unique. It includes guidance counselors, one vocational rehabilitation counselor, one special education coordinator, two instructional media specialists, and one person to coordinate both the independent study program and action learning program. (See chapter 9 for more detail about these two programs.) The three principals share the school's administration, with one of the assistants responsible for buildings, grounds, lunch-room, transportation, office management, and some discipline. The other assistant's major responsibility is the curricular and instructional program and the coordination of volunteer services.

Department Head— Role and Responsibilities

A department head coordinates the activities of each department and serves as a member of the principal's advisory council. The department head's responsibilities are:

1. Coordinate the inventory of textbooks and audiovisual materials.
2. Coordinate the development of an instructional budget for the department.
3. Provide the department staff with information regarding advances and subject matter and promising instructional materials.
4. Coordinate the placement and supervision of student teachers and interns in the department.
5. Recommend special resources and personnel needed to aid the department's instructional staff.
6. Direct department staff in selecting or preparing a written behavioral objective for each curricular area.
7. Seek the advice of a counselor or principal in handling special department problems.
8. Assume responsibility for completing routine reports.
9. Participate in the development of the school's inservice teacher education program.
10. Observe on request the instructional presentations of department staff and provide feedback aimed at improving instruction.
11. Provide individual assistance to new and beginning teachers.
12. Hold the staff accountable for student achievement.

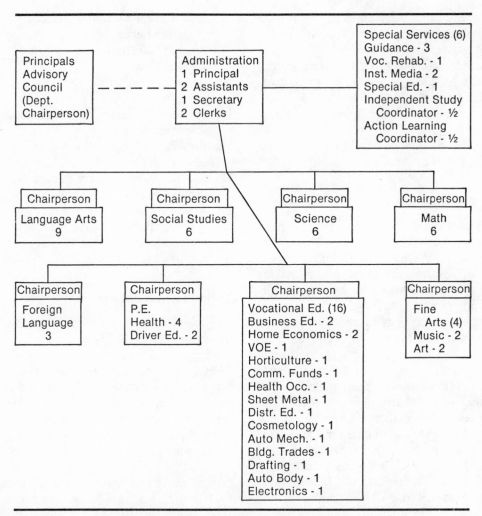

FIGURE 12–4. Standard departmental high school staffing pattern

13. Evaluate paraprofessionals assigned to the department.
14. Attend all meetings of the principal's advisory council.
15. Schedule and chair department meetings.
16. Channel information from a variety of sources to the department teachers.
17. Conduct demonstration lessons for department staff members using new materials and procedures.
18. Coordinate the assessment of students and the department based on individual objectives.
19. Plan with appropriate personnel to research activities for the department.
20. Schedule department meetings for goal setting, problem solving, and evaluation.
21. Coordinate the assessment of student's characteristics prior to any grouping.
22. Cooperate with other department chairpersons in coordinating school-wide facilities and resources.

23. Confer informally with department staff members to discuss ways of improving instruction.
24. Facilitate communication between central office personnel, consultants, and department staff.
25. Participate in the selection of professional staff assigned to the department.
26. Participate in the evaluation of professional staff assigned to the department.

Principal's Advisory Council

The advisory council is made up of all department heads (or team leaders) and the three principals. It is charged with the major responsibility of assisting the principals in making decisions regarding the curricular and instructional program of the school. The council should meet regularly, at least once a week, and work from an agenda to which all council members have had the opportunity to contribute. Items brought to the council should relate largely to discussions of curriculum and instruction and not to the daily management of the school. Neither should advisory council meetings be used as a substitute for school-wide faculty meetings, but rather they should focus on participatory decision making relative to curriculum and instruction. The following list suggests some of the responsibilities of the principal's advisory councils:

1. Coordinate inservice programs.
2. Conduct assessment of the school's program and determine needs.
3. Participate in the training of aides.
4. Formulate school-wide policy and operating procedures relating to curriculum and instruction.
5. Plan the orientation of new teachers.
6. Study curricular offerings to insure they are sufficient to meet the needs of all students.
7. Plan how special resource teachers can best benefit the entire school.
8. Provide direction for the independent study program.
9. Be an advisory group for the action learning program.
10. Provide direction for the community volunteer program.
11. Provide leadership in the development of school philosophy and goals.
12. See that these goals are published and distributed to teachers, parents, and students.
13. Assure the continuity of educational goals and learning objectives throughout the school and assure that they are consistent with the broad goals of the school system.

Team Staffing Pattern

The basic staff of a typical high school, as shown in figure 12–5, can be used to create numerous variations in team arrangements. Appropriate team designs, however, must provide a good relationship with a planned curricular design, good instructional strategies, and desirable patterns for student grouping. A summary of previous information concerning good design for curriculum, instruction, grouping, and staffing includes: (1) team members from two or more disciplines; (2) a differentiated staff including a team leader, team members, aides, clerks, etc.; and (3) a group of 75–150 students in a block of time appropriate in length to the number of subjects included in the team. The interdisciplinary team allows for the best options in integrating the curriculum, ease of scheduling, flexibility in grouping, and student control.

Interdisciplinary teams can be organized in a variety of ways. The Webster County High School in West Virginia organized a series of two-subject, four-teacher teams, consisting of two language arts teachers and two social studies teachers in a three-hour block of time

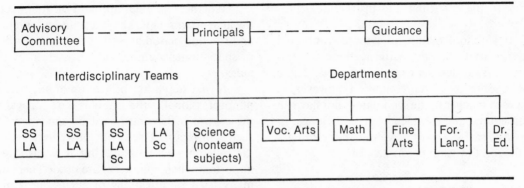

FIGURE 12–5. Interdisciplinary team staffing for fluid block schedules

coordinated with a free-floating elective.[2] Each team met with one group of approximately 120 students in the morning and worked with another block of students during the afternoon. The other half of the day for the students involved participating in a regular elective program.

Using the staff outlined in figure 12–5, the fluid block design organizes language arts, social studies, and science teams. One of the main advantages of the fluid block design is its allowance for three basic styles of instruction, ranging from traditional, to team approaches, to individually-paced labs. Hopefully, most of the teachers in the basic required subjects of language arts, social studies, and possibly science will be willing to work in a team arrangement. Teachers in other subject areas may join teams, may wish to set up their instruction as an individually paced laboratory (typing, art, foreign languages, and certain math courses lend themselves nicely to individualized labs), or may operate in a traditional type schedule as in the past.

SCHOOL-WIDE STAFF COMMITTEES

The principal has several school-wide staffing responsibilities. Gone is the day when the principal could make major instructional and curricular decisions for the school without the direct involvement of the staff. In many cases, the teachers are more knowledgeable than the principal regarding particular problems and solutions, because curricular and instructional decisions affect the teachers most directly. Good organizational theory has also shown that people have greater commitment to decisions in which they are involved.

An excellent way to involve the faculty is by forming a faculty council to improve the school's curricular and instructional program. If the school has a multi-unit learning community using interdisciplinary teams, the faculty council should be made up of the head of each team and the principal. In a similar fashion, special coordinating committees can deal with curricular areas such as science, math, social studies, or any area that requires cross-unit coordination. These committees may be permanent or temporary in nature, depending on the assignment.

If a multi-unit staffing design is used, these committees can best be formed with one teacher from each team. The curriculum committee thus formed provides representation from each of the teams as well as communication back to each team. Each staff member also shares in the school-wide efforts to provide continuity and thrust to the curricular and instructional program.

If a school maintains a more traditional departmental staffing pattern, these school-wide staffing designs can still be used. There will be some loss of representation, however, in that each teacher in the school does not have an instructional unit to which he or she belongs. In any case, staffing must be viewed in the context of the total mission of the school.

PARAPROFESSIONALS

Many daily tasks performed in the secondary school do not require professional training. Some tasks relate directly to improving instruction, while others are noninstructional in nature. The move toward individualized instruction, the multiple activity classroom, and the many additional services of a food, health, or welfare nature that are provided in schools increase the demand for nonprofessional employees.

In some schools, clerical and instructional aides have performed these functions. Other communities, without funds for aides, have used volunteers.[3] Paid or volunteer aides can be a great asset to the school, but schools must properly select and train these aides in order to avoid problems.

Types of Aides

There are two types of aides: the instructional or classroom aide, and the clerical or support aide. Instructional aides usually work directly with a classroom teacher or team and assist in instructing children under the direction of a teacher or team. In addition, they fulfill a variety of clerical, support, and supervisory tasks assigned by the teacher or team. A clerical or support aide usually does not work directly in a classroom but in the office, clinic, school store, library, or resource room.

Whether the aides are paid or volunteers, the aide program must have a sound orientation and training period as well as careful appraisal of special talents and abilities possessed by the aides.

A first step in the utilization of any special nonprofessional in the school is the approval of the central office and board of education for such a program. This is obviously necessary if the aides are to be paid, but it is also very important when volunteers are used. There are many legal ramifications of such a program, and a policy regarding the aide program should be developed in each school district and ought to include recruitment, selection, orientation, and training.

Recruitment and Selection of Aides

Aides can be drawn from the entire community. If most aide positions are established on a part-time basis—three to twenty hours per week—the potential available work force is very large. Available persons might include college students, high school students, housewives, retirees, and men or women who work evening shifts. Professional people may also often be available as resource people and for short special assignments.

Recruitment can occur through newspaper articles, letters to parents, the PTA, church announcements, telephone, or any other contacts available. After an aide program has been initiated, a television news story on the aide program followed by a call for assistance may be an effective recruitment device.

Each aide should be interviewed before acceptance into the program. In the initial interview, the principal should attempt to gauge the individual's motivations, assess potential contributions, and decide the kind of responsibility the person can most effectively assume. Factors that should be considered during an interview include educational background; the use of language; appearance, poise, and personality; interest in children; willingness and ability to follow directions; special interests, abilities, and training; past employment; general health (a physical examination should be required); and the home situation. By far, the most overriding consideration is the aide's dedication to the welfare of children and a willingness to commit time and energy on their behalf.

The interview serves to inform the aide of the goals of the school, and helps the aide decide if the school is a desirable place to work. The interview also can be used to determine whether a volunteer would work well directly with children. If not, the aide can receive other kinds of assignments, providing, of course, the person has the appropriate technical skills.

Orientation and Training Program Each aide should attend at least one formal orientation session. Additional sessions can be scheduled as the year progresses and as needs arise. Aides should be familiar with basic principles before they begin work. They must understand lines of authority within the school and must know where to turn in a conflict situation. An introduction to administrative and supervisory personnel will smooth relationships and give aides an understanding of who to contact if a problem arises.

Aides must realize that they have undertaken an important service with a fixed schedule, specific demands, and supervision of some activity. They should understand that the school expects a high quality of effort, reliability, and cooperation. They must learn to be friendly, tactful, helpful, and fair to all students. They must be instructed not to discuss children with parents and not to divulge any information from private records to anyone. They should be aware that disciplinary action is the responsibility of the teacher only, and that the teacher handles all parental problems.

A third phase of the training program for aides should involve a discussion of psychological aspects of their work. This discussion would cover general characteristics of children and the implications of working with them, along with their physical, social, mental, and emotional attributes. It should focus on the procedures and attitudes that are conducive to the best psychological atmosphere and climate within the classroom. This phase of the program should help aides learn the general approach to children used by the staff. The instructors for the aide-training program should include aides who have been successful in the program, teachers, and the principal.

The final phase of the training program is continuous. It is truly on-the-job training as it constitutes participation in the daily activities and operation of the school. In addition, instructional aides should participate as much as possible in teacher inservice training. The training program for clerical and support aides is similar to that of the instructional aides, but also includes specific training regarding clerical duties.

Training for Teachers

A volunteer program can be effective only if teachers want aide assistance and know how to use it. Most teachers are used to working alone and often are not skilled at delegating work to other adults. A must in the program is a training component for teachers in how to use aides, what tasks to give them, how to treat them, and how to delegate certain responsibilities to them.[4]

Creating a Supportive Atmosphere for the Aides

Aides, as well as teachers, must have a warm working climate within the school. They need a gathering place and time for a coffee break as well as the opportunity to share activities and responsibilities. An advisement committee of aides should meet with the principal on a regular basis to discuss improving the role of the aide within the school. Schedules for aides should be made as flexible as possible to accommodate outside responsibilities.

Administration of the Aide Program

If the aide program consists largely of volunteers, day-by-day scheduling becomes an important task. A principal does not have time to manage this on a daily basis and should use others to administer the work program. Two people should be identified for this function. One should be a staff member, for example, an assistant principal who can function as the staff liaison for the volunteers. The second should be a most capable volunteer who can head up the recruitment, coordinate the orientation, and manage the assignment of volunteers, either directly or by delegating portions to other volunteers.

Liability Implications for Aides

One particular caution needs to be raised regarding the use of aides: the legal questions of tort liability. Training aides for the jobs they hold is important. Specific supervisory training as well as the development of clearly defined supervisory policies, including lines of authority and responsibilities, are recommended. A training program for aides should consider techniques of supervising children, what to do in a variety of situations, how to handle the children who need disciplining, and how to handle emergency situations.

If each aide, whether paid or voluntary, receives this training, the potential for a negligence charge stemming from a personal injury situation will be greatly reduced. Some states require liability insurance for aides. Education associations usually provide this insurance in those states requiring it.

SUMMARY

Three dimensions of staffing were considered in this chapter: the teacher's involvement with the curriculum as either a generalist or a specialist; the teacher's interaction with other school personnel, functioning either as an individual or as a member of a team; and the various teaching functions that must be carried out as part of the act of teaching. These three dimensions interact and should be reviewed collectively when organizing a school staff.

When teachers work independently, decisions about curricular responsibilities and teaching function are limited. When teachers are organized into teams, many more staffing options are available. The multi-unit pattern for staffing, curricular organization, and student grouping makes maximum use of staffing potential. Delegation of tasks is a must in a large high school. Department heads and team leaders need to be charged with specific duties and responsibilities to successfully implement this delegation.

Paraprofessionals can be used to augment a school's staff by performing tasks that do not reuqire the professional skills of the teacher but that do demand the attention of an adult. These people may be paid staff or volunteers. In either case, it is important to provide the aides with adequate orientation and training to maximize their use in the schools.

ENDNOTES

1. J. Lloyd Trump, *Images of the Future*. Experimental study of the utilization of staff in the secondary schools and the National Association of Secondary School Principals, 1959.

2. Gerald C. Ubben, "A Fluid Block Schedule," *NASSP Bulletin* 60 (February 1976): 104–111.

3. An excellent source of information and ideas for volunteer aide programs can be found in the publications of the National School Volunteer Program, Inc., 300 North Washington Street, Alexandria, Virginia 22314.

4. Audry Jackson, *School Volunteers Program Leaders Handbook*. School Volunteer Program of Miami, Dade County Public Schools, Miami, Florida, 1975.

BIBLIOGRAPHY

Bechtol, William M.; Braun, Sister Janine; Slominski, Sister Suzanne; and Johnson, Sylvia. "Objectives, Competencies, and Trust —They're All Essential for Effective Group Functioning." *Journal of Teacher Education* 29 (Fall 1976): 229–231.

Biggs, David W. *Team Teaching*. Bloomington: Indiana University Press, 1964.

Casburn, Edwin H. "Bureaucracy vs. Shared Decision Making." *NASSP Bulletin* (April 1976): 62–68.

Dempsey, Richard A., and Smith, Rodney P. *Differentiated Staffing*. Englewood Cliffs, N.J.: Prentice-Hall, Inc., 1972.

Gibbons, Maurice. *The New Secondary Education*. A Phi Delta Kappa Task Force Report. Bloomington, Ind.: Phi Delta Kappan, Inc., 1976.

Glass, Thomas. "Community Involvement and Shared Decision Making." *NASSP Bulletin* (October 1977): 5–9.

Glines, Don E. *Creating Humane Schools*. Makato, Minn.: D. M. Printing Company, 1971.

Hall, Gene E., and Rutherford, William L. "Concerns of Teachers About Implementing Team Teaching." *Educational Leadership* 34 (December 1976): 227–233.

Hayes, Paul C. "The Volunteer." Worthington, Ohio: Buckeyes Association of School Administrators. Entire issue of *The Administrator* 3 (Summer 1973) ED 094 313.

Hedges, Henry G. *Extending Volunteer Programs in Schools*. St. Catherines, Ontario: Niagara Centre, The Ontario Institute for Studies in Education, 1973. ED 085 846.

Helgerson, Linda, et al. *Manual for a Volunteer Services System*. Columbus, Ohio: Columbus Public Schools, 1974, ED 116 284.

Hughes, Larry W. *Education and the Law in Tennessee*. Cincinnati, Ohio: W. H. Anderson Co., 1971. See especially chapter 10.

Hunter, Madeline. "Staff Meeting: Madeline Hunter Discusses Volunteers in the Classroom." *Instructor* 83 (May 1974): 20.

Jackson, Audrey. *Leader's Handbook*. School Volunteer Program of Miami Dade County Public Schools, 1410 NE Second Avenue, Miami, Florida 33132.

Joyce, Bruce, and Well, Marsha. *Models of Teaching*. Englewood Cliffs, N.J.: Prentice-Hall, 1972.

Martin, Lyn S., and Pavan, Barbara N. "Current Research on Open Space, Nongraded, Vertical Grouping and Team Teaching." *Phi Delta Kappan* 57 (January 1976): 310–315.

Marx, Leo. "Can We Create Together What We Can't Create Alone?" *Change* (Summer 1975): 38–43.

Mastors, Charlotte. *School Volunteers: Who Needs Them? Fastback Series, No. 55*. Bloomington, Indiana: Phi Delta Kappa Educational Foundation, 1975.

McCuaig, Susannah M. "Large Scale Unbudgeted Elementary School Tutorial Programs." *Educational Leadership* 32 (February 1975): 331–334.

Mott Institute for Community Improvement. *The Use of School Volunteers*. East Lansing: Michigan State University, 1973.

National School Public Relations Association. *School Volunteers: Districts Recruit Aides to Meet Rising Needs*. Arlington, Virginia, 1973.

Nolan, Robert R., and Rope, Susan Stavert "How to Succeed in Team Teaching by Really Trying." *Today's Education* (January-February 1977): 54–61.

Ohio State Department of Education. *Utilizing Volunteers for Children with Behavioral Disabilities*. Columbus: Division of Special Education, 1974.

Petrie, Hugh G. "Do You See What I See? The Epistemology of Interdisciplinary Inquiry." *Educational Research* 5 (February 1976): 9–14.

Recruitment Leadership and Training Institute. *Volunteers in Education: A Handbook for Coordinators of Volunteer Programs.* Philadelphia, 1975.

Sorenson, Juanita S., Poole, Max; and Joyal, Lloyd H. *The Unit Leader and Individually Guided Education.* Reading, Mass.: Addison-Wesley, 1976.

Sorenson, Juanita S.; Rossman, Pat A.; and Barnes, Donald E. "The Unit Leader and Educational Decision Making." *Journal of Teacher Education* (Fall 1976): 224–225.

Stoops, Emery, et al. *Handbook of Educational Administration.* Boston: Allyn and Bacon, 1975. See especially chapter 24.

Templeton, Ian. "Differentiated Staffing." *NAESP School Leadership Digest Series No. 8, ERIC* (1974), ED 095 608.

Thurber, John C. "Project VUE: Volunteers Upholding Education." Practicum report, submitted in partial fulfillment of requirements for national Ed.D. program, Nova University, 1973.

Trump, J. Lloyd. *Images of the Future.* Experimental study of the utilization of staff in the secondary schools and the National Association of Secondary School Principals, 1959.

Wendel, Frederick C. "Attitudes of Principals Toward Participatory Managerial Practices." *The Clearing House* (March 1977): 322–326.

Williams, Polly Franklin. *A Philosophical Approach for Volunteers.* University, Miss.: School of Education, University of Mississippi, 1974.

Zahorik, John A. "Teacher Planning Models." *Educational Leadership* 33 (November 1975): 134–140.

Chapter Thirteen

Scheduling Staff and Students

The school schedule is considered by many to be the command performance of the principal. It is here that the abilities to conceptualize, to organize, and to carry out detailed planning are most visible. If well done, the schedule will strongly support the instructional and curricular program of the school. On the other hand, if poorly designed, the schedule will be a roadblock to a balanced curriculum and instructional flexibility.

Scheduling can be defined as the plan to bring together people, materials, and curriculum at a designated time and place for the purpose of instruction. Its basic purpose is to coordinate the requirements laid down by previously reached decisions regarding curriculum, instruction, grouping, and staffing.

Several important concepts in scheduling should be reviewed before actually beginning the construction of a schedule. These include the flexibility, simplicity, and complexity of the schedule, and the timeliness of the schedule. Other concepts to consider are: previously made decisions concerning the design of curriculum and instruction, staffing and grouping patterns, and space availability and utilization.

SCHEDULE FLEXIBILITY

The schedule should have either the potential of being legitimately changed with great frequency or the internal elasticity to meet a variety of curricular and instructional requests within its regular structure. For example, the teacher who would like to take a group of children on a half-day field trip should be able to do so without disrupting the entire school schedule. Or, the group that needs an extra hour to complete a project should be able to have that hour with an easy adjustment in the schedule. Timeliness is part of flexibility. Schedules must be designed so that daily and weekly instructional and curricular needs can be met as they occur. This is seldom done in high school schedules because it is extremely difficult, but nevertheless it remains a desirable trait.

Simplicity and Complexity

The schedule needs simplicity to prevent interdependence of the components of the schedule, so that the modification of one component does not require the modification of several others. Complexity, on the other hand, is also needed in order to meet the demands of individual differences of students. To meet individual differences, intricate schedule and grouping designs often need to be constructed. This seemingly creates a paradox, but it is not as difficult as it seems. An analogy that seems fitting to describe this relationship is found in the new modularized television sets. The complexity of their circuitry is an amazing example of modern day technology, but on the other hand, this complex design is constructed in such a way that if a failure occurs, a circuit module can be removed and replaced very quickly without having to disassemble the entire set once the trouble spot has been identified. So it is with a good schedule. It must permit the complex construction required for individual differences while maintaining simplicity to allow easy changes.

TYPES OF SCHEDULES

The secondary school schedules can be classified under the following types: (1) group schedules, (2) mosaic schedules, (3) modular schedules, and (4) fluid block schedules.

Group Schedules

This schedule of single subjects is most often used to place groups of students who are registered for the same subjects, and where the elective offerings are very few. Students are scheduled by groups and stay together through the day. Only two steps are required for this scheduling procedure: (1) determine the number of students taking the same subjects and identify how many sections are needed; and (2) arrange the classes into a schedule according to their groups, rotating through the subjects as illustrated in figure 13-1.

The group schedule is used most often for traditional junior high school schedules. Its major advantages are its ease in scheduling and simplicity of design. Disadvantages are that students do not mix outside of their basic assigned groups and all classes are single-teacher responsibilities with very limited time flexibility. The block schedule, discussed later in this chapter, is a variation of the group schedule.

Mosaic Schedules

This is the most popular form of secondary school scheduling. It is designed to allow the scheduling of a large number of student electives. It is based on the concept that students register for courses first and then a schedule is built which fits *all* their requests. The term *mosaic* comes from the method of schedule construction. Each course to be offered is written on a small card or tile and moved about on a scheduling board so that it can be assigned a teacher, time, and room that is free of conflicts from other parts of the schedule. When the board becomes full of these small squares, it resembles a mosaic.

The steps in building a mosaic type schedule are as follows:

1. Determine the educational offerings of the school. Each year a needs assessment is conducted to determine what the curricular offerings for the following school year should be. New courses may be proposed by new district or state requirements or by the requests from students and staff. The initial list should consist of courses that are desired and for which there is some probability that they can be taught. With computer scheduling, all possible courses can be initially put on request.

	Group 1	Group 2	Group 3	Group 4
English	1	2	3	4
Social Studies	2	3	4	5
Math	3	4	5	6
Science	4	5	6	1
P.E. and Health	5	6	1	2
Elective	6	1	2	3

FIGURE 13-1. Group schedule (numbers indicate period of the day)

2. Provide an appropriate means for pupils and parents to review the curricular offering and to select courses for students to take with appropriate guidance from teachers and counselors. A booklet listing all courses with a brief description can be prepared. The booklet can also list requirements for graduation and suggested courses of study. Tentative planning worksheets for each year of a student's school career may also appear in the booklet so that complete programs can be worked out. Figure 13-2 shows excerpts from a booklet of a brief course outline and figure 13-3 shows a sample planning sheet for individual high school cur-

---

BUSINESS EDUCATION

Typewriting

Typewriting is a one-year course in which students learn how to operate a typewriter with speed and accuracy. They type letters, graphs, themes, reports, envelopes, booklets, and manuscripts. This course is necessary for those who wish to become secretaries or businesspersons, and is valuable for everyone—homemaker or college student.

Typewriting is a prerequisite for Shorthand II, Office Skills, and Secretarial Skills.

ENGLISH

English 10

English 10 marks the beginning of the study of the language at a more mature level. It seeks to help the student acquire the basic tools of communication through reading, writing, speaking, and listening. Opportunity for such activity may frequently be found in current problems of interest to students. Correctness in grammar and usage are stressed, but not as ends in themselves. It is emphasized that these things have real meaning only in relation to language and literature as means of communication, and that they cannot be separated. Hence, literature becomes an important part of the course, a part through which students are helped to appreciate the traditions, the ideals, and the aspirations of men of all countries.

FOREIGN LANGUAGES

French II

In the second year, emphasis is placed on readings in French culture, history, and literature, and on increasing the student's ability to comprehend and to carry out discussions in the language. The formal study of grammar is begun. There is continued use of tapes and facilities in the language laboratory. All French II students are eligible to join the French Club.

INDUSTRIAL ARTS

Architectural Drawing

Architectural drawing introduces a student to house construction and design through the drawing of various parts of a house. These drawings will include such parts as: footings, sills, framing methods, windows, kitchen layouts, symbols, etc. These drawings take about one-half of the year. The final project is to draw a set of house plans to include all elevations and a perspective drawing.

FIGURE 13-2. **Excerpt from senior high school course guide**

Instructions: Use this form to plan your three years in high school. Circle the courses that you tentatively plan to take each of your three years in high school. Record next year's courses on the registration form and return this sheet to your homeroom teacher.

Sophomore	Junior	Senior
English 10 (Required)	English 11 (Required)	English 12 (Required)
American History (Required)	World History	Creative Writing
World Geography	(Required)	Social Studies (Required)
Physical Education	World Geography	World Geography
(Required)	Elementary Algebra	Humanities
Elementary Algebra	Integrated Mathematics	Elementary Algebra
Integrated Mathematics	Plane Geometry	Integrated Mathematics
Plane Geometry	Higher Algebra	Plane Geometry
Biology	Biology	Higher Algebra
French I, II, III	Chemistry	Trigonometry/Advanced
German I, II, III	French I, II, III, IV	Algebra
Latin I, II	German I, II, III	Advanced Mathematics
Russian I	Latin I, II, III	Biology
Spanish I, II, III	Russian I, II	Chemistry
	Spanish I, II, III, IV	Physics
		French II, III, IV
		German II, III, IV
		Latin II, III, IV
		Russian II, III
		Spanish II, III, IV
Art I	Applied Physical Science	General Mathematics
Commercial Art I	Art I	Applied Physical Science
Typing I	Art II	Art I
Beginning Business	Commercial Art I, II	Art II
Electricity I	Typing I	Commercial Art I, II
General Metals	Office Skills	Typing I
Power I	Secretarial Skills	Office Skills
Wood I	Shorthand I	Secretarial Skills
General Graphic Arts	Bookkeeping &	Sales and Merchandising
Home Economics I, IV	Accounting	II
Journalism	Architectural Drawing	Office Education
Speech	Electricity I, II	Shorthand II
Gym & Choir (Alt. Days)	General Metals	Bookkeeping and
Gym & Band (Alt. Days)	General Graphic Arts	Accounting
Gym & Study (Alt. Days)	Machine Drawing I	Law/Sales
Orchestra	Machine Shop I	Architectural Drawing
	Power I, II	Electricity II, III
	Wood I, II	Machine Drawing I, II
	Home Economics I, II,	Machine Shop I, II
	IV	Power II
	Journalism	Wood II, III

(continued)

Sophomore	Junior	Senior
	Speech	Home Economics I, II,
	Band	III, IV
	Choir	Journalism
	Orchestra	Speech
	Boys' Physical	Drama
	Education	Band
	Girls' Physical	Choir
	Education	Orchestra
	Sales and Merchan-	Boys' Physical Education
	dising I	Girls' Physical Education

Graduation Requirements

1. English 10, 11, 12
2. American History
3. World History
4. Social Studies

5. One mathematics course
6. One science course
7. Passing grade in 10th grade phys. ed.
8. Total of 14 credits plus 10th grade phys. ed.

FIGURE 13-3. **Senior high school course guide**

ricular planning. Student requests should be gathered on a standard registration sheet that allows for easy tallying. A form such as the one in figure 13-4 can be used for either manual or computer scheduling.

3. Tabulate student choices by subject to determine the number of students in each as a basis for the needed number of sections of each subject. The tabulating can be done either by hand, placing the tallies on a sheet similar to the ones the students have used for registration, or by preparing input data for the computer indicating the student's request. The computer can provide an accurate total listing of all subjects and the number of requests for each. See figure 13-5.

4. Determine the number of sections needed for each subject. This can be determined by selecting a maximum class size for each subject and dividing the total students by that number. In the case of small enrollments, a determination must be made of adequate staff numbers to offer all requested courses. In some cases, small enrollments may require dropping some electives and asking those students to select another option. The feedback from the computer can

aid the principal in rapidly determining the enrollment feasibility of offering a particular course. The computer specialist can assist the principal in reviewing course offerings. The number of small enrollment electives that can be offered is ultimately determined by the total student-staff ratio.

5. Determine the teaching staff needed and compare with the teaching staff believed to be available, considering areas of certification, budget, etc. Teaching staff available can be determined roughly by multiplying the number of classes taught by each full-time teacher plus the number of sections to be taught by part-time personnel. This can then be compared to the number of sections indicated as being needed in the course tallies calculated in step 4.

Sections needed based on
student requests.........................350

Teacher sections available
based on total staff.....................335

Sections that must be cut from
student request tabulations or
provided for by the employment
of three additional teachers...............15

Student's name_____

Directions: Encircle the code number, in *red,* of all subjects for your next year's schedule as approved on your Proposed Program of Studies sheet. Recheck for accuracy. The homeroom teacher may reserve the responsibility of checking those subjects where ability-grouping is involved.

Miscellaneous

____060 Unassigned
____065 Driver Education
____067 Library Training

Work Periods

____071 First
____072 Second
____073 Third
____074 Fourth
____075 Fifth
____076 Sixth
____077 Seventh

Special Education

____081 & 082 Spec. Educ.
____083 Individual Acceler.
    Prog.

Coop. Voc. Trng.

____091 Job not yet assigned
____092 Dist. Ed. (assigned)
____093 Ind. Coop. (assigned)
____094 Ind. Coop., Part G.

Mathematics

____321 Alg. 2R
____330 Analysis A
____331 Analysis R
____351 Analy. Geom. (1/2)
____352 Probability (1/2)
____354 Comp. Prog. (1/2)
____355 Comp. Prog. (1)
____356 Comp. App. (1/2)
____358 Trig. (1/2)
____360 Calculus
____361 Calculus AP

Science

____400 Spec. Ed. Biol.
____430 BSCS Biol. A (1/2)
____431 BSCS Biol. B (1/2)
____435 Botany (1/2)
____440 Biol. 2A (1/2)
____441 Biol. 2B (1/2)
____445 Radiation Biology
    (1/2)
____450 Chemistry A (1/2)
____451 Chemistry B (1/2)
____454 Chemistry 11 A
____455 Chemistry 11 B
____461 Physics A
____462 Physics B

Business Education

____604 Typing IV (1/2)
____605 Office Practice
____606 Pers.-Use
    Typing (1/2)
____608 Voc. Off. Ed.
    —Jr.
____610 Shorthand I
____611 Shorthand II
____612 Voc. Off. Ed.
    —Lab.
____613 Voc. Off. Oc.
    —Coop.
____620 Acct. 1
____621 Adv. Acct.
____631 Bus. Law (1/2)
____632 Off. Mach.
    (1/2)
____641 Bus. Arith.
____642 Cons. Ed. (1/2)
____643 Bus Comm.
____099 Cl. Off. Aide

Homemaking

____681 Homemaking
    1A (1/2)
____682 Homemaking
    1B (1/2)
____683 Homemaking
    2A (1/2)
____684 Homemaking
    2B (1/2)
____685 Homemaking
    3A (1/2)
____686 Homemaking
    3B (1/2)
____687 Chef's Course
    (1/2)

FIGURE 13–4. Registration code sheet and teacher's tally sheet

COURSE	MALES	FEMALES	TOTALS
060	249	198	447
065	26	32	58
072	1	1	2
073		1	1
075	3	8	11
076	40	61	101
077	45	66	111
080	36	11	47
081	4	2	6
082	8	4	12
083		1	1
091	4	3	7
092	25	27	52
093	14	17	31
094	28	17	45
099		14	14
103	5	12	17
104	8	11	19
107	15	29	44
108	7	23	30
128	5	10	15
130	20	24	44
201	53	66	119
210	10	12	22
220	10	21	31
225	1		1
231		9	9
240	7	5	12
241	14	27	41
250	12	12	24
301	12	10	22
303	12	5	17
304	10	4	14
310	2	3	5
311	25	34	59
312	7	4	11
320	25	33	58

FIGURE 13–5.   Course numbers and registration totals

A more detailed analysis must now be carried out to properly match teacher assignment requests and certification areas to student course tabulations. This is done by comparing specific subject section needs with available staff. Some flexibility is usually available in determining staff assignments where additional positions are to be filled or staff turnover exists. Figure 13-6 is an illustration of the matching of teacher specialties and student requests drawn from figure 13-5.

Assignments may need to be moved around in order for all to be matched with qualified staff. In some instances, modifications may be made based on appropriate assignments for staff yet to be hired or yet to be employed by putting together logical assignments for new faculty, i.e., math-science, social studies-P.E.-coaching, etc. Ultimately, job descriptions for new staff can be formulated from these data.

6. Determine the number and length of class periods and the time for extracurricular activities. The number of periods in the school day should now be determined. Six or seven periods is usually typical for mosaic type schedules. Additional school periods over and above the number of classes taken by the average student usually become study halls or early dismissal periods. In most cases, experience shows that unless students are on work assignments of some type these additional hours are not used productively. Therefore, it is suggested that the number of periods in the school day match fairly closely to the number of courses for which each student registers. It is somewhat more difficult to build a no-study hall or limited study hall schedule requiring students to take courses each hour, but the productivity for a student is usually improved; thus, such tightly organized schedules are worthwhile. A five- or six-period day is recommended, which includes a large block of time plus several hour-long elective classes.

Extracurricular activities are most often scheduled after the regular school day. This works well when the students either walk to school or provide their own transportation. When a large number of students ride school buses, however, an after school activity period greatly restricts the number of students that can participate. A number of schools have had good success in establishing mid-day activity periods during the early afternoon. All students are then expected to select and participate in an activity, club, intramural program, or may use the period as a study period if no other opportunities are available.

Staff Roster	Desired Assignment	Areas of Certification	Proposed Assignment
Bailes, Cris	English 10-11	L.A.	L.A. 3-10, 2-11
Bray, Gail	S.S. 10	S.S., L.A.	5-10th
Brewer, Max	Sc. 11-12	Sc., Math	2 - Chem. 1 - Phys. 1 - Biol.
Crockett, Reba	Typing, Bkk.	Business Ed.	4 - Typing 1 - Bkk.
Dietz, Pat	S.S. 10-11	S.S., P.E.	S.S. 5-11
Edison, Freda	Algebra	Math, Spanish	Alg. - 4 Germ. - 1

FIGURE 13-6.   Teacher assignment worksheet

7. Make a conflict chart to determine the subjects that must not be scheduled at the same time if pupils are to have the program they have selected. Any subjects for which only one section is offered that are placed in the schedule at the same time prevents students from taking more than one such course. Therefore, in order for single section subjects not to conflict, they must be scheduled at different hours of the day. Two-way conflicts can also frequently occur. This happens when two single section offerings are matched with a request for a double-section course offered the same hours as the singles. Three-way conflicts are also possible, but the probability is relatively low.

The underlying philosophy of a good mosaic schedule is to design a schedule that is capable of honoring all student requests, and to then build a schedule that eliminates all possible conflicts. The smaller number of irresolvable conflicts within the schedule, the more perfect the schedule is considered to be.

A well-designed mosaic schedule should be able to reduce irresolvable conflict to around 2 percent of the total student population. An irresolvable conflict is defined as a set of student course requests which cannot be honored because of conflicts within the schedule and which requires the student to select one or more alternate courses in order to complete a program.

A conflict chart sets up a matrix of at least single, double, and triple section offerings and shows how many students have signed up for the various possible combinations. The conflict matrix shown in figure 13–7 shows that three students want to take both courses 107 and 111. While a conflict matrix is a vital part of the mosaic scheduling procedure, it is also an extremely time-consuming task if done by hand—particularly in a large school. It is accomplished by taking each student course request and comparing it to the other courses also requested by that student. The comparison is indicated by placing a tally mark on the matrix at the bisecting point. Up to fifteen comparisons could be required for six course requests from one student if they were all single subjects. Computer-assisted scheduling will produce a complete conflict matrix for all subjects generated from the same data which was used to determine student tallies. The computer specialist will often circle those conflicts that they feel to be particularly significant.

8. Assign classes to the master schedule in terms of the conflict matrix. A small card, approximately one-inch square, should be prepared for each section of each subject to be offered in the schedule. It is often desirable to color code the card into predominant grade levels, also reserving an additional color for classes that draw heavily from all or several grades. The mosaic cards should contain the course title and the section designation such as 1-1, 1-2, or 2-3, indicating which section the

Course No.	107	111	121	142	451	455	621	697	704
107		3	2	78	17	17	2	9	0
111			1	0	2	0	12	22	0
121				1	2	7	9	4	0
142					8	0	0	1	
451						3	2	0	
455							54	14	
621								0	12
697									2
704									

FIGURE 13–7.   Conflict matrix

card represents in the total number of sections of that type.

The mosaic cards are now to be placed on a scheduling grid, listing all proposed teacher positions and the periods of the day. See figure 13–8 for an example.

The following order is usually helpful in constructing the schedule with a minimum of conflicts. Use the conflict chart for all decisions.

a. Assign twelve grade sections, proceeding downward in grade order. This is desirable because often the greatest number of singletons are twelfth-grade courses. Also, it is often thought desirable to design the twelfth-grade schedule first to insure no conflicts since it is their final year in high school.

b. Assign subjects having only one section, scattering them throughout the school day. The scattering will reduce conflicts. Next, check each single section course against other single sections offered during that hour to insure no conflicts. If some exist, move sections until all are conflict-free.

c. Be careful not to assign two or more classes to one teacher during the same period.

d. Classes having double or triple periods should be assigned next. Included are the core classes, vocational classes, team-taught block classes, etc. Because of the larger block of time for these subjects, fewer options exist for scheduling; therefore, it is necessary to place them in the schedule early.

e. Subjects having only two or three sections should be scheduled next, checking each placement against the conflict matrix. By now, some moving of earlier placed sections will probably be necessary. Be sure to follow each through an analysis on the conflict matrix with other sections offered that hour.

f. Finally, multiple section subjects should be filled in, taking care to properly balance teacher load. Care should be taken to assure reasonable balance each hour for teacher preparation time, as well as to insure adequate availabil-

	BAILES	BRAY	BREWER	CROCKETT	DIETZ	EIDSON	EVERETTE	KIDD	KNIPPERS	LINTZ	MABRE	MCGREGOR	MILLER
PERIOD 1													
PERIOD 2													
PERIOD 3													
PERIOD 4													
PERIOD 5													
PERIOD 6													

FIGURE 13–8.   Scheduling board for mosaic schedules

ity of staff for teaching purposes. Each time a previously placed mosaic is moved, care must be taken to check out all other ramifications of that move on the conflict matrix. Consideration must also be given to available special facilities each hour, such as music rooms, science rooms, typing rooms, etc.

9. A room assignment sheet is prepared to prevent the assignment of two or more classes to the same room the same hour. A chart similar to the one shown in figure 13-8 can be used simply by replacing the top row of teacher's names with classroom numbers, and then also entering each room assignment on the appropriate mosaic of the master schedule.

10. Students may now be assigned to the classes of the proposed master schedule. As each student is assigned to a class, the information needs to be recorded on the pupil's individual assignment sheet, as well as on the separate class tally worksheet in order to balance class size. Each student must be scheduled individually for each of his or her course requests. Previously undetected conflicts will now come to light if the information from the conflict matrix was not completely adhered to or if certain conflicts were overlooked.

Computer-assisted scheduling procedures once again can save hours of clerical time by electronically loading students into the planned master schedule. The IBM scheduling programs such as STUDENT or CLASS are programmed to provide class loading procedures. A particular advantage of computer loading is the opportunity for a trial run, as the computer printout indicates any problem with student requests that cannot be scheduled. These student conflicts can now be reviewed by the schedule designer and result in additional scheduling modifications to avoid previously overlooked conflicts. All schedule modifications at this time should be to the master schedule only. Until the master schedule is perfect, no individual student schedules should be changed because of supposedly irresolvable conflicts.

A good master schedule should result in required schedule changes on an individual basis for no more than about 2 percent of the students. The computer specialist frequently will offer additional suggestions as to how the schedule can be improved. See figure 13-9 for an illustration of a computer printout on an individual student schedule conflict. Any number of simulated runs of the schedule can be made with additional schedule modifications each time. This will finally confirm its soundness and minimum conflict level before all other forms are printed.

Computer packages can include, in addition to the tally lists and conflict matrix previously mentioned: (1) study hall control, (2) common course scheduling (the same students in more than one class), (3) simulated runs, (4) alternate course schedules in case of conflicts, (5) balanced class enrollments as to size, and (6) class lists of students for each teacher for each hour of the day. These computer programs do not build the schedule, but they are of tremendous assistance in clerical operation. While costs vary for scheduling services around the country, it is generally believed that when a school reaches an enrollment of three to four hundred that the clerical and administrative time saved by its use more than offsets the costs.

The individual student schedules can be printed in multiple copies on paper as well as cardstock, providing one copy to the student, one for the office, and additional copies for school files such as attendance, counseling, etc. Individual schedules can also be printed with home addresses for summer mailing if this is desired. (See figure 13-10 for an illustration of a computer printed student schedule.)

Mini-Courses The same computer schedule can be used to schedule mini-courses for a variety of subjects on either a six- or nine-week cycle. From a scheduling standpoint it is easiest to schedule students into mini-courses each cycled in the same period of the day as their

```
C6720    TRENT MORRIS W     11 M 77-78  HANCOCK HIGH

                  STUDENT SCHEDULED EXCEPT FOR COURSE 433

      COURSE     PERIODS AVAILABLE
      REQUESTED  ..1......2......3......4......5......6....

        C00      3 PS
                 11111

        221                               3 PS
                                          11111

        655                                                        3 PS
                                                                   11111

        611               3 PS            3
                          11111           11111

        123                        3      3      3 PS
                                   11111  11111  11111

        402      2                 1 PS   2
                 11111             11111  11111
                 1                 2      1
                 11111             11111  11111

        433      1       1       1 CL   2      2      1
                 11111   11111   11111   11111  11111  11111
                 2       2       2 CL   1
                 11111   11111   11111   11111
```

PS - SECTION CHOSEN IN PARTIAL SCHEDULE.
CL - SECTION CLOSED.

FIGURE 13–9.   Computer printout of an individual student schedule conflict

13930	WILBURN ANGLIA R	10	F	78-79	MARYVILLE	
	STUDENT NAME	GRADE	SEX	NUMBER	HIGH SCHOOL	
PERIOD	SUBJECT NUMBER	SUBJECT	ROOM NUMBER	SEM.*	TEACHER	028	
						HOME ROOM	TELEPHONE
1	121	ENG 2 COL PR	014	3	014		
2	606	GEN BUS 1/2	013	1	117		
2	605	PERS TYP 1/2	017	2	117		
3	925	PHYS ED 1/2	025	1	106		
3	929	DR ED SEM 2	105	2	105		
4	821	HOME ECON 2	001	3	001		
5	211	ALGEBRA 1	020	3	020		
6	311	BIOLOGY	023	3	023		

13940	WILBURN DAVID M	10	M	78-79	MARYVILLE	
	STUDENT NAME	GRADE	SEX	NUMBER	HIGH SCHOOL	
PERIOD	SUBJECT NUMBER	SUBJECT	ROOM NUMBER	SEM.*	TEACHER	028	
						HOME ROOM	TELEPHONE
1	211	ALGEBRA 1	020	3	020		
2	925	PHYS ED 1/2	025	1	104		
2	929	DR ED SEM 2	005	2	205		
3	121	ENG 2 COL PR	014	3	014		
4	311	BIOLOGY	023	3	023		
5	491	LATIN 2	015	3	115		
6	021	BAND	026	3	026		

FIGURE 13-10.   Computer printed student schedule

mini-course the previous quarter. If not, the classes other periods of the day all become disrupted with incoming and outgoing students. Mini-courses can be rotated each cycle so that the variety of options will be available that period over the course of the year. Figure 10–9 in an earlier chapter on curriculum illustrates this rotation.

Modular Scheduling

Modular flexible programming is a scheduling design that attempts to more effectively allow for individualized instruction. It does this by allowing greater variability in the scheduling of time, space, staff, and students. The conventional 7-period day of fifty-five minutes is changed to a series of 21 twenty-minute modules each day or 105 each weekly cycle. Modules of twenty minutes each may be combined to provide for classes of any length. Class size can be varied allowing for small group seminars, large group lectures, or laboratory classes of predetermined size.

The variables to be considered in constructing a schedule of this type are many. Classes are of varying size and length. Even within a particular course of study, classes will be of several different types and will meet in different configurations on different days of the week. One schedule cannot be built for the entire cycle; a new schedule virtually has to be built for each day of the cycle. For these reasons, computer programs have been developed to deal with the huge array of variables and actually build a schedule for the school. However, the basic logic for modular schedule is fundamentally the same as for mosaic schedules. A computer program carries out many of the actual tasks of schedule building that were done by hand under the mosaic schedule, constantly checking back against a conflict matrix for individual student problems. Such programs, under the names of GASP, EPIC, and SOCRATES, are available to actually construct the modular master schedules.

While this technology exists to construct modular schedules, and many have been successfully built, these schedules have never gained a great deal of popularity across the country. This is probably true for several reasons:

1. The expense for computer time in schedule construction is substantially higher for modular scheduling than to use the computer only for its clerical function as outlined in the previous section on mosaic scheduling.
2. Modular schedules are still not very flexible. Once they are built they tend to become locked in, partly because of their complexity and partly because of their cost of construction.
3. Unscheduled time for students occasionally is excessive. This is because the varying length and size of classes leaves students left over here and there, waiting for one or two modules for another class to begin. In traditional schedules this unscheduled time becomes study hall. In modular scheduling similar solutions must be found with student lab study areas or library areas made available for their use.

An illustration of a portion of a modular schedule is shown in figure 13–11.

Fluid Block Schedules

A fluid block schedule is one which provides an extended block of time (two to three hours) to an interdisciplinary team of teachers for them to schedule to the needs of their instruction. The schedule within the block of time can be varied from day to day by the team at their discretion. In order to properly establish a fluid block schedule, the plan must provide an adequate amount of space (for example, four classrooms clustered together), a two- to three-hour block of time, and a common team of teachers along with an appropriate ratio of students. As

Reg. Room H50

Name Maver   Tara   Eve
      Last   First   Middle

Sex = M (F)   Year in School = /11/

PER.	TIME	Monday COURSE	RM	TCHR	Tuesday COURSE	RM	TCHR	Wednesday COURSE	RM	TCHR	Thursday COURSE	RM	TCHR	Friday COURSE	RM	TCHR
Reg.	8:05															
1	8:15	BG-Lg	H4	WESS	BT	H6	SAGE	BG-Lg	H4	Kart	BT	H6	SAGE	Activity Period		
2	8:35	BG-Lg	H4	WESS	BT	H6	SAGE	BG-Lg	H4	Kart	BT	H6	SAGE	Activity Period		
3	8:55	BG-Lg	H4	WESS	BT	H6	SAGE	Bg-Lg	H4	Kart	BT	H6	SAGE	Activity Period		
4	9:15										E-Mg	B3	MILO	MU	B5	LEE
5	9:35										E-Mg	B3	MILO	MU	B5	LEE
6	9:55				SS-Sg	B7	ELY				E-Mg	B3	MILO	MU	B5	LEE
7	10:15	MU	B5	LEE	SS-Sg	B7	ELY	MU	B5	LEE	MU	B5	LEE			
8	10:35	MU	B5	LEE	AG-Lg	AU	MOY	MU	B5	LEE	MU	B5	LEE			
9	10:55	MU	B5	LEE	AG-Lg	AU	MOY	MU	B5	LEE	MU	B5	LEE			
10	11:15	BG-Sg	H4	WESS				BG-Sg	H4	WESS				BG-Sg	H4	WESS
11	11:35	BG-Sg	H4	WESS	LUNCH			BG-Sg	H4	WESS				BG-Sg	H4	WESS
12	11:55	SS-Lg	AU	WADE	LUNCH						LUNCH					
13	12:15	SS-Lg	AU	WADE							LUNCH					
14	12:35	LUNCH			AG-Lab	A2	LIMA	LUNCH			Ag-Lab	A2	LIMA	LUNCH		
15	12:55	LUNCH			AG-Lab	A2	LIMA	LUNCH			Ag-Lab	A2	LIMA	LUNCH		
16	1:15	E-Lg	H9	RES	AG-Lab	A2	LIMA				Ag-Lab	A2	LIMA	E-Lab	B6	TROY
17	1:35	E-Lg	H9	RES	AG-Lab	A2	LIMA				Ag-Lab	A2	LIMA	E-Lab	B6	TROY
18	1:55				AG-Lab	A2	LIMA				Ag-Lab	A2	LIMA	E-Lab	B6	TROY
19	2:15	SS-Sq	B7	ELY				SS-Sg	B7	ELY				E-Lab	B6	TROY
20	2:35	SS-Sq	B7	ELY	E-Sg	B8	LEM	SS-Sg	B7	ELY				SS-Lg	AU	WADE
21	2:55	SS-Sq	B7	ELY	E-Sg	B8	LEM	SS-Sg	B7	ELY				SS-Lg	AU	WADE
	3:10	DISMISSAL														

FIGURE 13–11. Student program 1963–1964

long as this group remains mutually exclusive from other aspects of the schedule, the team has the power to control variations within it. For example, a team of four teachers, two social studies teachers, and two language arts teachers, and their assigned 120 students could use a three-hour block of time as shown in figure 13–12.

Option 1 suggests a large group presentation to sixty students in each subject, with the students rotating to a second subject at the end of the hour. Students would have one hour remaining for supervised study.

Option 2 suggests a large group/small group teaching with an overall student-teacher ratio of thirty to one. It is accomplished by trading off very large classes for the opportunity for the teacher to work with as few as fifteen students in a discussion group. By following a two-day cycle, students can be in a large group each day and a small group every other day in each subject. A third day can be incorporated into the cycle for study time and teacher preparation time, or the large group time can be converted to study time every other day.

Option 3 illustrates how a film or guest lecturer may be used for the entire group of students, eliminating the need for multiple presentations.

Option 4 shows how a team might schedule an interdisciplinary unit with each teacher contributing to a specialized part of an overall common topic.

The fluid block schedule is most applicable to required subject areas because of greater enrollments. It can best be scheduled when combined with two or three single hour courses selected as electives to be taught during the balance of the day. (See figure 13–13.)

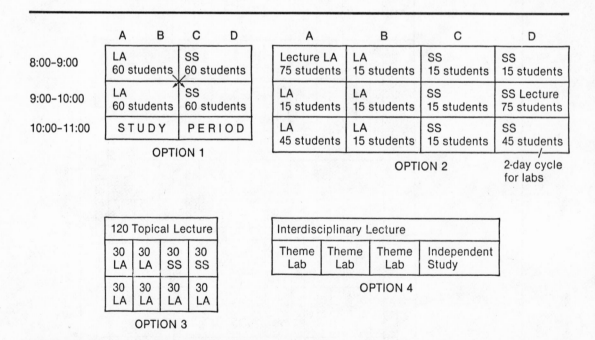

FIGURE 13–12.   Variations in fluid block schedules

Period 1 (4)	3-hour fluid block
2 (5)	2 required subjects,
3 (6)	i.e., LA - SS

Period 4 (1)	elective	elective	
5 (2)	elective	elective	Vocational Block
6 (3)	elective	elective	

FIGURE 13–13.   One half-day fluid block schedule

When the students elect another large block of time, such as a vocational selection, the schedule becomes a fluid block for required subjects during half of the day and an elective block during the other half.

Every team on the fluid block schedule teaches two blocks each day, one in the morning and one in the afternoon, or a block program half of the day and regular electives the other half. When teaching two blocks, the team schedule differs from the traditional in that the teams are assigned students for a full six periods. Part of this time, of course, is to provide supervised study and part of it can become preparation time as the team schedules planning time for themselves. Class loads can most easily be adjusted to limiting the overall number of students assigned to the team.

Fluid block scheduling has a number of advantages over mosaic scheduling. Accountability for students' instruction is achieved because each child is scheduled to a specific team for at least half a day. The organization of the team, the advisement of the students, and the variations in the student program all become the responsibility of the team. There is no study hall, but rather the team is responsible

for supervising study. Flexibility has been obtained for the major portion of the school day by passing on to the team decision-making responsibilities for each student, his or her curriculum, and his or her instruction. The schedule no longer inhibits flexibility. Large group and small group instruction are possible, but more important is that the schedule for any size group can be determined by the team on virtually a daily basis without confounding other parts of the schedule.

The fluid block schedule is realistic. It is highly compatible with traditional scheduling demands when this is preferred during the other half of the student's day; but it is also highly compatible with other large blocks of time schedules, such as required for most vocational subjects. This makes fluid block schedules particularly attractive to comprehensive high schools where the vocational offerings are many.

Finally, as has been pointed out in the chapter on student discipline and control, the fluid block design would greatly restrict the movement of children throughout the school. It keeps them within a specific core group of students and staff, thus creating a cohesive element which is a major factor for student control.

SUMMARY

This chapter has developed several different concepts of scheduling a high school, from the simple group schedule to the complex modular schedule of some of our more experimental type institutions. Complexity is not always best, however. More traditional mosaic schedules, when properly constructed, are most functional. However, when all aspects of school organization are considered, such as staffing, student grouping, curriculum, instruction, and student advisement and control, the fluid block schedule must be given a high rating.

Under all circumstances, scheduling is a major determinant of the school program. While it should not control, it must be designed in such a way as to not limit the desired instructional program for the school.

BIBLIOGRAPHY

Bush, Robert N., and Allen, Dwight W. *A New Design for High School Education.* New York: McGraw-Hill Book Company, 1964.

Campbell, Lloyd P. "Humanizing Schools Through Mini-Courses." *The Clearing House* 50 (November 1976): 127–129.

Cunningham, Donald C. "Observations on a Modular Schedule." *The Clearing House* (October 1973): 113–116.

DeLucia, Joseph J. "R.E.O.—A Flexible Modular Schedule with Accountability." *NASSP Bulletin* 61 (September 1977): 115–117.

Garvelink, Roger H. "Anatomy of a Good Middle School." *The Education Digest* 39 (February 1974): 14–16.

Gerhard, Brenda. "The Role of the Principal in a Flexible Modular Program." *The Clearing House* 50 (September 1976).

Gibbons, Maurice. *The New Secondary Education. A Phi Delta Kappa Task Force Report.* Bloomington, Ind.: Phi Delta Kappa, Inc., 1976.

Glines, Don E. *Creating Humane Schools.* Mankato. (Minn.): D. M. Printing Company, January 1971.

Heintz, Ann Christine. "Short Courses: Pathways and Pitfalls." *Media and Methods* 13 (Fall 1977): 14–18.

Hillson, Maurie, and Bongo, Joseph. *Continuous Progress Education: A Practical Approach.* Palo Alto, Calif.: Science Research Associates, 1971.

Parker, Jack. "Intangibles in the Master Schedule." *NASSP Bulletin* (October 1974): 79–83.

Petrequin, Gaynor. *Individualizing Learning Through Modular-Flexible Programming.* New York: McGraw-Hill Book Company, 1968.

Saville, Anthony. *Instructional Programming. Issues and Innovations in School Scheduling.* Columbus, Ohio: Charles E. Merrill Publishing Company, 1973.

Sturm, Barnett. "Surviving Mini-Course Registration." *NASSP Bulletin* 59 (September 1975): 99–100.

Tilwich, Richard L. "Student Self-Scheduling: An Unintentional Deception." *NASSP Bulletin* (November 1975): 114–117.

Ubben, Gerald C. "A Fluid Block Schedule." *NASSP Bulletin* 60 (February 1976): 104–111.

Ubben, Gerald C., ed. "School Scheduling and the Use of Time." Panel, J. Lloyd Trump, moderator. *Principal's Audio Journal* 1 (May 1974): Side B, Cassette Services, Inc.

Wilson, L. Craig. *The Open Access Curriculum.* Boston: Allyn and Bacon, Inc., 1971.

Chapter Fourteen

Staffing the School: Recruitment, Selection, and Termination

Recruitment and selection policies of local schools vary. The principal's involvement in the recruitment and selection process will depend on local district practice and policy. Central office personnel often assume the initial responsibility for the recruitment and screening of applicants for teaching positions. The principal should maintain a major role in the process and aggressively pursue this, if necessary. Central offices, often as a means of expediency and sometimes as a policy of control, limit the input of principals and staff in the selection process. If the principal is to be held in any way accountable for the quality of instruction in his or her building, he or she must have a major voice in the selection of personnel.

The major recruitment efforts of the principal begin with completing good position and person descriptions. Figures 14–1 and 14–2 depict sample position and person descriptions. If the principal finds it difficult to locate appropriate candidates, central office personnel should be contacted to review the recruitment process. For example, if the principal, in an effort to diversify the staff, has asked for a teacher from somewhere other than the local college, and the personnel office has not posted vacancies at other colleges, the recruitment drive will be ineffective. The principal is responsible for seeing that recruitment policies are broad enough to meet personnel needs.

The selection of personnel should be a cooperative effort between the district personnel office and the local school. The central office role is to screen applicants and then to send those best matching the position descriptions to the principal for final selection. In some large school districts, a personnel office may employ teachers unassigned to specific buildings, but even in this case, the building principal should have the final decision regarding who works in the building.

Care must always be taken to abide by the federal laws regarding recruitment and selection of staff. The Civil Rights Act of 1871 and the Equal Employment Opportunity Act of 1972 make it unlawful to discriminate on the basis of race, color, religion, sex, or national origin.

THE SELECTION PROCESS

The selection process has several steps. The first is application clarification. Prior to an interview, the principal should carefully review the candidate's application file, comparing the application with the person description. Few candidates will possess all the qualifications that have been specified, but the principal should try to find candidates with most of them.

The second step in the selection process should be a discrepancy analysis of the applica-

---

Lakeview Schools
219 Lakeview Ave.
Lake City

POSITION DESCRIPTION

Position Title: Teacher (team) Senior High School
Language Arts

Purpose of Position: To plan, organize and instruct high school students.

Starting Date:

Salary Range: Beginning teacher, B.S.—$10,200
M.S.—$11,000

Principle Duties: The teacher will be a member of a four-teacher team working with tenth- and eleventh-grade students. Instruction is organized on an interdisciplinary basis with social studies with cooperative planning units. The team has four assigned classrooms and schedules students in a flexible manner into these spaces. Major instructional responsibilities for the team include L.A. and S.S. Each group of students will remain for two hours. Each team will teach two groups each day.

FIGURE 14–1.   Sample position description

Lakeview Schools
219 Lakeview Ave.
Lake City

PERSON DESCRIPTION

Position: Language Arts teacher.

Sex: Prefer male.

Teaching Experience Necessary: None.

Training Requirements: B.S., prefer graduates from other than local college.

Certification: Secondary Language Arts, prefer SS minor.

Teaching Strength: Strong reading training, interest in social studies.

Other Skills: Prefer someone with training or experience with team teaching or I.G.E.

Other Interests: Prefer someone with avocational interests that would appeal to boys, such as camping, hiking, sports, flying, automobiles, etc.

FIGURE 14–2.   Sample person description

---

tion materials. Applicants present themselves in the best manner possible, minimizing weak points. One technique used to uncover discrepancies is searching the file for missing information. Common problem areas are efforts to conceal unfavorable past activities by excluding dates and not listing appropriate reference sources. Other areas include health and legal problems.[1]

The reviewer should look particularly at references from previous employers to make sure each employment situation is represented.

Read between the lines on health records. Look for gaps in employment or school records. The interviewer can request more detailed explanations concerning those areas where possible discrepancies have been identified. Most often, candidates will give perfectly acceptable explanations regarding the discrepancies, but occasionally interviewers uncover serious problems by a discrepancy review.

If the job candidate has had previous teaching experience and is one of the final candidates being considered for the position, a personal telephone contact with the previous principal or other school administrator who is acquainted with the candidate is usually helpful. Often, interviewers can obtain more information during a phone call than from a written reference.

THE JOB INTERVIEW

The job interview has several basic functions. It provides an opportunity for the candidate to clarify any apparent discrepancies found in the written job application. The job interview, however, goes beyond the written application by allowing the principal to gather information in greater depth than can be obtained from written materials only.

Another purpose of the interview is to gain insights into the personality and interpersonal skills of the applicant. Teaching is a "people" business, and teachers must be able to relate well to other adults and children. Research has shown that good verbal skills are particularly significant in determining the quality of a teacher. These skills can best be assessed through an interview.

If the interview can be arranged in the school where employment is to take place, it is helpful to involve teachers from the staff in the interview process. Department heads particularly should play a major role in interviewing perspective teachers for their departments.

Teaching teams should always have the opportunity to interview a prospective addition, to focus on personality match and compatibility of educational philosophy, as well as discuss how the team functions. Whenever possible, the employment recommendation should be based on group interaction of the principal and the existing staff.

Finally, in an interview a candidate must receive, as well as give, information. Two decisions must be made before employment can take place: your decision to employ the candidate and the candidate's decision to want to work in your school. The candidate needs a good information base from which to make the decision. This feedback of information to the candidate should include an expansion of the position description providing more detail about the organization and philosophy of the school and the kinds of children who attend. Also, the specific assignment as well as working conditions should be outlined. If the candidate is not from a local area, a brief orientation to the community might be helpful. Many principals or recruiting officers prepare a brief slide presentation on their community.

At the close of the interview, the principal should outline the next steps. If a decision has been made not to employ, the individual should know. The principal should indicate more candidates are to be interviewed before the final decision and should state an approximate date for the final decision. The candidate should also know if the principal's authority is simply to recommend to the central office. In addition, contract information and such specifics as when the school year begins, what the individual might do in the meantime for preparation, and when the new employee might expect to receive the first paycheck should also be discussed.

The selection process does not end with employment, but should continue through the first several years of employment until the recommendation for permanent employment-tenure.

ORIENTATION OF NEW STAFF

The basic purpose of staff orientation is to provide a rapid adjustment to the new position and early integration into the working environment. The main focus of orientation should be on instruction, operating procedures, and interpersonal relationships. Orientation of the new staff can be divided into three basic phases and should begin shortly after the decision to employ. Phase one is based on the assumption that the new employee is under contract for a month or so before the begining of the school term.

Phase One

Phase one should be initiated with a welcome-aboard letter from the principal and an invitation to visit the school before the start of school, if convenient. Pertinent information regarding the teacher's specific assignment should be provided as soon as it is available. A second letter to the new teacher should include items such as a staff policy manual or handbook, last year's faculty roster or, better yet, a yearbook that includes teachers' pictures. This will aid the new teacher in geting acquainted.

If a summer visit to the school is arranged, the new teacher should be provided with teacher editions of major texts that will be used. Teachers have more leisure time to review materials in the summer than after the school year begins. If new teachers are not going to visit the school during the summer because of distance or other commitments, they should be sent the material anyway. Providing advance information is one of the most productive ways of helping a new teacher get off to a good start.

Phase Two

Phase two begins with the preschool teacher conference and lasts into the first week of the school term. Now that the entire staff is present, the first priority should be developing good interpersonal relationships. Many of the questions and concerns of the new staff member can be handled informally if people are acquainted. Even returning staff members may need some help in redeveloping an effective working relationship. Two good opening group activities to aid in orientation as well as the renewal of acquaintances are useful.

Pairs and Squares Everyone identifies the person in the room they know the least well. When everyone is paired up with another person, each partner takes three minutes for an introduction. After the six-minute interchange is completed, step two begins. Each pair instructed to look around, find another pair of staff members whom they know least well, and join them to create a new group of four. Each person introduces the new friend, taking one minute for each introduction. This second phase takes approximately four or five minutes. The entire exercise takes only about fifteen minutes. If the group is large, it can form groups of eight and repeat the introductions.

Getting to Know You The second game organizes staff members into groups of four to six members. Again, those who know each other least well should be grouped together, mixing new members of the faculty with returning staff members. One member of each team is appointed timekeeper. Each member of the group takes five minutes to describe interests and background. If the individual runs out of things to say before the five minutes are up, the group asks questions for the remaining time. After each person has talked for five minutes, the group feeds back to each participant what they collectively remember about that individual, taking one minute for each individual. Feedback activity is important to the process and should not be overlooked.

A good way to begin this activity is for the principal to model the activity by spending the first five minutes talking to all the groups. The groups should also have to provide timed feedback.

Both activities will begin to open up communication lines within the staff and cause new teachers to feel very much a part of the group, as well as help the returning staff to become better acquainted.

Phase two of the orientation should continue with a session conducted by the principal specifically for the new teachers, focusing on basic operating procedures and discussing the schedule, room assignments, discipline, accounting procedures, and records. Ample opportunity should be provided for questions. This session should be conducted in addition to a regular staff update on similar topics because often a beginning teacher will not feel free to ask certain questions in front of the total staff. Department heads should also play a major part in this phase of orientation for new teachers.

Phase two should also include an orientation to the instructional program—acquaintance with supplementary texts, library materials, etc. If the school is organized into teams, the instructional orientation as well as much of the orientation of the basic operating procedures can be automatically handled within the team. Otherwise, a buddy system, with an experienced teacher assigned to a newcomer, should provide counsel and help in orienting the new staff member to the job. The department head may wish to assign a second- or third-year teacher who has performed well and who is often perceptive to the problems of the beginning teacher.

Phase Three

Phase three of orientation takes place during the entire first year of school. The buddy system or team support continue. The principal continues orientation sessions for the new staff, even if there is only one new member. These sessions should be scheduled at anticipated critical times during the school year. As the year proceeds, they will be needed less frequently. The first session should come after the first two weeks of school with a "how are you doing?" focus. Maintaining a warm, helping relationship with the teacher is important. Another conference should occur near the end of the first marking period to assist new staff members in evaluating students and reporting to parents.

Much of the responsibility for training a good teacher falls upon the principal. Colleges cannot provide all the technical detail necessary to operate successfully on the job. The inservice training program, a prime responsibility of the principal, can accomplish much.

EMPLOYEE PROBATIONARY STATUS

The selection process for staff does not end with employment, but continues through the probationary phase. Most states have a one- to three-year probationary period during which the employee is on a continuing contract before receiving tenured employment. During this period, the principal and department head must reaffirm the original decision to employ a particular staff member. Usually the contract renews automatically around April 15 unless notification is given to the teacher for nonrenewal. Through the continuation of the orientation phase and evaluation of instructional competence, which is discussed in more detail in a subsequent chapter, the emphasis for staff development is upon improving the quality of teaching. The selection process is usually considered complete only when tenure is granted. During this probationary period, the principal must consider the possibility of termination or nonrenewal of the contract when there is reason to suspect that the original selection was not wise.

TEACHER TENURE

One of the most misunderstood concepts in education is tenure. It is not, as often believed, a guaranteed job from which dismissal is all but impossible. Rather, in most states, it is simply a statement of the guarantee of due process assuring exercise of academic freedom for the teacher by allowing dismissal only for specific causes listed in the tenure law. Tenure does not guarantee the right to a job. If the job is abolished, or a teacher is found to be incompetent, insubordinate, or guilty of a variety of socially unacceptable behaviors, that teacher can be dismissed, with proper due process.

In the last few years, federal courts have broadened their decisions regarding due process and human rights to the point that due process guarantees, including many of the guarantees found in the tenure laws, have been extended to most employees. As a result, probationary teachers are now guaranteed many of the same due process rights afforded tenured teachers in the past.[2]

INVOLUNTARY TERMINATION

An extremely poor or incompetent teacher should never be kept on the staff of a school simply because dismissal is difficult. The law establishes definite rights for employer and employee. Procedural due process is guaranteed, but due process does not mean that teachers cannot be dismissed. What it does mean is that teachers have specific rights, such as the right to a hearing, the right to be treated in a fair and nondiscriminatory fashion, and the right to require that just cause be shown for the dismissal action.[3] The law may be more specific about the causes and process of dismissal for teachers under tenure, but dismissal can still be accomplished.

Every dismissal action should be carried out on the assumption that it will ultimately go to court. This attitude is the best way to prevent court action. Rarely will an attorney engaged by a dismissed teacher, or provided by a teacher association, take a case to court if the school district has prepared its action carefully.[4] When the courts reject the dismissal and order reinstatement of a teacher, it is most often because of improper procedure on the part of the school district and less likely the direct issue of teacher behavior.

Preparation for Dismissal

Dismissal decisions should not be made quickly. A tentative decision not to rehire a first-year teacher for the following year should be contemplated three to four months before the deadline for contract renewal. For a tenured teacher, often two or three years are needed to build a case defensible in court to reverse earlier recommendations that were positive enough to have resulted in tenure, even though the recommendations may have been a mistake. Unfortunately, poor personnel records and poor evaluation procedures are common in school districts.

The defensive attorney will often demand to see an entire personnel file for a teacher being dismissed. If positive evaluations have been given in the past, even though unjustified, a greater collection of data of a negative nature is required to offset them. Evidence that the teacher received specific notice of inadequacy and was offered help is important.

In a hearing, the courts will try to answer the following questions: Was procedural due process used? Is the evidence appropriate and supportive of the case? Was the employee discriminated against? Were efforts made to help the employee? Did the employee have prior knowledge that his or her work was unsatisfactory? The following suggestions will be helpful in preparing dismissal actions.[5]

Due Process Teachers must be given timely notice of the decision not to rehire. If contract renewal comes on April 15, with a two-week hearing notice deadline, employees should be notified by April 1. A certified letter is the best way of assuring a record of such notification. Employees must be informed that they have the opportunity for and the right to a hearing. The hearing time, date, and place should be stated in the letter. If the teacher is tenured, the letter should also include the specific causes or charges for dismissal. Recent due process decisions from the courts in some cases make it highly advisable to provide this opportunity for a hearing to nontenured teachers as well as to those who have tenure.[6]

Appropriateness of Evidence Evidence should be firsthand, factual, and documented accurately with appropriate dates. If the offense is accumulative in nature, the collection of data should also be accumulative. Descriptive notes of supervisory meetings and conferences, for example, expressing agreed upon outcomes and a statement describing the extent of the implementation or the lack thereof on the part of the teacher should be included. The statements should be objective. Rather than stating, "This teacher did a poor job of teaching today," the note should state that in presenting a lesson on the civil war the teacher did not hold the interest of the class, the students did not understand the lesson as presented, and the class became unruly while under the teacher's direction. Include the date, the time, what led up to the lessons, such as the previous involvement of the supervisor, and any immediate follow-up action that was taken. A note might simply read, "Mr. Smith arrived at school at 8:30 on December 2, 3, 4. His designated time of arrival is 8:00. He has been notified of this deficiency." This is not a judgmental statement, simply a statement of fact. Such items, properly collected, can be used to support the claim of incompetence or insubordination. The important thing to remember is to record facts, not opinions, and to do it in a timely fashion.

Equal Rights Was the employee treated in a fair and nondiscriminatory manner? Was anything done to or for this employee that was not done or available to other employees? Was the assignment unfair? Was the teacher asked to do more or less than the rest of the staff? Was supervision uniform? A grossly unequal schedule for supervision, for example, can be construed to be harassment. When problems arise, however, it is not unreasonable for supervision to increase as long as the time sequence can be demonstrated. Supervisory appointments and documentation included only in the file of the teacher being dismissed with no evidence of supervision included in the files of the other members of the staff, however, will often be looked upon as discriminatory action by the courts.

Were Efforts Made to Help the Teacher? The courts will want to know what was done to make this individual an effective employee. Was adequate supervision of a helping nature developed? If not, the courts may not uphold the dismissal action but may reinstate the employee, suggesting that the supervisory staff provide assistance.

Most often, when the principal is well prepared and has central office support, teacher dismissal, while serious, will take place quietly. A teacher who knows that school officials are well prepared most often will not request a hearing and will simply resign. Most cases resulting in the failure to dismiss are a result of poor preparation and improper procedure on the part of the school district. See figure 14–3 for a flowchart for employee dismissal procedures.

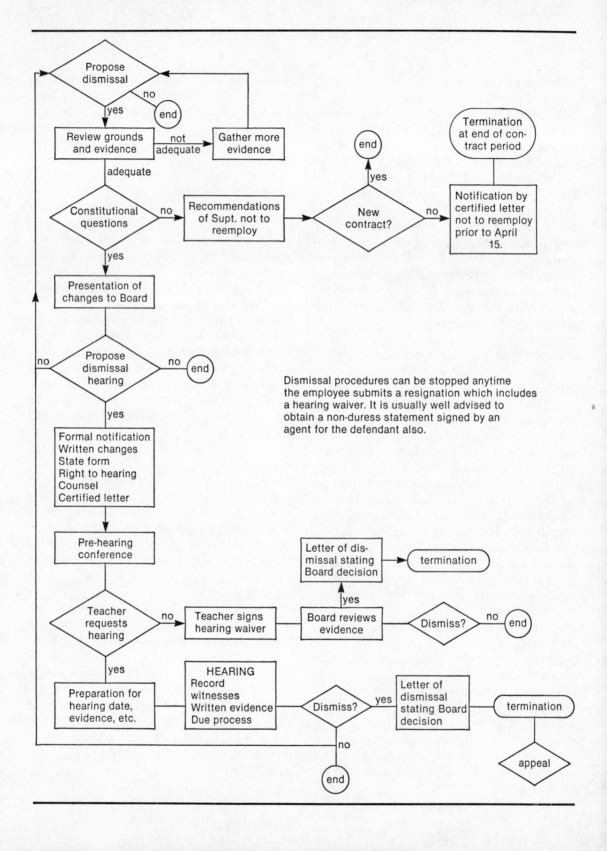

Dismissal procedures can be stopped anytime the employee submits a resignation which includes a hearing waiver. It is usually well advised to obtain a non-duress statement signed by an agent for the defendant also.

VOLUNTARY TERMINATIONS

Each year staff members will resign from a school for a variety of reasons: retirement, transfers, better jobs, starting a family, going back to school, and incompetence. In every case the principal should hold a termination interview before that person departs. Several basic purposes exist for such an interview. Of primary concern is the help the school might offer the individual in adjusting to a new life situation.

Second, the interview should be an opportunity to investigate the perceptions of the departing employee regarding the operation of the school. At times principals have difficulty getting good information about the operation of the school and the existing climate within the staff. Often, departing employees will be very candid about their perceptions concerning existing problems. They may even identify some previously hidden reason for leaving.

Finally, the interview can be useful in identifying prospects for substitute, part-time, volunteer, and future employment when the departing employee is remaining within the community. Retired teachers, or those who are staying home to rear a family, are particularly good candidates for part-time employment or volunteer positions.

SUMMARY

The search for and the employment of new staff members is one of the most important tasks of a school administrator. The process begins with the determination of staff needs, including recruitment, selection, orientation, and staff development, and culminates with the placement of the employee on tenure.

Termination of employees, voluntarily or involuntarily, will occur in most schools each year. The principal needs to conduct exit interviews with all terminating employees. Involuntary termination is usually a difficult, but sometimes necessary, task. An important point in staff dismissal is following due process and insuring that the employee's rights have not been violated.

ENDNOTES

1. Gerald C. Ubben, "Selecting Personnel," *Principals Audio Journal* 1 (December 1974). Cassette Services, St. Paul, Virginia.

2. A good discussion of the future of tenure can be found in Larry W. Hughes and William M. Gordon, "Frontiers of Law," *The Courts and Education, 77th Yearbook of the National Society for the Study of Education,* ed. Clifford Hooker (Chicago: University of Chicago Press, 1978), final chapter.

3. See chapter 5 for information about the steps in procedural due process.

4. See chapter 5, especially the reference to *Illinois Educational Association* v. *Board of Education,* 320 N.E. 2nd 240 (Ill. App. 1974).

5. Cases Related to Due Process—Teacher Dismissal
   a. *Board of Regents* v. *Roth,* 92 S. Ct. 2701 (1972) and *Perry* v. *Sunderman,* 92S Ct. 2694 (1972). These are the precedent cases regarding due process just like *Brown* v. *Board of Education* is for discrimination cases.
   b. *Paul* v. *Davis* 424 U.S. 693 (1976); *Bishop* v. *Wood* 246 U.S. 341 (1976); and *Meachum* v. *Fano* 427 U.S. 215 (1970).
   c. 7th Cir., the Court of Appeals in *Confederation of Police* v. *City of Chicago* 547 F. 2d 375 (1977).
   d. *Codd* v. *Velger* 97 S. Ct. 882 (1977).
   e. *Arnet* v. *Kennedy* 416 U.S. 134 (1974).
   f. *Peacock* v. *Board of Regents* 510 F 2d 1324 (9th Cir.).
   g. *Withrow* v. *Larken* (421 U.S. 35, 1975).
   h. Hortonville 96S Ct. 2308.
   i. *Mt. Healthy City School District* v. *Doyle* 97 S. Ct. 568 (1977).

◄ **FIGURE 14–3.** Flowchart for employee dismissal procedure

6. While most state tenure laws and continuing contract laws in and of themselves do not require a hearing for nontenured staff, the federal constitution and the Civil Rights Act of 1871 might. In a series of court decisions over recent years, a teacher is considered to have certain rights under the 1st and 14th amendments to the constitution. While non-renewal of a contract does not require a hearing, dismissal does. If a denial of freedom of speech claim is made, a hearing is advisable, and if the case is receiving much publicity so as to endanger the individual's opportunity for other employment a hearing should be held. Also, if discrimination is charged a hearing should be held. If an opportunity for a hearing is not granted, the teacher may later file a complaint of a violation of due process.

BIBLIOGRAPHY

Beach, Dale S. *Personnel: The Management of People at Work,* 2nd ed. New York: MacMillan Company, 1970.

Bishop, Leslee J. *Staff Development and Instructional Improvement.* Boston: Allyn and Bacon, Inc., 1976.

Bolton, Dale L. *Selection and Evaluation of Teachers.* Berkeley, Calif.: McCutchan Publishing Co., 1973.

Castetter, William B. *The Personnel Function in Educational Administration.* New York: MacMillan Company, 1976.

Crowe, Robert L., "The Computer and Personnel Selection." *School Management* 16 (August 1972): 40.

Dipboye, Robert L.; Avery, Richard D.; and Terpstra, David E. "Sex and Physical Attractiveness of Raters and Applicants as Determined by Resume Evaluations." *Journal of Applied Psychology* 62 (June 1977): 288-294.

Drake, Frances S. "The Interviewer and His Art." *The Personnel Man and His Job.* New York: American Management Association, 1962.

"Evaluating School Personnel." *The National Elementary Principal* 52 (February 1973): 12-100. The entire volume is devoted to evaluating personnel.

Flippo, Edwin B. *Principles of Personnel Management.* New York: McGraw-Hill, 1971.

Hooker, Clifford, ed. *The Courts and Education, 77th Yearbook of the National Society for the Study of Education.* Chicago: University of Chicago Press, 1978. See especially chapter entitled, "Frontiers of Law."

Hughes, Larry W., and Ubben, Gerald C. *The Elementary Principal's Handbook: A Guide to Effective Action.* Boston: Allyn and Bacon, 1978.

Hyman, Ronald T. *School Administrator's Handbook of Teacher Supervision and Evaluation Methods.* Englewood Cliffs, N.J.: Prentice-Hall, Inc., 1975.

McKenna, Bernard H., and Charles D. McKenna, "How to Interview Teachers." *American School Board Journal,* 155 (June 1968): 8-9.

Redfern, George B. *How to Appraise Teaching Performance.* Columbus, Ohio: School Management Institute, Inc., 1963.

Chapter Fifteen

The Principal as Supervisor

Staff supervision and evaluation are essential activities of the secondary school principal. Just as a teacher manages student learning by using a diagnostic prescriptive model, so can the principal direct staff improvement using staff evaluation as a diagnostic tool and the co-operative establishment of job targets as a prescriptive tool.

Staff evaluation in today's complex school faces many difficulties. The advent of collective bargaining has often placed many restrictions and regulations that must be adhered to in order to stay "within" the contract. The immense responsibility of the principal of almost any school makes it extremely difficult, if not impossible, to administer an evaluation system without the assistance of a vice principal and/or department heads. As a result, for proper staff development and evaluation the principal must take an initiating, rather than reacting role, and the comprehensive plan for staff evaluation must be based on a sound rationale.

Staff evaluation has two basic purposes: (1) to improve the performance and provide direction for the continued development of present staff; and (2) to provide a sound basis for personnel decisions, such as awarding tenure, promotions, transfers, or dismissals.

These two purposes create a dilemma for many administrators, even though both support quality education. Staff improvement is largely a helping relationship, most effectively carried out when built on trust between the teacher and the principal. On the other hand, personnel decisions of staff evaluation are judgemental in nature and often cause teacher apprehension.

CHARACTERISTICS OF A GOOD EVALUATION PLAN

A desirable evaluation model should include the following specific characteristics:

1. The opportunity for teachers to establish individual goals or job targets based on individual needs as well as school-wide goals for total staff development.
2. Participation by both the individual and the supervisor in setting goals with a provision for input from other appropriate groups.
3. A plan to identify activities by which goals or targets might be reached.
4. A list of instruments to be used for data collection, including observation guides, checklists, and survey forms.
5. Data collection on teacher performance from appropriate information sources, including students, parents, administrators, peers, and self.

6. A uniform means of summarizing, analyzing, and interpreting observation data.
7. A means of providing evaluative feedback directly to the teacher or through the immediate supervisior or principal.
8. A means of recording evaluative information to be used for personnel decisions.
9. A means of using evaluative information for individual staff development as the basis for setting new job targets.
10. A means of collecting evaluative data as the basis for planning building-level or district-level staff development activities.

ATTRIBUTES OF AN EVALUATION MODEL

Each school district should develop a set of suitable evaluation procedures. A staff evaluation plan should include the following basic considerations as desired attributes of an evaluation system:

1. Development of a positive teacher attitude. Every evaluation plan should make a strong effort to create a positive teacher attitude. Teachers should want and anticipate evaluation because of the insights they will gain.
2. Multiple performance perceptions. The data collection phase of evaluation should include the gathering of information about teacher performance from all appropriate sources, such as students, parents, administrators, and other community representatives with a legitimate contribution.
3. Teacher participation. Teachers should take part in the development or selection of observation instruments, checklists, and summary sheets that make up the evaluation package so that they will know the criteria and process by which they are being judged.
4. Comprehensiveness. The evaluation process must be comprehensive, reflecting all aspects of the daily working environment of the staff. When an evaluation component reviews only a portion of work responsibility, it should be kept in proper perspective in relation to the total work load.
5. State philosophy and objectives. The evaluation process should be based on local philosophy and objectives. Individual evaluations should be designed to consider the particular goals and objectives of the staff member while keeping in mind the overall goals of the school.
6. Self-improvement focus. The evaluation process must recognize that from the vantage point of staff development, the end product is one of self-improvement.
7. Validity and reliability. The evaluation design must emphasize the truly significant aspects of job performance and measure them with a high degree of accuracy and consistency. The use of multiple perceptions by one or more evaluators usually improves validity and reliablity.
8. Good use of time. The evaluation procedure must not be too lengthy, but should take enough time to ensure justness and fairness.
9. Benefits. The evaluation system must improve staff performance in order to justify the cost of its operation.

These nine considerations provide the underpinning for the development of an evaluation plan. Based on these considerations, a number of different evaluation processes are possible.

THE STAFF EVALUATION CYCLE

Staff evaluation and development is a cyclical process. Staff evaluation leads to a staff development prescription that is checked once again through evaluation.

Seven basic steps in the evaluation cycle focus on the ultimate purpose of improving instruction. The cycle begins when the teacher and principal plan goals and targets for the year and includes other people in the evaluation process. (See figure 15–1.) The seven steps of the evaluation cycle are as follows:

1. Identify and integrate individual and institutional goals.
2. Select specific objectives or activities for observation.
3. Determine the observation method, time, and place.
4. Observe and collect data.

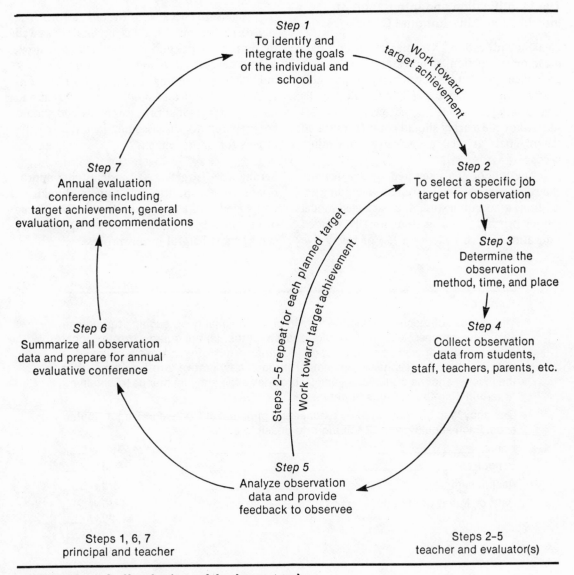

FIGURE 15–1.   Staff evaluation and development cycle

5. Analyze data and provide feedback.
6. Summarize and interpret collective observational data.
7. Report evaluation results and target achievement; make recommendations for individual and staff development at annual conference.

The Identification and Integration of Individual and Institutional Goals

Goal Identification   To maximize improvement of instruction, a necessary first step is goal identification. A principal should meet yearly with each staff member to select goals and specify job targets for that year.[1] The goal selected by the teacher should come from stated school goals as well as perceived individual needs.

The school goals selected by the teacher can come from numerous sources, including accrediting association studies, a packaged model school progam (such as Individually Guided Education[2] which includes a list of thirty-five

goals), or simply a local assessment. No matter what its source, each school should have a list of school goals and this list should be the basis for individual teacher planning and goal setting for personal improvement. The kinds of goals that come from a school-wide assessment process are often broadly stated and must usually be restated as a series of specific objectives. (See chapter 7.)

A general checklist of overall performance categories for individual needs can be reviewed by both principal and teacher. This list, however, is never the *only* source of information for individual goal setting. In the goal-setting conference, the principal should aid the teacher in identifying personal problem areas and should be prepared to discuss and identify specific targets for improvement.

Setting Job Targets   After identifying appropriate goals, specific job targets should be designated for each goal. A planning document, such as the one shown in Figure 15–2, can be most helpful in this process.

Purpose

The purpose of teacher evaluation is to improve the quality of teaching through an evaluative process which: (1) recognizes strengths, (2) encourages professional growth and improved competency, (3) identifies areas of weakness and provides specific plans for teacher improvement through cooperative effort on the part of the teacher and the evaluator(s), and (4) provides a fair and just means for retaining or terminating the services of personnel.

One copy is to be completed by teacher and principal at Goals and Target Conference. Each should give prior thought to possible entries.

Name_____   Experience: 1st yr.____
School _____   2nd yr.____
Assignment_____   3rd yr.____
Date of Initial Conference_____   4–10 yr.____
                                                              11–20 yr.____
                                                              over 20 yr.____

(continued)

Goals, Targets and Activities for Personal Professional Growth:
(Use separate sheet for each goal.)
Goal I _____

_____

_____

Target IA_____
date_____/_____.

    Activity IA1_____

_____

_____

    Activity IA2_____

_____

_____

    Activity IA3_____

_____

_____

Target IB_____
date_____/_____

    Activity IB1_____

_____

_____

    Activity IB2_____

_____

_____

    Activity IB3_____

_____

_____

Target IC_____
date_____/_____

    Activity IC1_____

_____

_____

    Activity IC2_____

_____

_____

    Activity IC3_____

_____

_____

FIGURE 15-2. Evaluation form for teachers

Probably the most difficult technical task in setting goals is focusing on the general goals by creating specific job targets. This task is very similar to organizing instruction for the classroom. For example, appropriate goals might be as follows:

Goal I: To more effectively individualize instruction.
Goal II: To organize instruction to include greater student participation in learning activities.

These goals are very general in nature and, while they provide a sense of direction for the teacher, they are not specific enough to direct action.

A variety of targets must be developed to fit each goal. For example, appropriate targets for goal I might be as follows:

Target IA: To build and use three good learning packages for a fall science unit.
Target IB: To develop and use a skills grouping plan for science laboratory skills instruction.

Targets should be written as behaviorally-stated objectives. These targets provide the teacher with something specific to work toward and accomplish. It is also appropriate to identify dates for the completion of targets.

Activities   Activities or tasks must be carried out to successfully meet a target. For example, meeting target IA might depend on the following activities:

Activity IA1: Read the book *Learning Centers* by John I. Thomas.
Activity IA2: Take a summer course on learning package construction.

Activity IA3: Build a practice learning package, and ask a colleague for an opinion. Try it out on the children.
Activity IA4: Attend an inservice workshop on learning package construction.

These activities should give a teacher the basic skills necessary to fulfill the target of building and using learning packages for the science unit. The activities are not the significant items; completion of the target is because it indicates movement toward the goal of improved individualized instruction.

This initial step in the evaluation cycle is extremely important. It provides direction, focus, continuity, and purpose to the entire evaluation process. Through this process, each individual within the organization receives a specific charge that sets direction. The principal's involvement in setting goals and targets for each teacher keeps the staff moving in the same direction, while the involvement of the teachers allows the evaluation cycle to become an individual self-improvement process.

The planning schedule of the evaluation process is completed with the scheduling of the activities and the selection of dates for the completion of the various targets. Figure 15–3 illustrates an evaluation cycle time schedule. Upon completion of the planning document, the staff members proceed to initiate the plan, carrying out the activities as outlined. As the first target date approaches, the teacher plans for an evaluation of that target, beginning with a pre-observation conference.

Pre-Observation Conference

The pre-observation conference has two basic purposes: (1) selecting a particular topic for observation, and (2) planning the details of the observation.

By June (or end of September for new staff) principal and teachers:

Plan goals, targets, and activities jointly by teacher and principal (Step 1)
(This can be on extension of the Annual Evaluation Conference for returning staff.)

By end of November (teachers and evaluators):

Achieve at least one job target using a pre-observation, observation, post-observation conference (Steps 2–5)
(This date, of course, assumes the appropriateness of both the observation cycle and type target planned)

By end of January (teachers and evaluators):

Achieve additional job targets (Steps 2–5)

By March 1 (teachers and evaluators):

Achieve additional job targets (Steps 2–5) and submit all evaluative data to principal (Step 6)

March 15 (principal and nontenured teachers):

Complete all annual evaluation conferences with nontenured teachers. All appropriate evaluation forms and recommendations to be forwarded to personnel office (Steps 6 and 7)

By April 1 (principal and teachers):

Complete all other annual evaluative conferences where transfer or termination is to be recommended. All appropriate evaluation forms and recommendations to be forwarded to personnel office (Steps 6 and 7)

April 15 (principal and teachers):

Complete all other annual evaluative conferences for all other tenured staff. All appropriate forms and recommendations to be forwarded to the personnel office (Steps 6 and 7)

End of the school year (principal and teachers):

Plan conferences to set goals, targets, and activities for returning staff (Step 1)

FIGURE 15-3.   Calendar for evaluation cycle

Target Selection (Step 2)   The several job targets of a teacher are usually too many or too varied to be properly observed and evaluated all at one time. Individual job targets should be selected one at a time for observation and evaluation.

Planning the Observation (Step 3)   Once the particular target has been selected, plans should be made for data collection regarding its achievement.

Observers   A pre-observation conference should include the teacher to be evaluated and those responsible for the data collection. The principal should not attempt to personally conduct all observations. Sometimes the principal is an appropriate data collector, but students, other teachers, parents, and other supervisors are also available. Numerous research findings support the position that others besides a principal who come in contact with the teacher at work can make valid and reliable judgments about that work.[3] Also, good data collection for evaluation takes time, usually more time than most principals have available.

Observation Tools A variety of observation instruments are available or can be created through various types of data collection for teacher evaluation.[4,5] There are instruments available to measure student perceptions of a teacher and his or her performance in the classroom and its effect on the student. There are also the more standard type instruments to be used by a professional as evaluator measuring teacher performance in the classroom, classroom organization, classroom environment, teaching strategies, etc.

Time and Place The time and place for the observation also need to be arranged during the pre-observation conference. Steps 2 and 3 determine the specific target to be observed, the method by which data will be gathered, when data collection will be done, and by whom.

Collection of Observation Data (Step 4) Data collection is simply carrying out the plan outlined in Step 3.

Observations need not be long, particularly if the job target is narrow in scope. Separate observation cycles for different job targets are often better than trying to combine a whole series of observations into one command performance. Fifteen minutes is usually adequate time to observe one technique or activity. The observation should take place at a scheduled time and place, and should maintain as normal an atmosphere as possible so the data will be reliable.

Post-observation Conference (Step 5) The observer should report and analyze the observation and provide feedback to the person observed.

The post-observation conference should be conducted by the person in charge of data collection. In some cases it will be the principal; often it will be another teacher. Information gathered from students or parents is returned to the principal or other designated person. Confidentiality of responses should be maintained.

Feedback on direct observation as well as other recorded data should be provided to a teacher the same day as the observation, or at least within a day or so. This immediacy will be helpful to both the observer and the observed. The results of the observation should be filed with the principal for the annual review and report.

The post-observation conference should include a review of the target or goal, a review of the activities leading up to the observation, and a description of the data collection itself. Post-observation conferences should take a positive direction. Praise goes much further than criticism in bringing about improved performance. Often it is wise to have the person observed describe their perceptions of the observation period or their expectations of the results of the questionnaire first. Most people are more critical of themselves than others will be, and self-criticism is usually the least destructive criticism for an individual.

If the self-criticism is close to being accurate, then the evaluator can say little of a negative nature. Remember, one of the first attributes listed for the evaluation model was that teachers should have a positive attitude toward evaluation. Negative criticism can destroy positive attitudes or prevent its development.

A positive note on which to end postobservation conferences is to ask the person observed to indicate how the observation cycle helped them. After they have responded, it is appropriate for the evaluator, teachers, principal, or supervisor to share with them any new insights gained by functioning as the evaluator.

A Cyclical Process (Steps 2–5) Steps 2 through 5 of the evaluation cycle may be repeated numerous times during the year for different job targets or for repeated evaluations of a particular job target. The relationship of the steps to each other over time are illustrated in figure 15-3. Steps 1, 6, and 7 are usually done only once each year.

Preparation of the Annual Individual Evaluation Report (Step 6)   At the end of each annual evaluation cycle, and in time to meet the legal deadlines for contract renewal or termination, the evaluative data gathered during the year should be summarized. Each teacher should be sure that all the necessary data collection has been done for each target established. The actual task of analyzing and summarizing the evaluative data belongs to the principal.

Each set of goals and targets should be evaluated for the degree of achievement. The principal should not expect teachers to meet all targets, however. Teachers should work toward goals through the completion of set targets, but if they must achieve all targets each year, teachers will very quickly learn to set only achievable targets and will never reach out to challenging ones. Therefore, some targets may not have been reached. Each case, of course, must be judged on its individual merits.

Comments should be written about each job target and its degree of achievement. Recommendations should be considered as proposals for job targets for the following year. This evaluative summation can be recorded on a form similar to the one on which job goals, targets, and activities were entered earlier (figure 15-2).

The principal should prepare a general overall performance evaluation at this time, reviewing the normal expectations of the teachers within the organization. Such items as meeting certification requirements, following general rules and regulations of the school district, teacher effectiveness, personal characteristics, management of students, and effectiveness in working with others may be included. The overall performance evaluation should only indicate whether a teacher is or is not performing satis-

factorily in each of these categories. An unsatisfactory rating, however, requires an explanation. Figure 15-4 illustrates a checklist evaluation form for teachers. This summarized performance evaluation should be shared with the teacher along with the recommendations developed in Step 7.

Annual Evaluation Conference and Recommendations

The annual evaluation conference, usually held in March or April with each teacher, includes three distinct tasks:

1. A review of the year's targets and the determination of the degree to which they have been achieved, using a form such as the one shown in figure 15-2.
2. A summary evaluation by the principal of each teacher's overall performance, using a summary checklist similar to the one shown in figure 15-4.
3. Recommendations for future targets for further staff development.

Recommendations for staff development should take two forms. The first is the identification of a proposed set of individual targets or goals as recommended improvement points for the next cycle of staff evaluation. These recommendations become the basis for generating new goals.

The second major thrust focuses on staff development on a school-wide basis. Gathering the criticisms and target recommendations for teachers in a school portrays a particular pattern of staff training needs. This is a most useful planning tool for outlining group staff development activities. (See figure 15-5.) If, for example, a staff needs profile indicates a need for learning center development or improvement, it would be helpful to organize a collective improvement program in that specific target area.

One copy is to be completed by the teacher and one by the principal evaluator.

Check the appropriate response under each statement. List any areas of strength you want to point out under each statement. If your response is "unsatisfactory" for any statement, substantiate the response and give recommendations for improvement.

1. The teacher is meeting the *Rules, Regulations, and Minimum Standards* of the State Board of Education:

Satisfactory ☐   Unsatisfactory ☐

_____

_____

2. The teacher is meeting the policies, procedures, rules, and regulations set forth in this school's handbook:

Satisfactory ☐   Unsatisfactory ☐

_____

_____

3. The teacher's effectiveness in working with students is:

Satisfactory ☐   Unsatisfactory ☐

_____

_____

4. The teacher's personal characteristics are:

Satisfactory ☐   Unsatisfactory ☐

_____

_____

5. The teacher's student management is:

Satisfactory ☐   Unsatisfactory ☐

_____

_____

6. The teacher's effectiveness in working with others is:

Satisfactory ☐   Unsatisfactory ☐

_____

_____

7. The teacher's professional ethics are:

Satisfactory ☐   Unsatisfactory ☐

_____

_____

(continued)

Recommendations: This teacher is recommended for (check appropriate boxes):

1. ☐ Continuation in his or her present position at this school.
2. ☐ Transfer to another position in this school system.
3. ☐ Termination of employment with appropriate notice according to the Conditions of Employment (contract).
4. ☐ Tenure in this system.

We discussed the above report in a conference_____.
(date)

Signed _____ Teacher

Signed _____ Principal

FIGURE 15-4.   Checklist evaluation form for teachers

Teachers	Group interaction	Learning centers	Small group instruction	Discipline	Record keeping	Reading skills instruction	Team skills	Other
Abbott, C.		X	X	X		X	X	X
Henderson, F.	X	X		X		X		X
Carson, B.			X	X	X			X
Dole, J.	X	X		X			X	X
Goff, R.	X	X			X			X
Harris, S.		X	X	X		X	X	X
Jones, B.	X	X		X			X	X
Nance, D.		X	X	X	X			X
Poriera, L.	X		X				X	X
Smith, T.		X			X	X		X
Wall, W.		X	X				X	X

FIGURE 15-5.   Staff development needs survey

A collective staff development program can also be used on a school district level if similar evaluation programs are used in each individual building. The more teachers available for the various parts of a planned, personalized inservice program, the greater its efficiency and effectiveness.

SUMMARY

The evaluation plan outlined in this chapter has two major components that operate on an annual cycle. One component consists of an annual review that pulls together the evaluative data for a particular teacher, summarizes those data with the teacher (Step 6), and recommends appropriate goals to be included in next year's agreement. In addition, it notes those recommendations for input into the school staff development program (Step 7). The annual evaluation conference ends with the beginning of the new cycle, and the development of a new set of goals and targets based on the individual needs of the teacher as well as school-wide goals.

The second major component of the evaluation cycle consists of the identification of particular targets and activities for immediate attention (Step 2), the planning of the particular observation (Step 3), the actual observation and data collection (Step 4), and finally, the postobservation conference where feedback is provided to the teacher on performance (Step 5). Steps 2 through 5 can be repeated numerous times during the year for the various goals and targets selected by the teacher in preparation for the annual evaluation conference.

ENDNOTES

1. A goal is something to strive toward, while a job target is a specific objective to be met.
2. Individually Guided Education is a model elementary school design focusing on individualized instruction and team teaching, disseminated by the Institute for the Development of Educational Activities, Kettering Foundation, Dayton, Ohio.
3. An excellent reference for client-centered evaluations is the publication of the Educational Research Service, *The Evaluatee Evaluates the Evaluator,* Washington, D.C.: American Association of School Administrators and Research Division, NEA, Nov. 5, 1970.
4. For an excellent source for variety of observation tools, see Gary D. Borich, and Susan K. Madden, *Evaluating Classroom Instruction: A Sourcebook of Instruments* (Reading, Mass.: Addison-Wesley Publishing Co., 1977).
5. Available instruments useful in assessing student information about the teacher include:

- *The Purdue Teacher Evaluation Scale,* by Ralph W. Bentley and Allan R. Starry. Available from the University Bookstore, 360 State Street, West Lafayette, Indiana 47906.

  The Purdue Evaluation Scale asks junior and senior high school students to provide information to their teacher regarding their performance. The instrument contains sixty questions divided into ten scales including: (1) the Ability to Motivate Students, (2) the Ability to Control Students, (3) Subject Matter Orientation of Teacher, (4) Student-Teacher Communication, (5) Teaching Methods and Procedures, and (6) Teacher Fairness. The instrument has been used extensively and has good reliability and validity data supporting it.
- *Student Evaluation of Teaching I,* by Donald J. Veldman and Robert F. Peck. It can be obtained through the Dissemination Department, Research and Development Center for Teacher Education, The University of Texas, Austin, Texas 78712.

  The Student Evaluation of Teaching, Set I, is a scale consisting of ten items designed to measure the way students perceive their teachers. It can be used through junior and senior high school. Five dimensions describing student perceptions of teaching style are included. These are: Friendly and Cheerful, Knowledgeable and Poised, Lively and Interesting, Disciplined, Non-directive (Democratic).

  Information about student perceptions of classrooms can often be important for the evaluator. There are several instruments designed specifically to collect these data. An instrument of this type is:

- *Learning Environment Inventory,* by Gary J. Anderson. Available from the Atlantic Institute of Education, Halifax, Nova Scotia, Canada.

The Learning Environment Inventory is designed to measure the climate within a classroom as perceived by secondary school students. Fifteen separate dimensions are included, reflecting both interpersonal relationships among students and the organizational characteristics of the classroom. These are Cohesiveness, Diversity, Favoritism, Cliqueness, Satisfaction, Disorganization, Difficulty, Apathy, Democracy, and Comprehensiveness.

A whole series of instruments for teacher evaluation to be used by a professional as observer are available. Some of the more useful include:

- *Observation Schedule and Record Form No. 4,* by Donald J. Medley, J. T. Impelliteri, and L. H. Smith. Available through the Department of Research Methodology, Ruffner Hall, University of Virginia, Charlottesville, Virginia 22903.

The OSCAR 4V is a system designed to assist in the observation of verbal behaviors in the classroom. The instrument is quite sophisticated but relatively easy to use. The focus is on the teacher rather than on the student. Teacher behaviors are categorized under three headings: (1) Teacher Statements, (2) Substantive Interchange, and (3) Non-Substantive interchange. The instrument is particularly useful in guiding the observer to follow the flow of interaction within the classroom over the course of a lesson.

- *Performance Assessment Record for Teachers,* by Bob Burton Brown. Available through the Institute for Development of Human Resources, College of Education, University of Florida, Gainesville, Florida.

The Performance Assessment Record for Teachers provides a framework for observing the classroom performance of both teachers and pupils. It is designed primarily for teacher self-assessment through the playback of an audio or video recording. The instrument consists of twenty-two items that describe what does or does not happen in the classroom. The instrument is not intended to represent universally "good" or "bad" behavior, but rather as a means of gaining insight in the classroom processes and effective teaching procedures. In that sense, it is an excellent instrument to use for this portion of a teacher evaluation system in that it provides descriptive feedback for a classroom teacher.

- *Spaulding Teacher Activity Rating Schedule,* by Robert L. Spaulding. Available through the Institute for Research in Child Development, Room 200, School of Education, San Jose State University, 125 South 7th Street, San Jose, California 95192.

The Spaulding Teaching Activity Rating Schedule is designed to assess the cognitive instructional methods as well as the affective and control strategies of teachers. It is an observational coding system that provides feedback to the teachers about their cognitive and affective styles of instruction. The instrument has a variety of different subsections which can be used independent of one another for focusing on particular teacher activities.

A variety of specific observation instruments are also available to look specifically at the classroom environment rather than at the teacher. The following instruments are basically this type:

- *Classroom Observation Scales,* by Edmund T. Emmer. Available at the Research and Development Center for Teacher Education, University of Texas, Austin, Texas 78712.

This instrument measures the classroom process through twelve variables. Included are: Pupil Attention, Teacher-Initiated Problem Solving, Pupil-to-Pupil Interaction, Teacher Presentation, Negative Affect, Positive Affect, Higher Level Cognitive Student Behavior, Passive Pupil Behavior, Convergent-Evaluative Interaction, Task Orientation, Clarity, and Enthusiasm. The observation scales are easy to learn and use and care for the most part behaviorally based.

• *Cognitive Component System,* by Edmund T. Emmer and I. Dorothy Albrecht. Available at the Research and Development Center for Teacher Education, University of Texas, Austin, Texas 78712.

The Cognitive Component System is an instrument designed to measure teacher and student behaviors within the classroom. Thirty classifications of cognitive behavior are tallied. The system may be used with audio or video tapes for teacher self-analysis.

• *Flanders System of Interaction Analysis,* by Ned A. Flanders. Available through Addison-Wesley Publishing Company, Reading, Massachusetts 01867.

The Flanders System of Interaction Analysis is probably one of the best known in education. This system focuses primarily on teacher behaviors that restrict or increase student freedom of action. The behaviors are recorded and tallied on a 10×10 matrix which provides a visual diagram of classroom interaction. Ten categories are used to classify teacher-student behaviors. They are: indirect teacher influences of accepting feeling, praise or encouraging, accepting or using student ideas, and asking questions. Direct teacher categories include: lecturing, giving directions, or criticizing or justifying authority. Two student categories are included: student talk as in responding and student talk as in initiating. The tenth category is one of silence or confusion.

• *Nonverbal Interaction Analysis,* by Peggy Amidon. Available through Paul S. Amidon and Associates, Minneapolis, Minnesota.

The Nonverbal Interaction Analysis is designed to parallel the categories from the Flanders Interaction Analysis, but deals with observing and recording nonverbal behaviors in the classroom. Four dimensions are included: (1) room arrangements, (2) materials, (3) nonverbal behaviors, and (4) activities. The first two categories deal with the physical arrangements within the classroom. The third dimension references the teacher's nonverbal behavior, while the fourth combines the first three and adds the dimension of the student interaction within.

BIBLIOGRAPHY

Abramson, Paul. "When Teachers Evaluate Each Other." *Scholastic Teacher* 43 (September 1972): 26-28.

Amidon, Edmund J.; Kiss, Kathleen M.; and Palisi, Anthony. "Group Supervision." *National Elementary Principal* 45 (April 1966): 54-58.

Bishop, Leslee J. *Staff Development and Instructional Improvement.* Boston: Allyn and Bacon, 1976.

Bolton, Dale L. *Selection and Evaluation of Teachers.* Berkeley, Calif.: McCutchan Publishing Corp., 1973.

Borich, Gary D. *The Appraisal of Teaching: Concepts and Process.* Reading, Mass.: Addison-Wesley Publishing Co., 1977.

Borich, Gary D., Madden, Susan K. *Evaluating Classroom Instruction: A Sourcebook of Instruments.* Reading, Mass.: Addison-Wesley Publishing Co., 1977.

Cogan, Morris L. *Clinical Supervision.* Boston: Houghton Mifflin, 1973.

Delano, June S. "In-Service for Change." *Educational Leadership* 32 (1975): 520-523.

Educational Research Service. *Evaluating Teaching Performance.* Washington, D.C.: American Association of School Administrators and Research Division, *NEA* 3 (1969); 3 (1972); (1979).

Goldhammer, Robert. *Clinical Supervision.* New York: Holt, Rinehart and Winston, 1969.

Green, Jay E. *School Personnel Administration.* New York: Chilton Book Co., 1971.

Harris, Ben M. "Supervision Competence and Strategies for Improving Instruction." *Educational Leadership* 33 (February 1976): 332-335.

Krajewski, Robert J. *Journal of Research and Development in Education* 9 (Winter 1976).

Lane, Willard, et al. *Foundation of Educational Administration: A Behavioral Analysis.* New York: Macmillan Co., 1967. See especially chapters 11 and 13.

Mosher, Ralph L., and Purpel, David E. *Supervision: The Reluctant Profession.* Boston: Houghton Mifflin, 1972.

Newton, Robert R. "Three Dilemmas of Supervision." *NASSP Bulletin* 56 (December 1972): 52-64.

Reeves, Billy B. "To Change . . . To Grow . . . /I/D/E/A/'s Clinical Training Workshops." *Educational Leadership* 31 (March 1974): 541–544.

Rosenshine, Barak. "Evaluation of Classroom Instruction." *Review of Educational Research* 40 (April 1970): 279–300.

Sergiovanni, Thomas J. "Human Resources Supervision." *Professional Supervision for Professional Teachers.* Washington, D. C.: Association for Supervision and Curriculum Development, 1975, pp. 9–31.

Sergiovanni, Thomas J., and Starratt, Robert J. *Emerging Patterns of Supervision: Human Perspectives.* New York: McGraw-Hill, 1971.

Stoops, Emery, et al. *Handbook of Educational Administration.* Boston: Allyn and Bacon, 1975. See especially chapter 27.

Trusty, Francis M. *Administering Human Resources.* Berkeley, Calif.: McCutchan Publishing Corp., 1971.

Tuckman, Bruce Wayne. "Feedback on the Change Process." *Phi Delta Kappan* 57 (January 1976): 341–344.

Chapter Sixteen

The Principal's Role in Contract Administration

The advent of collective bargaining by teachers brought to school administration, and particularly the principalship, a whole realm of new responsibilities. Written master contracts between teacher organizations and school districts create an added burden for principals of administering the personnel agreements. The school official with the greatest amount of direct contact with the teacher is the building principal who functions in a labor-management sense as the first-line supervisor. The principal is responsible for administering the employee contract and, as a result, must handle most of the grievances or problems that arise from the agreement.

CONTRACT ADMINISTRATION

The principal functions at the school level as part of the management team because of the basic responsibility of administering the employee contract once it has been negotiated.

The principal must be schooled as to the intended meaning of the contract and be able to interpret the agreement reached with the teachers and to apply it to an acceptable manner. Each year, principals should request a briefing from the school district negotiator about the new contract and an interpretation of agreements and information regarding implementation of that contract.

Great care must be exercised to accurately enforce the contract. Teachers will readily inform the principal if they are not granted all of the privileges called for in the contract, but also will most willingly accept privileges that extend beyond the contract. This is costly. Principals can inadvertently grant permanent privileges to teachers by simply giving them certain extra privileges.

Administrators should be aware of a key concept called *past practice*. It is the acceptance of duties based on the practice experienced over an extended period of time that becomes part of the contract by accepted practice. Arbitrators will invoke the term *past practice* in dispute cases when the teacher organization claims that a principal has, for an extended period of time, allowed a certain privilege or action to take place. Past practices become a part of the contract and thus a privilege to be exercised by the teachers.

GRIEVANCE PROCEDURE

Most master agreements include a procedure to guarantee employees a clear channel of communication to air complaints or grievances within the school system and to seek a just solution to problems. Most contracts state that employees may file a grievance if they believe they have been treated unfairly, or if they disagree with

Grievances and Complaints

A "grievance" is a claim by a teacher and/or counselor based upon an event which affects a condition of employment of a teacher and/or counselor or group of teachers and/or counselors and/or an alleged misinterpretation or misapplication of any of the provisions of this agreement.

An "aggrieved" person is the teacher, teachers, counselor, counselors having a grievance.

The purpose of the grievance procedure is to secure, at the lowest possible level, proper solutions to grievances. Both parties agree that the grievance proceedings shall be kept confidential at all levels of the procedure.

It is important that grievances be processed as rapidly as possible, consequently, the number of days indicated at each level are maximum. Every effort should be made to expedite the procedures; however, the time limits may be extended by mutual agreements of both parties.

The aggrieved person or persons may be represented at all stages of the grievance procedure by any person of his own choosing.

The teachers' association shall have the right to have its representatives present at all stages of the grievance procedure affecting an association member.

Grievances shall be resolved as follows:

Level One

An aggrieved person shall first discuss his grievance with his principal, either by himself or in the company of a teachers' association representative, with the objective of resolving the grievance informally.

However, if the grievance is not initiated within fifteen days after the aggrieved person knew, or should have known, of the event or condition upon which it is based, the grievance shall be considered waived.

Level Two

If the aggrieved person is not satisfied with the disposition made at Level One or if no disposition is made within five (5) days after such discussion, he may file a grievance in writing with his building principal with copies to the President of the Association and the Assistant Superintendent for Professional Personnel. The principal shall, within five (5) days after receiving the grievance, submit a written answer to the grievance to the Assistant Superintendent for Professional Personnel with copies to the President of the Association and the aggrieved person.

Level Three

If the aggrieved person is not satisfied with the answer provided at Level Two the aggrieved person may request in writing that the Association Professional Rights and Responsibilities Committee review the grievance and answer, and if the PR&R Committee desires, it shall refer the matter in writing to the Assistant Superintendent for Professional Personnel.

Should the PR&R Committee decline to refer the grievance to the Assistant Superintendent for Professional Personnel, it shall notify the aggrieved person and the Assistant Superintendent for Professional Personnel in writing of such decision. In such event, the aggrieved person may forward the grievance in writing to the Assistant Superintendent for Professional Personnel independently. However, if the written grievance is not referred by the aggrieved person to the Assistant Superintendent for Professional Personnel within thirty days after the PR&R Committee has declined, in writing, to refer such grievance, the grievance shall be considered waived.

The Assistant Superintendent for Professional Personnel will within five (5) days after receipt of the grievance hold a conference involving the aggrieved person, the building principal, the Assistant Superintendent for Professional Personnel and a representative of the association and/or attorney for the aggrieved person. Within forty-eight hours after the conclusion of the conference the Assistant Superintendent for Professional Personnel shall give a written response to all persons concerned.

Level Four

If satisfaction is not achieved by the aggrieved person under Levels Two or Three, the aggrieved person or the association PR&R Committee may submit the grievance to the Superintendent of Schools.

The Superintendent of Schools shall request that the grievance be reviewed by a panel consisting of three (3) disinterested members of the administrative staff appointed by the Superintendent and three (3) disinterested members of the association appointed by the President of the association.

Within ten (10) days after the grievance is submitted to the Superintendent the panel shall report its findings to the Superintendent and within forty-eight hours thereafter, the Superintendent shall give a written response to all parties concerned.

Level Five

If a satisfactory solution has not yet been attained, the aggrieved person and/or the association PR&R Committee may appeal in writing to the Board of Education requesting a formal hearing at which time the aggrieved person may represent himself, or be represented by the association, or be represented by legal counsel, or be represented by any combination of the persons itemized above.

Within fifteen (15) days after such request, a committee of the Board shall meet with the aggrieved person for the purpose of resolving the grievance. The Board shall at its next meeting by official action make its answer to the grievance.

Level Six

Grievances not settled in Level Five shall, until a declaratory judgment action or the enactment of legislation will permit the Board to agree to binding arbitration, processed as follows:

The Association PR&R Committee may, if requested in writing by the aggrieved person, within fifteen days after the Board's answer, notify the Board of its intent to submit the grievance to an Advisory Panel.

An Advisory Panel shall be selected and shall function as stipulated in Article X of this agreement.

In the event of a declaratory judgment action or the enactment of legislation defining the legal remedies available to the Board in cases of impasse, the Association and the Board, or its representative, shall meet and draft a Level Six section of this Grievance Procedure within the guidelines set by the judgment or legislation.

FIGURE 16–1.   **Grievances and complaints procedure**

their supervisors as to the application of the contract. The word *contract* refers primarily to written agreements negotiated with the teacher organization. However, in some cases it also includes written policies, procedures, and standards established by the school administration unilaterally. When differences arise between a negotiated contract and an administrative policy, the negotiated contract takes precedence.

The expression *treated fairly* relates to matters not covered by policy. It might relate to a substantial deviation from customary practice, or it might challenge a practice. It might also relate to an action that discriminates against an employee as a person. *Treated unfairly* does not have to apply to a disagreement with the negotiated contract; an employee who attempts to file a grievance on the basis of such a disagreement would be better advised to present these views to the union or association representative.

Occasionally the term *supervisor* will be used interchangeably in contracts with *principal,* but more often, the term *supervisor* refers to any administrator with direct responsibility for the actions of a certain group of employees, teachers, and other personnel. The negotiated agreement will probably provide different ways to handle grievances within the district, depending on the subject of the grievance, and the level of which it is introduced.

Some contracts require the person with whom the grievance is being filed to inform the local representative of the teacher organization (if the employee is not represented by a union or association) so that the union may take part as provided in the agreement. If the person bringing the grievance to a supervisor is not satisfied with the supervisor's determination, the agreement usually has a carefully defined set of appeal procedures.

While grievance procedures will vary in terminology and the number of appeal levels from contract to contract, they all seem to follow the same basic format. Figure 16–1 presents

the Grievance and Complaint section of a recently negotiated contract. This six-level grievance procedure presents an elaborate plan for "communication within the organization."

Most grievances are filed against the principal. In most schools, from 60 to 70 percent of all grievances are conflicts within the building. Most grievances, however, can be resolved at Level One, in a fairly informal manner.

HOW TO HANDLE GRIEVANCES

What is a principal's role during a grievance procedure? When a grievance is filed, a principal has the opportunity to reestablish the effective relationship with the employee and to improve the relationship. The most can be made of this opportunity by observing the following principles:

Be Approachable Principals should not place obstacles in the way of employees or their representative that will suggest that the principal is not interested in discussing their problems with them. An appointment should be made for a definite time at a specific place to discuss the grievance in private.

Listen Many times the grievance results from an action the principal has taken. The great temptation is for the principal to defend the action without further thought. However, if a principal adopts a defensive attitude, the employee may feel even more grieved. When teachers or other employees have a complaint, they should have the opportunity to talk it out. If the employee is excited, or if the basis of the complaint is not clear, the complaint should be clarified. Calm, interested, listening is required. Sometimes, in the process of putting the complaint into words, the grievance will disappear.

Get the Facts The principal should repeat the story after the employee has told it to clarify that both parties are discussing the same issue. Those facts agreed upon or accepted as true by both parties should be confirmed. Those aspects not perceived the same should be discussed further and if an agreement is not reached, more information should be secured before a decision is rendered.

Take Notes   During the discussion, the principal should take notes about the facts presented. The notes will be helpful in reviewing the facts with the employee and, when the matter is discussed later, with the superintendent or personnel director. Notes are also helpful for a written report of a grievance discussion.

Make Decisions with Care   An immediate decision is not usually required and the principal should carefully weight all the facts. Employees must be reassured that they will receive a fair hearing based on the facts of an issue.

In all cases, it is prudent, even necessary, to discuss the matter with the superintendent or personnel director before making a decision. This is especially important if the issue involves interpretation of a policy or a negotiated agreement. However, undue delay needs to be avoided in acting on the grievance.

Since action taken may result in the employee exercising the right of appeal, the principal's responsibility is to render the initial decision and inform the employee of his or her appeal rights.

It's the Principal's Decision   When the principal makes the decision, it should be clear that it is not that of the board, superintendent, or personnel director. Even though the action that is the subject of the complaint may be based upon some policy of the school district the principal did not help make, it is still the principal who applied that policy and who must accept first-line responsibility.

If grievances at this level are handled properly, most problems covered under the teacher's contract can be solved. If administrators follow reasonable procedures for the rapid but fair handling of grievances, relatively few grievances will need to be appealed to the next level in the established grievance procedure.

APPEALED GRIEVANCES

When an employee is dissatisfied with the initial responses of the first-level supervisor or principal, a formal hearing may be requested to move the grievance procedure to Level Two. This appeal is usually made by written statements, affidavits, hearings, or a combination thereof. A hearing is usually held at the request of the employee or the appeal administrator. As grievance procedures become more formal, standard forms may be desirable in processing and recording the grievance decision. Figure 16–2 depicts a suggested format to be used at the building level by the aggrieved employee. The administrator also needs documentation. Figure 16–3 depicts a suggested format.

THE PRINCIPAL'S ROLE IN COLLECTIVE BARGAINING

The school principal has two major responsibilities in the collective bargaining process. The first responsibility is as a member of the administrative team. Every school district should have an administrative team consisting of building level principals, supervisory staff, and central superintendent staff who will represent management in negotiation. Often, questions arise regarding various aspects of the principal's responsibility. A principal should be part of the management team to adequately defend that role and responsibility. However, there is some controversy over this matter. In some states, principals may be represented

Formal Grievance Presentation
(To be completed by aggrieved person.)

Aggrieved person(s) _____

Date of formal presentation_____

Home address of aggrieved person

_____

School _____

Principal_____

Subject area or grade_____

Name of association school representative

_____

Statement of grievance_____

Contract article, section, and clause in question

_____

Action requested_____

_____
(Signature of aggrieved)

FIGURE 16-2.

Decision of Administrator
(To be completed by principal, or other appropriate administrator, within three days
of formal grievance presentation.)

Aggrieved person(s) _____

Date of formal presentation_____

School _____

Principal_____

Decision of principal (or other administrator) and reasons therefore:

Date of decision_____   _____
(Signature of principal)

Aggrieved person's response: (To be completed by aggrieved within three days of
decision.)

    I accept the above decision of principal (or other administrator).

    I hereby refer the above decision to the Association's Professional Rights and
Responsibilities Committee for appeal to the superintendent of schools.

Date of response_____

FIGURE 16-3.

during negotiation by the employee bargaining unit.

Each principal in small school districts with few principals should be an active member of the administrative team and participate in an advisory capacity when called on during negotiations. In larger communities, principals may find it both necessary and effective to have representation on the negotiating team to express their viewpoint. Principals should be represented because to a great extent negotiation topics represent areas of direct concern to the building principal. In many cases, the ensuing negotiations result in erosion of the power or responsibility of the principal, often reducing administrative effectiveness.[1]

PRINCIPAL INVOLVEMENT IN TEACHER ORGANIZATIONS

A real danger for the administrator is membership or a leadership role in the teacher organizations of the school district.[2] In many areas, of course, the day is long past that this option for a principal still exists. But in many school districts, prior to the institution of negotiations, teachers and administrators functioned effectively within the same professional organizations, and principals often held leadership responsibilities. Formal negotiations has changed this. Now a principal usually cannot act effectively as an administrator and an employee under the contract simultaneously.

If the teacher organization decides on militant action and the principal represents the local leadership, that principal is placed in the untenable position of being leader for both parties in a conflict. Numerous cases can be cited where the principal was caught in this dilemma, faced with the demand of the teacher organization to go on strike and the demand of the school district to keep the schools open. In these situations, either the principal gains the

enmity of the teachers or loses the job, and, in some cases, both. Partly because of this power erosion, there has been a gradual evolving of principal groups toward the creation of their own middle management bargaining units.

SUMMARY

Collective bargaining by teachers has changed the role of the principal. Contract administration and the grievance procedures provide formal guarantees of communication between teachers and administrators. Principals now must abide by a specific set of rules, as spelled out by the contract, in dealing with teachers. Principals must reevaluate their active involvement in professional organizations. If militant teacher action is at hand, principals must consider removing themselves from any active leadership role in the organization and perhaps from membership. In many areas, the decision no longer rests with the administrator, as the teachers have long since made them unwelcome.

ENDNOTES

1. An increasing number of school districts provide for the direct negotiation of principals or negotiation in cooperation with other administrators or supervisors. Several states already have legislation requiring boards of education to recognize and negotiate with administrator units.

2. This is declining. The AFT does not permit it, and the NEA has taken many actions to discourage it.

BIBLIOGRAPHY

Bailey, Stephen K. "Political Principles for Political Principals." *NASSP Bulletin* 60 (January 1976): 17–21.

Castetter, William B. *The Personnel Function in Educational Administration.* New York: The MacMillan Co., 1971.

Lieberman, Myron, and Moskow, Michael. *Collective Negotiations for Teachers: An Approach to School Administration.* Chicago: Rand McNally, 1966.

Randles, Harry E. "The Principal and Negotiated Contracts." *National Elementary Principal* 55 (November–December 1975): 57–61.

Smith, David C. "Professional Negotiations and the Principal." *National Elementary Principal* 52 (January 1973): 84–87.

Smith, David C. "What's Negotiable? Professional Negotiations." *National Elementary Principal* 53 (March–April, 1974): 73–75.

Stoops, Emery, et al. *Handbook of Educational Administration.* Boston: Allyn and Bacon, 1975. See especially chapters 25 and 26.

Williams, Thomas R. "Principals: Political Kings or Pawns?" *NASSP Bulletin* 60 (January 1976): 30–37.

Chapter Seventeen

Pupil Personnel Services

INTRODUCTION

Many activities go on in the name of pupil personnel services—so many that the term demands definition. What is to be included under this rubric? And why have the number of persons and activities included grown so rapidly in recent years? It may help to think about the nature of individual students.

Students are comprised of four interacting "selfs": an intellectual self (inquiring mind in need of systematic development); a physical self (a developing body); an emotional self (a psychological demension); and a social self (a need to be encultrated and to be accepted in groups of interacting humans). All of these selfs come to school with the students and affect individual growth. If the only self educators had to be concerned about was the intellectual self, it would be a much simpler professional world, but this is not possible. The interaction of each of the other three precludes ignoring any. Thus, there has developed in school systems a variety of services designed to facilitate an integrated approach to the education of young people. The forces within any of the selfs are sufficient to retard growth in all or any of the others.

To be sure, alert classroom teachers have always recognized these forces and taken them into consideration. A good pupil personnel service program does not attempt to replace the need for teacher interest in the development of each of the selfs of students. Pupil personnel services are simply to augment the role of the teacher through the delivery of expert technical and professional services to the point of need.

Thus, pupil personnel services include all of those special classroom supportive services outside of the curricular and cocurricular offerings that impinge upon the maturation of the four selfs of the student. The pupil personnel services professional becomes a member of the instructional team, providing technical services and additional professional insight in the diagnosis, prescription, and treatment of individual learner difficulties as well as balanced programs for all learners.

The principal's role in this is crucial. It is the principal (in collaboration with team leaders and teachers) who must provide for the organization, coordination, and articulation of pupil personnel services at the building level.

COORDINATION OF PUPIL PERSONNEL SERVICES

Most frequently, school systems will designate one person to be responsible for coordinating the array of pupil personnel services on a dis-

225

Title: Coordinator of Pupil Personnel Services

Qualifications: Master's degree, with certification and experience in guidance and counseling. Certification in administration is recommended.

Supervisor: Assistant Superintendent for Instruction

Supervises: Certified and noncertified personnel assigned

Responsibility: The coordinator of pupil personnel services is the system-wide coordinator and administrator of guidance, testing, and health services. In addition, the person in this role supervises the coordination and administration of the special education programs. These duties are to be performed within the framework of the philosophy and objectives of the educational programs established by Board policies, consistent with statutes and standards of regulatory agencies, and in accordance with regulations and procedures developed in the District. The coordinator of pupil personnel services

- provides leadership in the development, operation, and interpretation of plans and strategies for the assessment of pupil learning needs
- coordinates interschool guidance and counseling program
- coordinates and evaluates standardized testing program
- supervises the special education program
- assists in the planning of the evaluations of Title I, Compensatory, and other specially funded instructional programs
- assists principals in ascertaining appropriate placement for students enrolling in the District without proper credentials from previous school
- processes and examines required immigration forms and reviews school records of foreign pupils, determines eligibility for enrollment, and recommends grade/level placement to principals, when necessary
- coordinates the school health program
- maintains direct communication with principals in regard to serious discipline cases
- serves as the review agent for all secondary discipline cases which involve long-term assignment, long-term suspension, recommendation for expulsion, and as mediator of serious discipline cases

(continued)

- supervises the suspension and alternative programs
- coordinates the regular visiting-teacher program
- plans and implements staff development programs and activities to strengthen all areas of pupil personnel services
- determines staff needs for the department and for special programs and projects conducted by the department and cooperates with the personnel department in securing qualified personnel
- supervises and evaluates professional and nonprofessional staff assigned
- prepares a budget for programs involving the department, based on identified needs and priorities of the District
- supervises the maintenance of school records for graduates and former students according to District guidelines
- coordinates the student accident insurance program
- promotes positive community relations through effective communication and involvement of community members
- analyzes personal characteristics and strengthens areas of behavior as necessary for the fulfillment of the assignment
- performs other duties and functions as assigned by the assistant superintendent of instruction

FIGURE 17–1. **Job description of a coordinator of pupil personnel services**

Port Arthur Independent School District, Port Arthur, Texas.

trict-wide basis. Insight about the extent of the potential impact of pupil personnel services and the variety of support services available to individual schools can be gained by examining the job description of one district-wide coordinator. Figure 17–1 is such a description.

Note that pupil services in the district to which figure 17–1 relates includes among others:

1. The testing program
2. Guidance and counseling programs
3. Special education
4. Evaluation of externally funded instructional programs (Title I, compensatory education programs, etc.)
5. Student placement

6. Student health programs
7. Coordination of extreme disciplinary cares
8. Visiting teachers program
9. Alternative education programs
10. Maintenance of student records of graduates and others who are no longer in school
11. Student accident insurance programs.

In the school system illustrated, there is also an assistant coordinator for special education who reports to the coordinator for pupil personnel services. The duties of this person are described in figure 17–2. The extent of the pupil personnel services program is further explicated by a review of that person's specific responsibilities.[1]

Title: Assistant Coordinator for Special Education

Qualifications: Master's degree with supervisor's certificate

Supervisor: Coordinator of Pupil Personnel Services

Supervises: Special education personnel assigned

Responsibility: The role of the assistant coordinator for special education involves the system-wide coordination and administration of the special education programs within the framework of the philosophy and objectives of the educational programs established by Board policies, consistent with statutes and standards of regulatory agencies, and in accordance with regulations and procedures developed by the District. The assistant coordinator of special education

- supervises the total special education program of the District
- cooperates with other departments in providing assistance to personnel in diagnosing student learning and/or behavior problems
- prepares a budget for programs involving the department based on identified needs and priorities of the District
- assists supervisory personnel in planning and implementing staff development programs and activities to strengthen identified areas
- determines staff needs for the department and for special programs and projects and cooperates with personnel department in securing qualified personnel
- supervises the educational program and PAISD personnel in Hughen School for Crippled Children
- assists in the evaluation of professional and nonprofessional staff assigned
- coordinates noninstructional activities and services as a support to the instructional program
- processes referrals of pupils for medical, psychological, neurological, and psychiatric services

FIGURE 17–2.   Job description of a coordinator for special education

Port Arthur Independent School District, Port Arthur, Texas.

Other Professional Support Personnel

There are other professional roles to be filled in a well-functioning pupil personnel services program.[2] No attempt will be made here to be exhaustive; rather, the roles to be described are simply representative.

Educational Diagnostician   The role of the diagnostician involves interpreting the results of student assessments to principals, counselors, teachers, nurses, and parents. It also includes administering diagnostic instruments and/or batteries of tests to students. Normally, a person trained in psychometrics will be required for this role. Many states now have sp - cific certification requirements for educational diagnosticians.

School Psychologist   The school psychologist will normally engage in both diagnosis and prescription. Frequently, the school psychologist is looked to for leadership in planning, implementing, and evaluating a comprehensive pupil appraisal program, as this program relates to identifying individual needs about appropriate educational and social placement. A specific task is often that of diagnosing learning and behavior disorders of certain individual pupils.

Visiting Teacher   Replacing the old-time truant officer is the visiting teacher—a professional educator trained in counseling techniques as well as law enforcement. The position includes such responsibilities as:

1. Counseling students and parents concerning discipline and attendance.
2. Liaison between law enforcement agencies, state and county welfare agencies, and the schools.
3. Assisting individual schools when disruptive behavior occurs.
4. Assisting in the enforcement of school attendance laws.
5. Representing the school district on legal activities pertaining to compulsory attendance laws and other legal matters involving students.

A variety of titles are used to designate the person fulfilling this function. Woodbury and Achilles,[3] for example, call this person "Juvenile Specialist." They describe the role as follows:

> The juvenile specialist can effect fundamental changes in the educational structure through various functions that may alter deviant behavior in adolescents. The school-oriented

functions include: (a) the development of educational and social strategies for delinquency-prone youth, (b) the use of information and appraisal data concerning delinquency as a staff training aid, (c) the development of school-community resources. Specialists working closely with teachers, counselors, and the school administration provide curriculum and social alternatives to delinquency-prone students who cannot cope with the structure of the regular school program.[4]

Special Education Supervisor   The role of the special edication supervisor requires the systematic study and analysis of the teaching learning process as it applies to the education of exceptional students. The supervisor serves as a resource person and a process specialist in support of the principal's role of instructional leader at the building level. This role becomes a critical one as PL 94–142, the "mainstreaming" act, is implemented. (The implications of PL 94–142 will be discussed later in this chapter.) The position includes responsibilities for evaluating and selecting instructional programs, materials, and equipment to support endeavors to educate exceptional students. Required as well, are skills in planning and implementing staff development programs, and the ability to help staff evaluate the effectiveness of individualized instructional plans.

Principal's Role in Coordination and Articulation

In a sense, with respect to the delivery of the described pupil personnel services, the principal is a person in the middle—not as a gate keeper but rather as a facilitator. While an organizational structure is frequently developed to deliver many of the pupil personnel services, it is still incumbent on the principal to take the lead in the orderly provision of these services to teachers and students in the building. Referrals, if not routed directly through the principal, should at least be made with an information copy to the principal. Why? Everything that goes on in and around the school is the responsibility of the principal—and that includes the proper delivery of support services. The reason for centralizing many pupil personnel services is because of their system-wide impact and because individual school needs vary enough to make it more efficient to house the services in such a way to provide maximum access in time of need.

Such a mode works well, provided the principal recognizes a responsibility to continually be aware of student and teacher needs in the building, and to investigate whether or not their needs are being met in a timely and efficient manner by the pupil personnel services division.

Thus, system-wide cooperation and coordination is a must. With it, a great positive impact on student growth, generally and specifically, will occur; without it, only incidental or accidental interventions of short-lived efficacy will occur.

IMPLICATIONS OF PL 94-142

The Education for All Handicapped Children Act (Public Law 94-142), The Developmentally Disabled Assistance and Bill of Rights Act (Public Law 94-143), and the Rehabilitation Act (Public Law 93-112) made certain rights to education and treatment for handicapped children a federal law. The rights include:

- Right to a free appropriate education at public expense, without regard to severity of handicap.
- Right to service in the least restrictive setting when the handicap requires service in something other than the normal school setting.
- Right to prior notice before any decision is made to change services to a child.

- Right of parents to consent before child is evaluated, placed in a special program, or changed in placement.
- Right to a full due process, gearing to challenge services; including representation by counsel, right to confront and cross-examine school personnel, right to a verbatim transcript, right to appeal, and right to be heard by an impartial hearing officer (not a school employee).
- Right to assessment without descrimination on the basis of sex, race, or culture.
- Right to placement in a program without discrimination on the basis of sex, race, or culture, and placement in a facility which is comparable to that offered to nonhandicapped clients of the system.
- Right to be served in accordance with an individual program plan which states annual goals, measurable intermediate steps, name of persons who will provide services and their qualifications, a timetable for beginning each step in the service and its anticipated duration, a schedule for evaluating success of the program, and the right to be transferred if the program is failing.
- Right to be protected from harm through use of unregulated experimental approaches, untrained staff, inclusion in a program with others who are physically assaultive, freedom from unreasonable corporal punishment, and freedom from work assignments without compensation.
- Right to see all records and to contest them in a hearing, with the right to place in the record information which the client feels presents a balanced picture.

Thus, "separate but equal" as a concept appropriate to the education of handicapped children has been found to be generally unsound.

The passage of PL 94-142 was the culmination of many years of litigation and legislation to protect the civil rights of children who are handicapped. The legislative act insures specified substantive and procedural provisions for handicapped children, as well as an escalating funding formula, to insure a free and appropriate public education for all handicapped students.

Of specific importance to the principal is that the law insists on:

1. A zero reject policy.
2. Specific due process procedures.
3. Non-discriminatory testing.
4. A written and promulgated individual educational plan (with specific evaluation procedures about its effectiveness) for every handicapped child. This plan is to be developed jointly with the parents and reviewed at least annually.
5. Provision of a least restrictive environment.

There are several ways to meet the objectives of the act, and, while the ways are not mutually exclusive, each will require careful planning. Among the ways to accomplish the purposes of the act are:

1. Employ paraprofessionals to assist those regular teachers receiving handicapped students.
2. Schedule special education teachers in the regular classroom to work directly with handicapped students.
3. Arrange for diagnostic-prescriptive teachers to work with regular teachers to plan instructional strategies for those handicapped children in the class. (The diagnostic-prescriptive teacher would provide no direct assistance to the student.)
4. Purchase individualized sequential materials for use by regular teachers to work with handicapped students.
5. Schedule handicapped students as needed, and include in the individual educational plan, with a special educator teacher in a classroom for less than half of the school day.

The implications of PL 94–142 to inservice education seminars is apparent. Resource people for such seminars are available from universities, if not readily available within the district.

SUMMARY

This chapter examined the varied aspects of a district pupil personnel services program. Educational programing which focuses only on the intellectual development of students is not sufficient to the task because the student brings not only an intellectual self to school, but also social, emotional, and physical selfs. These selfs impinge on each other.

The principal's role in the delivery of pupil personnel services at the unit level is that of coordinator and facilitator. The task requires well-developed insights about the nature of the services and the needs of students and teachers.

ENDNOTES

1. It must be noted that some of these responsibilities refer to coordinating activities at special schools for handicapped children. With the new emphasis on "mainstreaming" and the provision of a "least restrictive environment" in regular schools, these responsibilities will shift to the principal.
2. In smaller school districts more than one of these roles, if not all, will probably be filled by a single person. Described here are *functions* that might be carried out to meet pupil personnel needs.
3. Roger Woodbury, and Charles M. Achilles, "Schools and Delinquency: Where Are We Going Now?" *NASSP Bulletin* 59 (January 1975): 29–35.
4. Ibid. p. 33.

BIBLIOGRAPHY

Ballard, J., et al. *PL 94–142, The Education For All Handicapped Children Act*. Reston, Va.: Council for Exceptional Children, 1976. (This is a package including three captioned filmstrips and audio cassettes.)

Cochrane, Pamela V., and Nelson, Jane C. "Compliance with PL 94–142: A Plan for School System Accountability." *SAANYS JOURNAL* 7 (Fall 1977): 17–21.

Glasser, William. *Schools Without Failure*. New York: Harper and Row, 1969.

"Public Law 93–112, Final Regulations." *Federal Register*. Washington, D.C.: U.S. Government Printing Office, May 4, 1977.

"Public Law 94–142, Final Regulations." *Federal Register*. Washington, D.C.: U.S. Government Printing Office, August 23, 1977.

Simon, Sidney; Howe, Leland; and Kirschenbaun, Howard. *Values Clarification: A Handbook of Practical Strategies for Teachers and Students*. New York: Hart Publishing Co., 1972.

Stoops, Emory, et al. *Handbook of Educational Administration*. Boston: Allyn and Bacon, 1975. See especially chapter 21.

Woodbury, Roger, and Achilles, Charles M. "Schools and Delinquency: Where Are We Going Now?" *NASSP Bulletin* 59 (January 1975): 29–35.

Chapter Eighteen

The Counseling Program

INTRODUCTION

Although many of the pupil personnel services are actuated and delivered from the central office, one very important one is not: the guidance counselor. While this person does operate in frequent concert with other pupil personnel services, professionals at the district office level, most frequently the activities of the counselor's office are under the administrative control of the principal. Moreover, as will be developed further in this chapter, the counseling function devolves not just to a person designated as guidance counselor, but is really the responsibility of all professional personnel in the building. Organizing for this immense but critical task will require a deft administrator. In these days of troubling anonymity in the larger school units, of drop-ins and spiritual dropouts, a different approach from that which locates all counseling responsibilities in one office is required. The conceptual bases and environmental conditions described in chapter 17 demand total school commitment to the counseling function. In point of this fact, the earlier quote from Giles bears repeating:

> . . . the school counselor today can properly and adequately assist the student with academic planning, but the same school counselor cannot be a mental health worker responsible for the emotional adjustment toward the school setting and toward life in general.[1]

Cusick adds further to the substance of the problem:

> Do any of us who presume to understand, work in, and make decisions about high schools have any basic understanding or any feeling for what students see or think about when they look at their school and their relationship to that school? Despite the vast body of literature on high school students, the answer to the question is probably "No." There is actually very little that gives us any feeling for the way high school students actually deal with their classes, teachers, desks, assignments, books, papers, rules and regulations. Nor do we have satisfactory answers to a host of related questions: How do students regard their role of "student"? What part of the school is important to them? Why do they choose to ignore other parts? What accommodation do they work out with the rules and regulations which confront them? What, after all, are they really learning?[2]

Guidance counselors suffer from highly unrealistic expectations placed on them by their colleagues. The answers to the questions Cusick raises, especially in the light of the telling observations of Giles, are hardly manageable by one person operating out of the guidance office.

A different mode of organizing counseling services in the secondary schools is needed—not because trained guidance counselors aren't important, but because as presently organized in most secondary schools their skills are not being maximally used. The function of counseling is so critical to the development of students that a better approach must be employed.

THE COUNSELING PROGRAM

What is usually meant by the phrase *student advisement and guidance?* Traditionally, the guidance progam is one that is assigned to a particular person called a guidance counselor within the school, who is given the responsibility for everything that deals with psychological services, testing, and individual student programs.

Needs of Students

For a proper analysis of the functions of the counseling program, one must first examine the needs of adolescent students. The needs will, of course, be diverse, but they normally include:

1. A mother or father surrogate.
2. A friend.
3. A personal counselor for problems indigenous to family, peer, and teacher relationships.
4. An academic counselor to oversee and direct the student's learning in a personal way.
5. Someone to talk to about careers.
6. Insights about self.
7. A liaison with the home to share the school's perception of the child, both in academic counseling as well as to receive information about the student and to engage in cooperative goal setting.

The basic advisement and guidance functions to be performed for a particular student need to be in the hands of a single professional, someone who has a picture of the whole student. A person designated as school guidance

counselor with the usually recommended pupil-counselor rates of three to four hundred to one obviously cannot be expected to develop very many such relationships. It would be absurd to think otherwise; only perfunctory interpersonal encounters are probable.

Teacher-Advisor System

Although not a new concept, the teacher-advisor system has gained current momentum at least in part because of the NASSP Model Schools Project. In this approach, the high school is divided into clusters with a counselor and a principal or assistant principal acting as administrative head. The counselor serves as a "Master-Advisor" for fifteen to twenty teacher-advisors. The teacher-advisor has no more than twenty-five students for whom guidance services are performed.[3]

The difficulty in organizing an effective student advisement/guidance program around the teacher is often one of time. However, there are ways in which to gain time for student counseling. Organizing the activities and dividing some of the responsibilities with other appropriate personnel will assist in this endeavor.

The teacher-advisor's primary role is to work individually with students in much the same way that formerly was expected of the guidance counselor. The school guidance counselor's role is that of expert consultant to groups of teachers.

Speaking to the role of the teacher-advisor, Jenkins has written:

In working with students, the teacher-advisor is first and foremost a friend and advocate. He strives to get to know the student in ways beyond what a teacher could be expected to do with 150 students per day or 300 counselees. The teacher-advisor is above all else a listener and is someone with whom the student can talk openly and freely about school problems. The solutions to school problems very often involve various problem-solving techniques that not all students possess equally. The teacher-advisor by nature of the relationship with the student is in the position to help the student with important decisions. In any high school, there are many opportunities for students to exercise their decision-making skills. Having a friend in court with whom the student can easily consult in these matters is one of the major strengths of the teacher-advisor system.[4]

Organizing Counseling Activities

There are three basic counseling activities that should be carried out: group counseling, individual student counseling, and parent conferences.

Group Counseling   Group guidance activities can be of a variety of types, but the underlying concept is the advisor's responsibility to aid the students in developing good peer relationships, good personal problem-solving skills, and a good learning community climate. Group process methods such as Glasser's class meetings,[5] or the group guidance activity entitled "Innerchange," produced by the Human Development Institute,[6] are appropriate group activities.

Individual Counseling   This type of meeting is used for two purposes. First, it is to provide the opportunity for each student to interact with his or her advisor as a friend and confidant. Second, it is to provide for frequent program planning and evaluation conferences. It is suggested that at least bi-weekly conferences be held and that these should function as the main stage for academic planning between the advisor and the student. It can be best described with this teacher-advisor report.

For each of my students, I have a file folder in a box next to my desk. Every paper completed by that student is placed in that folder after it has been appropriately graded or reviewed. It remains there until the night before our scheduled appointment. Each night I take home the three folders of the students I plan to see the next day and regroup and review their papers according to subjects. I also review my notes from earlier conferences with each student and look at the goals we established in previous weeks. I then write down tentative goals that I have in mind for the student for the next two-week period. The next day when that student comes to my desk for his conference, I review with him his schedule of activities and the amount of time that he has spent in each subject area. We then go over his papers and I ask if he is having any particular problems. I will note for him problems I have identified from my review. Next, we look to see whether previously set goals have been achieved and begin our discussion of which goals and learning activities should come next. I prefer that each of my students set goals for themselves rather than for me to always have to suggest them. We each write down the goals agreed upon and identify some of the activities to be done toward each. As might be expected, most are continuations of previously laid plans but if new interests or needs have developed, these are to be included. Finally, a cover letter is stapled to the entire collection of papers to be taken home to the parent.

Figure 18–1 is an example of a letter such as the one referred to above.

Some teachers prefer to use a form on which to set and record goals that can also be shared with parents or at least made a part of the student's yearly diagnostic file. An example of such a form is shown in figure 18–2.

Selection of Advisor

The effective advisor must be able to communicate with each student on a friendly, personal basis. In order for this to be accomplished, a good personality match between advisor and student is desirable. This can be achieved if several choices for advisor assignment are available. Alternatives for advisor assignment for each student exist when the guidance program is operating on a team or expanded team basis.

Gordon Junior High School
Oxford, Ohio

Dear Parent:

Here are the samples of papers completed by your child during the past eight weeks. I have reviewed with _____ and we have made plans for the next set of activities.   (name)

While not all items in the packet show an evaluation, the general concepts have been reviewed.

If you have any particular questions, please call me at school and leave a message for me to return your call.

Gene Atkinson, Teacher-Advisor
Tiger Learning Community

FIGURE 18–1. Example of cover letter to accompany papers sent home

After staff and students have become acquainted in the fall term, the team can assign to each of its members an appropriate number of advisees, keeping in mind the needs of each individual student and which team member might best meet those needs.

One approach which has worked particularly well for a number of schools is for students to select advisors. After a three- or four-week get acquainted time in the fall, each student lists his or her first, second, and third choices from among five or six available team members or teachers to be his or her advisor. The team, learning community, or guidance counselor then sorts those requests, balancing the students among faculty members.[7]

Another organizational technique which greatly aids in the effectiveness of the advisement program is a multi-age grouping practice. This approach places students with a particular team for two or three years, each keeping the same advisor during that entire period. This long-term arrangement gives the teacher a much better opportunity to become well-acquainted with each student and to apply this knowledge over that extended period.

Advisement Conference Report

_____   _____
Student name   Term

_____   _____
Advisor   Date

A. Goals set by student and teacher
B. Adjustments/accomplishments toward previously set goals
C. Additional teacher comments
D. Additional student comments
E. Next conference date

FIGURE 18–2. Example of setting and recording student goals

An excellent opportunity to reduce the student-advisor ratio can be created by going to the expanded team concept for student guidance. This concept calls for participation in the guidance program by professionals within the school not ordinarily assigned to teams for purposes of instruction. Included would be teacher specialists (music, art, P.E.), resource teachers, librarians, and the principal.[8] By expanding each team with one additional professional for purposes of guidance, each regular teacher's advisement load can be reduced by five or six students.

If people outside of the team are to be used as advisors, it is necessary that they find adequate time to commit to the task. This includes time for individual as well as group activities with the students, and some planning time with the team in order to adequately coordinate with team instructional operations.

Establishing a Good Advisement Program

Maximum flexibility in advisor assignments can be achieved by the expanded team concept previously suggested. This will help keep the advisor-student ratio as low as possible.

Advisors should schedule meetings regularly with advisees, both on a group basis and individual basis. Figure 18–3 shows four different types of advisor-advisee activities with group and individual application.

The total weekly commitment to advisor-guidance functions of an individual nature is

Teacher-Student Made	Academic	Personal Development	Parent Reports	Administrative
Individual	Diagnostic-prescriptive goal setting evaluation 1 15-minute conference every two weeks (avg.)	Counseling as needed Average of 10 additional minutes every four weeks per child	Pupil-teacher conferences Parent phone contact 1 30-minute conference each semester plus 30 minutes planning time for each conference 2 conferences per week (2 hours) beginning after first six weeks of school	Unscheduled
6 hours per week (4 during school day 2 after school)	3 hours per week total	1 hour per week total		
Group	Standardized tests Orientation of advisor-advisee relationship General goal setting	Group process problem-solving class meetings	Parent orientation	Administrative announcements, records completion, attendance
2-1/2 hours per week in school	(2 30-minute periods per week) 1 hour per week	(2 30-minute periods per week) 1 hour per week	(1 1-hour after school or evening each semester)	(1 30-minute period per week)

FIGURE 18–3. Advisor-guidance activities and suggested average times needed

approximately four hours per week during the school day while students are available, and two hours after school, or when parents are available. Group guidance activities can be built into the regular school schedule, setting aside approximately thirty minutes each day, for a total of two hours and thirty minutes each week. The approximate time commitment per week, assuming an advisee load of twenty-four students, is also shown in figure 18-3.

Teachers are well-advised to build in advance the schedule for individual conferences as well as the group activities. If time is not set aside in advance for individual conferences, they tend to be easily forgotten in the press of time. A regular appointment calendar on a two-week rotation should be established, with each student knowing the designated time in advance for the conference. Figure 18-4 is an example of such a schedule.

Speaking of time allotment, Jenkins states about the Wilde Lake High School program:

Finding time to allow teachers to confer with advisees is a number one consideration. The more flexible the school program, the better the chance that teacher-advisors have time for individual conferences on school time. One easy way to achieve this end is to lengthen the school lunch period to 50 or 60 minutes, provide for student activities to keep students interested, and open up the media center or study areas, so that when teacher-advisers and students' finish their lunches they can have time for conferring. Time before and after school along with the regular planning period can also be used.[9,10]

With an advisee load of twenty-four, a teacher can plan to see approximately three advisees each day, leaving Fridays open for make-up appointments. Most of these appointments can be scheduled during off-instructional hours, either immediately before or after school, or during a noon break.

Each advisor should collect and file information about each student in a systematic manner using simple forms. Diagnostic information collected from student and parents, personal data sheets, interest information recorded by the teacher, learning style, observations, as well as reports in academic progress are all appropriate.

		15 minutes each conference			
	Monday	Tuesday	Wednesday	Thursday	Friday
8:00 Early bus arrivals	Barbara Greer	Leah Dunaway	Pete Husen	Eliz Shufford	Make up
	Classes begin				
	Lunch				Make up
12:15	Stewart North	Tom Goodman	Ellen Tang	Shirley Bascom	
3:00	Classes End				
3:10 Late bus departing	Larry Zinn	Brenda Manning	Bill Thomas	Norman Whisler	Make up

FIGURE 18-4. Student advisement schedule (Week 1 at a two-week cycle)

It can be seen then that an effective student guidance program is basically teacher-centered program, and time and activities must be specifically identified and scheduled if the program is to function successfully.

THE ROLE OF THE GUIDANCE COUNSELOR

The guidance counselor has a particularly important function to play in the advisement-guidance structure of the school. The tasks are several. Specifically, the guidance counselor can be expected to assume five responsibilities.

1. In order to keep close touch with the program, become attached to a team and assume an advisor responsibility; the same as the other specialists within the school.
2. Function as a school referral agent for problems identified by the teacher-advisor and faculty. A major role for the guidance counselor is the diagnostic work beyond that possible for the teacher to do.
3. Administer and supervise the advisement program. The level of advisement activities proposed in this chapter far exceeds that typically carried out in school. In order for it to operate well, a good advisement program requires constant attention and encouragement.
4. Provide and direct staff development activities in the techniques of advisement, including teacher training for both group guidance functions as well as individual student academic diagnostic work and techniques for personal counseling. A major portion of the guidance counselor's role should be spent directly in staff development activities.
5. Assist the teachers in establishing and maintaining a good in-class pupil personnel record system. These are the records maintained by the teacher for day-by-day counseling and academic prescriptions.

Student Referral System

Most school systems have a number of specialists available to the student to meet needs beyond those that can be carried out by the regular school staff. Each school should have someone designated to coordinate the special service needs for the school. The guidance counselor is an appropriate referral agent to determine the need of services, as well as identifying the proper source for those services.

It is suggested that each school prepare a list of available services and people to contact for those services so that teachers, parents, and other community members might know to whom they can turn for help with particular problems. Included on such list would be counselors, including guidance, special education, and attendance; the school psychologist; special education resource teachers; pathologists; home-bound teachers; reading specialists; and so on. An example of such a list is shown in figure 18–5.

PUTTING ORDER AND ACCOUNTABILITY INTO THE COUNSELING PROGRAM

A good counseling program will not just happen, no matter how much good will and interest there might be on the part of the professional staff. The Port Arthur (Texas) Independent School District has gained national repute for its systematic approach to the guidance function of the schools. Through careful analysis of the objectives of the program, a series of specific activities, responsibilities, and indicators of achievement of objectives has been developed. The following is an examination of what one school system has done to put order and accountability into the counseling program.[11]

The counseling and guidance functions are divided into three "domains": educational, career, and social. Each domain is explicated by

1. *Hillman Guidance Counselor*—Mr. Robert Ward is a full-time staff member at Hillman offering counseling, testing, and referral help to parents and students. Telephone: 699-3194.

2. *School Psychologist*—Dr. Albert Miller is available to all Hillman parents and students. His services are available by referral through the Pupil Services Department. Telephone: 699-2860.

3. *Special Education Counselor*—Ms. Dell Felder is the school counselor responsible for coordinating placement and for assisting parents and students involved within the learning disability classes. Her services may be available by calling 699-2860.

4. *Special Education Teacher*—Mr. Clyde McDougle is a regular Hillman staff member teaching students experiencing learning problems in our school.

5. *School Pathologist*—Ms. Sandy Sloan is a full-time Hillman staff member. She is responsible for diagnosis and treatment of speech and hearing problems.

6. *Home-Bound Teacher*—Mrs. May Lunden is available at the physician's request to every pupil who is unable to attend school for a period of four weeks or longer. Requests are made through Pupil Personnel Department.

7. *Diagnostic Center*—This center is being operated by Mrs. Cathy Yasilli to diagnose and prescribe educational programs for students experiencing problems in school. Contact the school counselor.

8. *Home-School Coordinator*—Miss Phyllis Selter serves as a liaison between the home and school. Her services are available by calling 699-2860.

9. *Attendance Counselor*—Mr. Howard Jones coordinates all attendance and data processing. He is responsible for attendance problems, juvenile court contacts, enrollment projections, report cards, secondary and junior high scheduling, and processing of test data. Telephone: 699-1658.

10. *Reading Specialist*—Hillman High School has three reading teachers who work with students to develop reading skills needed for high school work. The teachers are Mrs. Helen Davis, Mrs. Mary Pearson, and Mr. L. Y. Hollis.

FIGURE 18–5. Pupil services personnel available at Hillman Senior High School

a series of goals which, in turn, are further disaggregated into objectives, activities and responsibilities, and indicators of attainment. The time the activity is to occur and the grade level on which it is to focus are also stated.

Figure 18–6 depicts examples of goals and objectives of that part of a program which is concerned with the educational domain.

Two of the three goals in this domain concern providing students with an awareness of all aspects of the school environment and with an awareness of how they fit into that environment. The third goal is concerned with helping professional staff, parents, and community members understand the school's guidance program.

Figure 18–7 shows an example of the goals and objectives of that part of a program which focuses on career development activities for students. Goal A is concerned with providing students with an expanding awareness of career possibilities, whereas the accomplishment of

EDUCATIONAL DOMAIN

Goal C: To serve as a resource person to teachers, administrators, parents, and community.*

The goal is that teachers, administrators, parents, and other persons in the community understand the school's guidance program and become involved in support of the guidance program.

Objectives	Activities	Indicators	Time	Grades
1. The school staff should demonstrate an awareness of available guidance services and an understanding of counselor functions.	a. Counselors will conduct inservice training for all school personnel to explain available guidance services and counselor functions.	(1) School personnel will indicate an awareness of guidance services and counselor functions as determined through an evaluation.	As needed	All grades
	b. Counselors will summarize and organize data for use in curriculum planning, and will serve as members of the education team in developing and modifying the curriculum.	(1) A curriculum will be designed based upon student needs and interests.	Continuous	7–12
	c. Counselors will discuss students' academic problems with department directors and/or teachers and/or parents, seeking to develop plans for appropriate placement of each student.	(1) Students' grades will improve as a result of more appropriate placement.	As needed	7–12

FIGURE 18-6. Illustration of an accountable guidance counseling program

*Goals A and B (not illustrated) are "To develop an awareness of the educational setting" and "To develop an awareness of self in the educational setting."

CAREER DOMAIN

Goal A: To develop an awareness of the world of work.*

The goal is that students become aware that people work to meet needs; that there is a wide variety of work in the world; and that there are certain work standards, practices, and life styles in each area of work.

Objectives	Activities	Indicators	Time	Grades
1. Students should become aware of job clusters, training requirements, necessary job skills, and economic and personal rewards at different occupational levels.	a. Counselors, teachers, and career personnel will serve as resource persons to provide information in these areas.	(1) ____% of the students will be involved in these activities, as observed by counselors and teachers.	As appropriate	7–12
	b. Counselors will consult with librarians and administrators to provide, expand, and update career materials available in the library.	(1) All counselors and teachers will receive updated lists of career materials available in the library.	Annually	7–12
2. Students and other interested members of the community should become aware of the concept of work in our society, the occupational structure, and significant job trends.	a. Counselors and other District personnel will be available to serve as resource persons in providing activities in areas related to career education, new occupational trends, and the importance of attitudes and values in the world of work.	(1) A ____% increase in teacher requests for resource assistance will be evidenced.	As requested	7–12

FIGURE 18–7.   Illustration of an accountable guidance counseling program

*Goal B (not illustrated) is entitled, "To develop an accurate occupational self-perception."

Goal B is to result in accurate student self-perceptions about his or her career interests and abilities.

The third domain is the social domain, example goals for which are shown in figure 18–8. Goal A is illustrated and focuses on developing an awareness of social responsibilities, opportunities, and expectations. The other goal of the secondary program is accomplished when students learn to constructively cope with the expectations of social and cultural groups with which they are affiliated.[12]

SOCIAL DOMAIN

Goal A: To develop an awareness of social responsibilities, opportunities, and expectancies.*

The goal is that students become knowledgeable about the social setting within which they operate —including such groups as family, peers, and significant others. The emphasis is on awareness of the opportunities and requirements within the social environment, such as social expectations and social customs, and that students be able to differentiate their roles in the social groups with which they are affiliated.

Objectives	Activities	Indicators	Time	Grades
1. Students should become aware of the need to identify and affiliate with basic social groups.	a. Counselors will conduct, and/or coordinate with teachers, group guidance activities to help students become aware of the basic social groups and the need to identify or affiliate with social groups, i.e., family, peers, and other significant persons. Counselors may provide or use the following or similar materials for group interaction: • Focus on Self-Development • Developing an Understanding of Self and Others (DUSO) • Toward Affective Development (TAD) • Filmstrips • Awareness Center • Human Development Program (HDP)	(1) ___% of the students will be able to identify verbally the basic social groups and the reasons for affiliating with these groups.	Continuous	All grades

FIGURE 18–8.   Illustration of an accountable guidance counseling program

*Goal B (not illustrated) focuses on the elementary school program; Goal C is "To cope constructively with the expectations of social and cultural groups with which students are affiliated."

SUMMARY

The counselor is a person. The counseling program is comprised of a variety of functions and activities, the carrying out of which is the responsibility of many professionals on the school staff. To expect one or a few persons designated as guidance counselors to be totally responsible for all of the guidance functions is absurd.

This chapter has attempted to put the counseling program of the high school into better perspective. The depressing anonymity which characterizes many high schools, the incidences of dropping-out, of misdirected career patterns, of kids in trouble in ways no one is aware of, to name but a few pathologies, demand better ways of organizing building level pupil personnel services. A teacher-advisor system has been developed as one way to organize the counseling program. In such a system, the guidance counselor becomes a coordinator of services and has much more opportunity to effectively employ his or her specialized skills. In such a system, the student becomes more than a member of a faceless crowd.

The principal will need to support teachers as they perform this critical role and provide teachers with the necessary time, materials, and training. Further, it will need to become a criterion in performance evaluation. The counseling program and those who carry out its function should be held accountable for positive student growth in specifically designated skill and attitude areas.

ENDNOTES

1. John Robert Giles, "Positive Peer Culture in the Public School System," *NASSP Bulletin* 59 (January 1975): 23.

2. Philip A. Cusick, *Inside High School: The Student's World* (New York: Holt, Rinehart and Winston, Inc., 1973), pp. 1–2.

3. See John M. Jenkins, "The Teacher-Advisor: An Old Solution Looking for a Problem," *NASSP Bulletin* 61 (September 1977): 29–34 for a description of the program at Wilde Lake High School, Columbia, Maryland.

4. Ibid., p. 31.

5. William Glasser, *Schools Without Failure* (New York: Harper and Row, 1968).

6. Human Development Training Institute, Inc. *Innerchange Human Development Program.* LeMesa, California, 1977. Program focuses on secondary school level.

7. Several years ago, one of the authors was working with a team of seven members where this technique was used. It was a newly-formed team of teachers, most of whom had taught in the school, however, for a number of years. When the student requests were all in and the team sat down to sort them, it was found that one of the seven members had received only two third-place requests and no first or second. The teacher apparently had the reputation of being a hard disciplinarian, aloof, and unfair. As the tally of student requests was completed, this particular teacher became angry and then turned to tears and left the meeting. The principal was called in and informed of the difficulty, and then he and the team leader sat down with the teacher in question and discussed the problem. She, of course, attempted to defend her teaching style, but admitted that she was unaware of the fact that the students disliked her so. A temporary solution was found by assigning her team tasks of importance other than advisement. She became relatively open to suggestions from the team leader and principal, with respect to her relationship with the students. By the beginning of the second semester, a group of students was identified who indicated their willingness to shift to her for advisement.

8. This offers a good opportunity for the principal to have a direct one-to-one relationship with a group of students without having to be tied permanently to an instructional responsibility. It gives one that kind of contact that a principal often needs to keep in touch with the real world of teaching.

9. Jenkins, "The Teacher-Advisor," p. 33.

10. If this use of teacher time violates a master contract, as it might in some areas, then the issue will need to be subjected to negotiation at the next possible time.

11. Readers interested in more fully exploring the Port Arthur approach could direct an inquiry to Dr. Verlie A. Mitchell, Coordinator of Pupil Personnel Services, Port Arthur Independent School District, Port Arthur, Texas 77640.

12. Goal B in the social domain is not shown because it is of relevance to the elementary school guidance program only.

BIBLIOGRAPHY

Bohlinger, Tom. "Implementing a Comprehensive Guidance Program." *NASSP Bulletin* 61 (September 1977): 65–71.

Chase, Larry. *The Other Side of the Report Card.* Pacific Palisades, Calif.: Goodyear Publishing Co., 1975.

Cusick, Philip A. *Inside High School: The Student's World.* New York: Holt, Rinehart and Winston, Inc., 1973.

Ernest, Kenneth. *Games Students Play and What to do About Them.* Millbrae, Calif.: Celestial Arts Press, 1972.

Foster, Herbert. *Ribbin', Jivin', and Playing the Dozens.* Cambridge, Mass.: Ballinger Press, 1974.

Giles, John Robert. "Positive Peer Culture in the Public School System." *NASSP Bulletin* 59 (January 1975): 22–28.

Glasser, Willian. *Schools Without Failure.* New York: Harper Row, 1968.

Hubel, Keigh; Tillquist, Paul; Riedal, Robert; and Myrbach, Charles. *The Teacher-Advisor System.* Dubuque, Iowa: Kendall Hunt Publishing Co., 1974.

Jenkins, John M. "The Teacher-Advisor: An Old Solution Looking for a Problem." *NASSP Bulletin* 61 (September 1977): 29–34.

Larson, Robert, and Mable, Ted. "The Teacher-Advisor Role in an Open Secondary School." *NASSP Bulletin* 59 (April 1975): 37–43.

Trump, J. Lloyd. "Are Counselors Meeting Student and Teacher Needs?" *NASSP Bulletin* 61 (September 1977): 26–28.

Chapter Nineteen

Maintaining Positive Control of Students

INTRODUCTION

Poor Harry. We all have a Harry in our school. In fact, we would consider ourselves lucky if we only had one Harry. Harry, in truth, is the name of a whole group of students.

Harry has difficulty attending school on a full time basis. On those 3-1/2 days per week that he is present he cannot always make it to classes. He is too busy harassing and abusing students and staff. He spends a significant amount of time disrupting instruction and vandalizing the bathroom. Between parent conferences and visits with the psychologist, Harry sets fires, extinguishes imaginary fires and pulls alarm boxes in anticipation of a fire. Harry "borrows" purses and occasionally a car. Harry spends more time in your office than you do and contributes more to the disruption of the office than a visiting board of education member. When a police car pulls up to the school Harry goes into hiding. As the year progresses, Harry usually gets worse.

What can you do with Harry? Parent conferences, psychological evaluations, special programs, mental health team conferences, home visits, and Harry gets worse. And all of this is complicated by his age, fifteen years, one month and eight days. Can you continue to allow his disruption of the school? Or, maybe his parents will agree not to send him anymore.[1]

Bane of the professional educator's life, Harry causes a lot of stomachaches. Harry comes in different forms, intensities, and numbers. While one Harry may be problem enough, several Harrys will determine a school climate and materially affect the degree of productivity of the high school. This chapter will examine positive approaches to managing student life in such a way that there is orderly development within an unrepressive environment.

In Gallup poll after Gallup poll, discipline is reported to be one of the top five problems facing the public schools.[2] What is meant by discipline as a problem in the school varies with each respondent, but it can be generally summed up as control of student (mis)behavior.

In its charge to principals, one school district stated the principal's responsibilities with respect to creating a positive learning climate as follows:

It is recognized that there are no short cuts or easy-to-follow rules for establishing and maintaining discipline in a school. Discipline is based on the overall school purposes and program. A strong instructional program geared to individual student needs is the foundation for good discipline.

The primary task of the principal is to establish a proper learning environment, one which affords the opportunity for both students and teachers to successfully engage in the teaching-learning process. The central position which the principal occupies in the school requires that he be aware of disciplinary problems and appropriate disciplinary procedures. Ideally, his awareness of potential problem areas affords him the opportunity to prepare more effectively to deal with problems as they arise.

Schools should be dedicated to the twofold task of helping students understand that (1) every human being inherently possesses dignity and worth and (2) inalienable rights are accompanied by inescapable responsibilities. Such responsibilities, however, cannot be learned in the absence of freedom. *Children generally learn better from what educators demonstrate than from what they advocate.* [emphasis supplied]

When it is obvious to students that administrators are responsive to the serious concerns of young people, the school administration and staff can focus upon preventive discipline rather than punitive discipline.[3]

MAINTAINING GOOD DISCIPLINE

Developing a good disciplinary policy within the school is threefold; first is the development of "positive" climate, second are the actions which are preventive in nature, and third are those activities which can be described as corrective.

The percentage of disciplinary cases found within a school corresponds inversely with the quality and the effectiveness of the program operating within that school. Schools that provide meaningful learning experiences that are relative to student needs have fewer discipline problems.

Students who are in real contact with problems which are relevant to them wish to learn, seek to discover, endeavor to master, desire to create, move toward self-discipline.[4]

However, many discipline problems are created as a result of difficulties within the social or cultural environment, rather than any-thing within the school. Disruptions in family life create problems for the student as do hunger and poverty. Schools located in strife-ridden areas where riots, fighting, and racial upheaval are common have these problems carried into the school.

The principal of the school has a particular responsibility to lead the staff in developing school policies for controlling student behavior. This does not mean the principal personally should write the policy, but rather he or she should set up procedures by which the staff can establish a behavior philosophy, disciplinary procedures to be followed, and techniques for corrective action.

A good policy statement should include a referral system where teachers know under what circumstances they should ask for assistance, and of whom, and a statement of who accepts responsibility for the youngster's behavior with the referral.[5]

For example, a teacher should refer a student for disciplinary action when the situation has gone beyond a reasonable ability to handle it in the classroom. At that point, the problem is turned over entirely to the referral agent. In this way, changes and modification in teacher assigned punishment can be made and understood without seeming to undermine the teacher's authority.

The involvement of a second professional in all extreme discipline cases is required. This person should serve as an advisor and as a level head in treating the problem.[6]

An adequate follow-through reporting system must exist so that all staff members involved are aware of any action taken. Any policy developed at the building level must fall within the policies established by state rules and regulations and local board of education policies.

Good student behavior in the school comes as a result of adequate supervision and the use of good student management techniques. There are certain areas of the building and school grounds, for example, that must be appropriately supervised if a good preventive program is to be maintained. Guidelines drawn up by teachers themselves often offer the best solution, both in insuring that all such areas are supervised, as well as in good teacher cooperation in carrying out the plan.

A PROMISING PREVENTIVE TECHNIQUE: PROJECT ORDER

B. C. Elmore Middle School (grades 6–8) is located in the North Forest Independent School District (Houston, Texas). The school is located in a depressed economic area, predominately inhabited by Black families. In socioeconomic terms, its enrollment resembles that of many inner-city schools and, typical of many of these schools, it has been depicted as a violent and disorderly place. Ninety-nine percent of the students attending B. C. Elmore are minority group members. Within four years, the school was completely reorganized, and through formal evaluation the following results have been documented:[7]

1. Discipline problems are down 63 percent.
2. Referrals to the principal are down 17 percent.
3. Corporal punishment is down 93 percent.
4. Suspensions are down 20 percent.

Four Crucial Assumptions

Project ORDER (Organization for Responsibility, Dependability, Education and Reality) employs a systems model for reorganizing an inner-city middle school. The project is designed to develop an atmosphere of positive, constructive, orderly, acceptable student behavior in which learning can occur, and is intended to overcome the adverse effects of minority group isolation. The four basic assumptions made were:

1. Much of the disorder and lack of control in secondary schools is due to the existence of large, impersonal, anonymous masses of students. Their feelings of alienation and the teachers' feelings of helplessness must be recognized and addressed by the administration through reorganization of the school.
2. In the recent past the teaching of attitudes and values has been neglected. Behavior may be improved by affective education which uses modern theories of psychology and sociology.
3. A large percentage of severe discipline problems are caused by a small percentage of the students. Special facilities and methods are needed to handle the more severe disruptive behavior of these children if it cannot be handled effectively in the classroom.
4. Much alienation and misbehavior is caused by a curriculum which is irrelevant and inappropriate for many students. Curriculum which is appropriate and relevant to the students' environment can do much to improve behavior.[8]

Organization of Students

The student body is organized into four clusters of 250 to 300 students each. Clusters are composed of one team leader, a group of teachers, and a teacher aide, with a counselor for each two clusters. Students developed a new sense of group identity and importance through cluster-related activities. In becoming acquainted with the cluster, its purpose, and function, the student learns that the cluster operates as a unit and that there are general cluster rules which are posted in the classrooms. Within the cluster, the homeroom has become a means of increasing knowledge through direct teaching of values, attitudes, and behavior. The student becomes closely identified with one teacher.

Organization of Administration

Although a principal and assistant principal serve as administrative heads of the school, the four team leaders representing each cluster are also especially important. They give instructional leadership, have guidance duties, and also share the responsibility for control of the behavior of students in clusters. Team leaders work with regular classes for three periods each day, lead instructional planning, and coordinate the team teaching units.

Organization of Cocurricular Activities

To increase the active participation of the total student body, Elmore Middle School has expanded its program of cocurricular activities to involve all students. The activities are coordinated with the academic curriculum and are structured consistent with the objectives of Project ORDER. There are twenty-four clubs and intramural athletics in which *both* faculty and students participate.

The Crisis Intervention Center

One of the most unusual aspects of the cluster make-up is the existence of the Crisis Intervention Center for students who cannot or will not adapt to the regular classroom. Placement into the Crisis Intervention Center begins with the Admission and Dismissal Committee. This committee is composed of students, teachers, and administrative personnel. They listen to charges against students and reports of misbehavior. When all information has been reviewed by this committee, a decision is made as to whether or not the student will be referred to the Crisis Intervention Center. Assignment to

the center prevents these students from continuing to disrupt the school program, but makes suspension from school unnecessary.

Once the student has been assigned to the Crisis Intervention Center, each of his or her teachers makes lessons and assignments available to the Crisis Intervention Center teacher. The Crisis Intervention teacher and an aide work with all students, helping them with their daily assignments. When students become a part of the Crisis Intervention Center, contact with other students ceases until they are ready to return to their regular classes.

Reality therapy, among other techniques, is used with these students to help improve their behavior. When a student feels that he or she is ready to leave the Crisis Intervention Center, he or she must develop an acceptable plan of conduct that will be approved by the Crisis Intervention Center teacher. This plan is then submitted to the Admission and Dismissal Committee for their consideration. Once a student is allowed to return to regular classes, he or she is on probation for the first two weeks and must receive acceptable ratings from each teacher or return to the Crisis Intervention Center.

What Can Be Learned From ORDER?

The critical element in having a school relatively free from disorder and dissonance appears to be an organizational structure which reduces anonymity and an educational program which has a great amount of relevance to student needs.[9] The following are of prime importance:

1. Structuring the environment in such a way that a sense of identity is provided and anonymity reduced by organizing teaching-learning communities. Teams of teachers and specialists (really clinical teams) are created to work with relatively fewer children, but for longer periods of time.

2. A sound inservice training program for existing staff to focus not only on refining academic and methodological skills but also to contain skills development in the affective side of education.

PROMISING CORRECTIVE AND PREVENTIVE TECHNIQUES

Schools nationwide are facing the issue of maintaining positive student control in a variety of creative ways. The discussion which follows describes some of the more promising methods. Many of these techniques require the cooperation of several public agencies; all require careful organization and a sensitive and well-trained professional staff. Some of the techniques are preventive in nature, others are corrective.

Student Referral Centers

As an alternative to suspension, the Houston Independent School District created the Student Referral Center (SRC) in 1974. A relatively small operation (eight such centers exist) the SRC began as an experiment to do something positive about students who were consistently disruptive in class, repeatedly broke school rules, or were habitually truant.

The SRC is an alternative suspension program, operated jointly by the Houston school system and the city's Juvenile Probation Department, a community youth services division that has as its goal the prevention of delinquency. A center's staff includes three kinds of specialists: a school counselor-coordinator, teacher(s), and a youth services specialist from the probation department. They form, in effect, a clinical team.

The suspension class operates in much the same way as the traditional one-room school house where students do all of their school work under the direction of one teacher (whose classload is kept small and who has been designated a master teacher by the district). Regular teachers in the school from which the student was removed send assignments and the SRC teacher oversees the work.

Pupils are assigned to the center for as few as three days or as long as a full school term. The center does not get maximally severe discipline problems, such as students considered dangerous or who have threatened teachers with weapons.

The counselor-coordinator and the youth service specialist complete the clinical team. Their task is to work with the student, the family, and other public agencies to address the causes of the problem. The SRC teaching staff insures that in the process the student is able to maintain his or her learning progress. Thus, the program is not simply a "holding tank" wherein disruptive students are placed out of sight, but rather it becomes a diagnosis and prescription center.[10]

Positive Peer Culture

A much different technique focusing on improving student behavior is a new concept of group therapy, called Positive Peer Culture (PPC). It has had some success in treatment centers for delinquent youth and has been implemented in some public schools, the Omaha, Nebraska, schools among these.[11] Esssentially, peer groups of students are formed. Members of each group discuss problems and each other's behavior. The groups are small (seven to eleven members), composed of members of the same sex, and have an adult group leader.

The two kinds of PPC groups are leadership groups and student advisory groups.

Leadership Groups These are composed of students identified by faculty and students as leaders—either in a positive or negative sense. (That is, they are students to whom other students listen, are persuaded by, and/or emulate.) Identified leaders are invited to join the group after interviews with faculty members. With a trained adult group leader they meet two or more times per week throughout the year, including during summer school. The meetings focus on school and student problems, and form the nucleus of PPC. Members also learn counseling techniques.

Student Advisory Groups These groups are formed by individual members of the leadership group. Students with school problems such as misbehavior, attendance, truancy, etc., may accept this group's help. Meeting in vacant classrooms, the cafeteria, or any convenient place, individuals are subjected to peer influence. The attempt is to work with students before they get into serious trouble.

> The philosophy for Positive Peer Groups stems from the belief that delinquent behavior can be contained and modified by giving the student a positive role in a group process and within a sub-culture specifically designed to help young people help themselves. The *goal* is simply to present students with the opportunity to meet as a group in a positive relationship where they can learn to better solve problems and to develop a sense of responsibility for their own behavior.[12]

The program is probably best suited for senior high school because it does require somewhat greater maturity. The emphasis in the group is in helping members behave responsibly in a school and life setting (in a way in which the individual hurts neither himself or herself or others).

With great insight, Giles establishes the need for programs functioning in concert with, but separate from, the regular school program:

> The present *problem* faced by parents, students, and schools is the lack of recognition that stu-

dents have two areas of achievement to contend with in the educational system: they are expected to achieve academically, and they are expected to accept all demands made upon them without question and with good grace. There is no separation of academic attainment from the emotional reactions to the academic system.

> Neither is there an allowance made for the mental stability of the student in routine problem-solving situations. This means that the school counselor today can properly and adequately assist the student with academic planning, *but the same counselor cannot be a mental health worker* responsible for the emotional adjustment of the student toward the school setting and toward life in general. [emphasis supplied]

> In order to assist the student with the emotional component of the school system, some type of unique service is needed.[13]

PPC type programs do appear to offer some promise for helping large numbers of students who are having severe adjustment problems and who manifest this either in overt acts of hostility or in more difficult to discern withdrawal behavior.

THERE MAY BE TROUBLE COMING IF ..

Things aren't the best perhaps, but classes are running smoothly and there have been no serious disruptions. Yet, the principal wonders. Is this the way it's supposed to be? How does one know if the school is on the slide? While any school may have a bad week or even a bad month, there are some signs that may indicate that attention is needed. These indicators may be grouped under three rubrics: school climate, student actions, and parent and/or community members' attitudes.

School Climate

1. Inordinate complaints about curriculum and instructional practices.

2. General complaints that minority group members are being "tracked" or too frequently placed into nonacademic courses or special education classes.

3. Insistent complaints that certain kinds of students are subtly excluded from membership in identified school activities, including clubs, honor societies, or sports.

4. Charges that disciplinary procedures are being unfairly applied.

5. Teacher complaints that the "kids are running wild" or that the administrators are being too lenient in punishing miscreants.

6. A general drop in achievement levels of students or a significant increase in the number of students given failures for a grading period.

7. Charges (and countercharges) by identifiable ethnic or racial groups that the "other guys" get preferential treatment.

Student Actions

1. Increased vandalism to school or community property.

2. Marked increase in use of drugs or alcohol.

3. Increased absenteeism and tardiness rates (including marked change by a racial or ethnic group).

4. Increase of seemingly minor conflicts between ethnic or racial groups.

5. Consistent and/or increasing infractions of school rules.

6. Increase in number of police-student contacts.

7. Reports of threats made to teachers.

8. Weapon carrying.

Manifest Attitudes of Parents and Community Members

1. Appearance of hate literature.

2. Requests by a community group that the school must "crack down" on disruptive students.

3. Attempts on part of community group to circumvent the administrators concerning a school problem and to directly complain to the board of education.

4. Declining attendance at school events.

5. Continual and increasing appearance of nonstudents on school grounds.

6. Increasing requests for student transfer to another school by parents, or withdrawal of students to attend privately organized schools.

If some of these conditions are present, leading action is required. This may be the time for the principal to present the faculty, and perhaps a group of interested parents and students, with a list of concerns about the existent conditions preparatory to the constitution of a task force for problem identification and problem resolution. Action ahead of a crisis is the best mitigating force. The case study in decision making described in chapter 2 may provide some insights about the appropriate processes to be employed. The project management approach which is the subject of chapter 23 offers a systematic way of addressing the issues. Figure 19–1 suggests some preventive steps.

A Concluding Word About Techniques

The preceding discussion of promising techniques is hardly exhaustive. The intent has been to provide an examination of some educationally sound alternatives to positively address the more severe symptoms of an unproductive school climate. Trump puts the issue in perspective:

> The usual approaches that schools use to deal with students who persist in violating rules involve suspension or expulsion. Some schools even list the number of days that a student will be suspended for committing specified offences. For example, one school automatically suspends a student for three days when the stu-

1. Develop school discipline policies consistent with board policies and make sure that parents, teachers, and pupils are familiar with them. This may be done through a school handbook.

2. Base all rules and regulations upon whether or not the educative process is disturbed *rather than whether or not the educator is disturbed.*

3. Require teachers to keep records of recurrent misbehavior. A simple card file will suffice for this.

4. Encourage teachers and parents to make the initial attempt to solve problems.

5. Emphasize the responsibility that parents have in regard to their child's behavior.

6. Let minor infractions be handled by the teacher, recognizing that some teachers need more help than others with discipline.

7. Ask teachers to submit a disciplinary report along with the request for help from the principal.

8. Use some convenient method to inform teachers of the disposition of referred discipline problems.

9. Encourage teachers to assume responsibility for school discipline. A word from a teacher to students running, scuffling, etc., is often a sufficient deterrent.

10. Identify trouble spots such as restrooms, halls, and cafeteria, and assign faculty members to duty at certain specified times.

11. *Be visible.* Often the principal's presence in the halls, cafeteria, or playground serves as a deterrent to misbehavior and gives the teacher a feeling of support.

FIGURE 19-1.   Maintaining control: Tips for secondary school principals

dent is truant for a day—which almost seems like contributing to the offense. Wide variations exists in determining what constitutes causes for expulsion from schools.

A school that seeks to develop the maximum potential of each student must use positive steps to rehabilitate those persons who defy the system. . . . The basic approach is diagnosis of individual problems. Why does a student stay at home or go some other place in the community? Why did the student commit a violent act against another student or a member of the school staff? Equally necessary is the decision on what prescriptive remedy to follow. Alternatives are considered and decisions made to implement one or a combination of them.[14]

SUMMARY

This chapter has focused on specific ways to achieve positive student control. In a real sense it has examined the issue of what to do after the handbook on rules and regulations has been developed and promulgated.

Normative student behavior varies widely from school to school. Schools where students' behavior is positive are characterized by:

1. A lack of anonymity.
2. Relevant educational programming.
3. A fair, consistent, and well-understood system of rules and regulations.

ENDNOTES

1. Donald P. Riley, "What to Do About Harry," *SANNYS Journal* 7 (Fall 1977): 5.
2. For the past several years Gallup, in cooperation with the Kettering Foundation, has surveyed the public about attitudes toward public schools. These surveys are reported in the November issues of *Phi Delta Kappan*.
3. Memphis City Schools, "Helpful Hints for Discipline," Memphis, Tennessee: Department of Pupil Services, undated, pp. 4–5.
4. Carl Rogers, *Freedom to Learn* (Columbus, Ohio: Charles E. Merrill, 1969), p. 114.
5. If the school is operating on a team arrangement, teacher-to-team-to-principal is a good order to follow.
6. Chapter 5, "Students, Staff and Administrator Rights and Responsibilities: A Legal Focus" contains suggestions about specific procedures. Included also is a sample "Report of Disciplinary Action" Form.
7. The project was initially funded as a pilot program with federal assistance under the Emergency School Assistance Act. Project ORDER is an acronym for Organization for Responsibility, Dependability, Education and Reality.
8. Stanley G. Sanders; Janice S. Yarborough; and Raquel Bauman (eds.), "Project ORDER," an E.S.A.A. III Project (Houston, Texas: North Forest Independent School District) (mimeo), p. 12.
9. See Stanley Sanders and Janice Yarborough, "Achieving a Learning Environment With ORDER," *The Clearing House* 50 (November 1976): 100–102.
10. Similar programs exist around the nation. Donald P. Riley (see note 1) writes about another such program in Rochester, New York, schools.
11. PPC is a national corporation, Positive Peer Culture, Inc., based in Clinton, Michigan. At the time this book is being written, it is under a $60,000 yearly contract with the Omaha Public Schools and partially funded by the Nebraska Drug Commission. PPC is administered through the schools' Department of Human-Community Relations Services.
12. John Robert Giles, "Positive Peer Culture in The Public School System," *NASSP Bulletin* 59 (January 1975). See also, "Creative Discipline," *NASSP Bulletin* 1 (November 1977–January 1978), published by AFSC Southeastern Public Education Program, American Friends Service Committee, 401 Columbia Building, Columbia, S.C. 29201. See also, Harry H. Vorrah, "Positive Peer Culture—Content, Structure, Process," Michigan Center for Group Studies, 400 N. Penn Avenue, Lansing, Michigan.
13. Giles, "Positive Peer Culture," pp. 22–23.
14. J. Lloyd Trump, *A School for Everyone* (Reston, Va.: National Association of Secondary School Principals, 1977).

BIBLIOGRAPHY

Berger, Michael. *Violence in the Schools: Causes and Remedies.* Bloomington, Ind.: Phi Delta Kappa Educational Foundation, 1974 (order Fastback #46).

Cusick, A. *Inside High School, The Student's World.* New York: Holt, Rinehart and Winston, 1973. Cusick's book is disturbing because it reveals how little adolescents are really affected by teacher and administrator behavior. It is peer behavior that seems to control the life of the student. Yet, there is so much energy among students. How to harness this raw energy in a way which produces a productive learning environment is the professional challenge.

Dinkmeyer, Don, and Dinkmeyer, Don, Jr. "Logical Consequences: A Key to the Reduction of Disciplinary Problems." *Phi Delta Kappan* 57 (June 1976): 664–666.

Doyle, Walter. "Helping Beginning Teachers Manage Classrooms." *NASSP Bulletin* 59 (December 1975): 38–41.

Estadt, Gary J.; Willower, Donald J.; and Caldwell, William E. "School Principal's Role Administration Behavior and Teachers' Pupil Control Behavior." *Contemporary Education* 47 (Summer 1976): 207–212.

Foster, Herbert L. *Ribbin', Jivin', and Playing' the Dozens: The Unrecognized Dilemma of Inner City Schools.* Cambridge, Mass.: Ballinger, 1974. This book focuses on developing a creative learning climate and good discipline in inner-city schools. It contains proven techniques and provides great insight about the nature of street corner behavior.

Giles, John Robert. "Positive Peer Culture in the Public School System." *NASSP Bulletin* 59 (January 1975): 22–28.

Johnson, Christopher. "Secondary Schools and Student Responsibility." *Phi Delta Kappan* 59 (January 1978): 338–341.

Kindsvatter, Richard. "A New View of the Dynamics of Discipline." *Phi Delta Kappan* 59 (January 1978): 322–324.

Maynard, William. "Working with Disruptive Youth." *Educational Leadership* 34 (March 1977): 417–421.

Meares, Henry O., and Kittle, Helen A. "More Advantages: In-House Suspensions." *NASSP Bulletin* 60 (February 1976): 60–63.

McKean, Robert C., and Taylor, Bob L. "How to Reduce Discipline Problems." *Educational Leadership* 34 (April 1977): 557.

Riley, Donald P. "What To Do About Harry." *SAANYS Journal* 7 (Fall 1977): 5–6.

Rogers, Carl. *Freedom to Learn.* Columbus, Ohio: Charles E. Merrill, 1969.

Sanders, Stanley G., and Yarborough, Janis S. "Achieving a Learning Environment with ORDER." *The Clearing House* 50 (November 1976): 100–102.

Sinner, Greg, and Sinner, J L. "Options in High School Discipline." *Phi Delta Kappan* 59 (February 1978): 407–409.

Trump, J. Lloyd. *A School for Everyone.* Reston, Va.: National Association of Secondary School Principals, 1977.

Chapter Twenty

Financial Planning and Record Keeping

INTRODUCTION

The role of the principal in fiscal planning and management is crucial. Leading a staff in creative, far-sighted budget development requires well-honed human relations skills, intimate knowledge of curricular needs, skill in systematic planning, and a good understanding of the fiscal realities of the school district as a whole. A sound budget enhances the ability of the school to deliver on its promises to young people and the ability of the secondary school principal to persuasively advocate the school's needs before district-wide budget committees.

Managing the budget, once approved and allocated, also requires great skill. Poor record keeping and other unsound fiscal practices result in mismanaged dollars. Such mismanagement is always indefensible, but in an economy of scarce resources and Proposition 13, it becomes unconscionable!

Schools are big business. In many communities, the school system is the single largest employer of personnel and the largest industry in terms of capital flow. School districts receive and disburse huge amounts of money for a variety of services and materials over the period of a year. Similarly, at the individual school building, principals have the responsibility for administering sizeable financial resources—resources which come from the cen-

tral district office as a result of local, state, and federal support programs, as well as much smaller sums which come from places such as PTA's, school clubs, plays, etc. Budgeting and managing financial resources is a major responsibility accruing to most secondary principals, even though the board of education has the overall responsibility for the legal distribution and accounting of monies.

BUDGET PROCESS

Good bugeting is commonly thought of as containing four distinct steps: planning and allocating of all costs, consideration and adoption, administration and coordination, and review and appraisal. These four steps reveal that the budget process itself is cyclical and continuous. The review and appraisal step, for example, immediately precedes the following fiscal year's planning and preparation step.

Budgeting must be more than simply categorically allocating anticipated revenues and subsequently recording the expenditures made for these categories. Being able to specifically "cost out" the various activities and components of an educational program is a meager accomplishment unless it is viewed as just the first step in evaluating the effectiveness of those activities and components in terms of educational goal attainment by students. Thus, budget development must begin with a careful examination of the goals and objectives of the educational program. It requires general staff participation in the formative stages as well as in the implementation stage. (See figure 20–1.)

Priority Setting—Where the Dollars Must Go

Foremost in budget building is educational planning. The relationship between the educational goals and objectives of the school and the budget to support these must be made obvious.

Good budgeting is the result of careful educational planning; it is not a catalog of "outgoes" so that one knows retrospectively where the money went.

Many school staffs get caught in the "incremental budgeting game," thereby performing a great disservice to their clients. Incremental budget requires simple acceptance of the status quo. Any increases or losses in student population are projected for the next subsequent year, and, on the basis of what was required for the current year, dollar needs are established. Such a budget development process is simple, requires very little thought, and can

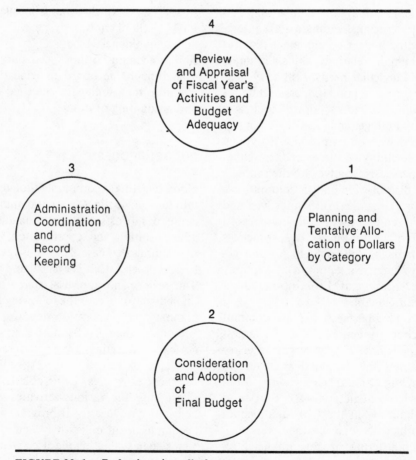

FIGURE 20–1. Budgeting: A cyclical process

be accomplished in a short period of time with a calculator and a census tract. It is also dysfunctional.

Preferable is a budget procedure which uses basic elements of Program Planning Budgeting System (PPBS).

Program Planning Budgeting System[1]

As its simplest, PPBS involves five steps:

1. Establishing the general goals to be achieved.
2. Identifying the specific objectives which define this goal.
3. Developing the program and processes which it is believed will achieve the objectives and goals.
4. Establishing the formative and summative evaluation practices.
5. A review and recycle procedure that indicates whether or not the degree to which the program and processes resulted in the achievement of the objectives and the goals, and, if not, to help determine other procedures, processes and programs.

In other words, PPBS is a system designed to help a school staff decide specifically what is to be accomplished and how to go about it. PPBS focuses upon goal accomplishment and, if sensitively and sensibly applied, will provide for efficient expenditures of monies.[2]

Often, educational planning has primarily been concerned with the "inputs" of education. The school budget typically has been concerned with the numbers game; the numbers of staff, books, equipment, and buildings which must be secured, purchased, and assembled in order to "educate" a determined number of children. It is in this regard that PPBS differs substantially from other budget building procedures because PPBS focuses on desired "outputs" of the effort (goals and objectives) and afterward considers the numbers of staff,

books, equipment, and buildings which must be engaged to obtain the desired end.

There are other values to a PPBS plan, however. A recent publication of the School Management Institute points out:

> PPBS. . . provides new opportunities and involvement which are critically needed today. [Educators] point to the impersonalization and bureaucracy of bigness, the militancy of teachers, frustrated parents, restless students and critical taxpayers, as evidences that school districts must find new avenues to gain understanding and support.
>
> Being a very public enterprise, a school district is forced to win the consent of adult citizens, employees, children and distant lawmakers, in order to operate successfully. Hence, there is a special need for communication and involvement on the part of those who use the school facilities, share direct and indirect benefits and pay the bills.
>
> . . . As enterprises have become more complex and diversified, as well as more demanding of money, manpower, and time investments, there has been greater anxiety about results. As the stakes get higher, there is a more pressing desire to know more precisely what the investment is producing and to minimize the chances of error or failure. The basic premise of PPBS is to help assure success.[3]

Implementing a Systematic Budget Building Process

The aphorism that budget should issue from planning the education program need not be so many words in a graduate textbook on school finance. The answer to the question, "How do you build an educationally sound budget?" is that one starts at the base—the educational program—and develops outward. How does one find out what the program needs are? One asks the people in the best position to provide the answer—the instructional staff. However, careful organization is required to provide an effective mechanism so that the needs of the program can be efficiently translated into dollar amounts in the budget. If budget building is to be anything more than a means of classifying outgo, it must involve dealing in futures.

Many principals will make at least a modest effort to involve instructional staff in the budget building process, but too frequently this simply is a matter of asking the staff for their ideas about needed equipment or supplies. The responses are often mundane and short-sighted suggestions, many of which may be of doubtful overall significance to the educational endeavor. The reason for this is that many staffs really have not had much practice in planning expenditures of significant amounts of money to improve their departments. Frequently, the nature of the request from the principal causes staff members to think solely in terms of additional "things" for their department, rather than thinking of the direction the educational program ought to be taking.

"What do you need now?" is too often the question, when the question really should be "Where do you see this school, or your department, legitimately heading in the next few years, and what is it going to take to get there?" Since staff involvement in decision making is the most effective means for bringing about real change, the effort to involve staff in curricular study and change must extend to budget development.

Among the outcomes of such a budget development process is a concern for the future and a continuous assessment of current curricular and instructional practices.

Step 1: The Five-Year Plan The planning process begins with the development of a five-year plan, well in advance of any specific budget proposals for the next fiscal year. This is not a document that is developed quickly. The process does provide a good basis for inservice workshops with staff and lends a substantive focus to faculty meetings and workshops held throughout the school year.

The process may begin by organizing the preschool workshop to focus on planning for the future. Several school-wide or department brainstorming sessions are held, at which time the topics to be stormed are often stated as, "What a student at the end of grade twelve should know" or "what this school needs is" or "outcomes of the 7–12 social studies program should be," or any number of other topics which are generative of ideas which focus on curricular or student outcomes. Staff members are encouraged to not be encumbered by any real world constraints nor to think solely in terms of the current year, but rather to project their thinking to as much as five or ten years in the future.

Following the brainstorming sessions, staff members convert the product of these sessions into a series of goals and objectives by a process of synthesizing, summarizing, and combination.[4] Once the staff has refined the statements of objectives and goals, they identify, often through another brainstorming session, the processes, materials, personnel, etc., which will be necessary to implement these goals and objectives over the next five years or so. The statements are not "written on stone" and are subject to future modification and change if that appears to be important. Less than perfection must be accepted lest the staff and the principal be victimized by the "paralysis of analysis." The tentative five-year plan has four major components:

1. A written description of the current state of the art of discipline. This is relatively brief (no more than a couple of pages). The staff simply describes where the department, or subject matter, or curricular field is at the present time in relation to what the literature and research reveal is the ideal state.
2. Statement of goals, objectives, and reasonable indicators of achievement of objectives for the department. It is important to establish objective indicators of achievement. However,

this does not have to be done at this time; it can be done later. A staff could bog down at this point and engage in either superficial rhetoric or become fatigued at developing long lists of performance objectives based on lower level cognitive achievement. This should not be allowed to happen; indicators can be developed just as well later. It is important to move the staff as rapidly as possible (while still obtaining serious thought) through the initial five-year plan development into the actual budget development process so that they may achieve a reward for their hard work reasonably quickly. This establishes credibility and is psychologically most important for a school staff which is engaging in this kind of a process for the first time. Again, it needs to be stressed that less than perfection must be acceptable; the staff will become more sophisticated as they engage in the process over subsequent years. The five-year plan is subject to modification through the formative evaluation which will occur as it unfolds. Slavishly following the procedures suggested here would be unwise indeed; one must not let the principles of systematic budget development be subverted by attention to unthinking observance of procedures. The sophistication of staff and local conditions must be taken into consideration.

3. A list of processes to be engaged in to implement the objectives.

4. A statement of needed equipment, materials, personnel, and other resources supportive of the processes established in the previous section.

This is the culmination point for the five-year plan development. It is subject to refinement and modification and is ultimately submitted for executive review and discussion. It does not contain any dollar figures at this point. While care should be taken not to hurry the process, definite timelines should be established for the completion of this process. Otherwise, it may become a cumbersome intel-lectual exercise that never gets completed. The five-year plan for the high school plots a general direction; the one-year building plan provides budgetary substance.

Step 2: The One-Year Plan   The one-year plan, in effect, asks the staff to develop a proposal identifying the kinds of things that need to happen next year if the five-year plan is to be ultimately realized. Figure 20–2 provides the suggested format for the one-year plan.

The one-year plan is translated into equipment needs, supplies, supplementary materials, immediate changes of personnel or addition of personnel, remodeling, and other needed resources such as travel monies and consultants. Justification for each specific item should be available in the one-year plan document.[5] This need not be elaborate, but it will require some brief statement about how the budget proposal is consistent with the five-year plan. An additional feature is that the departments or grade levels are asked to list their needs in orders of priority. If "cutting" becomes necessary because of insufficient total dollars, such cutting then can begin with lowest priority items in each of the departmental proposals.

Timeline.   In the initial effort to provide a five-year plan and ultimately translate that into one-year budget proposals, sufficient time must be provided. It should be noted that during the first year of the process, it will be necessary to continue the former budget development procedure because "start up" and five-year development will require most of the first year, and the new one-year budget proposals will not be available until the next subsequent fiscal year.

Subsequent steps.   Subsequent steps involve submitting the budget and the curriculum proposals of the department or unit to the principal and the administrative staff, its subsequent approval or return for clarification or modification. Ultimately, the preparation of a

Department _____

Fiscal year_____

Prepared by _____

Amount requested_____

Amount allocated _____

Request (indicate after each item which long-term objective this is supportive of)	Estimated cost	Suggested source of supply	Suggested source of money (fed. proj., local funds, donation, state experimental funds, etc.
1. Needed personnel			
2. Needed equipment and materials			
3. Needed other resources (e.g., travel monies, consultants, etc.)			
Total requested			

N.B. Prioritize needs in descending order.

4. Brief statement about how this budget proposed is consistent with and supportive of the five-year plan.

FIGURE 20-2.   **The one-year plan**

total school budget in summary form is made by the principal and the staff for submission to the central office. Following this, there are negotiations and approval of the individual high school budget in some form by the ultimate fiscal authority in the school district.

Eventually an approved budget is returned by the principal to each department or unit—a budget from which requisitions throughout the year will be submitted to the principal and purchase orders issued. It is also a budget which relates to priorities in the five-year development of the school. Each month a recapitulation of purchases to date is returned to the department.

(Figure 20-3 is an example of a monthly budget sheet for a department.)

Expectations and product. Involvement of instructional staff in budget building does not make the administrator's job any easier. In fact, after going through the initial process, team leaders, department heads, and other instructional staff will put up some very formidable and well-conceived arguments in defense of their budget. Needless to say, however, the principal will be supplied with much of the data needed in order to go to the superintendent or the board of education to justify an adequate

DEPARTMENTAL BUDGET, 1981
Mathematics Department

Month_____

Budget area and item	Allowable	Exp. this month	Exp. to date	Remainder
Texts (B-4)				
Textbooks	$1500.00			
Programmed texts				
40 @ $15	600.00			
Supplementary texts	450.00			
Equipment (D-4)				
Volume demonstration				
set (1)	60.00			
Graph board (multi-				
purpose) (1)	35.00			
Tightgrip chalkholder (6)	6.00			
Rack of compasses	48.00			
Rack of protractors	46.00			
Supplementary (B-6)				
Universal Encyclopedia				
of Math. (2)	35.00			
Other references	175.00			
Audio Visual (D-7)				
Overhead projector	240.00			
Discretionary Supplies	400.00			
SUBTOTAL	$3585.00			
Personnel (A-3)				
2 consultants 2 days	1200.00			
each for inservice plus				
expenses				
SUBTOTAL	$1200.00			
TOTAL	$4785.00			

FIGURE 20-3. Sample of monthly budget sheet

budget. Moreover, never will the central office and the board be as well informed as to outgo and the reasons behind the outgo as they will be under this system.

The budget building process just described attempts to accomplish three things. It gives the appropriate personnel a large measure of responsibility for initial budget preparation in their areas of instructional expertise. Second, it causes foresighted curriculum planning. Third, it provides substantiation to the board and the community that tax dollars are being spent in an efficient and effective manner. Figure 20-4 depicts the process.

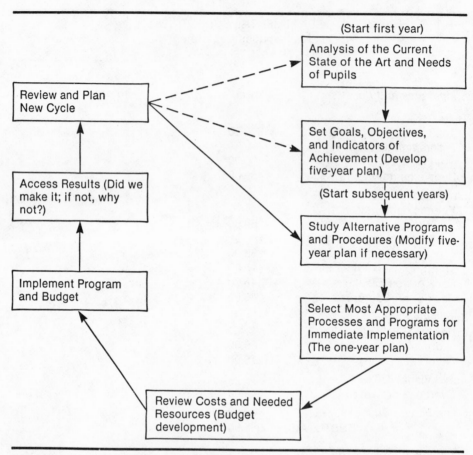

FIGURE 20-4. Systematic program and budget development: Developing and implementing the five-year and one-year plans

Once the budget is developed and approved, it becomes the responsibility of the principal to see that it is managed appropriately and wisely. Skillful budget management is the subject of the next section of this chapter.

MANAGING THE FINANCIAL RESOURCES

The responsibility of the secondary principal in the proper conduct of the business side of the enterprise is both active and supervisory. It is active in the sense that it will be the principal, within the guidelines set by the central office, who establishes the procedures governing the fiscal operation at the building level. It is supervisory in that the principal will regularly monitor the activities of those staff charged with properly recording and reporting financial transactions involving the school.

The degree of autonomy that the secondary principal has with respect to the final operation of the school will vary from school to school. In some systems, virtually all school financial decision making is made in the central office by the superintendent or the superintendent's designate. In other systems, the principal has wide latitude in the construction of budget and the expenditure of funds for personnel, operations, and capital outlay. It is encumbent upon the principal to immediately learn what expectations superordinates have with respect to financial decision making to be made at the building level. For the purposes of this chapter, we assume that the principalship does carry with it some degree of latitude in decisions with respect to fiscal matters. Principals need to be shrewd business managers if the goals of the education enterprise are to be effectively achieved.

Financial Record Keeping

All school systems have an accounting procedure and the principal will need to become familiar with it. Principals do have a bookkeeping function to perform or at least to oversee. Official accounting procedures vary between school system and by state, however.[6] Figure 20–5 depicts a typical array of accounts for a high school.

General Fund Free
General Fund Restricted

Instructional Fee
  Towel Fee

Instructional Fee and Shop
  Art

Instructional Shop
  Auto Mechanics
  Machine Shop
  Wood Shop

Other Instructional
  Music
    Band Uniform

Merchandising Service
  Bus Tickets

Profit Earning
  Coke Fund
  Concessions

Special Purpose
  Hospitality
  Library
  College Credit Course
  Sports Camp
  Oak Ridge Schools
  Scholarship
  Science
  Training & Technology

Student Organizations
  Anchor Club
  Bridge Club
  Class, Senior
  Class, Junior
  Combined Studies
  Debate Club
  DECA
  French Club
  German Club
  Gymnastics Club
  Home Economics
  International Relations Club
  Key Club
  Leaders Club
  Leo Club
  Literary Magazine
  Masquers
  Music: Band
  Music: Choir
  Musical Production
  National Honor Society
  Oak Leaf
  Oak Log
  Pep Club
  Red Cross
  Ski Club
  Spanish Club
  Student Council
  Tennis Club
  TOEC
  VICA

FIGURE 20–5.   Outline of accounts for a typical secondary school

In general, school principals will need to keep a journal of receipts and disbursements and provide proper monitoring of these. (See figure 20–6.) The principal may also have federally funded projects located in the building and will be expected to maintain appropriate records for these. Specific procedures will have been established for them and must be followed. Certainly, too, the principal will be responsible for securing supplies and materials, either by requisition from central warehousing using perhaps a system of transfer vouchers, or directly from a supplier. Probably most, if not all, of the principal's accounting responsi-

---

Monthly Statement of Receipts and Disbursements

Report for_____ 1971__ Prepared by_____Central treasurer

Account	Cash on hand, 1st of month	Receipts, this month	Total	Disbursements	Balance, end of month
TOTAL	$_____	$_____	$_____	$_____	$_____

Reconciliation of Bank Statement

Bank balance as of_____ $_____
   Plus deposits not shown on statement $_____
   Plus others_____ $_____
TOTAL $_____
   Minus outstanding checks_____ $_____
_____ $_____
Book balance as of_____ $_____

FIGURE 20-6.   A suggested monthly report form

bilities will occur in the "operations" (supplies, equipment, etc.) part of the budget. The principal is not likely to be required to account for personnel or capital income and expenditures. These will be handled in the central office of most school districts.[7]

In most secondary schools there will be a clerk or secretary on whom will rest the responsibility for keeping the books. This person will, under the principal's direction, generally make the journal entries and keep the records in order. This does not relieve the principal of executive responsibility, however. Regular review, as well as an independent annual audit, is essential. It is recommended that for the first few months on the job, the principal be involved directly in the accounting procedures, so to learn intimately the business side of the enterprise. Many curriculum and instructional decisions have great fiscal implications, and proper accounting and budget procedures are essential to a well-managed school.

The need for proper accounting procedures is often misunderstood by faculty. From time to time, they view the need for purchase requisitions, invoices, purchase orders, and receipts as unnecessarily cumbersome and designed to get in the way of their securing needed equipment and materials. Nevertheless, especially important in any good accounting system are supportive or original documents (bank deposit information, requisitions, purchase orders, etc.). The accounting system exists in order that the school may expend its funds efficiently and in accordance with the plan incorporated in the budget document. In a sense, it also provides a history of spending and may be used to evaluate how the plan developed in the budget document is proceeding.

Financial resources are always in short supply, and it is not likely that all the budgetary requests in support of the instructional objectives and school goals can be met in any one year. Thus, it does become most important for the principal to keep close record of outgo, making sure that this outgo is consistent with the budget plan and that sufficient funds remain for the purchase of high priority items throughout the school year. It is a sad fact that improper accounting procedures have too frequently resulted in an inadequate amount of money in April for the purchase of routine supplies necessary to complete the school year. Under such practices, teachers have been known to overpurchase and hoard supplies in their rooms. These practices are not healthy nor necessary in a well-ordered school.

Most school districts use an accrual accounting system, which means that as soon as a purchase order is initiated or a requisition for anything is approved, it is encumbered in the account book. Through such a process, the principal knows immediately how much money remains to be expended in any particular account. Under such a system, it is not likely that financial obligations will be made beyond the actual amount of money available.

It cannot be expected, however, that the faculty and nonacademic personnel will understand the intricacies of the accounting system and, as was pointed out earlier, it is possible that sometimes individuals on the faculty may view the entire process as a hindrance to the instructional program. Thus, the wise principal will spend some time in faculty and staff meetings (perhaps at a preschool workshop) generally informing the staff about the reasons why good record keeping and accounting procedures are important to an instructional program. Beyond this, it is the responsibility of the principal to make sure that the practices being followed are, in fact, efficient and do provide for quick delivery of materials and other services to the classroom. It is also the principal's responsibility to make sure that his or her decision making, with respect to expenditures, is consistent with the preestablished instructional budget.

The Transgressing Staff Member

It can be expected that some staff members may "transgress" and encumber monies without approval, or make purchases outside the usual channels for purchase making. How many times should a transgressing employee be "bailed out"? Once, perhaps, but probably no more. The unfortunate fact is that some people are not aware of the need for regularized accounting of expenditures and incomes (any bank official can attest to this!), but the principal must be aware of this need. The principal is the executive and is ultimately accountable for what goes on in the school fiscally and otherwise. The principal must develop sensible accounting procedures, instruct staff in the use of these, and insist that they be followed.

This insistence should, of course, be tempered with sensitivity and understanding. Chastising Ms. West because she did not unerringly follow procedures when purchasing cookies for a class Christmas party or an inexpensive instructional gadget from a traveling salesperson is not a good way to engender high morale or creative teaching. So, the principal might bail a person out—once. But, the situation can be capitalized on to show a teacher the budget for his or her department and the procedures to be followed to insure sensible purchasing and good record keeping, and the reasons for it.

There is a responsibility which must be accepted. One must make sure that emergency requests, unplanned expenses, unanticipated instructional opportunities, and similar "last minute" things that are important to a good teaching/learning climate do not get lost in a bureaucratic maze. Christmas cookies that get ordered in February, or a film strip on oxygen that arrives a month after the completion of the unit on oxygen are evidence of an unresponsive or inefficient administrative procedure. If this occurs often, it should not be surprising that teachers or staff attempt to circumvent established procedures. In other words, the principal must make sure that the procedures actually do facilitate rather than inhibit.

Regular Review

Once systematized, the accounting procedures need not absorb a vast amount of time, but require only regular monitoring by the principal. Care should be taken that materials ordered are received and properly inventoried. Keeping a separate set of books for district funds will provide the principal with a good check on expenditures against the accounts which the school has that are kept in the central business office. Mistakes do get made from time to time and when this occurs, it is to the principal's advantage to be aware of it and to rectify it.

In many school systems, the central business office will supply the principal with periodic financial reports in the form of ledger sheet printouts. These are easily checked against the school's set of books for accuracy. After careful examination of these ledger sheets and the reconciliation with the school's books, they will provide sufficient records of the financial aspect of the educational enterprise, especially if they are supplemented where necessary with additional notations by the principal.

Activity and Other Funds

Many schools receive and distribute monies other than those disbursed by the district office. Such sources and accounts run the gamut and commonly include PTA funds, classroom accounts, insurance monies, candy sales, athletic funds, club treasuries, petty cash, funds from charity drives, gifts, and so on. Individually, the accounts may be quite small, but collectively they often amount to a considerable sum.

A separate set of books should be maintained for these frequently unaudited (by the district) funds. It is in the use of these funds that the unwary principal may get into trouble.

No less precise bookkeeping procedures are required for these than for the district funds. Many states have passed special legislative acts which require the establishment of orderly procedures for the administration of school activity funds. Some states, as well as local school districts, have developed careful policies and procedures to guide individual schools in such financial accounting. Figure 20–7 contains a school district policy statement about activity funds. Further, help is also available from the federal government.[8]

In general, specific procedures must be established to control the collection and disbursement of the variety of activity funds. The following procedures provide a good guide.[9]

1. Official receipts should be issued for all money received.
2. All money expended should be expended by check, except for small cash purchases paid from the petty cash fund.
3. Supporting documents should be kept for all expenditures made.
4. Bank reconciliation statements should be made each month.
5. Monthly and yearly financial statements should be prepared.
6. An audit should be made each year and copies of the audit should be filed with persons having administrative authority for the school.

Figure 20–8 depicts a process for appropriate accounting of activity funds.

Also consistent with good financial practice is that each group having an account which the school is administering should file a simplified budget—indicating anticipated income, anticipated expenditures, and persons designated to approve monies to be expended from the account. Further, all school employees who are responsible for the fund should be bonded, with the amount of the bond to be determined

---

ACCOUNTING AND AUDITING PROCEDURES
STUDENT ACTIVITY FUNDS

Definition and Purpose of Activity Funds (Trust Funds)

The activity funds have been defined as funds consisting of resources received and held by the school, as trustee, to be expended or invested in accordance with conditions of the trust. Specifically, they are funds accumulated from the collection of student fees and various school-approved, money-raising activities. Activity funds are used to promote the general welfare of the school and the educational development and morale of all students.

Responsibility for Activity Funds

The school principal is personally responsible for the proper collection, disbursement, and control of all school activity funds. This responsibility includes providing for the safekeeping of funds at the school.

Monies on hand at the end of the school day should preferably be placed in a night depository at the school's bank. If this is not feasible, the principal may exercise his or her own discretion in protecting these monies. Only under unusual circumstances should the principal or other parties retain funds in their possession overnight. The school principal is not responsible, however, for funds collected, disbursed, and controlled by parent, patron, or alumni organizations.

FIGURE 20–7. Policy statement for activity funds

2.1 Enumeration of Basic Records

1. Activity Fund Cash Receipts

These receipts are the means of accurately recording cash received and provide support to substantiate each bank deposit. Activity fund cash receipt books are to be obtained only from the District Auditing Department.

2. Activity Fund Cash Disbursement Vouchers

These vouchers are the authority for the issuance of a check drawn on the activity fund checking account and provide support to substantiate each bank withdrawal. Activity fund disbursement voucher books are to be obtained only from the District Auditing Department.

3. Prenumbered Checks

These checks are used to disburse all funds from the activity fund checking account. Prenumbered checks must be secured from the bank handling the account. Checks must be printed with the school bank account name indicated thereon. Printed checks must also have two signature blanks for both check signers. When ordering additional checks, the new check numbers should begin with the number succeeding the last check in the old checkbook.

4. Bank Deposit Slips

These slips, when properly acknowledged by the bank, serve as a receipt for money deposited in the bank on specific dates. As such, these slips, when properly prepared and acknowledged, are vital supporting documents in the maintenance of accurate cash records. Deposit slips shall be obtained from the bank and must indicate the bank account name and number.

5. Monthly Bank Statements

This statement is a transcript of the official bank records reflecting all transactions affecting the cash balance on deposit during the preceding month. The monthly statement is accompanied by cancelled checks, validated deposit slips, and other memoranda which confirm the additions to and the subtractions from the cash balance during that month. When properly reconciled, the statement serves as official support for the cash balance indicated in the activity fund records. It is required that the monthly bank statement itemize the daily transactions. If this is not a regular practice of a particular bank, an itemized monthly statement will be rendered by the bank upon personal request.

6. General Ledger

The general ledger serves as a summary of all transactions included in the activity funds management.

FIGURE 20-8. Basic records required for activity fund accounting

by the estimate of the amount of money which the school will handle. Many school districts provide a bond covering all employees in the school system who are responsible for such funds. Whether or not this is so in any particular district should be checked by the principal.

In some school districts the school principal is required to make a monthly report about the state of the internal funds in the school. Such a report commonly contains specific and general conditions of the accounts and expenditures. Whether or not this is specifically required by district policy, it is an important procedure to be carried out by the principal and appropriately filed. It provides substantiation of the careful expenditure of funds and will assist in the annual audit. Figure 20-9 illus-

---

School_____ Report for month of_____
Bank Reconciliation

Bank _____

Balance per bank statement _____ $_____
                  Date

Add
  Deposits in transit   _____
  Other (specify)   _____

Total $_____

Deduct
  Outstanding checks

Check number	Date	Payee	Amount

                                                    $_____

Balance per general ledger _____ $_____
                  Date

_____   _____   _____
      Principal   School Treasurer   Date

FIGURE 20-9. **Monthly financial report of the school activity fund**

trates a monthly reporting procedure for an activity account.

The Audit

Every principal should have the internal account books audited annually by an outside accountant. The product of this audit should be filed with the district office. One should not misunderstand the purpose of the audit—it is not an attack on anyone's integrity. It has two primary purposes: it will provide good professional suggestions for improving accounting procedures being conducted in the individual school, and it protects all of those who have been responsible for handling school funds.

Before accepting a position as principal of a school, the incoming principal should insist on an audit of all funds as a means of being informed about current practices and improving upon these as necessary. The audit also establishes the state of the accounts before the new principal has responsibility for them. It, in effect, red lines the accounts, and the new principal starts with clear fiscal air.

SUMMARY

Financial resources are never in great supply. The proper allocation of the available resources requires careful budgeting. Good financial planning—the kind of planning which delivers resources in a systematic basis to the point of greatest need—requires procedures for the involvement of the staff and the challenge to look beyond the immediate needs of the current year. Stressed has been the need for long-range planning and a system for encouraging staff involvement in the planning process. The result will be an educationally sound budget.

Procedures to insure the efficient operation of the business side of the secondary school have also been the subject of this chapter. Dollars are always in relatively short supply,

hence, good management procedures as well as financial resourcefulness is vital.

The management of activity funds presents an especial problem for the secondary principal. These accounts often contain large amounts of money. Extreme care in properly accounting for these funds is required.

ENDNOTES

1. The discussion which follows is not intended to supplant a school finance course nor to argue the merits of a full scale PPBS, but the rationale undergirding Program Planning Budget Systems is a sound one. The fact that some who have tried to invoke it totally have been guilty of excesses in quantification and application is notwithstanding to the contrary.

2. An interesting comparison of two kinds of budgeting systems can be found in Builbert C. Hentschke, "Is Zero-based Budgeting Different from Planning-Programming-Budgeting Systems?" *Planning and Changing* 8 (Summer-Fall 1977): 128–139.

3. *PPBS for People Who Don't Understand PPBS* (Worthington, Ohio: School Management Institute, undated), pp. 8–10. (This well-written booklet is available from School Management Institute, 6800 High Street, Worthington, Ohio 43085, at a modest cost.)

4. A *goal* may be defined as a direction setting statement of general worth; which is timeless and not specifically measurable. An *objective* explicates the goal statement, is more specific, has a time dimension, and concludes with a series of "indicators"—subjective and objective evidence—that will be accepted as evidence that the objective has been achieved. These may not be absolutes, but simply conditions which, if present, the staff or an individual will accept as being sufficient to show that the objective has been achieved.

5. A similar process is used in the Dallas Independent School District although it also employs the concept of zero-based budgeting. Each department head and principal begins budget building each year at point zero and must justify or rejustify each line item and each program. As described in the

NSPRA publication, *Cutting Costs: Successful Ways to Reduce School Expenditures*:

> The budget includes a 'decision package' for each program, which describes the objectives for the activity, the consequences of not having the particular program, ways to measure the program's effectiveness, alternatives, and cost benefit analysis. (p. 5)

6.   Many states and individual school districts use a standard accounting system employing categories established by the federal government. Such a system does result in uniformity and comparability of income and expenditures. See the U.S. Office of Education Publication, *Financial Accounting: Classification and Standard Terminology for Local and State School Systems* (rev. ed.), Government Printing Office, 1973.

7.   Some school districts are, however, providing great fiscal latitude for their principals, including decisions with report to personnel and capital dollars. See Gerald C. Ubben and Taft Green, "Principal Accountability," *Principal's Audio Journal* I (November 1974) for a discussion of the Broward County, Florida, system.

8.   Edward E. Samuelson; George G. Tankard; and Joyt W. Pope, *Financial Accounting for School Activities* (Washington, D.C.: Government Printing Office, 1969). An example of a good state document on the same subject is *A Guide: Internal Accounting for School Activities* (State Department of Education, 1960).

9.   Ibid.

BIBLIOGRAPHY

Balls, Herbert R. "Planning, Programming and Budgeting in Canada." *Public Administration* 48 (Autumn 1970): 292–293.

Candoli, Carl, et al. *School Business Administration: A Planning Approach.* Boston: Allyn and Bacon, 1978.

Evans, Bruce, and Wagner, Hilman. "Have Student Activities Costs Gotten Out of Hand?" *NAASP Bulletin* 55 (September 1971): 22–32.

Greenfield, T. B., et al. *Developing School Systems.* Toronto: The Ontario Institute for Studies in Education, 1969.

Hentschke, Guilbert C. "Is Zero-Based Budgeting Different From Planning-Programming-Budgeting Systems?" *Planning and Changing* 8 (Summer-Fall 1977): 127–137.

Hughes, Larry W. "Better Budget Building." *American School Board Journal* 155 (February 1968): 19–21.

Nagle, John M., and Walker, Harold E. *SPECS: What It is and What It Does.* Eugene, Ore.: Center for Educational Policy and Management, 1975.

National School Public Relations Association. *Cutting Costs: Successful Ways to Reduce School Expenditures.* Arlington, Va.: NSPRA, 1977, p. 5.

Stoops, Emory; Rafferty, Max; and Johnson, Russell E. *Handbook of Educational Administration.* Boston: Allyn and Bacon, Inc., 1975. See chapter 10 especially.

Thomas, J. Alan. *The Productive School.* New York: John Wiley and Sons, 1971.

Thompson, Victor A. *Decision Theory, Pure and Applied.* New York: General Learning Press, 1971. This short monograph has an extremely fine critical analysis of Planning Program Budgeting procedures in public organizations.

Ubben, Gerald C., and Green, Taft. "Principal Accountability." *Principals' Audio Journal* I (November 1974).

U.S. Office of Education. *Financial Accounting: Classification and Standard Terminology for Local and State School Systems* (rev. ed.). Washington, D.C.: Government Printing Office, 1973.

Chapter Twenty-One

Managing the Building and Grounds

INTRODUCTION

Properly housing and equipping the secondary school presents some management priorities for the principal. Creative housing enhances educational programs, although this is not to say that innovative programs cannot be housed in traditionally designed buildings. In fact, much evidence exists to the contrary. Whether the building represents the latest in school design or reflects architectural thinking in the 1940s, the principal's responsibility is the same: to insure the maximum efficient use of the school plant for the educational program. An inefficiently used building, a poorly kept building, a building with unpleasant, colorless rooms, or a poorly maintained site all inhibit the development of a good educational program, as well as reduce staff and student morale. Similarly, a physical facility that is poorly equipped or has underutilized equipment also inhibits program development. This chapter focuses on management practices to get the best out of the school plant. There is also a discussion about the management of nonacademic support personnel.

EFFECTIVE CARE OF THE SCHOOL PLANT SITE

Of course, the principal is not going to spend the day in overalls with hammer in hand and shovel under arm, but he or she must assume the ultimate responsibility for operating the building at maximum efficiency. The principal will have two important reference groups: classified employees who are assigned to the building (custodians, cleaning personnel, cooks, kitchen personnel, etc.) and the school district-wide maintenance department personnel.[1] Working with nonacademic personnel to help them do their job better will require the same kinds of human relations skills as working with academic staff. Further, in any decision-making process, the counsel and advice of these persons should be sought and their expertise and insights capitalized on.

SITE UTILIZATION

The high cost of land is often reflected in small school sites. Unfortunately this is especially prevalent in urban areas where children are often most in need of wide open spaces in which to experience nature. Nevertheless, small site or large, there are maintenance and site development responsibilities which accrue to the principal. Frequent discussions with the custodial staff can result in maximum use of the site.

As a minimum, the site should be kept free of debris and safe, which suggests daily attention by the custodial staff and regular inspection by an administrator. Equipment must be kept in good repair or taken out of service. Preventive maintenance of equipment and outside surfaces is the most economical and sensible practice. No principal should tolerate less than this minimum, and an assertive principal will insure attention to the site, which will result in attractiveness, if not beauty.

Attention to the following is important and worthy of administrative supervision:

1. Essential
   a. Daily removal of debris.
   b. Weekly preventive maintenance checks and follow-ups (unsafe equipment, unsafe surface—rocks, holes in macadam, etc.)
2. Desirable
   c. Creative landscaping.
   d. Development of land laboratory.

Desirable Site Development

The two desirable tasks require some discussion. If the principal is fortunate to be the executive of the building located on a site which is not entirely composed of macadam, some creative opportunities may exist to enhance the attractiveness of the site, as well as extend educational possibilities.

The professional field of landscape architecture may be of considerable assistance to the principal interested in making the site both aesthetically pleasing and educationally sound. Help in developing or redeveloping a site is available from such diverse sources as the public library, the U.S. Department of Agriculture District Office, agricultural extension agents, appropriate university departments, and private landscape architectural firms with some commitment to public service. Such development need not be expensive; free labor may be available from a boosters club or similar organization, including a local garden club who might wish to take on the project. As a project for the horticulture or other vocational classes,

it is not only a good application of skills being learned but also an important service.

In all but the most macadamized school sites, the development of a land laboratory to enhance the science programs, as well as provide other kinds of educational experiences for students, is a good possibility. One need not be dissuaded from the development of a land laboratory by a small site. The effect of the size of the site will only be to determine the nature and kind of flora to be cultivated. Help and low-cost plantings are readily available, especially from the U.S. Department of Agriculture—specifically the Soil Conservation Office. It is possible for schools to become members of a Soil Conservation District through the simple application of the school board. Purchasing trees and bushes with help from Soil Conservation District personnel is inexpensive. The office also will assist in the proper placement of plants and give instruction on care and nourishment. Other help in the development of a land laboratory is also available from some of the same agencies mentioned previously. It does remain the responsibility, however, of the principal to initiate action in these matters.

MAINTENANCE OF THE BUILDING

The inside of the building requires the same sort of attention to create an attractive, safe learning-living-working environment for pupils and staff. Even old buildings can be attractively maintained. Many large districts have a director of maintenance and operations whose overall responsibility is to see that skilled persons are employed and deployed to respond to refurbishment and major maintenance needs of all the buildings in the district. However, it is the responsibility of the principal, working with the custodial staff, to identify, ahead of emergency conditions, those major needs and to insure that they are systematically attended to. The day-to-day custodial and light maintenance functions will, even in larger districts, usually fall to the building custodial staff.

At the beginning of each school year, the principal should meet with the custodial staff to chart the long-range objectives for building maintenance for the year and to work out a systematic plan for addressing those needs. Much of the custodial work will, of course, be routine and daily or weekly in nature. Cooperative development of a work schedule is desirable, and regular inspection by the principal or a designated assistant important.

The principal should anticipate the usual conflicts that occur from time to time between support service personnel, such as custodians, and the instructional staff. Unfortunately, neither often understands the others' problems and responsibilities very well and this is a frequent cause of disruptive conflict or, at the least, wary truces. Such conflicts often run the gamut—from the custodian's refusal to put the chairs in Ms. Smith's room back in circles because it is more difficult to clean that way, to out-and-out warfare between a department and the custodial staff over the unwillingness of the instructional staff to have the students keep classrooms and halls reasonably clean.

Many of these problems are simply human relations problems. The principal must be sensitive to these and take steps to engender cooperation. A successful process employed by some high school principals is a standing committee on school maintenance and development. The committee is composed of representatives of the faculty, classified staff, students, and in some instances, school patrons. The tasks of the committee include beautification projects, building utilization policy development, and cross-group communication, among others.

Routinizing Custodial Functions

Effective supervision of building maintenance programs need not require an inordinate amount of time, and can be regularized through the use of a simple checklist. Such a checklist is shown in figure 21-1.

The principal and the custodial staff should give particular attention to common internal building flaws, such as inadequate lighting fixtures, roof or wall leaks, dirt in the corners, broken windows, torn sashes, etc. The entire staff, including instructional personnel, should be asked to assist in identifying maintenance needs and to report them immediately to the office for attention. Many times, annoying maintenance defects are allowed to continue simply because a teacher or another staff member has not reported them and they have gone unnoticed by custodial staff. Defects such as a torn sash or graffiti on a restroom wall often breed others at an almost exponential rate until a major effort and expense is required to redo an entire wing. Overnight, it seems one torn sash becomes sixteen torn sashes—some torn to the point where no repair is possible. Similarly, one clever but obscene statement on a restroom wall provokes others at a geometric rate, to the point where the entire wall has to be repainted.[2]

Scheduling the Work

The custodial staff requires a regular routine which is consistent with the educational program conducted in the school building. The scheduled projects to be completed during the school year need to be supplemented by a daily and weekly time schedule to insure that routine custodial tasks and maintenance are taken care of. An example of such a work schedule with both a task and time dimension can be seen in figure 21-2. Times are approximate, of course, and the schedules need to be developed in concert with the custodial staff in order that the estimates are reasonable and appropriate to the unique features of the building.

School_____ Date_____
Building_____
Custodians _____

	Condition	Remarks
Roofs		
Roofing		
Flushing and Coping		
Skylights		
Gutters		
Vents		
Exterior Wood Trim		
Rakes and Facia		
Soffits		
Window Frames, Sash		
Louvres and Vents		
Ceilings		
Doors		
Exterior Plaster and Concrete		
Walls		
Ceilings		
Arcade Slabs		
Platforms		
Splash Blocks		
Exterior Plumbing and Electrical Fixtures		
Hose Bibbs		
Fire Hose Cabinet		
Fire Extinguishers		
Break Glass Alarms		
Water S O Valves		
Gas S O Valves		
Switches and Plates		
Exterior Lights		
Yard Horns and Bells		
Electrical Panels		
Drinking Fountains		
Exterior Metal		
Down Spouts and S Blocks		
Columns		
Louvres		
Grease Traps		
Doors		
Screens		
Sumps, Gratings		

(continued)

Exterior Concrete, Brickwork
A.C. and D.G.

	Condition	Remarks
Curb and Gutters		
Drive-ins		
Sidewalks		
Incinerators		
Water-Meter Boxes		
Gas-Meter Boxes		
Electrical Vaults		
Asphalt-Concrete Areas		
Decomposed Granite Areas		
Fences and Gates		
Bicycle Stands		
Flag Pole		
Parking Lots		
Splash Blocks		
Playground Equipment		

Exterior Areas

Turf		
Lawns		
Sprinkler Systems		
Trees		
Shrubs		

	Condition	Remarks		Condition	Remarks
Room No.____			Room No.____		
Floor			Intercom		
Walls			Amplifier		
Ceiling			System		
Wood Trim			Metal		
Venetian Blinds			Partitions		
Cabinets			Tile		
Drain Boards			Plumbing &		
& Splashes			Fixtures		
Furniture			Kitchen		
Heating &			Equipment		
Controls			Stage		
Hardware			Equipment		
Electrical			Towel &		
Fixtures			Toilet		
Educational			Tissue Cab.		
Equipment			Mirrors		

FIGURE 21–1. Checklist for regular inspections of individual maintenance

Emery Stoops, et al., *Handbook of Educational Administration* (Boston: Allyn and Bacon, 1975), pp. 384–385. Reprinted with permission.

Daily Custodial Work Schedule

7:00 A.M. to 12:00 A.M. (5-hour worker)

7:00–8:00 A.M.	Check heating temperatures. Inspect school premises—pick up trash as you enter. Put out hose for watering. Open administration unit at 7:30 A.M.
8:00–9:00 A.M.	Report to office at 8:00 A.M.—Do this every day. Open front gate at 8:15 A.M. Open vehicle gate at 8:15 A.M. Put up flags at 8:30 A.M. Burn trash.
9:00–10:00 A.M.	Sweep corridors and pick up paper blown and thrown on yard as you water lawns. Water lawns. Sweep patio with sweeper.
10:00–12:00 A.M.	Help set up cafetorium for lunch or special assembly. Do any odd jobs requested by principal.

10:00 A.M. to 6:30 P.M. (8-hour worker—30 min. for lunch)

10:00–10:30 A.M.	Report to office at 10:00 A.M. Dust administration unit. Inspect women's and men's toilets for paper, soap, towels, etc.
10:30–11:00 A.M.	Inspect girl's toilets for supplies, Set up cafetorium for lunch—morning custodian helping.
11:00–11:30 A.M.	Spot, wash windows, weed flowers, and do any small cleaning jobs needed.
1:00–3:00 P.M.	Work in cafetorium. This includes teachers' dining room and setting up for any afternoon or evening cafetorium use.
3:00–4:00 P.M.	Sweep, dust, clean toilets, clean drinking fountains, empty wastebaskets in rooms 21 and 22. Sweeping takes 20 to 30 minutes per room, depending upon the primary furniture in the rooms and including cleaning toilets and drinking fountains.
4:00–6:00 P.M.	Sweep, dust, clean toilets, clean drinking fountains, empty wastebaskets in rooms 1, 2, 3, 4, and 5.
6:00–6:30 P.M.	Clean administration unit.

(continued)

Nightly Custodial Work Schedule

2:00 P.M. to 10:30 P.M. (8-hour worker—30 min. for supper)	
2:00–2:30 P.M.	Report to office at 2:00 P.M. Empty garbage cans, clean, scald, let drip, replace. Help with cafetorium set-up when needed.
2:30–3:00 P.M.	Sweep rooms in primary dept. Dust, close windows, turn out lights, etc.
3:00–6:00 P.M.	Sweep, dust, clean toilets, drinking fountains in primary dept. rooms.
6:00–6:30 P.M.	Supper.
6:30–9:30 P.M.	Sweep, dust, clean toilets, drinking fountains in upper grade rooms. Finish by dusting all cleared surfaces in all rooms.
9:30–10:30 P.M.	Check all doors and windows throughout the plant even though you locked them as you finished in each unit. Check all gates as you lock up.

FIGURE 21-2.   Custodial work schedule
Emery Stoops, et al., *Handbook of Educational Administration* (Boston: Allyn and Bacon, 1975), p. 393. Reprinted with permission.

SUPPLIES AND EQUIPMENT MANAGEMENT

A major responsibility of the principal is securing, inventorying, and allocating supplies and equipment necessary to the educational program. It is essential that adequate quantities of soft goods (supplies) and the appropriate kinds of hard goods (equipment) be provided and available ahead of educational needs and secured in the most economical manner possible. It is equally important that a management system be provided which won't require an inordinate amount of supervisory time. If the school is operating under a budget development system, as that described in chapter 20, the selection and purchase of needed supplies and equipment in support of educational goals can become routinized. At most, it should require a regular review to see that (1) anticipated needs are being met on schedule; (2) estimated costs are remaining within budget; (3) advantage is being taken to the appropriate discounts allowed by suppliers; (4) inventories are adequate; and (5) equipment is being appropriately tagged, recorded, conveniently stored, and used.

Storage and Inventory Control

The daily needs of instructional staff are such that amounts of common educational supplies (mimeograph paper, art paper, chalk, etc.) can be relatively easily predicted and kept in sufficient reserve to handle needs over a period of a few months. One does need to be cautious about taking up valuable storage space with an over supply, but a quick review of projected needs and the previous years' experiences should be sufficient to avoid this. Responsibility for insuring that the appropriate amount of day-to-day supplies are available can become that of the school secretary or some designated person. This task need not and should not require much attention by the principal. An inventory control procedure set up by the principal working with the designated individual will permit routine replenishment of supplies. Adequate inventories of educational materials and supplies that are unique to special aspects of the program can be maintained by the person who is responsible for that special aspect of the program.

It should not be expected that most educational equipment will be housed centrally in the building. For example, equipment such as overheads and tape recorders should be located in almost all of the learning spaces or classrooms. Similarly, equipment and materials supportive of the science program, social studies program, the arts, etc., should be located in those parts of the building designated for these programs.

All equipment, irrespective of where it is housed, should be tagged or identified in some manner and listed in the inventory. Moreover, equipment must be kept in good repair and staff members made aware of the responsibility to report immediately any malfunction of equipment so that necessary repair can be made. The principal may wish to provide each teacher with a supply of "red slips"—a notice of needed repairs or equipment malfunction printed on red paper which identifies the particular piece of equipment which is malfunctioning and describes the nature of the malfunction. These slips should be turned in immediately to the office for action. Figure 21-3 is a specimen of such a form.[3] (A supply of replacement items such as projector bulbs, extra cords, etc., should always be kept on hand because these are the most common malfunctions.)

Staff Work Areas

Every school needs an instructional staff workroom for the preparation of transparencies, overlays, displays, and so forth. Large school systems may have educational technicians who will handle the preparation of elaborate audio-visual aids, but often the school staff itself will want to be able to prepare simple kinds of visuals for their immediate use. Supplies and

HELP!

Date_____

Instructor_____

IT NEEDS FIXING!

_____What malfunctioned?

_____Location and identifying number

_____Describe what went wrong.

_____

_____

Bring it to the office if you can. (Attach this slip to it if you do.)

FIGURE 21-3.   Red flag for equipment repair

equipment need to be provided to make this possible. Often, too, the production of less elaborate audio-visual aids can be made the responsibility of paraprofessionals or parent volunteers.

Using Equipment

A school will often invest in very expensive equipment only to find that it is not being used or is being underused by instructional staff. Many times the reason for this is that the staff is not trained in the use of certain equipment or does not understand the instructional possibilities which exist. Thus, care should be taken that the instructional and staff support services personnel receive training in the use and function of the equipment available in the school. Many principals take extensive advantage of the expertise of the sales personnel and technicians of the various suppliers, having these individuals available at inservice workshops to work with staff in putting the equipment to best use.

Central Warehousing

The responsibilities for supply management in school systems are frequently handled at the central office level. Even if the principal has a considerable amount of responsibility with respect to supply management, large systems will have a central warehouse from which most supplies and equipment are secured. There is considerable advantage to this because systems can develop standardized lists of materials, with precise specifications. These can be periodically reviewed to provide maximum use of school system dollar resources.

Certain kinds of educational materials may also be housed centrally in the school district. Materials such as films, filmstrips, audio and video tapes, and so on, which have use throughout the system but are not required in any individual unit of study except on an infrequent

basis, are often catalogued and housed centrally in the school district. Where this is the case, teachers must understand the need for more lead time in requisitioning and securing these for classroom use. This is not to say that last minute requests should not be acted upon to the degree possible. It is an unhealthy school system, perhaps characterized by abundant bureaucratization, which is not responsive to an unplanned "teaching moment," but in general it will be necessary for staff to anticipate need for centrally housed educational materials.

NONACADEMIC SUPPORT PERSONNEL

Before closing this discussion of building management, some comment is appropriate about the use of nonacademic support personnel in carrying about the business function of the school. Most of the nonacademic personnel will be persons employed to work in the business side of the enterprise. The selection, training, and careful development of responsibilities for these persons is an important managerial function, yet this has received very little attention in professional literature. Improperly trained workers or workers who are unsure of their responsibility, whether in the cafeteria, in the boiler room, or in the principal's office, are a liability. Similarly, the nonacademic staff member who does not understand or particularly like children, while perhaps not common, is also a liability that a school cannot really afford.

At times, entry into nonacademic school positions seems almost casual, yet such positions are a vital part of a well-functioning school building. For example, a secretary who does not understand that the position requires public relations skills as well as technical skills may produce beautifully typewritten reports and books which balance to the penny, while doing the school irreparable damage with the community.

It is incumbent on the school system, therefore, to develop personnel policies for the employment, inservice growth, and retention of good nonacademic personnel. Job descriptions, adequate compensation, and other benefits must reflect the school's interest in maintaining a nonacademic work force of the highest quality.

The standards of employment should not only evidence an interest in appropriate technical competence, but also a realization that most of these personnel will be working with children in some way or another. The latter simply suggests that the appropriate attitudes and understandings about young people may be one of the most important employment and retention criteria.

SUMMARY

The physical environment of the school contributes mightily to the learning environment. An attractive, well-kept school building is essential. It is also important that the principal ensure that there are appropriate response mechanisms so that teachers can go about their work with the right equipment at the right time.

A good school environment also depends on many kinds of personnel. It is the principal's responsibility to deploy these people in the most effective ways. To do so will require carefully developed job descriptions and the ability to help them see the importance of their job to the proper functioning of the educational institution.

ENDNOTES

1.   School districts are organized differently. In most school districts, custodians and cafeteria personnel are normally under the jurisdiction of the building executive; however, some districts have a more centralized operation with custodians, maintenance personnel, and cafeteria and clerical workers

selected and assigned by a central office division of plant maintenance or a division of business. It is important for the principal to establish the limits of authority and the latitudes of decision making with respect to school plant operation. In our opinion, those latitudes should be wide indeed and provide the principal with authority for decision making over all aspects of the operation of the building with the central office plant division serving as a service unit to provide expert kinds of help when necessary.

2.   We are reminded of the insightful principal who was faced with unlimited creative talent for graffiti among the students, resulting in extensive costs in repainting walls in the restroom and in an inordinate amount of time spent by the custodial staff. He took an easy and sensible way out. He had inexpensive chalk boards placed in the restrooms, over the urinals and in the individual stalls and made sure there was sufficient supply of chalk on hand. It effectively solved the maintenance problem, although at this writing, it has not yet been productive of any great poetry or reproducible art.

3.   This same type of form can be adapted for staff use to identify any immediate needs.

4.   Personnel being described include secretarial and clerical staff, cooks and kitchen helpers, custodians, maintenance workers, and school nurses, among others. Discussions about building level operation often overlook the contributions to the educational program which are made by these non-certificated employees. Yet, nonacademic support staff do have important jobs to perform and most come into daily contact with pupils. Recent years, too, have seen increasing use of paraprofessionals whose responsibilities are such that they are often directly involved in the learning activities of children.

BIBLIOGRAPHY

Castaldi, Basil. *Educational Facilities: Planning, Remodeling and Management.* Boston: Allyn and Bacon, 1977.

Feldman, Edward B. "Don't Neglect Your Cleaning Curriculum." *Nation's Schools* 91 (May 1973): 66-68.

Feldman, Edward B. "Twelve Ways to Save on Maintenance Costs." *American School and University* 44 (June 1972): 11-12.

Gardner, John C. "Safety and Maintenance." *American School and University* 43 (March 1971): 8.

Hughes, Larry W., and Simpson, Robert J. *Education and the Law in Tennessee.* Cincinnati: W. H. Anderson Co., 1971. See especially chapter 10.

Myers, W. M., Jr. "Common Sense Training for Custodial Personnel." *American School and University* 46 (March 1974): 32.

Stoops, Emory, et al. *Handbook of Educational Administration.* Boston: Allyn and Bacon, Inc., 1975.

Trotter, Charles E., Jr. "Are You Touching All Your Housekeeping Bases?" *Nation's Schools* 92 (July 1973): 40–41.

Chapter Twenty-Two

Techniques to Achieve Good Public Relations

INTRODUCTION

The school and the community it serves have grown increasingly psychologically distant from each other. Efforts to exchange information have often been left largely to report cards, single-spaced ditto bulletins sent home with children, and infrequent all-school meetings attended in most instances by middle-class moms and an uncomfortable father or two. The result: low-level understanding of the nature of the educational enterprise, suspicion, and often an overwhelming lack of support in times of crises or great need.

Because public schools are owned by and operated for the benefit of the community, educators do have a responsibility to keep the community informed about all aspects of the school program. The school, as the largest single public agency that serves the community, is most affected by a declining understanding on the part of the various publics. It is crucial that the public be aware of and sensitive to the needs, problems, aims, goals, and directions of the educational enterprise. Keeping the community informed, however, is not an easy task.

THE FOLKS RAISE A QUESTION: A CASE STUDY

The school system has made a departure from tradition. After considerable study, a decision

was made by the system to implement the concept of open education in the junior high and middle schools. Several professional task forces engaged in such necessary activities as material selection, leveling, and developing appropriate inservice activities. Within a little over a year, many of the schools were reorganized in such a way to provide for flexible scheduling, team teaching, individualized instruction, large group/small group arrangements, independent learning contracts, a new reporting system, and a host of other procedures and processes consistent with open education. Further, some of the buildings were open-space designed. In general, the professional staff in the schools in which the open concept of curriculum was implemented were there because they wanted to be. Teachers who were not favorably disposed to the plan were given the option to join the staff of other more traditional schools. The program has now been in operation two years.

Almost from the start, a number of parents began to complain about the program. The complaints were manifested first in phone calls to the principal, then in some heated discussions at PTO meetings, letters to the editor of local newspapers, a spurious mimeographed neighborhood "newspaper," and ultimately in the formation of a "Return to the Basics" committee. Members of this group called a public meeting in several of the schools to insist that "open education" be discussed, stating the committee's position that it was a fad which was not providing an adequate education for their children.

Specifically, the charges were:

1. The students are not learning the basic skills as well as they were previously.
2. Students are confused by so much independence and freedom.
3. The report card tells only individual progress; it does not tell parents how their child "stacks up" against others in the system or the nation. Thus, parents cannot set realistic goals for their children.
4. Discipline is missing; the students are running amok and not learning respect.
5. Students need a home base—a teacher who knows them well, not an impersonal team of teachers.
6. The students are not happy with the new program. They say, "Mom, I don't know what's going on and I can't get help from my teachers because there are too many other kids and they get help first."
7. It's a fuzzy-headed idea thought up by left-leaning educators. Children should be told what to do, then made to do it. You can't put kids in charge of their own learning. That's what teachers are paid to do.

Tomorrow evening one of the first citizens' meetings will be held at your school. Indications are that it will be well-attended by parents as well as by some other interested citizens who have followed the controversy as it developed. The meeting was billed as an open forum discussion of the issue, but you have the nagging feeling that it may turn into a donnybrook.

There are thirty-five hours to prepare for the meeting. What should be done?

An interesting dilemma is presented by this case study: how to overcome the lack of two years of public relations work in a two- or three-hour meeting charged with emotion. This type of situation seems to occur frequently in schools around the nation. While the specifics may vary, one thing is clear—educational decisions will be challenged and sometimes in dramatic confrontations.

This chapter will examine some of the more promising public relations practices so that the public's right to challenge will occur in a setting more likely to result in communication than the one just described.

School-community communication endeavors may take several forms, any of which have limitations. A high quality school-community relations program will use a variety of media, and an alert principal will suit the particular message to be conveyed to the appropriate medium. Too often, however, the communication endeavor has relied almost exclusively on one-way information dissemination devices. In this chapter, both one-way and two-way information exchanges will be discussed.

ONE-WAY PUBLIC RELATIONS EFFORTS

There are several one-way methods that may be employed to relate to the community. The hope is that the message will reach the intended receivers, be read or listened to, and acted upon in some kind of positive way. The one-way nature of the medium used, however, does not permit much opportunity for the broadcaster to find out whether or not this is so.

Newspapers and Other Mass Media

There are few communities which are not served by at least a weekly newspaper, and none is outside the reach of radio and television. These mass media are commonly used to impart information about the various public agencies serving the community. The following discussion will focus on newspapers primarily because of their more localized nature and because the activities of the school principal are more likely to involve working with newspapers. Irrespective of which mass medium is utilized, however, the same principles are appropriate.

Newspapers that serve the community or the neighborhood will vary from weekly or bi-weekly "advertisers," with perhaps a few columns given over the highly localized activities, wedding announcements, etc., to urban dailies with several editions. Similarly, depending on the kind of community in which the particular school is located, a principal may find his or her role varying from writing news releases that will be published mostly word-for-word, to meeting with news reporters who will recast the stories in their own words.

In any case, developing good relations with the working press is essential if the most effective use is to be made of the medium. Principals will be called upon by news reporters or editors for information about developing stories or fasting-breaking news items. Principals will less often be called upon to supply news stories that contain general information about what's going on in the schools. The latter instance will require initiative on the part of the principal to provide regular reports of ongoing school practices which are important for the public to know.

The news media have their problems too. Newspapers and television stations are businesses, with advertising to sell, bills to pay, and subscribers to satisfy. Further, news editors deal with just as many pressure groups championing various causes as do school administrators.

Also, school administrators are often surprised to learn that the recommended percentage of space devoted to stories and advertising is 70 percent advertising and 30 percent news. This percentage affects the amount of school news that will get printed.

Reporters complain that public agencies tend to engage only in "gold star" story writing. That is, for example, in the minds of many editors, school administrators are only too eager to have those news items printed which are praiseworthy, but they tend to back away from legitimate adverse criticism. An adverse story *is* legitimate news, and when such a story breaks, the school official and the newspaper both have a job to do. Covering up a weakness or refusing to respond to a legitimate inquiry into a potentially embarrassing situation can only lead to bad press relations and a widening credibility gap.

Public Information Officers

A recent study has indicated that almost 70 percent of the school systems in the United States have someone who performs at least part-time as a public information officer (PIO). Of those systems that have PIO's, approximately 50 percent are on a full-time basis. Full-time PIO's are concentrated among systems that have enrollments of over 25,000 pupils.[1] Figure 22–1 depicts how one district describes the PIO job.

The study concluded with the recommendation that even the smallest school system should have a designated information officer who will coordinate news releases and maintain a continuing relationship with news reporters. Increasingly, school systems are acting on this suggestion, but nevertheless, from time to time, it is the individual building principal who will be the first source of information for news media. Even where there is an organized systemwide public information program, the quality of that program will rely upon the kinds of information that the individual buildings in the system supply to the PIO.

Techniques for Dealing with Mass Media

There are a number of specific techniques that the principal may employ to insure balanced reporting.[2]

1. Articles and stories about scheduled events should be prepared well in advance, with

The Public Information Officer shall be responsible for keeping the public informed about the goals, programs, and activities in the district, for coordinating all public information activities for the school district, for evaluating current public information activities and practices, and for introducing new programs and activities in order to better inform the public of the programs and progress of the district as well as to receive feedback from the public regarding their attitudes and judgements about the programs within the district.

The Public Information Officer shall report to the superintendent of schools, and shall fulfill the following responsibilities:

1. Prepare and edit special publications such as recruitment brochures, district information pamphlets, district newsletters, special administrative reports, school bond election materials, and other desired publications.

2. Prepare and edit news releases regarding programs and activities within the district for release to the local and area media.

3. Prepare and distribute an internal publication for all district personnel relating matters of interest.

4. Survey the community systematically in cooperation with the Research and Evaluation Committee to solicit significant opinions, suggestions, and recommendations that bear importantly on the policies and operations of the Board of Education and the school district.

5. Provide inservice training in the field of public information for all school personnel.

6. Answer telephone inquiries and correspondence, and meet and guide visitors to the district, to assist the public in gaining an understanding of the programs of the district.

7. Assist staff in the preparation of special public information activities such as open houses, dedications, public school week programs, PTA and PTO programs, and other similar activities.

8. Initiate other public information activities as are necessary and desirable to fulfill the responsibilities of the position.

FIGURE 22-1.   Position description: Public information officer

Courtesy of Alief Independent School District, Alief, Texas.

photographs of speakers or others involved in the program provided to the news media before the event occurs. Often there is a media policy to not print information about or report any event which is past.

2. Follow-up reports should be prepared for the media as soon as possible after an event. It's important for school principals to know the news and film deadlines for all the media with which they may have to work. Deadlines are crucial for newspapers and television stations,

and missing a deadline will mean that the story will not get in at the appropriate time and, thus, may never get in.

3. A simple and fast way to get radio news coverage is to use a telephone hook-up and dictate stories to be taped and played on later newscasts.

4. News releases should be written to conform to the requirements of the different media. Releases for radio and television stations usually must be shorter, more repetitious,

and in a more conversational style than those reported by the newspapers.

5. Scheduling programs about local schools may be facilitated by taking advantage of the public service requirements that broadcasting stations must meet. However, Norman and Achilles recommend that "rather than producing programs which are scheduled at off hours, when the listening or viewing audience is small, it is better to concentrate on news stories, audio tapes, slides, and films for regularly scheduled newscasts."

6. Relationships with media representatives will determine if the principal or the public information officer concentrates on writing and distributing releases or on furnishing suggestions and information to journalists who themselves will develop their own stories. In urban settings, reporters will probably write more of their own material, but they will ask the help of school administrators to secure material, identify sources of news, and arrange interviews. Conversely, in rural or small town settings, the school administrator may write much of the material in finished form.

7. The public information program that uses the media should be continually evaluated. It really isn't very valuable to send out large numbers of news releases if few are used, and submitting too much material to the media in an indiscriminate way may result in few stories being published.[3]

The latitude a principal has with the press will depend in great part on the particular school district's press policy. News media personnel, however, are most sensitive to what they perceive to be censorship, and normally they respond negatively to the suggestion that every story or every interview must be cleared with the central office. A policy that requires all school personnel to refer reporters and editors to the central office rather than answer questions, or a policy that insists the news media go to the central office for all informa-

tion, if employed rigidly, will damage press relations. Obviously, fast-breaking news items of a potentially explosive nature will require discretion on the part of the school principal, but to attempt to close off the individual school building to members of the press will do little more than create media-school relations that are antagonistic.

An especially effective practice is the use of school news item files and forms such as that depicted in figure 22-2. There are many activities in the school that might be newsworthy—staff members are engaging in a variety of activities, unique instructional practices are being tried out, the school is engaging in an innovative project or two, etc. Each staff member should have a supply of the news item forms to jot down those projects that might be especially interesting. These forms should then be sent regularly to the principal's office. The principal or the secretary can simply file these reports in a folder (labeled according to the kind of project) and a news reporter can simply review the files, selecting any particular items to follow up. This helps both the reporter, whose responsibility it is to find news, and the principal, whose responsibility is to supply news but not necessarily to write it.

Newsletters, Bulletins, and Report Cards

Frequently, the principal and the staff will attempt to communicate with the home and other agencies through newsletters and bulletins. These can be useful if employed judiciously and if well done. But what kind of message is conveyed when a newsletter arrives home crumpled in the pocket of a student, printed on a smeared ditto or stencil copy, is hard to read, and often contains out-of-date information? If newsletters and bulletins are to be employed, the format should be simple; the information conveyed should be concisely written, to the point, and free of educational jargon; and the method of getting them home

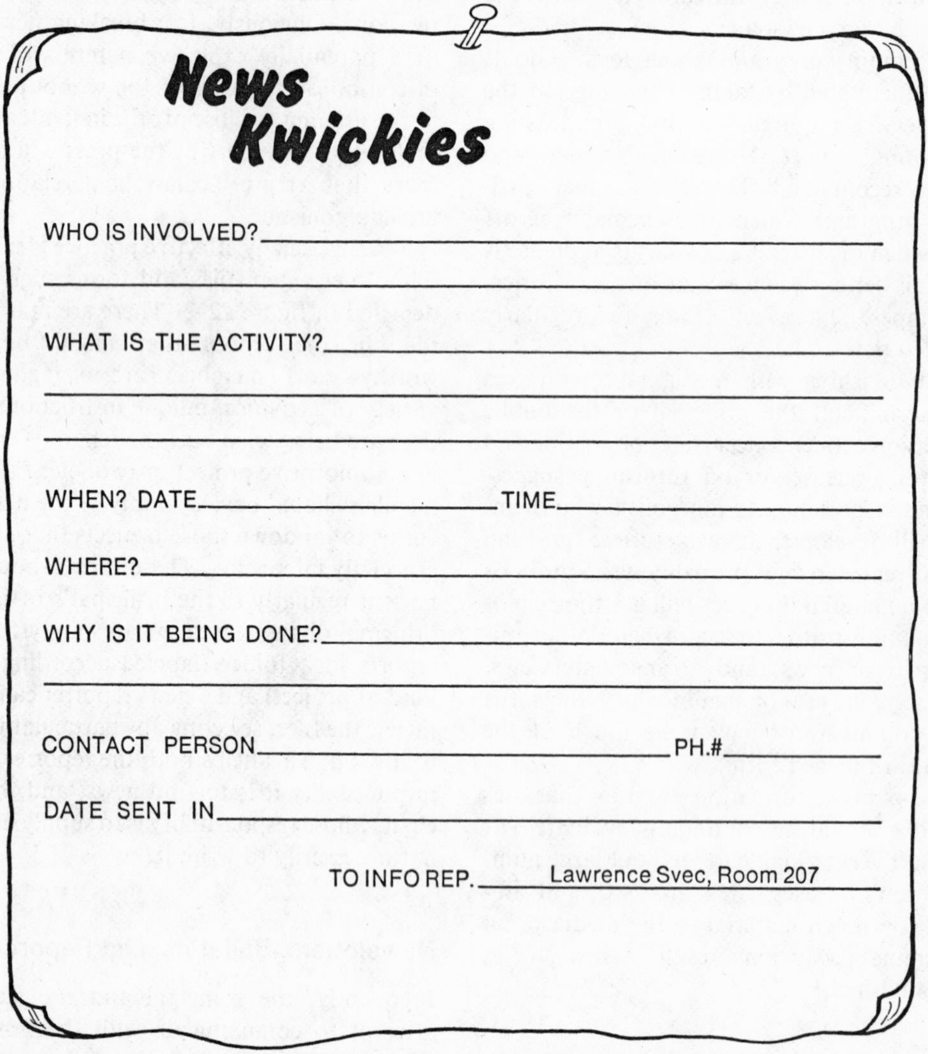

News Kwickies

WHO IS INVOLVED?_____

_____

WHAT IS THE ACTIVITY?_____

_____

_____

WHEN? DATE_____ TIME_____

WHERE?_____

WHY IS IT BEING DONE?_____

_____

CONTACT PERSON_____ PH.#_____

DATE SENT IN_____

TO INFO REP._____Lawrence Svec, Room 207_____

FIGURE 22–2.   A quick way to gather potentially newsworthy items

should be via the mails. Newsletters sent home with the students often do little but contribute to the neighborhood litter problem. If the newsletter is not produced with appropriate care and printed in an attractive manner, it is simply not worth the bother; it won't be read anyway, and the time spent preparing them, no matter how small, isn't worth it.

Remember, too, that the education profession has a language of its own, as do all professions. This language is not well understood outside the profession, therefore, care should be taken to report events and school happenings in such a way that information is shared rather than obfuscated. One method, called a "fog index," contains some implicit warnings for producing readable bulletins. The fog index is shown in figure 22–3.

Report cards are often overlooked as public relations mechanisms, but they are the single most regular way in which schools attempt to communicate with the home. Typically, both teachers and parents like report cards to be uncomplicated because of the ease of reporting and the ease of understanding. Yet, simple consideration of all the ways in which a child is growing, developing, and learning defies summing this up with the barest symbol of the English language—a single letter grade. Thus, the development of an appropriate reporting procedure will require careful study by the staff. It should include the use of a faculty-lay committee to develop a reporting format that is easy to understand, but that also contains important kinds of information relative to the child's progress upon which parents, teachers, and children can act positively.

Dictums of Communication

The *co* in communication means a closed loop. That is, communication means that the message was not only sent, but that it was received and responded to in a way which indicates it was understood. Following are important questions to ask when examining the quality of one-way informational devices:

1. If the message was received, was it read?
2. If it was read, was it understood?
3. If it was understood, was it understood in the right spirit?
4. If it was understood in the right spirit, will it be acted upon in a positive way?
5. How do you know?

TWO-WAY COMMUNICATION EFFORTS

Many formal mechanisms provide two-way information sharing. However, nothing about these mechanisms makes them automatically effective. Careful organization is required.

Parent-Teacher Organizations

Everyone is familiar with the PTA or PTO or boosters group that are a regular part of school-parent relations programs. Their effectiveness has varied markedly throughout the country. In some instances, these organizations have served well, with a membership characterized by broad participation in important activities. In other instances, they are moribund groups doing little but spending time listening to speeches and having bake sales in order to buy tape recorders and athletic equipment for the school, with little opportunity for interaction with anybody except themselves. Nothing good automatically happens just because an organization is labeled in such a way to suggest a formal relationship with the school.

Parent-teacher organizations can provide a useful avenue for interaction between school and community if the meetings are arranged to provide an opportunity for both formal and informal interaction, and if the organization is

---

1. Find the average number of words per sentence.
2. Count the number of words having three or more syllables.
3. Add the two factors above and multiply by 0.4. This will give the fog index. It corresponds roughly with the number of years of schooling a person would require to read a passage with ease and understanding.

FIGURE 22–3. Eschew obfuscation: Use the fog index

given important tasks to perform. The key would seem to be *active involvement in significant tasks*. Parent organizations, just like other community groups, are competing for the time of the members. Whether or not a parent elects to spend Thursday evening at a boosters meeting will depend upon whether or not that time is viewed as being productively occupied. No one wants to give time to an activity that is dull, nonproductive, and not even entertaining.

An effective parent group will spend less time meeting formally and more time in subgroups considering important tasks to be performed around the school and the community. Organizing business-industry-education activities for the career development program, developing after school special interest programs, training voluntary para-professional teams, and working on curriculum review committees are examples of activities which community-school groups can organize.

One problem that has become increasingly evident to principals when the value of traditional parent organizations is examined is the nature of the membership itself. Many principals realize that even though their school may serve a rather heterogeneous population, the actve membership of the parent group is often comprised almost entirely of those who reflect only one particular point of view. Or, as one high school principal said, "PTA meetings are attended by a lot of middle-class moms and an uncomfortable father or two who made the mistake of coming home early from work." Thus, the principal will need to examine the membership rolls of any organization carefully. If those who come to PTA meetings reflect only one ideological position, then the chances are most likely that important opinions are not being secured, nor is there an information exchange with the broader community.

One way to find out the degree to which an organization reflects the population of the school is to conduct a survey about the membership. Such a survey might be conducted as illustrated in figure 22-4.

Such a study can determine whether or not an organization serving the particular school is truly representative of the student population. If it is not, then it is an inadequate way to communicate with the total community. Further, even if it is representative, but it is not active or has a very small membership when compared to the possible membership, it will not serve as an adequate communication medium.

Principal-Organized Gripe Sessions

A practice used more frequently in recent years is a regular "tell it to the principal" gripe session. Principals concerned about establishing and maintaining good relationships with students and their parents have initiated two kinds of gripe sessions. One is a student-principal program conducted regularly in the principal's office. Attendance is limited to approximately ten students who sign up for the session in advance. An open forum discussion is held, and in these sessions students express interests and discuss grievances they have, making suggestions about the general improvement of the school.

The same thing can be done for parents and other community members. Patrons may be notified by mail or through the newspaper of the meeting dates, and a secretary can take reservations for a dozen or so patrons. The rules for the meeting are that any topic is acceptable, except personal complaints about individual teachers. Discussions planned for two or three hours are usually adequate. An important opportunity is provided for an informal exchange of ideas in a nonthreatening setting. For the principal, it is an excellent sensing mechanism to find out what is on people's minds in the community and to get some notion of impending problem situations. For the patrons, it's a good opportunity to find out the inside story of the operation of the school.

The initial effort would be to collect representative demographic information about the make-up of the student population of the respective school. Such information as general income levels or the nature and kinds of housing from which children come is what is sought. Such classifications that comprise Warner's Social Class Index or the McGuire-White Measurement of Social Status (Carson McGuire and George D. White, *The Measurement of Social Status,* Research Paper in Human Development, No. 3, revised, Austin, Texas: Department of Educational Psychology, University of Texas, March 1955) will prove helpful. Those classifications are "occupation, source of income, house type, dwelling area." These factors can be checked for a random sample of the students in the school if the school size is large.

Once the relevant demographic data about the student population has been collected, a questionnaire may be developed requesting the same general kinds of information and sent to the active membership. It is important in this instance to be straightforward and simply explain to the recipients of the questionnaire what you are attempting to find out, that is, the representative nature of the members.

A map of the attendance area served by the school should be developed and, by using a color code of some sort, locate active members according to where their home is on the map. Are some parts of the attendance area seemingly underrepresented? If it is available, secure a "pupil locator" map and compare the location of students with the location of members. Is there a discrepancy? Using the same locator map, you can now, by applying the indices of quality of housing, sources of income, occupation, etc., determine whether or not the membership is confined to certain social strata.

FIGURE 22–4.   An inquiry to determine the representative nature of a parent organization

One of the problems in engendering community support for the schools is the inadequacy of the information exchange between school and home. Organized parent-principal forums address this problem. Complex ideas are difficult to express in the usual one-way bulletins or news stories that serve as major sources of information for parents and other community members.

Neighborhood Seminars

Neighborhood seminars have been successful in both large and small school districts. There are two important ingredients: an informed staff and careful initial organization. Neighborhood seminars will not be effective if they simply become a way of providing a forum for someone from the school to lecture to a collected group of individuals from the community. A deft discussion leader, careful planning, and an attitude not of propagandizing but rather of providing the opportunity for interchange of ideas and facts are required. Many of the characteristics of a good neighborhood seminar are the same as those of principal gripe sessions. The principal doesn't have to do it all; a cadre of well-informed staff who are especially adroit in leading discussions and who have been provided with a sufficient amount of general information about the school can assist the principal.

Properly organized seminars attended by the people who represent a cross-section of attitudes in the community provide a most effective way to begin a new relationship with the community. The neighborhood seminar approach can provide the basis for sophisticated community involvement programs. The issues and problems discussed often lead to joint task force teams that engage in problem-solving efforts.

Program Analysis by Special Groups

Principals may invite identified groups in the community who might have an interest in certain parts of the school program to examine, in conjunction with appropriate school personnel, some of the special curricula of the school. A variation may be to simply involve a group in an analysis of the total school program. Many state departments of education have publications that might prove helpful.[4] These or locally developed instruments for analysis can be used to help structure the activities of citizen-school analysis committees.[5]

Citizen Committees

Similar to the special interest committees are general citizens' committees. The basic difference is simply that instead of looking at specific aspects of a program, such committees are issue-oriented. Asking citizens, students, and staff to study and recommend solutions to specific educational questions does not impinge on the principal's power. Various committees can work simultaneously on different educational questions. Citizen involvement in this manner can ease the professional workload, dispel apathy, and lead to valuable recommendations.

Committees may be formed to study and make recommendations about discipline, budget, construction of new schools, or vandalism. The committee should be representative and have a clear purpose. Forming one more committee as a way to simply occupy people who might become critical of the school is transparent to most community members. The purpose of committees is to secure good, creative problem resolution. Better school-community relations will result as a spin off from such activi-

ties, and better school decision making will result because intelligent resources are being tapped.

The committee must know what its anticipated product is, and it must know the limits of its decision-making powers. If the principal is after advice and counsel but not final decision making, this should be stated at the outset so the committee knows within which framework it is being asked to operate. The discussion in chapter 2 about setting decision-making limits is important. Groups formed by the principal to help in problem resolution need to know not only the limits of their responsibility, but also when their job is done!

Simulation Activities

Many schools have developed simulation games as a means of involving community members and students in a decision process. In such instances, a data book is prepared by the school in which certain relevant facts about the school and about the problem are provided.

For example, suppose vandalism is a continuing problem in a given school. A data book would contain information about the kinds of vandalism prevalent, the time of day when vandalism seems to occur, the costs of such vandalism, the negative effect the vandalism seems to have on school morale and attendance rates, and other relevant facts that impinge on the problem. Further, the data book might contain related school district policies, the limits of the school's police authority, and any relevant laws. The effort is to provide sufficient information that the group may study so that the limits which might affect the nature of the solution are understood.

Following a study of the information, the group may then assume the role of a task force team charged with significantly reducing vandalism. The technique of brainstorming would be appropriate. Through such game playing, an important problem may be attacked with productive results. The fact that it is a game reduces any threat that particular persons or groups might feel, especially if the topic is highly controversial or emotional.

Often, perhaps because of existing laws, firm school district policies, or community mores, there may be only a few alternative solutions that are acceptable. In this instance, the group discussion might become somewhat more formalized and be directed to achieving consensus on which alternative would be the most desirable, given the facts presented in the data book. Such a process will focus the discussion and define the parameters of the decision making.

Parent-Teacher Conferences

Planned parent-teacher conferences can become an important element in a school-community relations program. Excellent opportunities are provided in such conferences for direct relationships between the teacher and the home, but they require careful planning. Thought must be given to such factors as the increasing occurrence of both parents working during school hours, one parent in the home with responsibilities for other children or an occupation that would preclude attendance at conferences scheduled during the normal school day, or transportation difficulties. These and other constraints, however, can be overcome with diligent work on the part of teachers and other school personnel.[6]

Organizing for parent-teacher conferences can be a task of a joint community-teacher group, although, of course, the group assigned the task of organizing the effort should be generally representative of the neighborhood or the community.

School Advisory Councils and Mini-Boards

The differences between advisory councils and mini-boards concerns the nature of decision-making authority. Many principals have formed advisory councils to test ideas, but without decision-making authority; that is, the word *advisory* is definitive.

Some schools, where there has been school board mandate to do so, have formed neighborhood mini-boards that perform functions much like legally constituted systemwide school boards. In such instances, the mini-board exists as a creature of the system board, but may be imbued with broad decision-making powers. In the latter case, the principal of the school may assume a role much like that of the general superintendent.

The community group is involved in a continuous needs assessment process. Addressing the identified needs will require setting goals through a consensus process. This process allows for positive action to meet school needs without blaming anyone. Working together in consensus building activities reduces "we/they" schisms and any accompanying hostility.[7]

Questionnaires/Opinionnaires

Surveying community attitudes and opinions can be effective especially when a school district enters into an evaluation phase in an effort to establish or review educational goals, objectives, and priorities. Such a survey can lead to numerous community committees and a revitalization of community involvement in educational policy making and decision making.

There are a number of ways to conduct educational surveys. Mailed questionnaires to a random sample of the population living in a particular school attendance area is the most common, although it is not generally productive of many returns. A good technique to employ if the time and manpower are available is to conduct house-to-house interviews using a structured interview technique, calling on a ramdom sample of the population and making sure that all parts of the community are included in the sample.

Help is available in constructing such instruments. For example, the School Management Institute has a complete package entitled, *Citizens' School Survey: Surveying the Public's Educational Goals.*[8] The Kettering Foundation publishes a booklet entitled, *A Look into Your School District.*[9] Additionally, the National School Public Relations Association is the source of such publications as *Polling and Survey Research*[10] and *Communicating with the Public.*[11] The Ryans have developed a manageable technique for studying rural community influences.[12] Any survey has its limitations, but if conducted on a regular basis, it is a good way to get useful information. If the survey technique is utilized, the information should be acted upon and reported back to the community.

SUMMARY

Schools are a part of the greater social system, and people in the community have a right to be informed about the operation of the school.

---

1. One attempts to communicate for a reason: to disseminate information, to promulgate a decision, to change behavior, to present an important point of view, to challenge thinking, or to raise a question. When the idea to be communicated has to go from one person via someone else or something else to a third person, something is probably lost in the translation—the spirit in which it was intended, the background of thinking involved, or even the true meaning.

2. The device for communicating that is employed must be appropriate to the complexity and nature of the idea one is attempting to convey. Unless carefully produced and attractive, newsletters make good filler for wastebaskets, especially if single spaced.

3. Quality is more important than quantity. *Quality* in communication may be defined as that which is readily understood and is understood in the spirit in which it was given.

4. Communication systems must take into account all kinds of people. Perceptions of others are modified by individual drives, needs, and desires.

5. There must be sensitivity to the possible reactions of others to decisions, the reasons for which they have insufficient knowledge. Those most affected by a particular decision should know at least why the decision was made.

6. There are many devices for insuring better understanding of messages. Small group meetings, large group meetings, delivering the message in person, involvement of others in appropriate decision making, publications—ranging from bulletins and newsletters to organized releases in the news media—should all be employed, but only when they are most appropriate.

7. Communication requires an opportunity to react and for feedback. This is needed for two reasons: first, to be able to know whether or not what was sent was understood; and, second, because the reaction may indicate that some modification in the decision or practice may be called for in the light of the response.

8. In order for the communication effort to be effective, the receiver must pay attention, must be interested in what is being sent, must see some personal application to what is sent, and must be willing and able to act upon it.

FIGURE 22-5.   Important aspects of communication

Similarly, principals have an obligation to see that a two-way information flow is developed. By failing to interact with the community, the school system or the individual school will become static and unresponsive to changing community needs. The community itself may be undergoing great change, possibly as a result of population mobility or changing attitudes of people. The result is clear: a gap develops between the community and the school it serves. Specific objectives for a school-community relations program would include the following:

1. To implement a school-community communications network that will facilitate two-way communication. Traditionally, school-community relations programs have failed to include mechanisms for receiving information back from the intended receiver.
2. To implement procedures for the involvement and participation of community members in the school program development.
3. To monitor the community on a continuous basis.
4. To facilitate face-to-face communication between community members and school representatives.

Important aspects of the communication endeavor are presented in figure 22-5.

ENDNOTES

1. Douglas C. Norman and Charles M. Achilles, *Public Information Practices in Education: A Study of Techniques* (Knoxville, Tenn.: Bureau of Educational Research and Service, The University of Tennessee, 1973).
2. The Norman-Achilles study is a source of many of these recommendations.The study itself contained twenty-eight specific recommended public information techniques (See Norman and Achilles, *Public Information Practices in Education,* pp. 12-15).

3. An interesting case study simulation film dealing with press relations is available from the University Council for Educational Administration, 29 West Woodruff, Columbus, Ohio 43210. Entitled, "On the Spot With the Press," this film, written and produced by Larry W. Hughes and Frederick P. Vendetti, details a potentially explosive school situation and ends with two questions posed to administrators: "What do we tell the media this afternoon?"; "What should our general policy with respect to relations with the media be?" Discussion materials are included with the film. The film is one component of the Monroe City Urban School Simulation game, but can be rented or purchased separately.
4. For example, the state of Ohio has a publication entitled, "A Guide for Self Appraisal of the High School." Further help may be available from such publications as *Profiles of Excellence: Recommended Criteria for Evaluating the Quality of a Local School System,* published by the National Education Association, and, of course, the various accrediting bodies such as the North Central Association of Colleges and Secondary Schools, or the Southern Association of Colleges and Schools, among others, can also provide instruments and suggestions for such an analysis.
5. Two sources of help are Robert Feldmesser and Esther A. McReady, *Information For Parents on School Evaluation* (Princeton, N.J.: ERIC Clearinghouse on Tests, Measurements and Evaluation, 1974); and Helen T. Fedorko and Doris Rhodes, "Cooperation is the Key," *Momentum* 7 (December 1976): 17-20.
6. If the master contract under which the teachers perform precludes night meetings or restricts in other ways the development of parent-teacher conferences, then this might be an item for negotiation at the next contract review.
7. A good approach is presented in Roy Azarnoff, "A New Model for Working with the School-Community Council," *NASSP Bulletin* 58 (January 1974): 58-62.
8. 750 Brooksedge Boulevard, Westerville, Ohio 43081.
9. CFK Ltd. Publications, 3333 South Bannock Street, Englewood, Colorado 80110.
10. John H. Thomas; Stuart C. Smith; and John S. Hall, *Polling and Survey Research* (Arlington, Va.: National School Public Relations Association and

ERIC Clearinghouse on Educational Management, 1973).

11. Ian Templeton, *Communicating with the Public* (Arlington, Va.: National School Public Relations Association and ERIC Clearinghouse on Educational Management, 1972).

12. Thomas A. Ryan and Martin D. Ryan, *Power and Influence in a Rural Community* (Knoxville, Tenn.: Bureau of Educational Research and Service, The University of Tennessee, 1974).

BIBLIOGRAPHY

Azarnoff, Roy. "A New Model for Working with School Community Council." *National Association of Secondary Schools Principals Bulletin* 58 (January 1974): 58-62

Facos, Peter C. "An Analysis of Written Communications Distributed by School Districts." Doctoral Dissertation, State University of New York at Buffalo, 1968. This study analyzed various printed materials distributed by the schools to the community. Facos concluded that readability of these messages "is not sufficiently differentiated to take into account the variation of educational background of the audience to which the communication is directed."

Hughes, Larry W., and Foster, Car. "Community Advisory Councils and Neighborhood Mini-Boards." *The Principal's Audio Journal* (January, 1974), Side B.

Hughes, Larry W., and Hyder, Leslie R. "Public Relations Practices in Tennessee Public Schools." *Tennessee Education Quarterly* 4 (Spring 1974): 22-30

Hughes, Larry W., and Kayler, James. *Patterns of Influence: Educational Decision Making in Monroe City.* Columbus, Ohio: University Council for Educational Administration, URB/SIM Series, 1974.

Hughes, Larry W., and Venditti, Frederick P. *On the Spot With the Press* (a simulation training film). Columbus, Ohio: University Council for Educational Administration, URB/SIM Series, 1974.

Keller, Arnold J. "School and Community: Stimulating Open Dialogue." *SAANYS Journal* 7 (Fall 1977): 25-27.

Lewis, Anne C. *The Schools and the Press.* Washington, D.C.: National School Public Relations Association, n.d. This is a most helpful volume and includes, among a variety of topics, how to organize the news, what to do when there is unfavorable press, how to write copy, etc.

Norman, Douglas C., and Achilles, Charles M. *Public Information Practices in Education: A Study of Techniques.* Knoxville, Tenn.: Bureau of Educational Research and Service, The University of Tennessee, 1973.

Ryan, Thomas A., and Ryan, Martin D. *Power and Influence in a Rural Community.* Knoxville, Tenn.: Bureau of Educational Research and Service, The University of Tennessee, 1974.

School Management Institute. *Citizen's School Survey: Surveying the Public's Educational Goals.* Worthington, Ohio: The Institute, 1971.

Strongh, Charles S. "Getting Along with the Media." *School Management* 17 (January 1973): 56-57.

Templeton, Ian. *Communicating with the Public.* Arlington, Va.: National School Public Relations Association and ERIC Clearinghouse on Educational Management, 1972.

Thomas, John H.; Smith, Stuart C.; and Hall, John S. *Polling and Survey Research.* Arlington, Va.: National School Public Relations Association and ERIC Clearinghouse on Educational Management, 1973.

Trusty, Francis M. *Conflict Management at Janus Junior High School.* Columbus, Ohio: University Council for Educational Administration, URB/SIM Series, 1975. This publication is one of several interpretive content papers written to accompany simulation materials in urban administration produced under the auspices of UCEA. This particular publication interprets the conflict situation in the Venditti film, *Outside Advice.*

Venditti, Frederick P. *Outside Advice* (a simulation training film). Columbus, Ohio: University Council for Educational Administration, URB/SIM Series, 1971.

PART THREE

MANAGEMENT TOOLS

Two chapters comprise this final section. Performing successfully as a secondary school principal requires more than understanding the various dimensions of the role and more than having appropriate skills in functional areas. A pervasive need is the ability to engage in systematic planning irrespective of the issue area. Another pervasive need is the ability to manage one's activities so that the right things get done and in a timely manner.

Chapter 23 contains a discussion of project management that embodies the principles of systematic planning. A way of approaching these problems is proposed which has been shown to be both efficient and effective. The book concludes with an examination of the principles underlying the good management of executive time.

Chapter Twenty-Three

Systematic Planning and Project Management

INTRODUCTION

Much has been written about project management and systematic planning as processes for effecting change or solving problems. Great scientific achievements have occurred, largely as a result of systematically disaggregating a desired goal into a series of interrelated, interdependent tasks. These tasks are then organized into manageable components. Task force teams based on technical expertise are formed under the direction of a project manager who coordinates the efforts of the team in completing a component.

Putting a man on the moon (a goal) was an infinitely complex project. The number of people and agencies involved in the effort was myriad. Yet, in a relatively short span of time—less than a decade after President Kennedy made the initial decision—the mission was accomplished. How could a task with such magnitude be completed so quickly? Using concepts and procedures that were developed during the building of the Polaris submarine, thousands of people from a variety of agencies were involved in a step-by-step progression to the moon. Groups, often working independently of each other, systematically focused on components of the master plan. The following were characteristic:

1. Task-specific expertise of personnel.
2. Clarity of function and clear designation of responsibility.
3. A specified time line.
4. Allocation of dollars and other resources.
5. Intergroup communication system.
6. A general master plan specifying each of the interrelated components and the nature of the interrelationship.

Educating young people is also complex. Moreover, the school, even the smallest school, is itself a complex organism faced continually with problems and pressures from within and without. There is a need to adapt to new social conditions, to revise curricula, to address issues ranging from vandalism to the creative use of ESEA monies, to plan inservice education programs, to develop more effective ways to communicate with the public, to respond to apparent learning deficiencies of clients, and the list could go on and on. The point is that often too many of these issues never do get resolved, and they don't go away either. They linger, forming and reforming, manifesting themselves in different ways. They result not only in an ineffective operation, but they also reduce morale of staff, students, and community members who may feel as though they are on some sort of treadmill. Often, a school year is completed with "survival" being the most identifiable accomplishment.

A better way exists. While systematic planning and project management are not panaceas, they will result in an orderly progression to problem resolution. They will also provide something far more sound and satisfying than simple survival as the major year-end accomplishment.

It is possible to become battle weary and overwhelmed with the terms and acronyms that permeate written works about systematic planning. PERT, CPM, PPBS, Gantt Charts, complicated formulae for predicting completion dates, all might appear to the novitiate planner to confound rather than solve the problem. It need not be so. One does not have to be a graduate systems analysis engineer or a college major in educational futures to lead a staff in systematic planning endeavors. Systematic planning will facilitate goal achievement, not get in its way, and it does not make much difference what words or labels are used as long as certain identifiable and logical procedures are employed. Ultimately, the stress is on goal achievement—what it is that one is attempting to accomplish, and how it can be done most efficiently. What follows is an explication of this process.

PROBLEM IDENTIFICATION

A problem exists. Students don't seem to be reading as well as expected, or all is not well with the school-community relations program, or the social studies curriculum needs revision, or the incidence of vandalism is on the rise. *Something* is wrong.[1]

The problem identification phase defines the real issue, avoids stating problems as solutions, and avoids focusing on symptoms rather than problems. Suppose, for example, that one plaguing condition confronting the junior high school principal is that the students do not seem to be reading as well as they should. To state the problem as "the need to implement a new reading program" presupposes a solution. Similarly, to state the problem as "how to get students to read more books" focuses on a symptom. The problem stated, after careful collection and examination of facts, might be "to improve the functional reading skills of students at Hudson Junior High School."

To be sure, one solution might indeed be a revamping of the reading program, and one desired outcome might be that junior high youngsters read more books, but neither of these is the basic problem. This may seem tautological, but it isn't. Moving too hastily to solutions on the basis of uncertain facts will result in faulty planning, displaced energy, and unresolved problems. Tossing out the existing English and reading skills program will end with predictably poor results if what was really required was (1) better trained teachers, (2) a new partnership with the home, and (3) a wider range of supplementary books.

Once the problem has been clarified and the specific desired outcomes identified, project management, using a systematic problem resolution process, is possible.

Purpose of the Project

The initial step in project management is to specifically state the purpose of the project. To illustrate, assume that one problem confronting the school is increasing social distance between the school and the community. Several symptoms lead the principal and the staff to this conclusion. Attendance at school-sponsored programs and PTO meetings is poor or not representative of the community at large, criticism of the school curriculum often becomes emotional, student tardiness and attendance rates are not what is desired, communication with the home seems limited to report cards, student morale is low, and student attitudes toward the school seem to reflect parental disinterest, perhaps even distrust. These, among other symptoms, lead the principal and staff to conclude that the relationship between the home and school needs to be improved. The purpose of the project is stated "to improve home-school communication."

FORCE FIELDING THE PROBLEM

Kurt Lewin concluded that in an organization things stay as they are because a field of opposing forces is in balance.[2] His force field theory provides a useful way to engage in problem analysis as well as a basis for engaging in problem solution. One way to conceptualize a situation is to regard it as a product of forces pushing and pulling in opposite directions.

There are restraining forces and facilitating forces. The restraining forces are current conditions or actions which are such that change is inhibited. One might think of these forces as negative or "minus" forces. The facilitating forces are current conditions or actions which are such that a change is encouraged. These may be thought of as positive or "plus" forces.

The force field concept issues from the physical law that a body at rest (in equilibrium) will remain at rest when the sum of all the forces operating on it is zero. The body will move only when the sum is not zero and it will move only in the direction of the unbalancing force.

This can be observed in an organization whether one is examining the productivity of staff, the state of the intramural program, or the status of home-school communication among any of a number of examples. A thing is where it is because the counterbalancing plus and minus forces together equal zero. That is, conditions are such that the forces militating against improvement are equal to the existent forces pushing for positive change.

A school staff or project team dissatisfied with the current state of home-school communication should ask the question, "Why are things as they are?" This question leads to a force field analysis. A beginning analysis may look as follows:

Force Field Analysis: Why Aren't Home-School Communications Better?

Facilitating Forces for Change (+)	Forces Militating Against Change (−)
1. Faculty interest	1. Perceived community apathy
2. ESAA monies available	2. High student turnover
3. Media interest	3. Moribund PTO
4. Consultant help available	4. Little released time for teachers
5. State mandate	5. Lack of budget to support new approaches
6. Etc.	6. Etc.

Movement or change will take place when an imbalance is created by affecting the intensity or power of the forces. The imbalance "unfreezes" the current situation and the level will change to a new position where balance will be once again achieved (new state of equilibrium). An imbalance may be created by:

1. The addition of a new force (in the example given, the allocation of some ESAA monies for budget support).
2. The deletion of a force (e.g., revitalization of the PTO).
3. A change in the magnitude or strength of force(s).

Any plan that develops after the force field analysis will probably use all three processes to some degree. Also, as can be seen from the example, some forces may appear almost as reciprocals, so that an increase in one necessarily reduces the other in direct proportion. Other forces are such that there may be little direct action that can be taken. For example, it is not likely that a school faculty could do much to reduce transience of the school population.

In general, increasing only facilitating forces will likely increase tension in the system, and restraining forces may correspondingly increase. It is often more effective to first attempt to reduce the intensity of the restraining forces.

Engaging in a force field analysis will help a task force to focus its thinking on those specific environmental conditions in need of change if the project goal is to be reached. The brainstorming procedure discussed in chapter 2 or the problem resolution guide illustrated in figure 2–1 may be useful techniques. The result of this activity is the development of the project plan.

THE PROJECT PLAN

Figure 23–1 illustrates a comprehensive problem resolution document that reveals the project goal, delineates the components comprising the solution to the problem, establishes target dates for completion, and identifies the specific persons who have accepted responsibility for seeing to it that the various activities get carried out. There is a project director who assumes overall responsibility, and each component has a designated coordinator.

In a sense, the specific components are hypotheses. That is, the staff or the task force team involved in the problem definition phase decided that if all of these activities are carried out, better home-school relations will result.[3]

Component Coordinators and Other Key Personnel

Different people will be affected by the project. Some will be involved directly by coordinating components or carrying out other agreed-upon responsibilities. Others will be involved in ancillary ways, ranging from giving approval to certain acts to simply being kept informed. Figure 23–2 illustrates a way for the project manager, component coordinator, and the staff to keep track of who is to do what, who is affected by what, and what needs to be done about it.

Two things must be considered when responsibilities are assigned: the person accepting the responsibility must be capable of carrying it out and that person must agree to, and understand the nature of, the assignment. The assignment of responsibility must not occur in the cloister of an office by an individual unaccompanied by anything more than a sharp pencil. More jobs have been bungled because of unclear, unaccepted assignments than any other single factor. Further, the unique talents and the interests of staff members should be capitalized on and their inabilities mitigated.

Beyond the task force team charged with the implementation of the project will be others who are affected by the project, some in positions of authority, others who have a special competence to be used, and still others who simply have a need or right to know. The key personnel checklist depicted in figure 23–2 takes these into account.

Key personnel or groups are identified along with the several components comprising the project. The nature of the relationship of each person or group to each component is indicated.

Project: __To Improve Home-School Communication; Hudson High School__

Project manager: __Charles Achilles__

Completion date __July 1, 19--__

Start date __September 1, 19--__

Resolution components	Date for completion	Relationship to force field (if any). State which "plus" or "minus" the component relates to.	Component coordinator	Special notes
1. Monthly newsletters to clients	11/15	See Facilitating 2 and 3 See Inhibitors 4 and 5	Fred Hay	
2. Congratulatory letters system	11/1	See Inhibitor 1	Dennis Spuck	Trusty should facilitate
3. Parent rap sessions schedule	11/15	See Facilitating 4	Dorothy Kilburn	
4. Student rap sessions schedule	11/15	See Inhibitor 1	Brian Rocksborough	
5. Visitation days organized	1/1	See Inhibitors 1 and 3	Peter Husen	Get PTO involved
6. Report cards revised	3/1		Keith Waters	
7. Parent advisory council organized	7/1	Inhibitor 3	Jody Stevens	Board must be kept informed

Budget to support approved __8/15__   Amount __$1700__ (initial)   FY __19--__ (current)

(Date)

FIGURE 23–1. Comprehensive problem resolution document

PROJECT: To Improve Home-School Communication at Hudson High School					
		What part do they play?			
Project component	Who needs to know?	Must approve	Keep informed	Special skill	Other
1. Monthly newsletter	Secretary, PTO			X	
	Faculty Council		X		
	Achilles or Spuck	X			
	News Media		X		
2. Congratulatory letters	Class Advisors, PTO		X		
	Achilles			X	
3. Parent rap session	Achilles	X			
	Trusty			X	
	News Media		X		
	PTO		X		
	Board of Education		X		
	Superintendent		X		
4. Student rap session	Achilles, Spuck,	X			
	Trusty, Stevens,			X	
	Waters			X	
	Faculty Council		X		
	Board of Education				} Monthly reports
	Superintendent				
5. School visitation days	Achilles, Spuck, Husen			X	
	News Media		X		
	PTO		X		
6. Report card revision	Faculty Council	X			
	Superintendent, PTO	X			
	News Media		X		
7. Parents advisory council	Achilles	X			
	Faculty Council		X		
	Superintendent		X		
	Board of Education		X		
	Trusty, Hay			X	

FIGURE 23–2. Key personnel checklist for component coordinators

Putting the Specific Components into Operation

The project has now been disaggregated into a series of components which provide greater specificity. Depending on the nature of its complexity, each component may require further subdivision into a series of specific tasks, the carrying out of which will result in the accomplishment of the component. For this component, coordinators may need to develop a document similar to the comprehensive problem resolution document that disaggregates complex components into manageable units. Figure

23–3 depicts such a disaggregation. Again, target dates are established for each of the major units comprising components, and responsibilities are assigned. For those units that are themselves complex or composed of several related identifiable events, a further disaggregation may be required. It is important for component coordinators to note also what resources will be needed in the way of personnel, money, and facilities, and then to advise the project director about these.

Establishing Realistic Completion Dates

Establishing precise starting and completion times for the project as a whole as well as for the components of the project is very important. In not all cases will the completion of one component depend upon another, but often this will be so.[4] Even when this is not so, it is vital that all components be completed on time.

The best method of establishing realistic completion dates requires that those involved in

---

Project Improve Home-School Communication at Hudson High School

Component Development of Newsletter

Coordinator Fred Hay

Completion date 11/15 and continuing

Units	Completion date	Person responsible	Special notes
1. Develop format	10/1	Hay (with committee)	Limited to 4 pages
2. New sources identified	10/1	Hay (with committee)	Use Student Council if possible
3. Reproduction mechanics developed	10/15	Barbara Greer	Postage meter Required
4. Copy assignments out and collected	11/1	Hay	
5. Material edited	11/8	Leah Dunaway	Released time Required
6. Reproduce and mail out	11/15	Barbara Greer	Released time Required

Budget to support: $500 start up; $200 per quarter thereafter   TOTAL This FY $1300

Equipment and Space: Reproductive (available), postage meter, designated workroom

---

FIGURE 23–3. Problem resolution component sheet

Project: To improve home-school communication at Hudson High School   Target date: July 1, 19--

Activity Description	Month: Sept. week 1	2	3	4	Month: Oct. week 1	2	3	4	Month: Nov. week 1	2	3	4	Month: Dec. week 1	2	3	4	Month: etc. week 1	2	3	4
A 1 Newsletters	X								X											
t 1 Format	X				X															
t 2 News Sources			X		X															
t 3 Reproduction			X			X														
t 4 Copy out							X	X												
t 5 Mat'l edited								X	X											
t 6 Reproduction									X—X											
t A Congratulatory 2 Letters				X					X											

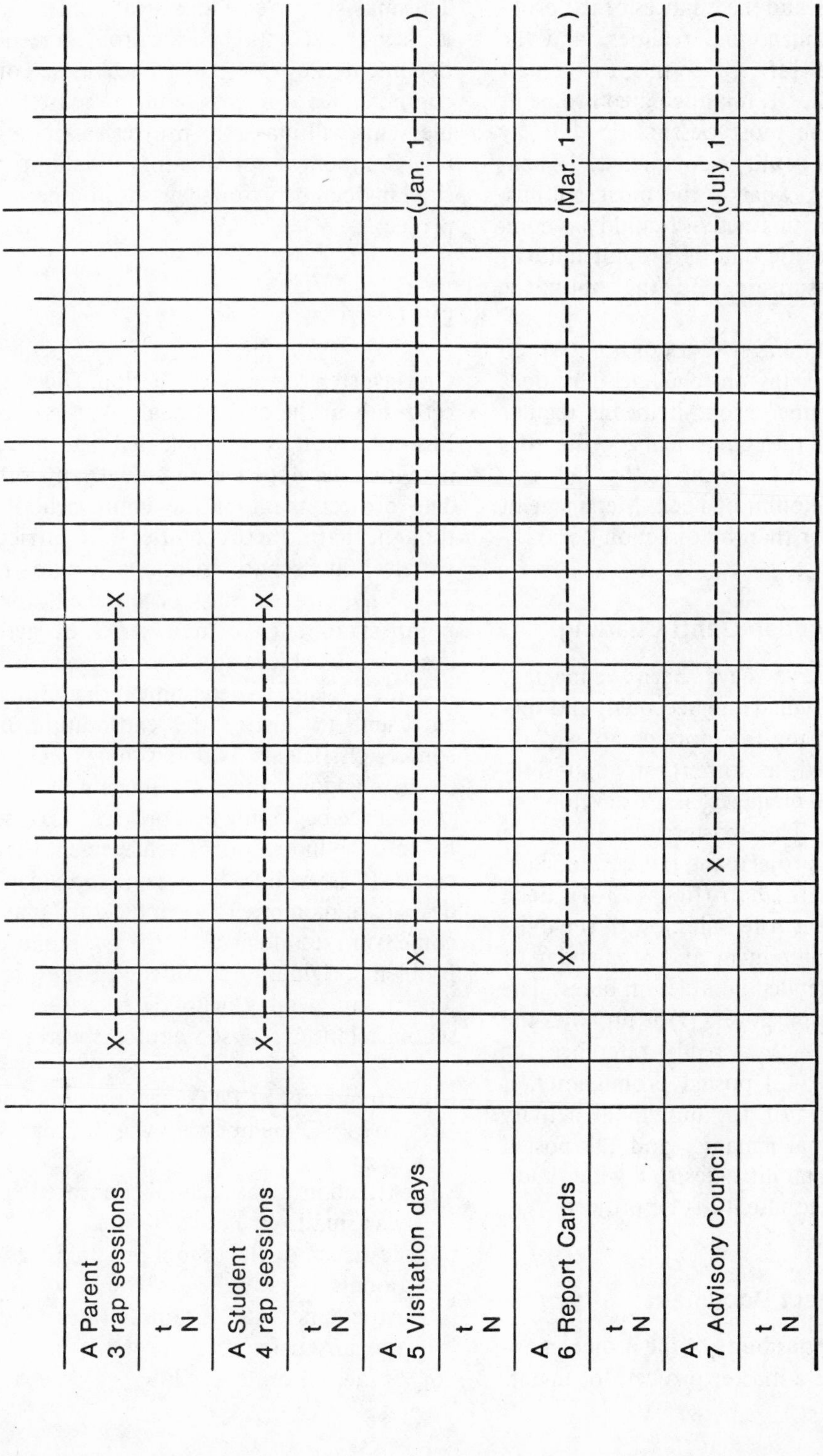

FIGURE 23–4. Project calendar of events

the project understand the nuances of the problem, certain organizational realities, and the capabilities of the staff. Given this, the project team can ask itself, "If unanticipated problems arose, what is the most pessimistic date by which this activity could be completed?" Then, "If all went well, what is the most optimistic date by which this activity could be completed?" The realistic date is a point midway between the pessimistic and the optimistic dates.

The project manager's responsibility is to help the task force stay on schedule. This does not mean daily supervision; it means regular conversations with the component coordinators about how the activity is going so that help can be provided at the point of need. Management by exception rather than by direction occurs.

The Project Calendar: Gantt Charting

After the comments have been delineated, responsibilities assigned and accepted, and specific tasks comprising the more complex components established, an important responsibility of the project manager' is to develop the master schedule. The master schedule is a chronology of the project, and it is developed in the form of a Gantt Chart (figure 23–4). Each major component is listed along with the units comprising the component and a calendar of beginning and intended completion dates. The chart serves three purposes: (1) it provides the project manager with a ready reference for checking progress; (2) posted prominently, it serves as a motivator for individual activity supervisors and participants; and (3) posted prominently, it communicates to a wider audience the nature and intent of the project.

The Master Project Document

An important responsibility of the project manager is to prepare a master project document.

This may simply be a loose-leaf binder in which is placed the comprehensive problem resolution document, key personnel checklists, complex component documents, and the master schedule. This will make the project easier to monitor. Component coordinators should prepare a similar document for their specific part of the project.

EVALUATION

One last step remains: evaluation. Did the project result in the desired goal? At the outset of this discussion, it was indicated that the several activities developed were actually hypotheses. The project team or the entire school staff thought that if these activities were carried out, better home-school relations would result. These hypotheses must be checked, for it is pointless to engage in a series of activities designed to achieve an outcome if one does not provide a means to determine if the results were sufficient to justify the expenditure of resources. Efficiency is doing things well; effectiveness is doing the *right* things well.

At the beginning of a project, it is essential to state the indicators of achievement the project staff is willing to accept as evidence of desired outcomes. These indicators may best come from restatements of the symptoms of the problem originally identified. In the previous illustration dealing with deteriorating home-school relations, those symptoms were:

1. Attendance at PTO meetings was poor.
2. The PTO membership was not representative.
3. Attendance at school-sponsored events was small.
4. Criticism of the school program was emotional.
5. Attendance and tardiness rates of pupils was unsatisfactory.
6. Student morale was low.

7. Communication with the home was limited to report cards.
8. Student attitudes toward learning were poor.

Changes in these conditions provide a means for evaluating the effectiveness of the project. Parent and student attitude inventories, attendance records, and informal and formal feedback from school and community persons and groups all serve as data sources to determine project effectiveness. Further, it may be that certain activities were efficacious and others were not. This, too, needs to be investigated.

SUMMARY

The process of systematic planning is applicable to any problem situation. It is designed to do two things: engender commitment to problem resolution by involving those who have expertise, insight, and interest in the specific problem in question, and marshalling those resources through a systematic process to get from problem identification to problem resolution. The result of such an endeavor will be productive change.

ENDNOTES

1. Uncovering issues to be addressed in the upcoming school year provides an excellent activity at preschool or year-end inservice workshops. Groups of teachers, and perhaps community members, may be set to work generating items, large and small, that seem to be getting in the way of maximum effectiveness. This list can then be turned over to a representative steering committee for refinement and ultimate identification of major issues for review by the staff.
2. See Kurt Lewin, "Quasi-Stationary Social Equilibria and the Problem of Social Change," in Bennis, Benne, and Chin (eds.), *The Planning of Change* (New York: Holt, Rinehart, and Winston, 1961), pp. 235–238. See also, in the same volume, David H. Jenkins, "Force Field Analysis Applied to a School Situation," pp. 238–244.
3. The need for an evaluation component is apparent. It is important to provide checkpoints throughout the project to see if desired outcomes are being achieved and, if they are not, to make midpoint corrections. Additionally, of course, a final evaluation and recycling stage must be provided for.
4. When the project is very complex and has several interdependent parts, it may be necessary to develop a PERT chart which depicts the order in which each of the activities has to occur and the relationship of one activity to another. An especially good treatment of this process can be found in Thomas Sergiovanni, *Handbook for Effective Department Leadership* (Boston: Allyn and Bacon, 1977). See Chapters 7 and 8.
5. The project manager is not necessarily the principal. He or she might be, of course, but any staff member with the requisite administrative abilities or other special expertise may serve in this position.

BIBLIOGRAPHY

Bennis, Warren; Benne, Kenneth D.; and Chin, Robert (eds.). *The Planning of Change*. New York: Holt, Rinehart and Winston, 1961.

Cleland, David I., and King, William R. *Systems Analysis and Project Management*. New York: McGraw-Hill Book Co., 1968.

McGrath, J. H. *Planning Systems for School Executives*. San Francisco: Intext Educational Publishers, 1972.

Sergiovanni, Thomas J. *Handbook for Effective Department Leadership*. Boston: Allyn and Bacon, 1977. Especially chapters 8 and 9.

Tanner, C. Kenneth. *Designs for Educational Planning*. Lexington, Mass.: D. C. Heath and Co., 1971.

Woodcock, Mike, and Francis, Dave. *Unblocking Your Organization*. La Jolla, Calif.: University Associates, Inc., 1979. This is a most useful volume for the practicing school administrator. It provides analytical techniques and exercises designed for immediate use with work groups and project task forces.

Chapter Twenty-Four

The Effective Management of Executive Time

INTRODUCTION

There are 168 hours in a week—no more, no less. Making the best use of the available hours requires planning and conscious action. To do otherwise will result in unaccomplished goals, missed deadlines, a briefcase filled with after-dinner work, and a less than satisfying professional and personal life. This chapter will focus on the principles and practices of good time management.

THE PRINCIPAL IS NOT THE PRINCIPALSHIP

The "principal" is a person; the "principalship" is a collection of responsibilities and specific tasks. The principal's job is to see that these responsibilities are met and the tasks performed well. We distinguish between principal and principalship to point out that while the principal is ultimately responsible for what goes on in and around the school, this does not imply that it is the principal who must personally perform all of the management and leadership acts. Only a foolish person would attempt to do so, for not only would it violate the precepts of good management, but it would also be impossible.

Some of the administrative tasks will, of course, be performed directly—and should be—because of their complexity and overriding importance or because the tasks are those for which the individual principal has great skill. Nevertheless, good management is mostly the science and art of achieving *planned objectives* through the efforts of other people.

Establishing a Responsibility Circle

Those things which require only the principal's attention must be identified. These things include tasks which, because of special training, insight, or designated responsibility, can only be done by the principal, or those tasks of an important kind in which the principal has the greatest skill. Once these are identified, the principal establishes the nature of his or her involvement. It is in these activities the principal participates directly; in all others, the principal will hold others responsible. The latter will require that the principal spend initial time working with the appropriate staff so they may (1) know what their responsibilities are, and (2) be trained in the proper dispatch of these responsibilities. The principal can effectively manage all of the functions of the principalship with attention to good delegative practices.

315

Among other things the various professions have in common is that each has a body of knowledge, experience, and skill that enables the professional to get the job done well because of his or her own efforts. Professional management is different only in that its body of knowledge, experience, and skills enables the professional manager to get the job done well because of the coordination of others' efforts.

HOW TO GET IT ALL DONE: TIME MANAGEMENT

The first chapter of this book suggested that it was unrealistic to expect principals to be either administrative paragons or obsequious book-keepers. The position does require a person with well-developed human, conceptual, and technical skills. It also requires an individual who can make maximum use of the time available for task accomplishment.

The Activity Trap

The frenetic activity characteristic of administrative offices at all levels of education often suggests accomplishment that is more apparent than real. Principals frequently find themselves parcelled out in so many different directions, responding directly to so many requests of others, that the important tasks do not get done, or get done in an inadequate way. But, even if the product of the effort is miniscule, the energy expended was great and the principal is tired. Ordione calls this the "activity trap."

> Most people get caught in the Activity Trap! They become so enmeshed in activity they lose sight of why they are doing it, and the activity becomes a false goal, an end in itself. Successful people never lose sight of their goals; the hoped-for outputs.[1]

Successful school executors know how to manage their time and avoid the activity trap. It is not easy, but it can be done. It is not easy because the "on line" executive often has the least control over his or her time. Principals spend a great deal of their time reacting to the problems of others. The issue in time management is how to get more time free to *act* rather than *react*; how to get more time for policy development and other leadership activities and spend less time focusing on other people's crises or engaging in pointless activity.

The key to spending time productively is in goal setting and the consequent establishment of job priorities in support of the goals. This will result in effectiveness rather than just efficiency. The first question to answer when confronted with a task is always, "Should this thing be done?" This is a goal and priority question. There is no way that one can get more than 168 hours from a week. The issue the principal must confront is not how to get more time, but rather how to spend more time on those things that are most important. The latter is achievable.

Four Questions to Ask Before Agreeing to Take On "One More Task"

1. How important is this?
2. Can someone else handle it with equal or better facility *OR* is there a more appropriate person who should handle it?
3. Does it need *immediate* attention from me or someone else?
4. What kinds of information will be required for the job to get done and where or from whom is this information available?

In the beginning of this book, five functions were identified as comprising the principalship: community-school relations, staff personnel development, pupil personnel development, educational program development, and business and building management. These functions and the skills necessary for implementation is the subject of this concluding chapter.

Ideal/Perceived/Real Use of Time

How would principals prefer to spend their time? How do principals think they spend their time? How do principals *actually* spend their time? These are three very different questions and, importantly, the answers seem always to be at some variance with each other. It is perhaps not surprising that how principals prefer to spend time (ideal time usage) would be different from how they think they spend time (perceived time usage) because few persons can always spend their professional or personal hours exactly as they want. Others in the organization will by right impinge upon the principal's work time. Similarly, the needs of family members and friends or other personal responsibilities will interfere with plans for nonwork time.

The most surprising thing is that how principals *perceive* they are spending professional time and how they are *actually* spending time *invariably reveals a disparity*! That is, principals (and other executives as well) not only are unable to spend time the way they most desire, they are not even aware of how they really are using their time.

Over the past few years, we have had the opportunity to work with many groups of school executives in seminars on time management. By collecting information from participants prior to the seminars, certain facts about time usage become apparent.

A time analysis questionnaire is shown in figure 24–1. Question 6 of the questionnaire asks respondents to tell what percentage of time they would ideally allocate among the five functions of the principalship. (There are two additional categories: unoccupied, and other. The latter category is listed in case the respondent doesn't feel the first five categories are adequate depictions.) Question 7 requests respondents to identify what percentage of their time they think they are *currently* spending in these same categories. The remainder of the questionnaire is used for further time analysis and other data collection.[2]

Initial Job Analysis Questionnaire

Few people are fortunate enough to spend all of their time doing exactly as they have previously planned. Burns said it, "The best laid plans of mice and men aft gang agly." This preseminar questionnaire is an effort to help you and us gain some insights about your job. *We aren't looking for textbook answers;* all that is wanted is a frank open response.* First, we need to have your name and a little information about the school or office you work in.

Name_____

School_____

Questions

1. _____What is your present position?
2. _____If you are a principal do you have an assistant?
3. _____What is the student enrollment of your school?
4. _____Level of school (h.s., jr. high, elem.)?
5. _____Best description of school population served; e.g., inner-city; urban but not inner-city; suburban.

(continued)

*You may wish to keep a copy of your responses so you can do some comparing with normative data available on the first day of the seminar.

6. If it was the best of all possible worlds this is the way I would allocate my time:

_____% Community-school relations activities (meeting with parents and civic groups; doing news releases; etc.)

_____% Developing personnel (helping teachers; inservice activities)

_____% Working with students

_____% Educational programming (developing innovative curricula; future planning; etc.)

_____% Managing the building (report writing; keeping the toilets flushing; keeping kids in and intruders out; etc.)

_____% Unoccupied (woolgathering; Monday morning quarter-backing; coffee drinking; etc.)

_____% Other (please specify)_____

7. Alas, it's not the best of all worlds and here's how I think I actually spend my time:

_____% Community-school relations activities (meeting with parents and civic groups; doing news releases, etc.)

_____% Developing personnel (helping teachers; inservice activities; etc.)

_____% Working with students

_____% Educational programming (developing innovative curricula; future planning; etc.)

_____% Managing the building (report writing; keeping the toilets flushing; keeping kids in and intruders out; etc.)

_____% Unoccupied (woolgathering; Monday morning quarter backing; coffee drinking; etc.)

_____% Other (please specify)_____

8. The things (people, objects, organizational constraints, whatever or whoever) that most often keep me from allocating my time the way I would like to are: (list 2 or 3)

_____

_____

_____

9. Respond to the following statement in a short, sweet, and "from the hips" fashion: I've got a good school (or this is a good system), but it could be better if__

_____

_____

_____

_____

Larry W. Hughes
Gerald C. Ubben

FIGURE 24–1.   Preseminar questionnaire sent to time management seminar registrants

Ideal Time Usage A typical group of principal responses to Question 6 is recorded in figure 24–2. Ideally, many of the principals would spend only 5 percent of their professional time on building and business management activities. (The average was 7 percent). A modal response of 20 percent was the ideal allocation for pupil personnel and educational programming activities. Staff personnel activities had a modal 10 percent allocation, but revealed a wide range of responses from one principal who would de-vote 75 percent of his time to this to another who would allocate only 5 percent. The most agreement among the respondents was to ideally devote about one-fifth of their time to program work.

Perceived Time Usage How do these principals think they really have to spend their time? Somewhat differently, as can be viewed in figure 24–3. Principals perceived themselves to be spending about 20 percent of their time in

A typical group of secondary school principals' responses to the statement:*

"If it was the best of all possible worlds I would allocate my time as follows."

| | Response by Percent | | | |
	Mode	Avg.	High	Low
Community-school relations	5	13	30	2
Staff personnel	10	36	75	5
Pupil personnel	20	32	80	4
Educational programming	20	22	50	4
Building management	5	7	20	0
Unoccupied	0	4	6	0
Other**	0	6	20	0

FIGURE 24–2. Ideal time usage

*N = 42 (Respondents were from urban and suburban junior and senior high schools.)

**Sample Statements: Extracurricular activities; crises; attending meetings; studying; workshop attendance.

A typical group of secondary school principals' responses to the statement:*

"Alas, it's not the best of all worlds and here's how I think I actually spend my time."

| | Response by Percent | | | |
	Mode	Avg.	High	Low
Community-school relations	5	11	30	1
Staff personnel	20	26	65	0
Pupil personnel	10	23	60	0
Educational programming	10	23	68	2
Building management	20	28	70	2
Unoccupied	0	6	15	0
Other**	0	14	50	0

FIGURE 24–3. Perceived time usage

*N = 42 (Respondents were from urban and suburban junior and senior high schools.)

**Self renewal; attendance at workshops out of district.

each of the categories "staff personnel" and "pupil personnel," a reverse of how they would ideally spend time. (One principal thought he was spending 80 percent of his time on pupil personnel issues.) Building management activities were perceived to be occupying 20 percent or more of the time by most, contrasted with the modal ideal of 5 percent.[3]

Thus, in most instances, these principals do not believe they are able to spend their time as they really would prefer. A discrepancy exists between ideal and perceived. One more step must be taken before the principal can effectively address the time management issue. That step is collecting information about how the principal *actually* spends time—because, and our studies strongly support this, how principals perceive they spend time frequently does not correlate with how they really do spend time!

The only way to gain insight into how time is actually being allocated is to record activities over time in a systematic way. There is need for the executive to develop an administrative log.

The Administrative Log

Keeping a log of administrative time is the best way to find out how the principal is actually spending time. It is necessary to know this if time is to be managed wisely because, as was pointed out earlier, depending on perception alone results in faulty judgments. Keeping a log of activities recorded at fifteen-minute intervals of random days over several weeks will provide the kind of insight needed. The use of an activity and time recording sheet such as that depicted in figure 24–4 will help.

A fellow administrator or some other person knowledgeable about the principalship

---

(Record major activities in appropriate fifteen-minute blocks and indicate leading action taken.)

Day_____	Activities (What are you doing, who are you talking with, what is it about?)	Leading action taken (Or, minutes wasted and why.)
7:00 A.M.		
7:15 A.M.		
7:30 A.M.		
7:45 A.M.		
8:00 A.M.		
8:15 A.M.		
8:30 A.M.		
8:45 A.M.		
9:00 A.M.		
9:15 A.M.		
9:30 A.M.		
9:45 A.M.		
10:00 A.M.		
10:15 A.M.		
10:30 A.M.		
Etc.		

FIGURE 24–4. Administrator's log

should probably be asked to do the initial analysis. This involves judging which of the seven categories the activities recorded fall into. To be sure, it is at times a very subjective judgment, but if the log has been kept for several days, a definite pattern will develop and a few erroneous subjective judgments will not skew the information. Computing the percentage of time spent in each of the categories is a simple arithmetic exercise. Categorical designations are made by fifteen-minute intervals; an eight-hour day would thus result in thirty-two, as a number against which percentage of the time spent in various categories would be computed.

How to Keep an Administrative Time Log

1. The log should cover different days of the week over an extended period of time (at least six weeks).
2. Avoid the first and last months of the regular school year.
3. The log needs to be as complete as possible with items listed every few minutes. Something needs to be written down at intervals no greater than fifteen minutes. There is no way that one can recall or reconstruct conversations, conferences, phone calls, personal dealings, etc., after several hours.
4. For those hours that you are in your office, ask the secretary to be a "shadow" and keep the log. Otherwise, carry the log on a clipboard as daily activities about the school are engaged in.
5. If the press of a particular situation makes it impossible to write it out in detail, make a brief note at the moment regarding that activity so it may be recalled and written in more detail at the end of the day.

Once the categorical percentages have been computed, the principal has information upon which to act. If there are discrepancies between the "what is" and the "what is desired," then it is time for an examination of some principles and procedures of good time management. Moreover, if an examination of the individual activities performed suggests that these activities run to the trivial, then this, too, must be a subject for reflection.

Reducing the Discrepancies

When principals are occupied at a task a substantially greater span of time than they would ideally like to be, something is wrong. How does one get control of the administrative day so that the tasks that are of high priority get done? Deciding how time should be spent (the ideal usage) is the first step. This involves also engaging in a careful analysis of one's own skills and interests.

Taking stock of actual time allocation is the second step in gaining control. This involves carefully recording daily activities by using an administrator's log and categorically defining on what types of activities the time has been used. The seven categories established in the questionnaire in figure 24–2 are useful in this context.

The third and final step is organizing one's time in such a way that the maximum effort is placed on high priority tasks. This entails also the responsibility for providing an administrative structure that results in other tasks being appropriately delegated and carried out. This third step, that of priority setting, is the subject of the section which follows.

Priority Setting

What's important anyhow? In a sense, this question can be answered by responding to the "best of all worlds" part of the question depicted in figure 24–2, because it asks principals to indicate how they would ideally spend their time. The degree to which responses to the question of "ideal" use of time are true, of course, depends on the candor and insight of the particular respondent. The first step in getting better control of time, therefore, is to make an honest appraisal of what ought to be done. This appraisal should consist of a careful self-examination of organizational expectations,[4] personal skills, and personal interests. These three forces in balance will provide a basis for job satisfaction and maximum productivity.

The most effective executives concentrate their energies on a few major tasks where superior performance will produce outstanding results. Contrast this approach with those executives who get caught up in the activity trap discussed earlier. The effective use of time requires the highest form of self-discipline.

Steps in Priority Setting   Once a decision has been made about how the individual principal can best utilize time, the task becomes one of establishing goals and setting priorities. The principal then spends time mainly in those predetermined priority task areas.[5] The individual "draws a circle" around those tasks and activities that he or she is most competent to do, and activities and tasks that fall outside of the circle become tasks for other persons.

The first step in this process is to establish specific year-long goals or targets for the school; things that the principal would like to see accomplished. Goals might be stated for each of the five functional aspects of the principalship. The next question becomes which of these goals require primary energy. These become the high-priority items in terms of personal time usage.

Each goal is defined by a series of activities, the completion of which will result in achieving the goal over an established period of time, in this instance, a school year. Figure 24–5 depicts part of such a list. The principal who developed the list intends to devote 30 percent of the time during the current school year to curriculum development activities. This principal, after analysis of personal interest and

skills, believes that the best deployment is for time to be spent in an instructional leadership role. In order to reach this goal, several priority activities have been developed. The principal in question will also devote considerable energy to developing better school-community relations, and again has specified a series of priority activities. Such a list can be developed very easily into an evaluation device as well. Figure 24–6 depicts an administrative performance objective derived from such a priority list.

The establishment of priority administrative goals and specific activities permits the principal to develop daily and weekly "to do" lists. (See figure 24–7.) The title "to do" is self-explanatory, except that the principal also attaches a priority to each item. Generally speaking, these priorities should reflect the statements of goals and activities developed for the year. If they do not, too much time is being spent on low priority or emergency items. This can be corrected if detected early.

Managing is not doing. One question often arises as priority lists are developed. The question may be stated: "How can a principal get away with spending most of the time on curriculum development and school-community relations when there are books to be balanced, kids to be seen, inservice programs to be run, and faculty meetings to be held?" To be sure, there are other functions of the principalship and they must be adequately performed or the school will not operate well, but managing does not mean doing everything. The principalship is not the principal. Careful assignment of tasks to others and delegation of authority will provide a structure for others to make decisions and help administer the enterprise. Then, the principal can spend time on those tasks which he or she performs best. The circle can be drawn.

Planning Time   Obviously, not all events and emergencies can be foreseen. Just as obvious is that the principal can control only a portion of

Functional Area	% Time to be Allotted	Goal	Activities
Curriculum Development	30	To provide instructional and curricular leadership	1. Visit each classroom four times per year. 2. Require teachers to develop behavioral objectives. 3. Organize an instructional council. 4. Introduce instructional or curricular innovation and provide for implementation.
School-Community Relations	25	Better relationships with the community	1. Develop regular newsletter home. 2. Organize Parent Advisory Council. 3. Organize neighborhood resources file.
Pupil Personnel	15		
Staff Development	15		
Business	10		
Self-Renewal	5		

FIGURE 24–5. Example of a principal's time priority list

time. One is required to spend much time reacting to the problems presented by others. Nevertheless, the workday can be planned and that plan can be followed.

Planning does require a willingness to not be dominated by urgent events. MacKenzie has written:

> Urgency engulfs the manager; yet the most urgent task is not always the most important. The tyranny of the urgent lies in its distortion of priorities—its subtle cloaking of minor projects with major status, often under the guise of "crisis." One of the measures of the manager is his ability to distinguish the important from the urgent, to refuse to be tyrannized by the urgent, to refuse to be managed by crisis.[6]

Being "managed by crisis" is the result of a failure to plan. In order to insure that time is spent daily on the most important tasks rather than just the urgent, it is essential that a daily planning document be prepared.

Goal: Provide more instructional leadership.

Performance Objective:

1. The principal will organize time in such a way that each classroom in the building is visited for a minimum of one hour per nine-week period.

2. The principal will organize an instructional council which will meet not less than once monthly to advise on school policy, curriculum development, and instructional practices.

3. The principal will require each teacher in the building to submit behavioral objectives each year for Instructional Council review and will meet individually with each teacher to discuss these.

4. The principal will introduce at least one instructional or curricular innovation adjudged by research evidence to be an important new approach to the teaching/learning process and will develop a PERT network to describe the implementation procedure.

FIGURE 24-6. Example of a principal performance objective

Day: Tuesday, October 31

	Priority
Set up conference with parents re: Advisory Council	1
Arrange meeting with department heads	2
Review monthly ADM	3
Visit Richard Hooker	1
Barbara Greer	2
Richard Strahan	2
Review school health insurance package	3
Meet with custodian re: faulty locks	1
Counsel Dennis Spuck	2
Call Stan Sanders re: Principal Association Program	2
Phi Delta Kappa meeting (4 p.m.)	2
Complete report to superintendent re: high school curriculum revision	1

FIGURE 24-7. "To do" list

PRIORITY 1 Activities	Relates to what goal?	Estimated time needed for completion	When is this time available?	Who else could do it?
PRIORITY 2 Activities				
PRIORITY 3 Activities				

FIGURE 24–8.   Daily planning document

The document should be developed at the end of each day. (See figure 24–8 for an example of such a document.) The document is divided into three priority areas: those of highest priority (priority 1), those of some importance (priority 2), and those of less importance (priority 3). Estimates of time needed for completion are made, judgments about when during the day the time is available, and a determination of whether or not someone else can do it. Further, a determination is made about which, and/or whether or not, the high priority activities are related to the yearly goals.

Next, a firm resolve is made: the principal *will not* work on any priority 2 activity until *all* priority 1 activities are completed—no matter what! If time has to be "stolen" it must be taken from priority 2 and 3 activities. If all priority 1 activities are completed, priority 2 activities may be engaged in, and the principal will not work on any priority 3 activities until all priority 2 activities are complete. At the beginning of each day, the principal should spend

fifteen minutes to half an hour going over the daily planning document with the secretary to develop the day's routine. One-half hour spent this way will save four hours later.

A weekly analysis of the planning document will insure that progress is being made toward the year-long goals and that high-priority activities are taking precedence. (Figure 24–9 depicts another kind of daily time planner which has been used to good advantage by practicing school executives.)

What Gets in the Way?

Emergencies do occur and a carefully planned day or week can explode in a flurry of unanticipated crises. These can be expected and need not have a long-range effect on the orderly achievement of the priorities of the week or the goals of the year.[7] Studies conducted in a variety of management settings have consistently revealed fifteen common sources of time control problems:

1. Telephone.
2. Drop-in visitors.
3. Meetings (scheduled and unscheduled).
4. Crises.
5. Lack of objectives.
6. Cluttered desk and personal disorganization.
7. Ineffective delegation and involvement in routine.
8. Attempting to do too much at once and unrealistic time estimates.
9. Confused responsibility and authority.
10. Inadequate, inaccurate, and delayed information.
11. Procrastination.
12. Lack of or unclear instructions.
13. Inability to say No.
14. Lack of controls.
15. Fatigue.[8]

In an inquiry conducted by one of the authors in the Houston, Texas, area, secondary principals completed the questionnaire shown in figure 24-1. It is interesting to compare the preceding list with their responses to item 8 of the questionnaire: "The things (people, objects, organizational constraints, whatever or whoever) that most often keep me from allocating my time the way I would like are. . . ." From their responses, it is possible to determine

Instructions: In the lefthand column, jot down all tasks which need to be done. On the right, list six of these, in order of their importance, which need to be done today. Start with the first and continue until you have completed all six. Begin a new priority list as soon as you finish the first six. Make frequent reference to your long-range goals to make sure you are on course.

Tasks to be done	Priority	Tasks to be done today
	First Second Third Fourth Fifth Sixth	
	First Second Third Fourth Fifth Sixth	
	First Second Third Fourth Fifth Sixth	

FIGURE 24-9. Principal's daily time planner for scheduling and setting priorities on immediate goals

six specific categories and a seventh general category which was simply labeled "others." Under each category below are listed synthe-sized responses comprising the category. The number beside the category is the percent of respondents identifying it as one of the major obstacles. Respondents were asked to name two or three such obstacles. Forty-two junior and senior high school principals comprised the sample. Note the great similarities between this list and its components and the list above based primarily on data about managers in private in-dustry.

*Obstacles Which Keep Secondary
Principals from Allocating Time the
Way They Would Like:*

1. Paperwork (76%)
   a. reports—forms from county, state, and federal
   b. surveys
   c. evaluations
   d. program evaluations and guidelines
2. Meetings (52%)
   a. central office
   b. due process hearings
   c. called by assistant principal and com-mittee chair
   d. unannounced teacher/parent confer-ences
3. Emergencies (50%)
   a. discipline problems
   b. unexpected drop-ins (parents, teachers, central office administrators, etc.)
   c. unexpected calls (parents, central office, or other administrators)
   d. truancy problems
   e. petty problems that need immediate at-tention
4. Communication Problems (14%)
   a. lack of proper programming for major assignments
   b. who handles what in district
   c. dealing with special programs and guidelines; TEA and Southern Asso-ciation
   d. organizational structure of responsi-bility
   e. lack of coordination between depart-ments
   f. dealing with central office
   g. central office functions assigned to one or more principals
5. Personnel Problems (12%)
   a. resolving staff personality conflicts
   b. teachers that can't control classes
   c. lack of supervision at peak periods
   d. lack of assistant principal
6. Building Management (12%)
   a. old building facilities (something al-ways needing repairs)
   b. managing building maintenance
7. Other (29%)
   a. organizational constraints
   b. outside demands
   c. extra activities
   d. inability to organize
   e. trying to maintain quality in a rapid growth school setting
   f. "misinformed or outright stupid people"
   g. scheduling
   h. computer service deadlines

A review of this list indicates many items over which the principal has control. Telephone interruptions, for example, can be controlled by a secretary who takes call-backs and who is able, when appropriate, to refer the caller to another person.[9] Telephones should not be tyrants.

Meetings can be made more efficient and need not interfere with the effective use of the principal's time. Some meetings, of course, need not be held at all; other meetings can be made shorter. Moreover, individual confer-ences with staff members—superordinates or subordinates—can also become more efficient.

To: All faculty

From: John Croft

Subject: Meeting about school drop-outs

All department heads and guidance personnel will be meeting with me on Thursday at 3:00 P.M. to discuss the organization of a task force on drop-outs. The intended outcome is the development of a mission statement and the formulation of a task force.

You are welcome to come if you are interested in serving or have information about the drop-out problem.

In any case, all will be kept informed.

FIGURE 24–10.   Announcement of meeting

Effective managers almost always work from tightly developed agendas with stated anticipated outcomes, which other participants have had a chance to review in advance. If the session is to be a problem-solving one, the group should be limited and only those directly affected should be invited to participate. To avoid misunderstandings and facilitate communication, an announcement such as that depicted in figure 24–10 may be useful. No one who may have special insights, skills, or interests is excluded, but neither is the whole staff required to attend. This helps conserve everyone's time.

Individuals who frequently meet together can organize meetings to make maximum use of time together. The key is to meet less frequently and cover more than one matter per meeting. Figure 24–11 displays a conference planner that

Instructions: In the spaces below enter the names of those with whom you have frequent conferences. As you are reminded of items you need to discuss with each, jot them down. When the timing is right for a conference, number the items in order of their priority. Eliminate unnecessary items or those that can be best dealt with in another way. Work toward avoiding one- or two-item conferences.

Name	Name	Name
Name	Name	Name

FIGURE 24–11.   Principal's conference planner

will provide greater specificity and a better product.

The Myth of the Open Door

The principal must be accessible. What has developed from the belief in reasonable accessibility is something called the *open door policy.* Unfortunately, "open door" has come to mean the door is supposed to be open all the time. How foolish. This is a certain way to insure that the principal will spend virtually all of the working day responding to other people's problems or engaging in Monday morning quarterbacking with any casual drop-ins who have time on their hands. The "always available" principal will find it impossible to get work done.

All executives need planned unavailability. If this is impossible to get in the office, then the principal should find a hideaway where he or she can develop those projects which require longer periods of time.

Some executives seem to have an illusion of indispensability and conclude that the organization could not survive without their immediate and continuous attention. Vacations and weekends are given up as the executive stays on the firing line, making decisions and putting out fires. This refusal to delegate authority leaves the principal with an underdeveloped staff, an overworked secretary, and no recourse but to wade daily through mountains of paper work and a morass of other people's problems.

There is a caveat, however. It is hoped that this discussion has not suggested that mechanical behavior and great rigidity is necessary to effectively administer the secondary school. That would be contrary to its intent. Good time management practices release the principal from time domination so that he or she is more productively available. These practices will provide greater opportunities to chat with students and teachers, visit with custodians and cooks, feel the pulse of the school, and see and be seen. Time consciousness is not a license to disappear behind the door and never be seen again.

SUMMARY

How to get the job done and on time has been the subject of this chapter. The five functions of the principalship are not manageable in a very large school if the principal believes in personally performing each task. Rather, the effective school executive organizes time in such a way that all the important things get done by those best suited by disposition, training, interest, and availability. Skills in delegation and time management are basic to this.

ENDNOTES

1. George Ordione, *Management and the Activity Trap* (New York: Harper and Row, 1974), p. 6.
2. No judgment is made here about how a principal "ought" to spend time. The principalship contains five functions and these functions must be performed adequately by somebody—either the principal or someone who has been delegated that authority by the principal. In either case, it is the principal who is ultimately responsible.
3. The "ideal" and "actual" time usage figures were obtained by a random sampling of forty-two junior and senior high school principals in the Houston, Texas, area in the spring of 1978. The mode represents the percentage of time most frequently responded to by the sample. The average is simply the computed average according to the range from high to low. The "high" and "low" columns represent the range of time allocation in percentages.

According to the "ideal" time usage chart, about one-half of a principal's time should ideally be devoted to pupil personnel, educational programming, and developing staff personnel. The responses indicate that only about 10 percent of a principal's time should be devoted to public relations (community and school) and managing the building.

As the "actual" and "ideal" time usage figures are compared, the greatest discrepancy is seen in managing the building. Apparently, principals spend much more time dealing with building maintenance problems than they feel necessary.

There was a wide range of responses, the most provocative of which frequently appeared in the "other" category of the actual time allocation responses. Two principals stated that they spent 50 percent of their time in "other" activities. One of these principals stated that at least 50 percent of his time was spent in extracurricular activities! The other reported that meetings and reports occupied 50 percent of his time.

4. Organizational expectations include the expectations of superordinates and subordinates.

5. "Mainly" is the word used because it is realized that no executive can totally control time; there are always emergencies, unplanned interruptions, and other unanticipated inside and outside organizational demands.

6. R. Alec MacKenzie, *The Time Trap* (AMACOM, 1972), pp. 42–43.

7. If the principal does appear to be continuously moving from crisis to crisis, something is wrong. A reassessment of the principal's role, organizational structure, delegation practices, and time management practices are immediately required.

8. Charles A. Lutzow, "Effective Time Management for the Public School Principal," *Chicago Principals Reporter* (Spring 1978): 10.

9. It is imperative that the principal return phone calls. An even better procedure may be to have a period of time set aside each day during which the principal will be in the office and available for phone conversation. The secretary indicates when the principal will be in the office and asks the person to call back at that time. This places a responsibility for returning the call on the initial caller rather than on the principal. Also, it frequently happens that the person does not call back, but resolves his or her problem in another way.

BIBLIOGRAPHY

Bliss, Edwin C. *Getting Things Done: The A B C's of Time Management*. New York: Charles Scribner's Sons, 1976.

Drucker, Peter F. *Management: Tasks, Responsibilities, Practices*. New York: Harper and Row, 1974.

Lakein, Alan. *How to Get Control of Your Time and Life*. New York: Peter H. Wyden, 1973.

Loen, Raymond O. *Manage More by Doing Less*. New York: McGraw-Hill Book Co., 1971.

Lutzow, Charles A. "Effective Time Management for the Public School Principal." *Chicago Principals Reporter* (Spring 1978): 4-11.

McConkey, Dale D. *No-Nonsense Delegation*. New York: AMACOM, 1974.

Odiorne, George S. *Management and the Activity Trap*. New York: Harper and Row, 1974.

Weldy, Gilbert R. *Time: A Resource for the School Administrator*. Reston, Va.: National Association of School Administrators, 1974.

INDEX